IRMA ADELMAN is professor of economics, Northwestern University, and author of *Theories of Economic Growth and Development.* ERIK THORBECKE is professor of economics, Iowa State University, and co-author of *The Theory of Quantitative Economic Policy: With Application to Economic Growth and Stabilization.*

The Theory and Design
of Economic Development

THE THEORY AND DESIGN
OF ECONOMIC DEVELOPMENT

EDITED BY
IRMA ADELMAN AND ERIK THORBECKE

PUBLISHED BY THE JOHNS HOPKINS PRESS, BALTIMORE, 1966
IN COOPERATION WITH THE CENTER FOR AGRICULTURAL AND ECONOMIC
DEVELOPMENT OF IOWA STATE UNIVERSITY (AMES)

PREFACE

Perhaps the most exciting advances in economics today are being made in the theory and planning of economic development. This is due primarily to the tremendous pressure for economic development among the newly emerging nations and to the resultant response of modern economists to their needs. A great many different routes to development are being tried, and a number of alternative theories have been propounded.

Because of the relatively large amount of experience which has been accumulating, and because of the almost embryonic state both of theoretical approaches to the explanation of the growth process in developing nations and of appropriate planning models, it seemed desirable, in the summer of 1965, to organize a conference to consider the "state of the art" of economic development. The conference was sponsored by the Center for Agricultural and Economic Development of Iowa State University and was held at Iowa State University in November, 1965. The program committee consisted of Irma Adelman, Gustav Ranis, and Erik Thorbecke.

The major objectives of the conference were to help bridge the gap between the theoretical and the practical approaches to development problems and to indicate to both groups the most promising directions for future research. To do this the conference planners brought together some of the most prominent of the development planning specialists with a number of the outstanding economic theorists in the growth and development field. The papers presented at the conference are therefore representative of the most advanced and fruitful techniques, both theoretical and applied, available for analysis of the development process in the emerging nations today.

The first group of papers in these proceedings is concerned with theoretical aspects of the development process. The first paper, by Ranis and Fei, is a rigorous analysis, based on a set of simplifying assumptions, of the interrelationship between the agricultural and the industrial sectors of a developing economy. It treats in some detail the growth of a dualistic economy, and it presents a model of a stagnant agrarian economy which is used to address the important question of how an economy can reach a stagnation point. The Jorgenson paper which follows examines the empirical consequences of two alternative theories of the growth process in a dualistic economy; the two theories are compared with existing empirical evidence, and one (the Ranis-Fei approach) is refuted. In the subsequent discussion by Marglin, the generality of these empirical tests used to compare the two theories is questioned. Thus, these two papers and the discussion constitute an interrelated unit which appears to leave open the question of the validity of the Ranis-Fei model.

Next, Fei and Chiang demonstrate that the level at which consumption should be set in order to maximize the economy's rate of growth is greater than the bare substitute level, and that, even in a socialist economy, the first austerity phase should be expected to be followed by an era of relaxation during the development process. The Tintner paper offers a probabilistic formulation of the process of economic development, which is used to estimate the dates at which important changes took place in the structural relationships governing the growth process of the British economy. Finally, Uzawa makes a pioneering attempt to analyze, at a very high level of abstraction, the optimum fiscal policy for economic growth. It is the first attempt by a theoretical economist to analyze rigorously the optimal use of such an important instrument of government policy for the promotion of economic growth and development.

The empirical work in this volume includes examples of the best economic techniques available for development planning, and, in the opinion of the editors, can well serve as reference material for planning agencies throughout the world, as well as for courses in economic development. The techniques employed in the several papers offer a progression from the most aggregative forms of planning to the most disaggregative, and from various feasibility and consistency analyses to optimizing approaches of both linear and nonlinear varieties. The Chenery-MacEwan paper is an interesting exploration, by means of parametric linear programming, of the effects of changes in foreign aid upon economic development. The macroeconometric approach is represented by the Thorbecke-Condos paper on Peru. Consistency analyses, of the input-output variety, are represented by the Seers paper on Zambia and the Bergsman-Manne paper on India.

Lefeber, in discussing the Bergsman-Manne paper, raises the question of the relative merit of consistency models versus optimizing models, and thus provides a good transition to the linear programming technique, the best and most sophisticated approach devised to date for development programming. Five of the papers presented use this technique to draw up sectoral investment plans. The paper by Manne is a summary of an actual planning job performed at the Bank of Mexico in conjunction with

Mexico's ten-year development program. Bruno's model of Israel is, in many ways, the most advanced and most seasoned application of linear programming to development planning and uses several imaginative simplifications to avoid the most serious deficiencies of perfectly linear programming models. The Adelman-Sparrow paper on Colombia offers a discussion of the sensitivity of results obtained by linear programming methods to various changes in the objective function. The empirical section ends with linear programming analyses of two sectors of particular importance in developing economies—agriculture by Heady and education by Adelman.

It was clear from both the papers and the discussion at the conference that there is really a dichotomy between the more pragmatic planning models in use today, on the one hand, and the theoretical growth models which attempt to explain the relevant phenomena, on the other. Most theoretical growth models tend to deal with a one- or two-sector stylization of the economy, and, with a few recent exceptions, they focus primarily upon the growth processes in a closed economy. The production functions used in these models are of the smooth, neoclassical type, with resultant continuous adjustment processes. Also, the time horizon typically is infinite.

By contrast, most practical development models are quite disaggregated and use production functions in which factor substitution is impossible within a given sector and is quite limited for the economy as a whole. The evolutionary paths traced out by typical pragmatic growth models are therefore characterized by abrupt changes as successive bottlenecks to economic growth are relaxed. More important, it is the optimization of foreign trade policy, aid policy, and investment in foreign exchange earning activities in an open economy over a limited period of time which is the crux of practical development planning. It is therefore evident that the relevance of current theoretical growth models to contemporary growth problems is at present rather limited.

As a result of considerations of this nature, the more theoretical contingent at the conference tended to conclude, with perhaps varying degrees of intensity, that theoretical growth models, to be of real assistance in practical development planning, must move strongly in the direction of taking into account precisely those effects which are of most interest to the planner. In general, it was agreed that the design of economic development policy would greatly benefit from a closer interaction between these two different approaches to development problems. Thus, the policy relevance of theoretical discussions would be greatly enhanced if trade problems were to be made an integral part of dual economy models.

By the same token, it would be extremely useful for the formulation of general propositions in economic development if the planners would construct simple stylized versions of their practical models. The systematic study of the properties of these simplified models in a large number of economies characterized by vastly different parameter magnitudes might enable the derivation of more general, empirically anchored, propositions which could then be used in the construction of improved theoretical models.

Our primary indebtedness is to Professor Earl O. Heady who originally conceived the idea of the conference and without whose constant efforts the conference could not have succeeded. We are also grateful to the Center for Agricultural and Economic Development of Iowa State University whose generous support made this conference possible. The local arrangements committee, and particularly William Stucky and Leo V. Mayer, contributed greatly to the smoothness of the conference and the comfort of the participants. One of us (I. A.) would also like to express her appreciation to the Ford Foundation for financial support during the current academic year which has permitted her to participate more effectively in the preparation of the conference and in the editing of the volume.

Irma Adelman and Erik Thorbecke

CONTENTS

ix

PART I
DEVELOPMENT THEORY AND STRATEGY

1. AGRARIANISM, DUALISM, AND ECONOMIC DEVELOPMENT

JOHN C. H. FEI, CORNELL UNIVERSITY
GUSTAV RANIS, AGENCY FOR INTERNATIONAL DEVELOPMENT

I. INTRODUCTION

From the beginnings of our science, economists have been trying to gain a better understanding of the economy's growth performance. In the recent resurgence of interest in development, after the long neoclassical interregnum, there has been some effort to glean as much helpful information as possible from the analysis of earlier work. Both the old writers and the new increasingly seem to agree that the real world essence of a developing system cannot be meaningfully "captured" by conventional aggregative analysis and that the search for significant intersectoral relations and intersectoral asymmetries may well provide the key to the enhanced understanding we seek.

Nevertheless, when endeavoring to extract the maximum transferable knowledge from the writings of the physiocrats and the classicists, for example, we must be painfully aware that each such formulation is inevitably the product of its own particular historical conditions and circumstances. The transferability of any particular set of concepts is circumscribed by differences in the social issues faced, in the tools available, and, consequently, in the vision of the future presented. Therefore the usefulness of past theories is limited for examining the problems facing us now in the lessdeveloped world.

In this general context we think it useful to distinguish among three major types of economic systems—agrarianism, dualism, and economic maturity. Economic maturity has been exhaustively treated by postKeynesian growth theorists[1] and is not our major concern here, but we

---

[1] See, for example, R. M. Solow, "A Contribution to the Theory of Economic Growth," *Quarterly Journal of Economics*, LXX (February, 1956), 65–90; T. W. Swan, "Economic Growth and Capital Accumulation," *Economic Record*, XXXII (November, 1956), 334–61.

3

believe the distinction between agrarian and dualistic economies to be of considerable importance for a fuller understanding of the relevance of earlier writers to our present concern with growth in the less-developed economy.

The central feature of agrarianism is the overwhelming preponderance of traditional agricultural pursuits. While other economic activities may be in evidence, they are of distinctly secondary importance in both a quantitative and qualitative sense. Those nonagricultural pursuits which exist are characterized by a modest use of capital. The agrarian economy is essentially stagnant, with nature and population pressure vying for supremacy over long periods of recorded history. Moreover, the prognosis for the future is likely to be "more of the same."

The central feature of dualism, on the other hand, is the coexistence of a large agricultural sector with an active and dynamic industrial sector. Industry uses capital, and both sectors undergo continuous technological change as they "interact" during the growth process. The dualistic economy strives to adjust the historical preponderance of agriculture by gradually shifting its center of gravity toward industry through factor reallocation. Its inherent condition is thus one of change, and its vision of the future is the ultimate graduation into economic maturity.

It is our view that both the eighteenth-century physiocrats and the later classicists were really addressing themselves to the problem of growth in an agrarian economy. The physiocrats' major contribution undoubtedly lay in the recognition—for the first time—that the growth of the economy must be viewed basically as an interrelated system of intersectoral flows. In their world, only the preponderant agricultural sector is capable of producing a surplus, as agricultural workers exploit the fundamental bounty of nature. Nonagriculture is peopled by the so-called "sterile classes" which cannot produce a surplus, but can only transform value created in agriculture. The owners of the land, the landlord, the nobility, or the church, "own" whatever "slack" there may be in the system, whether in the form of the emerging agricultural surplus or of redundant manpower available for personal services, feudal wars, and the like. These slacks are largely consumed by the propertied classes, either directly, in the form of food, or indirectly, in the form of the output of the sterile classes, as services and handicraft products, which are delivered in exchange for the wage goods provided. It is at least implicitly assumed that no marked changes in agricultural production techniques can occur and that the artisan and service sectors remain completely stagnant. Thus, to the physiocrats, growth was tantamount to the perpetuation of the cultural life of the ruling classes made possible by the assumed regularity of the circular flow mechanism described in their "tableau économique."

The classical school of economists was heavily influenced by its physiocratic predecessors and also turned its attention primarily to analysis of the agrarian economy. As Schumpeter points out, before 1790 "all countries—even England—were predominantly agrarian."[2] Thus, while the classicists referred to the growth of industry, their analytical attention was concentrated on distribution and on the long-run growth prospects of an undifferentiated, monolithic economy dominated by agriculture. The tripartite division of income, perhaps their major analytical contribution, is analyzed in a setting in which "the typical capitalist . . . was the 'farmer' in the British sense, who rented land [from the absentee landlord] and hired laborers, received the product at the end of the year and turned over to the two other claimants their respective shares."[3] There is occasional reference to nonagricultural activities now viewed as capable of producing a surplus along with agriculture,[4] but as Schumpeter put it, "the manufacturing industry that economists beheld and reasoned about was all along the manufacturing industry of the artisan."[5]

In the agrarian system there is still no clearly discernible industrial capital in the form of reproducible plant and equipment, but only the extension of production advances in the form of wage goods to industrial workers for the support of further production.[6] Technological change is once again either ignored or considered to be of only secondary interest. The classicists made a considerable advance in presenting a fully deterministic system capable of dynamic analysis, but they saw their problem in physiocratic terms and their prediction of the ultimate stationary state was one of continued agrarian stagnation. "Both groups [the classicists and physiocrats] viewed production as the creation of a 'surplus' of tangible wealth . . . available for such 'unproductive' uses as the support of government and the cultural life. [And both] shared the popular belief that agriculture is the only activity which is really productive."[7]

In sharp contrast to the essentially agrarian view of both the physiocrats

---

[2] Joseph A. Schumpeter, *History of Economic Analysis* (New York, 1954), p. 565.

[3] Frank H. Knight, "Capital and Interest," reprinted in *Readings in the Theory of Income Distribution* (Philadelphia, 1946), p. 385.

[4] Even though Smith still exempted services as nonproductive and sterile.

[5] "No author," Schumpeter went on to say, "not even A. Smith, had any very clear ideas of what the processes really meant that led to . . . the Industrial Revolution." Schumpeter, *History*, p. 150.

[6] Knight, "Capital and Interest," p. 386.

[7] *Ibid.*, p. 385.

and the classicists, modern writers, returning to a concern with growth in the underdeveloped world after the Second World War, have made dualism the central focus of their analysis.[8] This emphasis is primarily borne of the fact that while analyzing poor and largely agricultural economies, they see before them the vision of the wealthy and industrialized mature economy. Regardless of analytical differences among them, they are implicitly or explicitly interested in the process of transformation from an overwhelmingly agricultural dualistic economy to a mature industrial economy.

This dualistic outlook is characterized by the incorporation of a set of new analytical facets of growth which are largely absent in the earlier agrarian way of thinking. While economic events involving the nonagricultural sector represent a diversion from the main stream of agrarian thought, they occupy center stage in the dualistic framework of analysis. The postulation of two major production sectors (agriculture and industry) and the formal analysis of the asymmetrical structural relations between them may be said to constitute the heart of modern growth theory. The nonagricultural parasitic sector of agrarianism now becomes a bona fide industrial sector characterized by the use and the constant augmentation of a stock of real capital. Another major change in emphasis consists of the introduction of technological change in both the agricultural and industrial sectors and the major role assigned to it in the analysis of the growth process. The classical problem of population pressures on the land is now handled in conjunction with the problem of labor reallocation from the agricultural to the industrial sector. Economic surpluses can now be generated in the industrial sector as profits as well as in the agricultural sector; the intersectoral channelization of this savings fund constitutes an essential ingredient of the dualistic framework of thinking. Finally, the agrarian economy is isolated from the rest of the world and impervious to stimuli from abroad, but the dualistic economy enjoys the advantage of an international division of labor and the borrowing of technology from abroad.

Thus while agrarianism is primarily concerned with the maintenance and survival of a monolithic production structure, dualism strives for the demise of the agrarian system through a radical change in the production

---

[8] See R. Nurkse, *Problems of Capital Formation in Underdeveloped Countries* (Oxford, 1957); W. A. Lewis, "Economic Development with Unlimited Supplies of Labour," *Manchester School*, XXII (May, 1954), 139–91; J. C. H. Fei and G. Ranis, *Development of the Labor Surplus Economy: Theory and Policy* (Homewood, Ill., 1964); B. Higgins, *Economic Development* (New York, 1959); P. N. Rosenstein-Rodan, "Problems of Industrialization of Eastern and South-Eastern Europe," *Economic Journal*, LIII (June–September, 1943), 202–11.

structure. The agrarian view is one of resignation and fatalistic acceptance of the restraining hand of "natural law" while dualistic writers wish to attain a better future through a fuller understanding of the growth process and the application of relevant growth promotion policies. In summary, from the viewpoint of the technical equipment brought to bear, the assessment of the most pressing social problem of the day, and the vision of the future prospects of the society as a whole, agrarian and dualistic thinkers diverge in a fundamental sense.

Each system is characterized by its own internal rules of growth, the analysis of which is the major purpose of this paper. However, we believe that a fuller understanding of the total growth phenomenon will be achieved by viewing these separate regimes as occurring in a natural historical sequence. Ultimately, we must consider the transition from one phase to another, in which context such research into growth-promoting policies is likely to be most relevant and fruitful.

It is our view that at least one important type of growth proceeds via the natural sequence from agrarianism to dualism to maturity. For example, the agrarian pattern should by no means be viewed simply as a historical curiosity; in fact, much of the present-day underdeveloped world, particularly in Africa, finds itself in an essentially agrarian condition, with non-agriculture either totally absent or restricted to artisan handicraft and service activities. A relevant theory of development must be able to analyze not only the workings of the dualistic economy and the conditions for a successful transition from dualism to maturity,[9] but also the workings of the agrarian economy and the transition from agrarian stagnation to rigorous growth under dualism. We hope that this paper will contribute to this undertaking. Section II will explain the workings of the agrarian economy. In section III we present a preliminary view of the dualistic economy, which provides the guidelines for the construction of a formally deterministic growth model for such an economy in Section IV. Some conclusions are presented in Section V.

II. Development of the Agrarian Economy

The predominant form of economic activity in the agrarian economy is the production of agricultural goods by the application of labor (L) to land (T). In Figure 1a, labor (land) is measured on the horizontal (vertical) axis, and the curve, indexed by Y, is a typical production contour for agri-

[9] We shall not be concerned with this transition in the present paper. For a treatment of growth under dualism and the transition to maturity see Fei and Ranis, *Labor Surplus Economy.*

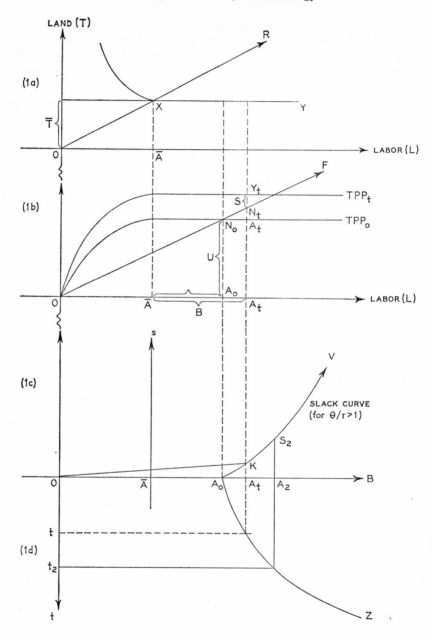

Figure 1. The Agrarian Economy

cultural goods. Following the classical tradition, we assume that land is fixed (at $\bar{T}$). For this amount of land, the total productivity of labor is represented by the curve TPP_0 in Figure 1b. As the figure indicates, at some labor input point (at $\bar{A}$) the TPP of labor levels off and becomes constant (the MPP_L approaches zero). Thus $0\bar{A}$ units of workers represent the non-redundant agricultural labor force. Any workers in excess of this amount do not make a positive contribution to output and thus represent the redundant labor force.[10] As long periods of time elapse and crop practices improve due to technological change, the TPP_L curve may shift upward to the position TPP_t (Figure 1b) at time t (from the initial position).[11] This summarizes the basic production conditions encountered in the agrarian economy.

To analyze the problem of population pressure endemic to an agrarian economy, let time be measured on the vertical axis (pointing downward) and population (or labor force) be measured on the horizontal axis of Figure 1d (vertically lined up with Figure 1a). The economy begins with an initial population of $0A_0$. The magnitude of this population through time can then be represented by the curve A_0Z in Figure 1d. The initial total output is A_0N_0 units in Figure 1b. This determines an initial level of per capita consumption as indicated by the slope of the radial line $0F$. At time t, with population at $0A_t$ and with total output of A_tY_t (Figure 1b), an agricultural surplus of $S\,(=N_tY_t)$ units appears if the initial consumption standard continues to obtain. We shall refer to S as the AS (agricultural surplus) as it is a genuine "surplus" of agricultural goods, after the consumption requirements of the agricultural population have been satisfied.

As indicated in the introduction, we believe a facet of economic life in the agrarian economy is the emergence and utilization of "slacks" in the dominant agricultural production sector. Such slacks are of two kinds, agricultural goods not required for the maintenance of traditional consumption

---

[10] The controversial assumption of a zero marginal product of labor (MPP_L) is not essential to the argument and is made only to facilitate exposition of our analysis of the "slack" phenomenon in the agrarian economy. Some writers (such as Theodore Schultz, *Transforming Traditional Agriculture* [New Haven, 1964]) object to the notion of a zero marginal product on regional peak demand and other grounds. We do not insist on an MPP_L of precisely zero, but we have little understanding for those who deny that there is considerable redundancy of full-time equivalent agricultural workers in many parts of the contemporary underdeveloped world, as well as in the agrarian past of other regions. If a man is needed only for the two-month harvest period, he can be considered five-sixths redundant.

[11] In Figure 1a, the ridge line $0R$ passes through point X vertically lined up with point A. The technological change depicted is assumed to be of the neutral variety (i.e., the output index in Figure 1a is simply "blown up" and the TPP_L curve in Figure 1b shifts up proportionally).

levels and manpower not needed for agricultural production. Referring to
Figure 1b, at time *t*, the surplus of agricultural goods is represented by *S*
while the surplus of agricultural labor is represented by the redundant labor force, *B*, of $\bar{A}A_t$ units. The magnitudes of these two types of slacks are
indicated in Figure 1c, where the vertical axis is now shifted to $\bar{A}s$ (origin
at *A*), with the redundant labor force measured on the horizontal axis and
the agricultural surplus measured on the vertical axis. The magnitudes of
the two types of slacks, through time, are indicated by the curve A_0V and
shall be referred to as the *slack-curve*. For example, at time t_2 (Figure 1d),
when the total population has grown to $0A_2$ the redundant labor force is
$\bar{A}A_2$ while the agricultural surplus is S_2A_2.

These two types of slacks in the agrarian system are obviously of key
analytical interest because they can both be used in any way the economy
sees fit (or even wasted) without interrupting the workings of the production system in the dominant agricultural sector in any significant way. After
all, the agricultural surplus, *S*, is an excess over consumption requirements
and the redundant labor force, *B*, is an excess over the labor force which
makes a positive contribution to agricultural production. The emergence
and utilization of these slacks over long periods of time determines to a
large extent the ultimate fate of the agrarian system.

The Emergence of Slack

We have depicted the case of slack emergence in Figure 1c in which both
B and *S* increase through time. To investigate the conditions leading to
this result, let us make the simplifying assumption that the production
function in the agricultural sector is of the Cobb-Douglas type, that is,
$Y = e^{\theta t}T^{\alpha}A^{1-\alpha}$. With *T* constant, we can define the unit of measurement of
output (*Y*) and obtain a production function of the type

(1.1)
$$Y = \begin{cases} e^{\theta t}A^{1-\alpha} \text{ for } A > A \\ e^{\theta t}U \text{ for } A < A \end{cases}$$

where θ is the rate of technological change, *A* is the nonredundant labor
force, and *U* is the initial total agricultural output ($U = A_0N_0$ in Figure 1b).
We assume here that the initial population $0A_0$ is greater than the non-
redundant labor force ($0\bar{A}$), that is, there are some disguised unemployed
or redundant workers in existence initially. Moreover, assuming the population to be growing at a constant rate, *r*, we have

(1.2)
$$A = A_0e^{rt}.$$

The initial per capita consumption standard, C^*, is then defined by

(1.3) $$C^* = U/A_0.$$

The magnitude of the redundant labor force, B, is given by

(1.4) $$B = A - \bar{A}$$

and the agricultural surplus is

(1.5) $$S = Y - AC^* = e^{\theta t}U - A_0 e^{rt}U/A_0 = U(e^{\theta t} - e^{rt}).$$

Using the population growth equation $(A/A_0 = e^{rt})$ to eliminate "t" from the above expression, we have

(1.6) $$S = U[(A/A_0)^{\theta/r} - A/A_0]$$

expressing a functional relation between A (size of population) and S (size of agricultural surplus). This expression can be simplified when we define

(1.7a) $A_0 = 1$ (the initial population A_0 is defined as one unit)[12]

and

(1.7b) $s = S/U$ (the unit of measurement of the surplus S is conveniently defined in terms of the constant U).

Under the above simplifications, (1.6) becomes

(1.8) $$s = A^{\theta/r} - A.$$

This curve passes through the point A_0 (now assumed to be "1") on the horizontal axis since $s = 0$ when $A = 1$ (Figure 1c). Finally we can derive the slack curve itself with the aid of relation (1.4):

(1.9) $$s = (A + B)^{\theta/r} - (A + B).$$

Thus we see that the slack curve of Figure 1c is derived under the assumption that both technological change and population growth proceed at an exogenously given constant rate with $\theta > r$. We shall assume that this inequality holds[13] and a slack emerges.

There exist a series of possible alternatives for the disposition of the

---

[12] Under this convention, the magnitude $\bar{A}$ is the fraction of the initial population which is nonredundant.

[13] If θ is less than r the slack-curve is negative and decreasing through time. The economy is not capable of generating either type of slack and hence the analysis of such an economy which cannot even maintain its initial consumption standard is not very interesting from the long run point of view—though at times undoubtedly of historical relevance.

emerging slack with major significance for the future prospects of the agrarian system. We shall deal in this paper with only two major alternatives, the consumption-population adjustment and the technological adjustment.

Consumption—Population Adjustment

The most obvious method of utilizing the surplus is to devote all of it to increases in per capita consumption. This, in turn, may have repercussions on the (no longer exogenous) population growth rate. To see this in greater detail, the possible increment in per capita consumption at time t (the amount of increase in per capita consumption possible over the "traditional" base year level) is given by the slope of the straight line $0K$ ($KA_t/0A_t$) in Figure 1c. As the point K moves upward on the slack-curve, the per capita consumption level increases.

In order to rigorously deduce the magnitude of this increase, we can easily, using (1.1), calculate the rate of increase of per capita output (η_Y^*) as follows:

$$(1.10a) \quad \eta_Y = \begin{cases} \theta + (1 - \alpha)\eta_A & \text{for } A \leq \bar{A} \\ \theta & \text{for } A \geq \bar{A} \end{cases} \quad \text{rate of increase of } Y$$

$$(1.10b) \quad \eta_Y^* = \begin{cases} \theta - \alpha\eta_A & \text{for } A \leq \bar{A} \\ \theta - \eta_A & \text{for } A \geq \bar{A} \end{cases} \quad \text{rate of increase of } Y^* = Y/A.$$

The relationship between the rate of increase of agricultural productivity (η_Y^*) and the population growth rate (η_A) for the two cases (labor not redundant and labor redundant) in (1.10b) is given in Figures 2a and 3a. In both cases, an inverse relationship exists between these two magnitudes, indicating that the higher the population growth rate, the lower the rate of increase of labor productivity. The only difference between the two cases is that in the second (the labor redundant case), which is the more relevant here, $\alpha = 1$. Thus in Figure 3a the curve linking η_A and η_Y^* is a negatively sloped 45-degree line.

The situation pictured in Figure 1c is therefore related to Figure 3a when labor is redundant. Since in the case of consumption adjustment all outputs are consumed, output per head (Y^*) is the same as consumption per head. From Figure 3a we see that per capita consumption will continue to increase ($\eta_Y^* + 0$) if and only if the population growth rate is less than the rate of technological change ($\eta_A < \theta$) which is the case depicted in Figure 1c.

When this consumption adjustment is assumed to take place and when the classical endogenous population growth theory is also accepted, we obtain what may be called the Jorgenson thesis of the "low level equilib-

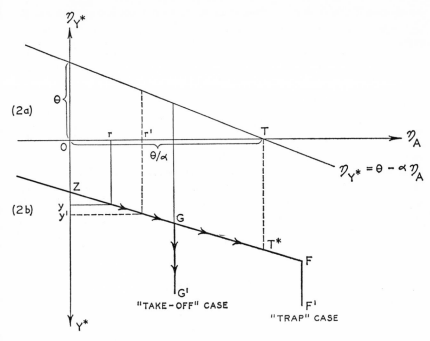

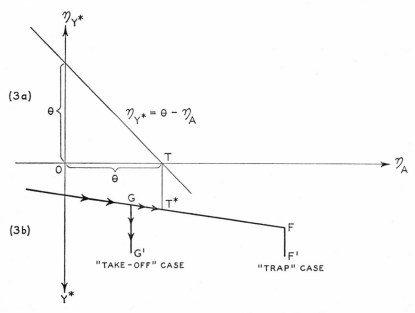

Figure 2. Long-Term Prospects: Labor Non-Redundant Case

Figure 3. Long-Term Prospects: Labor Redundant Case

rium trap."[14] According to this thesis, population growth is assumed to be dependent upon the level of per capita consumption, Y^*, in a manner described by the curve in Figure 2b. (In this diagram, Y^* is measured on the vertical axis, downward and η_A, as before, on the horizontal axis.) Two possible population response curves are given by the two broken lines, ZFF' and ZGG', which differ from each other in that in the first case the "turning point" (F) lies to the right of point T on the horizontal axis of Figure 2a, while in the second case the "turning point" (G) lies to the left of point T. The first case (ZFF') may be designated as the "trap" case, the second (ZGG') as the "takeoff" case.

In the "trap" case, starting from a low consumption level per head such as y (on the vertical axis of Figure 2b), the population growth rate implied (r) is positive and hence per capita income and consumption will increase in the next period. The higher level of Y^* or C^* leads to a still higher population growth rate (r'), a lower, but still positive rate of increase of Y^* (or C^*), and so on. This process continues with the time path indicated by the arrows until point T^* (and T) is reached, when (simultaneously) per capita income (and consumption) increases cease ($\eta_{Y^*} = 0$) and the population growth rate reaches a stationary equilibrium. At this level of population growth rate, θ/α, technological change and diminishing returns to labor just offset each other, keeping per capita output at a constant level. The economy is thus caught in a low-level equilibrium "trap."

In the "takeoff" case, starting again from such a point as "y" and the population growth rate implied thereby, the rate of growth of income (and consumption) per head is seen to be *positive* and hence the value of income (and consumption) per head will be higher in the next period. In Figure 2b, the time path will be as before, toward point T^*. However, at point G before T^* is realized, population is no longer responsive to increased per capita income (and consumption) because there exists a maximum rate of population growth.[15] In Figure 2b, the growth path will follow

[14] Dale Jorgenson, "The Development of a Dual Economy," *Econ. J.*, LXXI (Spring, 1961), 309–34; see also the article by Jorgenson in this volume and references cited therein.

[15] Dale Jorgenson, "Dual Economy," makes unnecessarily restrictive and unrealistic assumptions concerning this "turning point," namely that a saturation point for the per capita consumption of agricultural goods is reached at *precisely* the same point at which population growth becomes nonresponsive to further increases in Y^*. He utilizes this consideration to show the necessity of the ultimate evolution of an industrial sector, a subject to which we shall return later. Moreover, Jorgenson stipulates a constant death rate and a birth rate which rises with per capita income. What little we know about these matters indicates that the birth rate behaves unpredictably and that it is the decline in the death rate—related to preventive and public health expenditures (and not per capita income)—which causes the rise in population growth. Though Jorgenson claims to be neoclassical, his acceptance of the consumption adjustment and Malthusian population thesis gives his framework a distinctly classical cast, especially when θ is 0 or negligible.

the arrows toward G' once the turning point G has been reached. This constancy of the population growth rate implies a constancy henceforth in the rate of increase of per capita income (and consumption). The agrarian economy has thrown off its Malthusian shackles and continues to increase its per capita consumption level; it may be said to have reached a "takeoff."

Although the Jorgenson formulation is independent of the question of redundancy or nonredundancy of the labor force in the typical agricultural production situation, it is easily adapted to the case where this phenomenon is accepted. For this case a diagram similar to Figure 2ab, that is, Figure 3ab can be constructed. The explanation of the latter diagram follows exactly the same lines as the analysis just presented for 2ab. The only difference is that "the critical turning point," T (or T^*), occurs where the rate of population growth (η_A) is equal to the rate of technological change (θ) on the horizontal axis. Thus if the point at which population becomes nonresponsive to further increases in per capita income (and consumption) is to the left of T^* (for example, at G) we again have takeoff; otherwise the economy is "trapped."

The above analysis may be used to interpret Jorgenson's theory of the agrarian economy. Jorgenson's approach is important; his rigorously formulated dynamic model permits us to distinguish precisely between the trap and nontrap cases in the monolithic agrarian economy and thus between continued stagnation and takeoff. Nevertheless, the analysis is based on unrealistic or unduly restrictive assumptions. First, the assumption is made that the entire increase in the agricultural surplus is used for consumption by farm labor. This may occasionally be true in a completely freeholder economy but is highly unrealistic given most land ownership and tenure arrangements in the agrarian economy. Secondly, the acceptance of the Malthusian population theory is, at least according to much modern demographic testimony, subject to considerable doubt. Thirdly, and most important, in the Jorgenson world the rate of technological change in agriculture is mysteriously fixed and constant, which offends our sense of the real world. It rules out an important and perhaps more realistic alternative to the consumption-population adjustment mechanism as a method of disposing of the economy's agricultural slack. We shall call this alternative the "technology adjustment mechanism" and explore it at greater length.

Technology Adjustment

Any alternative adjustment mechanism is most conveniently discussed when, given a rate of population growth (r) and a rate of technological change (θ), per capita income is rising and two kinds of slacks are being generated. Both common sense and the lessons of the physiocrats and historical experience imply that a full consumption adjustment is unlikely to occur. Moreover, alternative and more realistic ways to dispose of the surplus may have an important feed-back effect on agricultural productivity increase itself.

As noted earlier, the physiocrats clearly saw the possibility of using the emerging agricultural slack for nonproductive purposes, that is, for an expansion of so-called sterile activities. Thus, in terms of Figure 1c, as a particular quantity of redundant workers (B) and agricultural surplus (S) is generated, those who own the slack, the landlords, the nobility, the church, may utilize it to expand their consumption of services, handicrafts, and other luxury products. Alternatively, as the income of the ruling classes rises they may choose to enlarge the military establishment, wage war with their neighbors, build pyramids, construct churches, or enhance the general "cultural attainments" of the society in some other way. There are an unlimited variety of uses to which the economy's slack can be put by those who have control over its disposition.

We contend that the choice of alternative uses of an economy's agricultural slack may have a considerable impact on the productive performance of agriculture through its effect on the rate of technological change, θ. In other words, as long as the economy is basically agrarian and not dualistic, when its nonagricultural activities are stagnant and parasitic, the rate of agricultural productivity increase may be adversely affected.

We should recall that technological change in the agrarian economy involves long-term, sometimes hardly perceptible changes in the state of the arts. The agrarian economy represents essentially a struggle between nature and numbers, with slight improvements in crop practices over the centuries. According to the testimony of agricultural economists, this slow improvement trend of agricultural labor productivity, θ, can be sustained only if the agricultural infrastructure is kept in decent repair and improved upon. Irrigation, for example, has been one of the oldest concerns of man. Without proper irrigation and drainage facilities or where such networks have fallen into disrepair it is very difficult, if not impossible, to translate the slow but persistent accumulation of human experience on the soil into secular, if slow, increases in productivity.

The human resource inputs of one period required to elicit such productivity increases in the next may thus be very important to technological change. While a portion of the agrarian economy's labor force may, for example, be redundant in contributing to this year's output (using this year's state of the arts), it is instead required for a variety of activities which may render agriculture more productive in the future. The unemployed and underemployed in agriculture can and do play a major historical role in digging irrigation ditches, constructing levees and dams, terracing, and in simply keeping existing facilities from falling into disrepair. The magnitude of θ is thus, at least in considerable part, a function of the extent to which the underemployed agricultural labor force is engaged in long gestation-period productivity-enhancing activities.

This is why determination of how the agrarian economy's slack is utilized is so crucial. Clearly, it is up to the owners of the agricultural surplus and those who control the human resources available whether the slack is to be deployed in θ-enhancing directions or dissipated in high living and conspicuous consumption. But it is almost typical of the agrarian economy that the owning classes do not have a clear vision of the future and do not associate productivity increases with current allocation decisions about the work and leisure of their resources. More likely, they respond to their rising income by increasing their demand for the products of the sterile classes, and the surplus of agricultural goods is used to hire away the surplus in manpower from agriculture-enhancing activities and provide more personal services, more luxury goods, more pomp and circumstance, larger armies, and more wars. In the Middle Ages the tithe was extracted for the support of the church and the plethora of feudal payments to support both the military and civilian manpower demands of king and baron. In Tokugawa, Japan, a high tax on land went almost exclusively for the support of the court and the warrior classes.[16] As surplus manpower is thus bid away the rate of agricultural productivity increase is likely to suffer. Thus, once we reject the rather untenable notion of a fixed, exogenously given, long-term rate of agricultural advance, we can see that in the typical agrarian economy there are forces at work tending toward a secular decline in θ. We believe that this technology adjustment is based on a realistic view of the long-run problem of the agrarian society. Ultimately this downward pull can bring the system to a halt, quite aside from the danger of the demographic trap of the Jorgenson consumption-population-adjustment school.

This hypothesis concerning "economic stagnation" brought about via "technology adjustment" may now be presented in a more rigorous formal fashion—not for the sake of precise model construction but because only in this way can the "logical consistency" of the above ideas be put to the test. In Figure 4, we reproduce the slack curve $\bar{A}FS$ of Figure 1c. Let "d" denote a wage premium, the amount of excess over the prevailing per capita consumption standard, C^*, which must be paid to the sterile worker if he is to be wooed away from agricultural pursuits. The number of sterile work-

[16] Thomas Smith, *The Agrarian Origins of Modern Japan* (Stanford, 1959).

ers is *T;* then the consumption per head of these workers is $C^* + d$, and the consumption per head of the nonsterile workers is C^*. The postulation of a positive wage premium, "*d*," is due to the fact that it generally takes a positive real social cost to mobilize, convert, and sustain each sterile worker

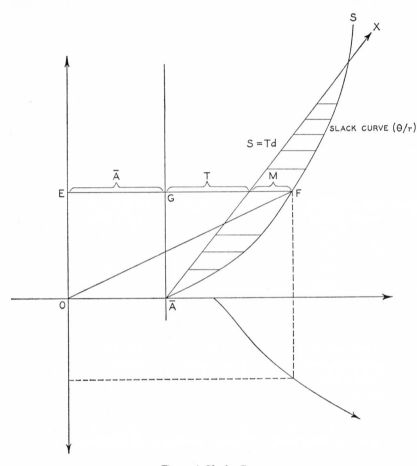

Figure 4. Slacks Curve

(soldier, priest, artisan, feudal servant) who has been induced (or forced) to leave his dependent life in agriculture. Since agricultural surplus, *S*, is the amount of surplus after allowing for consumption by the entire population at level C^*, *S* represents the "fund" out of which the wage premium to the sterile workers can be paid. Thus if all the surplus food is used to draw off workers for a variety of parasitic activities, we have

(1.11) $S = Td$

which is described by the straight line $\bar{A}X$ in Figure 4.

This line now permits us to determine the allocation of the economy's total labor force, A, at any point into three categories, nonredundant or productive labor, $\bar{A}$, sterile redundant labor, T, and nonsterile redundant labor, M:

(1.12) $A = \bar{A} + T + M$.

For example, point F represents a typical point on the slack curve (Figure 4). At F the entire population, EF, is divided into three portions: the nonredundant labor force, $\bar{A}$, the sterile redundant labor force, T, and the nonsterile redundant labor force, M. The latter (composed of M units of labor) represents redundant workers only from the *static* point of view; at any point in time they can be withdrawn from the agricultural sector without adversely affecting the total agricultural output of that year. However, from the dynamic point of view, they are productive in the sense that their removal from the agricultural sector will adversely affect future agricultural productivity by causing θ to turn down as a consequence of a relative neglect of agricultural overheads. The basic notion here is that the gradual, nonspectacular spread of new agricultural techniques is inhibited by the failure to maintain and improve irrigation and drainage facilities, feeder roads, and the like. These activities are bound to be heavily labor-using in the agrarian economy and once they are neglected, the long-run processes of slowly accumulating knowledge and passing it on from generation to generation are impaired.

In Figure 4, the shaded horizontal distances between the slack curve ($\bar{A}FS$) and the straight line ($\bar{A}X$) (1.11) represent various possible magnitudes of such redundant nonsterile workers. From the concavity of the slack curve (as previously derived) we know that, given a fixed value of both innovation intensity (θ) and population growth rate (r), the magnitude of the nonsterile redundant classes (M) will eventually decrease to zero as the absolute size of the economy's population continues to expand and the economy continues to move "upward" along the slack curve. This means that, sooner or later, the agricultural sector will begin to suffer from a "shortage" of this θ-maintaining type of labor, and the "dynamic efficiency" of agricultural activities cannot be maintained at the level of θ once M dips below a certain critical minimum level.

The above idea can be described rigorously by a behavioristic relation between θ and the labor force needed to sustain θ. For this purpose, let us denote $(\bar{A} + M)/L$ by "q"; "q" is the total nonsterile labor force as a fraction of the total labor force, L. For simplicity, we can postulate an increasing functional relation between θ and q:

(1.13a) $q = Q(\theta)$ with $Q' > 0$

where

(1.13b) $q = (\bar{A} + M)/L = (L - T)/L$

which states that a higher level of θ necessitates the application of a higher fraction of the total labor force as nonsterile labor.

Given fixed per capita consumption, C^*, the total consumption demand of the nonsterile workers is $C^*(\bar{A} + M)$ or $C^*(L - T)$ and that of the sterile workers is $(C^* + d)T$. Since total output is LY^*, we have

(1.14a) $C^*(L - T) + (C^* + d)T = LY^*$

which applies

(1.14b) $T/L = (Y^* - C^*)/d$

and hence (by 1.13b)

(1.14c) $q = 1 + (C^* - Y^*)/d = \phi(Y^*)$ with $\phi' < 0$.

The last equation states that the value of q is uniquely determined by Y^*, as indicated by the notation $\phi(Y^*)$. The value of q is inversely related to Y^*. Together with (1.13a) we see that θ is a function of Y^* and is, in fact, inversely related to Y^* (as per capita output increases, the value of θ decreases). This may be written as:

(1.15) $\theta = h(Y^*)$ with $h' < 0$.

We shall refer to equation (1.15) as the innovation response curve since it specifies the level of innovational intensity in response to per capita income changes. This relationship (which may seem contrary to common sense) is due to the fact that increases in the well-being of the propertied classes, as reflected in higher per capita incomes and surpluses, lead to an increase in demand for the services of the sterile classes to the point that agricultural productivity increases sooner or later begin to suffer. While there are good reasons to assume that such a relationship is not inevitable in every agrarian society, it seems reasonable. In both Tokugawa, Japan, and medieval Europe the evidence indicates that the ruling classes did not concern themselves with maintaining agricultural progress but rather devoted their energies to the "good life" and/or making war on their neighbors—both activities making substantial demands on redundant labor resources.

Turning now to Figure 5a, equation (1.10b) is written as $\eta_Y{}^* = \theta - r$ and represented by the positively sloped straight line. While $\eta_Y{}^*$ is plotted on the vertical axis, the magnitude of θ is indicated on the horizontal axis. Moreover, since in our analysis, the population growth rate is assumed to

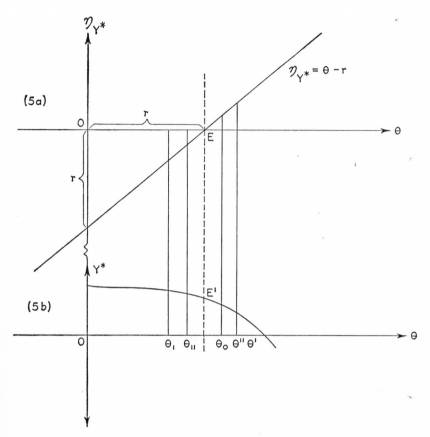

Figure 5. Technology Adjustment

be constant ($\eta_A = r$), the straight line is a 45-degree line which intersects both axes at distance r from the origin. In Figure 5b, vertically lined up with Figure 5a, Y^* is measured on the vertical and θ on the horizontal axis, and the innovation response curve (1.15) is represented by the negatively sloped curve. Moreover, a vertical dotted line is drawn from point E to obtain point E' on the innovation response curve.

Our theory of stagnation via the technology adjustment mechanism can now be summarized with the help of Figure 5b. Starting from a point such as θ' greater than r, for example, the value of θ necessarily decreases (from θ' to θ'') because the value of $\eta_Y{}^*$ is positive (see Figure 5a). During this process, output per head (Y^*) increases but at a decreasing rate (see Figure 5b). Eventually, the value of θ decreases to a stationary value (θ_0) at E, equal in magnitude to the population growth rate (r).[17] The economy will then be expanding in a stationary equilibrium state characterized by the constancy of Y^*. In this fashion, the phenomenon of long-term stagnation results from the workings of the technology adjustment mechanism.

Up to this point, our analysis of the agrarian economy has focused entirely on understanding the internal workings of that system and examining the plausibility of alternative mechanisms by which it either escapes from its low-level equilibrium trap or faces the prospect of long-run stagnation. This has entailed a view of growth within a fixed regime, defined by a given set of rules. The focal point of the analysis has been in terms of real resource behavior patterns in the agrarian regime.

In this context, the consumption-population adjustment mechanism was found to be unrealistic. Similar objections could undoubtedly be raised against the alternative technology adjustment mechanism, presented here, but we find it more reasonable since it includes in the explanatory model certain historical features characteristic of the agrarian economy neglected in the Jorgenson approach. This includes the existence of a nonconsumed agricultural surplus and of nonagricultural production activities and the importance of the forces which determine the rate of technological change. What is perhaps indicated for the future is a partial synthesis of the consumption-population adjustment and the technology-adjustment mechanisms in exploring the long-run behavior of the agrarian system; both mechanisms may be at work to some extent in yielding the observed "trap" outcome. In the real world undoubtedly all the potential surpluses are not consumed by the agricultural working population, nor are they likely to be entirely diverted to support the luxury life of the propertied classes. The extent to which increases in per capita income lead to increases in per capita consumption, or to surpluses available for other purposes, will depend on such institutional factors as the existing class structure, tenure arrangements, and the relative power of the landlord to adjust rental charges. Clearly, considerably more inquiry into such organizational characteristics of the agrarian economy is needed before we can be sure of the more precise causation of the observed long-run quasi-equilibrium in the system.

There is, however, a second issue to be addressed—the nature of the transition from agrarianism to dualism. This is no longer a largely quanti-

---

[17] Similarly, in the unlikely case that the initial θ is less than the population growth rate, r (e.g., at θ_1) , θ will be increasing to the same stationary value.

tative or real resource question, but one relating to an institutional transformation affecting the rules of growth themselves. The analysis of such a transition, for the nontrapped agrarian economy is much more complicated than any real resources calculus. If the regime of agrarianism is to be transformed into one of dualism, institutional arrangements must first be constructed so that the various economic functions endemic to dualism (bound to be vastly more complicated than those of agrarianism) can be performed. It is clear that we cannot even hope to analyze the transformation without a full understanding of the dualistic regime which follows.[18]

III. THE DUALISTIC ECONOMY: A BIRD'S-EYE VIEW

The dualistic economy exhibits structural characteristics which are markedly different from those of the agrarian economy—even though both are underdeveloped and heavily agricultural. A major distinguishing feature of the dualistic economy is the coexistence of a subsistence agricultural sector and a commercialized industrial sector. In contrast with the subsidiary and "sterile" handicrafts and services of the agrarian economy, using virtually no real capital, the industrial production sector is dynamic and vigorous (if initially small), and real capital formation plays an important role. The basic problem in this economy is not one of how to satisfy the growing luxury tastes of the leisure classes in the presence of diminishing returns in agriculture, but of how to shift the economy's center of gravity from agriculture to industry until agriculture becomes a mere appendage.

Specifically, the importance of real fixed capital in the industrial sector of the dualistic economy cannot be overstated. This is true because with the advent of real capital, we introduce important new analytical facets; a new source of income (capitalist profits) and a new source of surplus (capitalist savings), both absent in the agrarian economy. Associated with this new source of income is a new propertied class, the industrial capitalist, with ownership of the industrial capital stock being created out of the savings of the industrial sector. This emerging capitalist class is anxious to increase its ownership of the industrial capital stock as much and as quickly as possible. It wishes not only to siphon off the new surplus for reinvestment in industry but also to enhance the productive power of the

---

[18] Jorgenson's view varies from ours on this point. He says that as the agrarian economy ceases to be trapped by Malthusian pressures (phenomenon completely determined by real resources calculation) the transition to dualism is easy and automatic. Jorgenson does not differentiate the problems.

new capital through the incorporation with it of as much technological change as possible. The owners of the industrial capital—unlike the sterile classes in the agrarian society—thus have an incentive to innovate or to adopt and adapt the innovations of others along the economy's industrial production functions.

It should be clear that the dualistic economy's total saving fund is composed of two kinds of surpluses, industrial profits and agricultural surplus. This total saving fund must then be allocated to the two sectors—along with entrepreneurial activity—to increase agricultural labor productivity in one sector, thus freeing labor, and to increase industrial labor productivity in the other, thus creating a demand for the allocated labor force. At the same time, given the consumer preferences of the typical worker, the output generated in the two sectors must be such as to prevent a "shortage" of food or of industrial goods, as indicated by a marked change in the intersectoral terms of trade. Thus allocation decisions, taking into account both capital accumulation and technological change in each sector, must proceed in a balanced fashion so as to avoid the overexpansion of either sector in the course of the reallocation process. With the economy's saving and entrepreneurial energies expended so as to insure the synchronized forward movement of both sectors, the prospects for success are heightened.

While it is, of course, true that capital accumulation (as well as technological change) may enhance agricultural productivity in the dualistic economy, we accept the evidence of such successful agricultural revolutions as those in Japan, Taiwan, and Greece to the effect that physical capital plays a relatively less important role in agriculture; the labor-intensive adoption of new techniques, the application of fertilizer, and the like are considerably more important. Thus the net flow of capital resources (as well as labor resources) in the course of dualistic growth is out of agriculture and into industry.

Acceptance of this notion of a balanced intersectoral allocation process in the dualistic economy leads us directly to the idea that the ownership of industrial capital goods may be viewed as a possible reward for the generation of an agricultural surplus. Moreover, once the agricultural propertied classes, the landlords and nobility, begin to view the acquisition of industrial assets as more desirable than the making of war and the good life in the agrarian context, the transition to dualism is assisted directly and there is an important feed-back on the incentive toward further increases of agricultural productivity. The landlord views agriculture as a direct means of participating, along with the original industrial capitalist, in the ownership of the productive assets in the growing industrial sector.

These claims against the industrial sector are established in the course of facilitating the net flow of surplus (or savings) from agriculture to the rest of the economy. Surplus food is sold by the landlord in the intersectoral commodity market and the proceeds invested in the industrial sector. This is accomplished most easily by the dualistic landlord[19] who has one foot in each sector and directly owns and manages the newly created industrial production structure. Alternatively, the claims against the industrial sector can be acquired by the owner of the agricultural surplus through a system of financial intermediation, such as the purchase of savings certificates, bonds, and stocks, implying the more customary separation between ownership and control. But institutions of this type are difficult to establish in the typical underdeveloped economy and, once established, they may not be accepted. The most trusted financial intermediary is obviously oneself or one's close relatives, which is why the dualistic landlord (as encountered in Japan) or his counterpart are so important for the transition from agrarianism to dualism as well as for dualism's continued growth. The dualistic landlord as agricultural entrepreneur has an increasing interest in innovating in that sector as the potentialities of industrialization become apparent to him; similarly, as industrial entrepreneur he is anxious to innovate or to adapt the industrial innovation of others to the fullest extent possible. Technological change in both sectors is thus bound to yield increasing surpluses for the owning class and a more rapid accumulation of the desired industrial capital stock. In juxtaposition to the technology adjustment mechanism of the agrarian economy, which has a negative effect on θ, the dualistic economy is characterized by a technology adjustment mechanism which has a positive effect on θ. No longer are human resources and entrepreneurial attention pulled away from agriculture and squandered on luxuries and frills, but increasing agricultural productivity is viewed as a major engine for the balanced forward motion of the entire dualistic system. We may call this a positive technology adjustment mechanism.

One other facet of the emerging dualistic economy deserves further consideration—the determination of the nature and rate of technological change in the industrial sector. As long as the economy is basically agrarian it is relatively insulated from change domestically and from the rest of the world. Once the transition to dualism is under way, however, the economy becomes more fully exposed to the rest of the world, both through the exchange of primary products for imported consumer and capital goods and through the accompanying transfer of technology. As we have already pointed out, the incentive for the entrepreneurs to adopt new and more efficient production functions clearly exists; but the prior preoccupation

---

[19] For a fuller analysis, see Fei and Ranis, *Labor Surplus Economy,* Chapter 5.

of the propertied classes and their limited experience with industrial production causes them to turn for help, at least initially, to the outside.

As Veblen pointed out long ago,[20] considerable advantages attach to the "latecomer nation" attempting to industrialize. Such an economy is in a position to survey the technological shelf already perfected by others and to pick and choose that which seems most suitable—without itself incurring the considerable cost of trial and experimentation. But, while innovations with the highest payoff or yield are likely, at least initially, to emanate from abroad, this does not necessarily imply the adoption of the latest, most up-to-date techniques known, nor the mere transplantation of processes from one country to another. As the nineteenth-century Japanese experience illustrates,[21] technological transfers from the more advanced to the latecomer country are most effective when handled selectively, in some cases via adoption of methods already obsolete abroad and in others the transfer of the latest ("most modern") methods. The heavy borrowing of industrial technology from abroad in the early decades of the dualistic economy does not, moreover, preclude a considerable dosage of domestic innovational activity. Such activity will, however, be directed more toward the adaptation of imported techniques to different local conditions (such as the greater relative availability of cheap labor) than to the creation, from scratch, of new methods of production.

The role of technological change, both in its intensity or strength and in its slantedness or bias, can thus be of great importance in the early industrialization process. T. Watanabe concludes that "the most important causes for Japan's rapid industrialization can be found in the nature and growth of technological change."[22] Innovations, for example, were responsible for as much as 80 per cent of the absorption of industrial labor during the early period.[23]

It is also a fact of life, as Veblen points out, that the early advantage of the latecomer is ultimately dissipated. As the technological shelf of the more advanced countries is cleared of relevant techniques, the annual rate of technological advance of the industrial sector of the dualistic economy is likely to slow down. As the dualistic economy becomes more and more industrialized, however, in the course of a successful labor reallocation proc-

[20] Thorstein J. Veblen, "The Opportunity of Japan," *Essays in Our Changing Order* (New York, 1934), pp. 248–66.
[21] See G. Ranis, "Factor Proportions in Japanese Economic Development," *American Economic Review*, XLVII (September, 1957), 594–607, for a fuller statement on the subject of this paragraph.
[22] "Economic Aspects of Dualism in the Industrial Development of Japan," *Economic Development and Cultural Change*, XIII (April, 1965), 293–312.
[23] Fei and Ranis, *Labor Surplus Economy*, pp. 125–31.

ess its domestic skill and ingenuity levels will be rising; increasingly as the importance of borrowed industrial technology declines, the economy will be in a position to produce its own technological advances domestically. In fact, it may be the capacity to generate a sustained flow of indigenous technological change in a routinized fashion which separates the mature from the underdeveloped society.

IV. DEVELOPMENT OF THE DUALISTIC ECONOMY

The above discussion has emphasized the essential characteristics of development in a dualistic economy. Now, with a rigorously formulated growth model, we can explain how the time path of an interrelated system of economic magnitudes is determined. Such a dynamic system must, in addition, be capable of emphasizing all the essential growth-related phenomena in a dualistic economy outlined in the last section.

Although there are only two production sectors, the growth process in the dualistic economy is by nature very complicated. This process involves production-centered phenomena (such as the use of capital and labor and the generation of innovational activities) in two separate production sectors. Therefore, one must take account of such crucial intersectoral relations as the transfer of labor from the agricultural to the industrial sector, the intersectoral channelization of savings, and the possibilities of the intrasectoral and intersectoral stimulation of technological change. Central to this process are not only the forces of production (the production functions of the two sectors) and consumption (the consumer preference function), but also the impact of such "exogenous" forces as population growth and the substantial possibility of importing technology. Finally, we should recall that all these real production, allocation, consumption, and distribution decisions must be made within the context of a set of organizational devices to handle and coordinate the various disparate economic activities. For example, with respect to the particular institutional milieu of capitalism or the "mixed economy," this involves the use of wages and prices as instruments of stimulation and harmonization. When the workings of this entire system are to be understood, satisfying all the major conditions imposed by the real world, the dynamic general equilibrium model which emerges is, by necessity, complicated and cumbersome.

In order to introduce the model in its entirety, let us first present the following system of growth equations; our immediate task is to explain the economic significance of these equations individually and then to show that, collectively, they determine the entire growth process in an orderly fashion. (To facilitate our exposition a brief description of each variable and of the relationship in which it is involved is presented after each equation.)

(2.1a) $Y = \begin{cases} e^{\int \theta dt} A^{\alpha} & \text{for } A < \bar{A} \\ e^{\int \theta dt} V & \text{for } \bar{A} \leq A \end{cases}$ (production function in the agricultural sector where Y = agricultural output; A = agricultural labor force; θ = innovation intensity in agricultural sector).

(2.1b) $P = A + L$ (labor allocation equation; P = total population; L= labor force in the industrial sector).

(2.1c) $S = Y - A\bar{w}$ (definition of total agricultural surplus (TAS); S = TAS; $\bar{w}$ = institutional real wage in terms of agricultural goods).

(2.1d) $V = S/L$ (definition of average agricultural surplus (AAS); $V = AAS$).

(2.1e) $\tau = gL/S$ (definition of terms of trade; τ = terms of trade [units of industrial goods exchanged per unit of agricultural goods]).

(2.1f) $w = \phi(V)$ (determination of industrial real wage; w = real wage in terms of industrial goods).

(2.1g) $g = \lambda w$ (determination of surplus coefficient; g = surplus coefficient; λ = proportionality factor between g and w).

(2.1h) $\theta = f(\tau)$
$\theta' \geq 0$ (intensity of agricultural innovation function).

(2.1i) $\eta_P = r$ (population growth function; r = population growth rate).

(2.1j) $X = F(t) K^B L^{1-B}$ (production function in the industrial sector; $X =$ industrial output; K and $L =$ real capital and labor force in the industrial sector).

(2.1k) $J = \eta_F = b + ae^{-ut}$
                $a \geq 0, b \geq 0, u \geq 0$ (innovation intensity in industrial sector).

(2.1l) $\pi_1 = BX$ (profits in the industrial sector: π_1).

(2.1m) $\pi_2 = Lg$ (savings of the agricultural sector used in the industrial sector: π_2).

(2.1n) $\eta_K = (\pi_1 + \pi_2)/K$ (rate of growth of capital in the industrial sector).

(2.1o) $\eta_L = \eta_K + J/B - \eta_w/B$ (labor absorption equation in industrial sector).

The basic production conditions for the dualistic economy are given by (2.1a) for the agricultural sector and by (2.1j) for the industrial sector. For the latter, we have postulated a Cobb-Douglas function with neutral innovation in the Hicksian sense. The *intensity of innovation*,[24] denoted by J, is defined by

(2.2a) $J = (\partial x/\partial t)/x$

which, when applied to (2.1j), leads to

(2.2b) $J = \eta_F = (\partial F/\partial t)/F$.

Furthermore, for the production function in (2.1j), we have assumed that the innovation behavior (in the industrial sector) takes on a special form as depicted by the curve indicated in Figure 6 (the curve J, labeled "innovation intensity"). This assumption is due to the fact that, for a contemporary dualistic economy, arriving on the scene as a latecomer anxious to borrow technology from abroad, it is reasonable to postulate that J initially takes on this shape, monotonically decreasing to a stationary level, "b," as the advantages of the initial latecomer status are gradually exhausted (as innovations become increasingly "domestically" generated rather than imported). This innovation behavior in the industrial sector is approximated by equation (2.1k). From this equation, we easily have

[24] In words, J is the fractional increase of output due to the passage of time, only holding both K and L constant. See Fei and Ranis, *Labor Surplus Economy*, Chapter 3.

(2.3a) $\eta_J = -u/(1 + (b/a)e^{ut})$ (rate of increase of
                                          innovation intensity)

(2.3b) $F = F(0)e^{\int J dt} = F(0)e^{bt-(a/u)e^{-ut}+au}$ (level of innovation).

In Figure 6, η_J, the rate of increase of innovation intensity, is represented by the monotonically increasing curve below the horizontal axis. Thus the underlying assumption is "deceleration" of innovation intensity. The curve

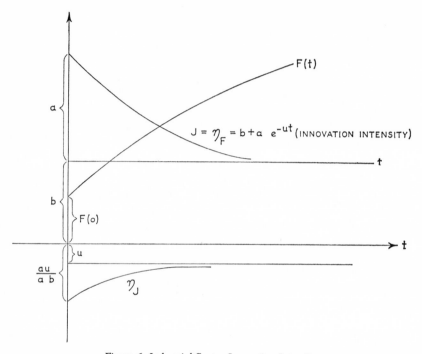

Figure 6. Industrial Sector Innovation Intensity

for $F(t)$ in (2.3b) is plotted in the same diagram and represents the cumulative output-raising effect of innovation. Figure 6 thus helps us to visualize the innovation behavior postulated for the industrial sector of the dualistic economy. Finally, using (2.3b), the production function (2.1j) takes on the following form through a redefinition of the unit of measurement of output:

(2.4) $X = e^{bt-(a/u)e^{-ut}+au}K^B L^{1-B}$.

Next comes (2.1a), the production function for the agricultural sector of the dualistic economy, which is seen to be similar to (1.1), the production function postulated for the agrarian economy. For example, when labor is not redundant, it is deduced from a Cobb-Douglas function with neutral innovations:

(2.5) $$Y = F(t)A^\alpha T^{1-\alpha}$$

where T stands for land and $F(t)$ is the "innovation level" factor similar to $F(t)$ in (2.1j) for the industrial sector. Denoting the innovational intensity in the agricultural sector by θ,

(2.6a) $\qquad \theta = \eta_F \qquad$ by (2.2a) applied to (2.5),

hence

(2.6b) $$F = F(0)e^{\int \theta dt}.$$

When (2.6b) is substituted in (2.5), we obtain (2.1a) after redefining the unit of measurement of output and assuming land to be fixed. The intensity of agricultural innovation, θ, is formally introduced into the production function because of our conviction, previously stated, that the analysis of changing innovational behavior in the agricultural sector is central to the performance of the dualistic economy. In this sense, the treatment given to agricultural innovations is completely symmetrical to that given to industrial innovations, J. Nevertheless, the symmetry in treatment ceases when we proceed beyond this formal level. The basic difference between J in the industrial sector and θ in the agricultural sector is that while J is assumed to be determined exogenously, the value of θ is determined endogenously.

Equation (2.1b) simply states that the total labor force (P) is to be allocated, at all times, either to the agricultural sector (A) or to the industrial sector (L) while equation (2.1i) states that the total population is growing at a constant rate, r. Together, these equations emphasize that the dualistic economy is subject to population pressure and that the reallocation of labor (from the agricultural to the industrial sector) is a crucial aspect of growth in the dualistic economy. In fact, *all* the remaining equations in (2.1), in one way or another, are related to the process of labor reallocation.

Equations (2.1c) and (2.1d) present definitions of *TAS* (*total agricultural surplus*, denoted by S) and *AAS* (*average agricultural surplus*, denoted by V) respectively. In order to deduce these concepts we assume that a fixed level of real wage, in terms of agricultural goods, $\bar{w}$, is given exogenously as the *IRW* (*institutional real wage*), as determined institutionally in the agricultural sector. In a poor, underdeveloped economy, the *IRW* may be close to the level of subsistence wage and remains fixed at this level as long as there are redundant workers in the agricultural sector. The total agricultural surplus, S, is the surplus of agricultural goods after the entire agricultural labor force has been fed at $\bar{w}$ (see 2.1c). The measure of the availability of agricultural goods per unit of worker already allocated to the industrial sector is AAS (see 2.1d).[25]

The economic significance of the AAS is as a measurement of the extent of commodity support that the agricultural sector furnishes to the industrial sector. The magnitude of the AAS directly determines the terms of trade when we know consumer preferences as well as the level of the institutional wage in terms of agricultural goods. This relation is fully analyzed elsewhere,[26] so we shall only present a brief summary here.

Let us assume that regardless of the ownership of TAS, the entire amount (S) will be exchanged for industrial goods in the intersectoral commodity market. On the other side of this transaction are industrial workers who, after receiving their wage in industrial goods, seek to acquire agricultural goods for consumption. Assume that the real wage (in terms of industrial goods) which prevails in the industrial sector is "tied" to the agricultural real wage (the $\bar{w}$) as they have the same exchange value.

In Figure 7, agricultural (industrial) goods are measured on the vertical (horizontal) axis and the indifference map of a typical worker in the industrial sector is given. The constant institutional level of the real wage, $\bar{w}$, in agriculture is marked off on the vertical axis and the price-consumption curve from point $\bar{w}$ is constructed. In case the amount AAS is known, its magnitude can be indicated by a point such as A on the vertical axis. This permits us to obtain point D on the price-consumption curve. It is then obvious that the slope of the straight line, $\bar{w}D$, represents the terms of trade (τ) between the two production sectors—for only at these terms of trade will the intersectoral commodity market be cleared and will the AAS be purchased by the typical industrial worker. This holds true under the assumption that the industrial wage *in terms of agricultural goods* is pinned at $\bar{w}$ units of food (the institutional real wage in terms of agricultural goods prevailing in the industrial sector not only is tied to the value of the agricultural real wage but—for simplicity's sake—is equal to it). The value of the real wage in industrial goods then is $0B$ and the distance g as noted on the horizontal axis is called the *surplus coefficient* (g). Specifically, the economic interpretation of g is the amount of industrial goods which the typical industrial worker gives up in exchange for the surplus of agricultural wage goods he has acquired. Since the total expenditure of all industrial

[25] *TAS* and *AAS* are defined in this same fashion in Fei and Ranis, *Labor Surplus Economy*.

[26] Fei and Ranis, *Labor Surplus Economy*, Chapter 5.

workers is *gL* units of industrial goods, the *terms of trade* (τ) between the two sectors is *gL/S* as in equation (2.1e).

The above analysis shows that the industrial real wage in terms of industrial goods is controlled by the relative availability of agricultural surplus through a mechanism operating in the intersectoral commodity market.

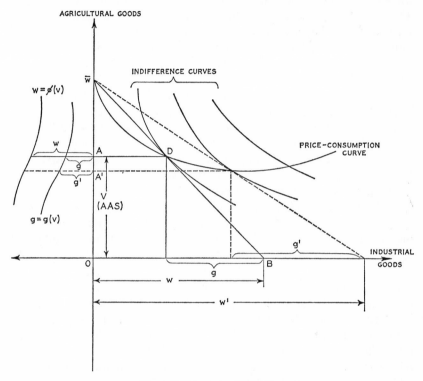

Figure 7. Intersectoral Relations

This functional relationship between the *AAS* and *w* (the real wage in terms of *industrial* goods) is given by equation (2.1f) and is represented by the curve in the second quadrant of Figure 7. As indicated in this diagram, any increase in *AAS* will depress the real industrial wage through a cheapening of food (a deterioration of agriculture's terms of trade). When this occurs, the value of the surplus coefficient (*g*) also decreases as the expenditure (in *industrial* goods) of a typical industrial worker declines. Thus, there is an inverse functional relationship between *AAS* (i.e., *V*) and the surplus coefficient (*g*) as is indicated by the curve (denoted by $g = g(V)$) in the second quadrant of Figure 7. From these two curves ($w = \phi(V)$) and ($g = g(V)$)

indicated in the second quadrant of Figure 7, we may, for simplicity, assume that w and g are proportional to each other. This leads to assumption (2.1g).

Equation (2.1h) states that the intensity of innovations in the agricultural sector (θ) is a function of and is positively related to the terms of trade (τ) as they are determined in the intersectoral commodity market. The economic justification for this assumption should be clear: a cultivator will make a larger effort in initiating new cultivation practices or imitating those initiated by others (both resulting in a higher intensity of agricultural innovation), when the terms of trade are more favorable to the agricultural sector.

The mutually beneficial relationship between the industrial and the agricultural sectors of the dualistic economy is due to the fact that, from the viewpoint of the agricultural sector, "access to the industrial sector" stimulates agricultural productivity and from the viewpoint of the industrial sector, "access to the agricultural sector" increases the savings fund. This latter beneficial effect is depicted by the two components of the savings fund, π_1, the reinvestment of the profits of the industrial sector (2.1l) and π_2, the savings of agricultural sector (2.1m) which, together, determine the rate of growth of capital in the industrial sector (2.1n). Equation (2.1l) defines total industrial profit, π_1, determined competitively in the industrial sector—as seen from the fact that "B" is the "profit share" in the Cobb-Douglas production function (2.1j). Equation (2.1m) defines agricultural savings, π_2, since Lg is the total amount of industrial goods which the owners of the agricultural surplus acquired through the intersectoral commodity market—as described in (2.1e).

Equation (2.1o) is the labor absorption equation which states that the rate of increase of employment of labor in the industrial sector is positively related to the rate of capital accumulation (2.1n) and innovation intensity, J (2.1k) and is negatively related to the rate of increase of the real wage (2.1f). This equation is obtained directly by computing the marginal productivity of labor (the competitive level of real wage) and its rate of increase through time from the production function in (2.1j):

(2.7a) $w = MPP_L = \partial X/\partial L = F(t)(1-B)(K/L)^B$ (competitive real wage)

(2.7b) $\eta_w = (dw/dt)/w = J + B\eta_K - B\eta_L .$

The rate of labor absorption (2.1o) is, of course, crucial in the development of the dualistic economy—as, when compared with the population growth rate (2.1i) we can determine whether an increasing fraction of the total population is gradually being employed in the industrial sector, that is, whether or not the center of gravity can be gradually shifted from the agricultural to the industrial sector.

Having explained the above fifteen equations individually, we now turn to the problem of the dynamic determinism of the growth process through the interaction of the forces summarized with the help of these equations. To assist us in achieving a firmer grasp of the workings of the dualistic economy as an organic analytical whole, a fuller understanding of the proposed causal order of the economic forces at work may be helpful. In Figure 8 a causal order chart is presented. The heavy horizontal line marks off two adjacent periods, such as $t = 0$ (above the line) and $t = 1$ (below the line). In each period, we find three large circles including three clusters of

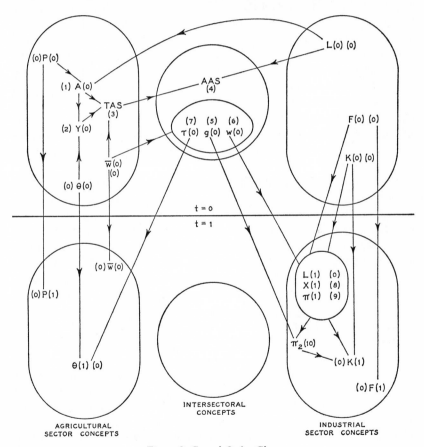

Figure 8. Causal Order Chart

economic concepts: agricultural sector concepts (circle on the left), industrial sector concepts (circle on the right), and intersectoral concepts (circle in the center). Although this grouping is not exact, it may help us to develop a sense of order for the growing system as a whole. The various arrows indicate the assumed direction of causation (or the order of determination of the system). For convenience we use the notation (x, y) to refer to an arrow which initiates from concept "x" and points to concept "y." Finally, numbers (1, 2, 3. . . .) are attached to the various concepts to identify their order of presentation in our discussion.

The initial values, at $t = 0$, are given of population $P(0)$, innovational intensity in agriculture $\theta(0)$, industrial labor force $L(0)$, industrial capital stock $K(0)$, level of innovation in the industrial sector $F(0)$, and constant institutional wage in agriculture, $\bar{w}$. The initial values of these six variables (and of only these) are assumed to be given. To determine the other economic magnitudes within the agricultural sector, given the size of the total population, $P(0)$, and the total industrial labor force, $L(0)$, we can immediately determine the size of the agricultural labor force, $A(0)$, by using (2.1b). Since the initial intensity of agricultural innovation, $\theta(0)$, is given, this, together with $A(0)$, determines total agricultural output, $Y(0)$, by using the production function (2.1a). We can then determine the size of the agricultural surplus by using $Y(0)$, $A(0)$, and the institutional wage, $\bar{w}$, according to (2.1c). In this way all the concepts in the agricultural circle at time $t = 0$ can be determined.

Next, given total agricultural surplus, TAS, and the size of the industrial labor force, we can, by using (2.1d), determine the magnitude of the average agricultural surplus, AAS. The AAS concept represents a crucial link between the two sectors of the dualistic economy since, together with the institutional wage, $\bar{w}$, it determines a set of three important economic magnitudes, the industrial real wage, $w(0)$ (by 2.1f), the surplus coefficient $g(0)$ (by 2.1g), and the intersectoral terms of trade, $\tau(0)$ (by 2.1e). This completes the determination of all the concepts in the intersectoral concept circle at $t = 0$.

The industrial sector circle at $t = 1$ indicates that the size of the previous period's industrial capital stock, $K(0)$, the level of innovation, $F(0)$, and the wage rate, $w(0)$, determine the amount of industrial labor absorbed in this period, $L(1)$, as per equation (2.1o). This, in turn, determines industrial output, $X(1)$, and industrial profits, $\pi_1(1)$, by use of the industrial production function (2.1j) and the distribution equation (2.1l). Furthermore, the surplus coefficient, $g(0)$, and the industrial labor force, $L(1)$, together determine the agricultural surplus contribution to the total savings fund, $\pi_2(1)$, in accordance with equation (2.1m). Once we know the total savings

$(\pi_1 + \pi_2)$ we can determine the capital stock in the next period, $K(1)$. The level of innovation in the next period, $F(1)$, is then determined as we have assumed that innovation in the industrial sector is exogenously given according to (2.1k). In this fashion all the concepts in the industrial circle at $t = 1$ are determined.

To complete this discussion of determinism, we see that the total population at $t = 1$ is given by (2.1i). However, more significantly we can determine the level of innovational intensity, $\theta(1)$, as a phenomenon directly related to the activities in the intersectoral commodity market; the terms of trade, $\tau(0)$, and the innovation intensity in the previous period, $\theta(0)$, determine the innovation intensity, $\theta(1)$, and hence the level of technology in this period according to (2.1h).

There are altogether fifteen variables $(P, A, L, Y, S, \theta, V, g, w, T, X, \pi_1, \pi_2, K, F)$ to be determined by the fifteen equations in (2.1). Furthermore, the five variables $(P(0), L(0), Q(0), F(0),$ and $K(0))$ whose initial values are assumed to be given at $t = 0$ (which are indexed by causal order "0") are again determined at $t = 1$. This means that the whole cycle can start once again and determine all the magnitudes in the next round $(t = 2)$. Finally, there are seven variables in Figure 8 (numbers 1–7) which appear in $t = 0$ but not in $t = 1$; and there are three variables (numbers 8–10) which appear in $t = 1$ but not in $t = 0$. This means that there can be no problem of inconsistency through overdeterminacy in any subsystem of the above equation system.

V. Conclusion

The main purpose of this paper has been to contrast two definable regimes—of agrarianism and dualism—relevant to the problem of development and to explore the rules of growth peculiar to each. We have endeavored to draw as much as possible on the growth-theoretic implications of the work of both the physiocratic and classical schools as well as the more modern writers concerned with development in the less-developed world.

The reasons for this inquiry are clear. On the one hand, we believe that agrarianism represents not only an important, if neglected, state of economic organization in the historical past but also accurately describes the modus vivendi of substantial portions of the contemporary underdeveloped world. On the other hand, we firmly believe that the growing interest in the analysis of growth under conditions of economic dualism constitutes a big step forward in our understanding of the essential facets of the growth process. Finally, we are convinced that in the idealized life cycle of historical development, a successfully evolving economic system is likely to proceed from agrarianism through dualism to economic maturity.

To bring our over-all framework somewhat closer to the real world and to the possibilities of empirical verification we have endeavored to move toward the evolution of a fully deterministic system to explain long-term agrarian behavior as well as a deterministic model to describe the dynamic interaction of both sectors in the growing dualistic economy. This attempt to describe the dynamic rules of growth of the agrarian and dualistic systems must be viewed as representing our best, and undoubtedly inadequate, thinking in the present state of our knowledge.

We have been even less definitive about the problem of the transition from one regime to the other. The reasons for this should be equally clear, namely, while the task of explaining the "machinery" which moves the system under conditions of agrarianism or dualism is challenging enough in and of itself, an adequate explanation of the transition from one regime to the other is considerably more complicated. An analysis of what permits an economy to graduate from agrarianism to dualism requires a change in the method of traditional analysis. It requires proceeding beyond the resources framework, in which the economist is at home, to the mutual interaction between the economy's human agents, the institutional framework within which they organize themselves, and these economic functions proper. As an illustration of the difficulty in analyzing this "transitional" problem, we can mention one of the most basic differences between dualism and agrarianism, the *causation of agricultural innovations*. This issue deserves a prominent place because it is likely to be the most critical issue in a contemporary underdeveloped economy. Stagnation in agricultural technique represents a development bottleneck which, to the present time, few underdeveloped countries have succeeded in overcoming.

In our view, in a dualistic economy, the motivation for an increase in the annual flow of agricultural innovations is directly tied up with the opportunities perceived, on the part of the decision-making units in agriculture, for acquiring ownership of the industrial sector capital stock or industrial consumer goods. The incentive to increase agricultural productivity is enhanced if it becomes clear that the proceeds from such increases can be utilized to obtain assets in the industrial sector—either directly or through financial intermediaries—or to obtain industrial consumer goods previously imported or not within the consumer's horizon. Once the relationship between either or both of these objectives and the human effort and toil involved in applying fertilizer and water, using better seeds, pesticides, crop rotations, and so forth becomes clear, marked changes in agricultural productivity can be realized. Historical experience in such diverse areas as Japan, Greece, and Mexico indicates that the dynamic outward-looking agricultural sector of the dualistic economy, in which activities on the soil are not hermetically sealed off from the rest of the system, can yield increases in θ over a decade larger than those achieved through centuries of inner-oriented agrarian isolation.

The importance of contiguity or "connectedness" between the agricultural and industrial sectors of the dualistic economy has been much neglected. If the owner of the surplus can invest directly in an extension of the industrial sector close to the soil and in familiar surroundings, he is much more likely to choose the productivity out of which further savings can be channelized. The experience of nineteenth-century Japan indicates that such intersectoral "connectedness" is much enhanced by the growth of decentralized rural industry, often linked with large-scale urban production stages via a putting-out system. The Japanese government's role, using the famous land tax, was undoubtedly of considerable importance in financing social and economic overheads in the early Meiji period. But it was really the flow of private voluntary savings through a large number of small hands which was responsible—increasingly throughout the nineteenth century—for financing of the prodigious Japanese industrialization effort. It was, in fact, mainly the medium-sized landlord, with one foot in the agricultural and one in the industrial sector, reacting to the intersectoral terms of trade and the changing relative returns to investments of his time and ingenuity, who propelled the dualistic system forward. As late as 1883, 80 per cent of all Japanese factories were located rurally, with 30 per cent of the still agricultural labor force engaged in rural industrial "side jobs."

A dualistic landlord, or his counterpart in another context, not only eases the difficulties of the required intersectoral financial intermediation but reduces problems attending the immobility of traditional rural labor, increases the potentialities of using efficient labor-intensive production functions, and avoids the overexpansion of capital-hungry urban centers.[27] We do not wish to deprecate the conventional wisdom about the importance of government experimentation and research, of education and extension activities, all of which undoubtedly facilitate the propagation of technological change; but we do want to emphasize the importance of a motivational dimension without which the chances of a really dynamic, balanced growth performance in the dualistic economy are considerably dimmed.

Herein, in fact, lies the essence of the difference between agrarianism and dualism. In agrarianism no active innovational inducement mechanism

[27] For a fuller discussion of the role of the dualistic landlord in nineteenth-century Japan, see Fei and Ranis, *Labor Surplus Economy*, Chapter 5.

is at play, no entrepreneurial group exists sensitive to surplus-generating opportunities within and outside of agriculture. In the dualistic setting, on the other hand, there is an entrepreneurial class with decision-making power and access to land which associates its personal well-being—either as industrial consumer goods or ownership of industrial capital goods—in a clear and direct fashion with the continuous improvement of agricultural practices. Such a group is unlikely either to be very large in number or to exhibit conventional Schumpeterian characteristics, but it is composed of leaders who are followed and imitated by the large mass of dispersed cultivators and make it possible for the dualistic economy to progress and ultimately graduate into economic maturity.

The above association obtained by deductive reasoning and buttressed by inductive evidence for nineteenth-century Japan must undoubtedly be subjected to fuller empirical testing. There seems to be little doubt about the general relevance of industrial proximity for agricultural productivity change in the United States.[28] With respect to less-developed countries, Nicholls has carried on some as yet unpublished work on Brazil which points in the same direction. The importance of the decentralized rural-oriented character of the Japanese industrialization effort has been documented elsewhere at considerable length.[29] Schultz acknowledges that "the process of development appears to have its mainspring in the industrialization complex,"[30] that divergences in the pattern of agricultural productivity are related to the proximity of an industrial-urban complex.

At the present state of our knowledge, we have barely scratched the surface in understanding the full workings and changing nature of the crucial innovations inducement mechanism in agriculture or elsewhere without which our progress is bound to remain limited.[31] We must learn more about tenure and other institutional aspects in agriculture which make it more likely for θ-enhancing activities to replace θ-obstructing activities as a routine matter. What is ultimately needed is a new deterministic transition theory to go along with any satisfactory deterministic theory of agrarianism and dualism, taken separately.

Our paper frankly espouses the notion that development is likely to proceed via the transition first, from agrarianism to dualism and, then,

---

[28] See, for example, W. Nicholls, "Industrialization, Factor Markets and Agricultural Development," *Journal of Political Economy*, LXIX (1961), 340; W. Nicholls and A. M. Tang, *Economic Development in the South Piedmont, 1860–1950: Its Importance For Agriculture*, (Nashville, 1958).

[29] See Fei and Ranis, *Labor Surplus Economy*, and John P. Lewis, *Quiet Crisis in India: Economic Development and American Policy* (Washington, 1962).

[30] Theodore Schultz, *The Economic Organization of Agriculture* (New York, 1953).

[31] This is still, lamentably, the case even for the mature industrial system.

from dualism to maturity.[32] Yet we think we differ from the stages theorists in that we proceed from a fairly well-defined analytical framework within which precise questions can be asked concerning the functions that need to be performed within each stage as well as to effect the transition between any two stages. Parts of our framework may well be inadequate and will need to be modified or replaced as more evidence is accumulated and better theorizing becomes possible. But retention of such an analytical framework is essential if a satisfactory refutable theory (or set of theories) of development is someday to emerge.

COMMENT

ROBERT E. BALDWIN, UNIVERSITY OF WISCONSIN

This paper is a valuable addition to the impressive work already done by these two authors in the development field. They are much more flexible in this paper as to the particular set of assumptions on which their models are based than in their previous work. Thus, one is less likely to become involved in long arguments about their specific assumptions and more able to concentrate upon what I think their main contribution has been—an analysis of intersector relationships within developing economies on a level of theoretical rigor and ingenuity that few have been able to match.

There is a growing recognition that analysis of the economic interactions among sectors is the most promising approach to the study of development. One obtains some useful results by analyzing the developing nations with simple aggregative models, but the payoff is much less than with developed countries. The rigidities and intersector misallocations that characterize less-developed countries make disaggregative sector analyses almost mandatory if one attempts to formulate a general theory of development. Although a number of other writers have followed the intersector approach, few have outlined possible interactions with such precision and insight as Professors Fei and Ranis.

The present paper extends and refines their analysis of development in a dualistic economy and also presents a model of nongrowth for the stagnant agrarian economy. Previously, they had begun their analysis of the dualistic economy at a stagnant level where technological progress in agriculture and industry was—for some reason—suddenly introduced. Now they present an analysis of how an economy gets to the stagnant point in the first place. As the

---

[32] The conditions for success in the latter transition have been elaborated earlier (Fei and Ranis, *Labor Surplus Economy*, Chapter 7).

authors point out, there is still the even more important problem of how and why an economy is transformed from a stagnant rural economy to a dynamic dualistic country, but this they do not attempt to handle in the current paper.

A standard explanation of the low-level equilibrium trap focuses upon the rate of population increase up to a certain point as per capita income rises in relation to a given rate of technological progress. Given some rate of technological progress and responsiveness of population to income levels, a particular per capita output is necessary if the economy is to "take off." Professors Fei and Ranis reject this explanation of the stagnant rural economy in favor of one that concentrates upon the slowing down of the rate of technological progress. Given an initial condition in which an agricultural surplus prevails, they postulate a relation between the way this surplus is used and the rate of technological progress. In particular, if it is used outside of agriculture to sustain the production of services and luxury products instead of to maintain and expand the agricultural infrastructure, then what little technological progress there is in agriculture will gradually decline. This in turn will bring about a cessation of growth in the economy.

In effect they are saying that investment in overhead capital in the agricultural sector is necessary to maintain technological progress in this sector. Since they define an agrarian sector as one in which such investment is largely absent, they conclude that such an economy will stagnate independently of the population trap.

An emphasis upon the relation between investment and technology is useful, but one would like a little more explanation—buttressed with empirical evidence —as to just how this relationship works. Writers such as Adam Smith tied technological progress and capital accumulation together very closely, but it is not obvious that the link should be as close as Fei and Ranis make it. One might also suggest that using the agricultural surplus to support the production of luxury products and services may create technological progress and labor skills in the nonagricultural sector that helps initiate development in the agricultural sector. In short, their analysis is ingenious, but it seems to me to rest on some special assumptions whose merits over alternatives are not as apparent as the authors believe.

In their analyses of both the stagnant agrarian economy and the dualistic economy, they also assume the existence of disguised unemployment. However, they do not insist upon it, but suggest it as a simplifying assumption that facilitates their analysis and that must be tested in more detail to determine its relevance. This, I think, is a welcome change from some of their earlier work which emphasized the existence of disguised unemployment. Although—as Professor Jorgenson points out in his paper—some of the uniqueness of the Fei-Ranis model is lost when this assumption is dropped, it is to be hoped that they do not get bogged down by tying all of their development analysis to this special condition. There is a growing body of empirical tests that do not support the redundant labor hypothesis in the sense that the marginal productivity of agricultural labor over a production cycle is zero. Professor Jorgenson summarizes this evidence in his paper, and there is no need for me to elaborate upon it.

Of course, Professors Fei and Ranis are well aware of these studies. They argue, however, that if an agricultural worker is employed full time for only a few months in the year he should still be considered at least partly redundant because of his idleness the rest of the year. This condition could be defined as redundancy, but the operational meaning attached to the term by most writers, including Fei and Ranis, is a condition in which the workers can be withdrawn from the agricultural sector without adversely affecting total agricultural output for the particular year when they are withdrawn. In the absence of some such change in agriculture as greater work from those who remain or technological advances that reduce peak-labor demands, it would seem that agricultural output will fall under peak-labor conditions except in the unlikely circumstances that the costs of transferring workers back and forth between industry and agriculture are negligible. Moreover, even if workers are not fully employed during the entire year, withdrawing some of them will, of course, reduce agricultural output unless those who remain work harder. This may require a wage increase for these workers that eliminates the surplus that otherwise would be available to feed the new industrial workers.

In short, the widening of the scope of assumptions in this paper by Professors Fei and Ranis is to be encouraged. They have begun to set forth the kind of dynamic interrelationships in developing economies that promise to lead to a much better understanding of the growth process. Unfortunately, the number of interrelationships that seem plausible on casual grounds is almost boundless. In addition to the kind of analysis in which Fei and Ranis excel, we need much greater efforts at careful empirical testing of the development hypotheses that already exist.

2. TESTING ALTERNATIVE THEORIES OF THE DEVELOPMENT OF A DUAL ECONOMY *

DALE W. JORGENSON, UNIVERSITY OF CALIFORNIA

I. INTRODUCTION

As a branch of general economic theory, that of development of a dual economy is of relatively recent origin. It is widely recognized that under contemporary conditions most backward economic systems have important relations with advanced economies, either through international trade or through the establishment of a modern "enclave" in an otherwise backward social and economic setting.[1] Either relationship gives rise to economic and social "dualism" in which a given economic or social system consists of two component parts—an advanced or modern sector and a backward or traditional sector. Neither theories of economic growth for an advanced economy nor theories of development for a backward economy are directly applicable to the development of a dual economy.

In a previous paper we have described two alternative approaches to the theory of development of a dual economy.[2] In order to facilitate comparison of the two approaches, we attempted to develop both within the same framework. The basic differences between the two are in assumptions made about the technology of the agricultural sector and about conditions gov-

* A longer version of this paper was presented at the Conference on Subsistence and Peasant Economics at the East-West Center in Hawaii and will be published in *Economic Development in Subsistence and Peasant Agriculture*, edited by Clifton W. Wharton, Jr.
[1] This point of view is elaborated in my paper, "The Development of a Dual Economy," *Economic Journal*, LXXI (1961), especially, pp. 309–11. The same point of view is expressed by Luigi Spaventa, "Dualism in Economic Growth," *Banca Nazionale Del Lavoro Quarterly Review*, LI (1959), especially, pp. 386–90. An excellent review of the literature on economic dualism through 1960 is given by Howard S. Ellis, "Las economías duales y el progreso," *Revista de economía Latinoamericana*, I (1961), 3–17.
[2] Dale Jorgenson, "Subsistence Agriculture and Economic Growth" (paper presented to the Conference on Subsistence and Peasant Economics, Honolulu, Hawaii, March 5, 1965).

erning the supply of labor. In the "classical" approach it is assumed that there is some level of the agricultural labor force beyond which further increments to this force are redundant. In the "neoclassical" approach the marginal productivity of labor in agriculture is assumed to be always positive so that labor is never redundant. In the "classical" approach the real wage rate, measured in agricultural goods, is assumed to be fixed "institutionally" so long as there is disguised unemployment in the agricultural sector. In the "neoclassical" approach the real wage rate is assumed to be variable rather than fixed; it is further assumed that at very low levels of income the rate of population growth depends on the level of income. These are the basic differences between the "neoclassical" and "classical" approaches to the theory of development of a dual economy.

The neoclassical and classical theories differ in characterization of the backward or traditional sector of the economy. These differences have implications for the behavior of the backward sector. Among the implications we may note that according to the classical approach, the agricultural labor force must decline absolutely before the end of the phase of disguised unemployment; in the neoclassical approach the agricultural labor force may rise, fall, or remain constant. The differences between the two approaches also have implications for the behavior of the advanced sector; unfortunately, these implications depend on the actual behavior of the terms of trade between the backward and advanced sectors. In the neoclassical approach the terms of trade may rise or fall; in the classical approach, they cannot be determined endogenously. Alternative assumptions about the course of the terms of trade may be made. Corresponding to each assumption, there is an alternative theory for the behavior of the advanced sector. Since any assumption about the course of the terms of trade is consistent with the classical approach, the behavior of these terms cannot provide a test of this approach. The classical approach may be tested only by deriving the implications of this approach for the advanced sector, given the observed behavior of the terms of trade, and confronting these implications with empirical evidence.

We have developed the classical theory in detail only on the assumption that the terms of trade between the backward and advanced sectors remain constant. Proceeding on this assumption, we have derived the following implications of the classical approach: (1) output and employment in the advanced sector grow at the same rate so long as there is disguised unemployment in the backward sector, that is, labor productivity in the advanced sector remains constant; (2) capital grows at a slower rate than output and labor so that the capital-output ratio falls; (3) the rates of growth of manufacturing output, employment, and capital increase during the phase of disguised unemployment. For the neoclassical approach, the corresponding results are: (1) output and capital in the advanced sector grow at the same rate, asymptotically, so that the capital-output ratio remains constant; (2) manufacturing employment grows more slowly than either output or capital so that labor productivity in the advanced sector rises; (3) the rates of growth of manufacturing output and employment decrease throughout the development process. Since the classical approach reduces to the neoclassical approach after the phase of disguised unemployment is completed, the two approaches have different implications only for situations where it is alleged that disguised unemployment exists.

In view of the similarities between classical and neoclassical approaches to the development of a dual economy, it is not surprising that many implications of one model are also implications of the other. For example, both models imply that if the proportion of manufacturing output to agricultural output increases, the share of saving in total income also increases. Thus, either model suffices to explain an increase in the fraction of income saved in the course of economic development. The fact that the implications of the two approaches for the share of saving are identical is of considerable significance. According to Lewis: "The central problem in the theory of economic development is to understand the process by which a community which was previously saving and investing [four or five per cent] of its national income or less, converts itself into an economy where voluntary saving is running at about [twelve to fifteen per cent] of national income or more. This is the central problem because the central fact of economic development is rapid capital accumulation (including knowledge and skills with capital)."[3] Both classical and neoclassical theories of the development of a dual economy provide an explanation of an increase in the share of saving. In each case the explanation is based on the relationship between saving and industrial profits. Disguised unemployment is neither necessary nor sufficient to generate a sustained rise in the share of saving. Ultimately, a sustained increase in the saving share depends on a positive and growing agricultural surplus and not on the presence or absence of disguised unemployment.

We conclude that tests of the classical versus the neoclassical approach to the development of a dual economy can be carried out only for situations in which it is alleged that disguised unemployment exists. For all other situations the implications of the two approaches are identical. Even where disguised unemployment is alleged to exist, some implications of the two approaches are identical. The implications that are different may be classi-

[3] W. A. Lewis, "Economic Development with Unlimited Supplies of Labour," *Manchester School*, XXII (1954), 155.

fied into two groups: (1) direct implications of the basic assumptions about agricultural technology and the conditions governing the supply of labor; (2) indirect implications about the behavior of both backward and advanced sectors of the economy. In reviewing the evidence pertaining to the development of a dual economy, we will first discuss the evidence for and against the existence of disguised unemployment and historical evidence for and against the constancy of the real wage rate in certain historical circumstances where disguised unemployment allegedly exists. Secondly, we will discuss the evidence for and against the indirect implications of the two alternative approaches. Since the indirect implications refer mainly to historical trends in economic development, we will concentrate on the historical development of the Japanese economy, which is cited in support of the classical approach by Fei and Ranis and by Johnston.[4]

II. EVIDENCE: DIRECT IMPLICATIONS

In Lewis's original presentation of the classical approach the scope of validity of the assumption of disguised unemployment is delimited as follows: "It is obviously not true of the United Kingdom, or of North West Europe. It is not true either of some of the countries usually now lumped together as under-developed; for example, there is an acute shortage of male labour in some parts of Africa and of Latin America. On the other hand it is obviously the relevant assumption for the economies of Egypt, of India, or of Jamaica."[5] In *The Theory of Economic Growth*, Lewis characterizes the phenomenon of disguised unemployment as follows: "This phenomenon is rare in Africa and in Latin America, but it repeats itself in China, in Indonesia, in Egypt and in many countries of Eastern Europe."[6] In a later presentation he states: "More than half of the world's population (mainly in Asia and in Eastern Europe) lives in conditions which correspond to the classical and not to the neoclassical assumptions."[7] Fei and Ranis are not so specific in delimiting the scope of application of their version of the Lewis model. However, they state: "The empirical support of both our theory and policy conclusions draw heavily on the experience of nineteenth century Japan and contemporary India."[8]

---

[4] J. C. H. Fei and G. Ranis, *Development of the Labor Surplus Economy* (Homewood, Ill., 1964), pp. 263–64; B. F. Johnston, "Agricultural Development and Economic Transformation: A Comparative Study of the Japanese Experience," *Food Research Institute Studies*, III (1962), 223–75.

[5] Lewis, "Economic Development," p. 140.

[6] W. A. Lewis, *The Theory of Economic Growth* (Homewood, Ill., 1955), p. 327.

[7] W. A. Lewis, "Unlimited Labour: Further Notes," *Manchester School*, XXVI (1958), 1.

[8] Fei and Ranis, *Labor Surplus Economy*, p. 6.

Lewis's allegations that disguised unemployment exists in Asia and eastern Europe are based on a substantial literature on the problem dating from the 1930's and early 1940's. This literature has been surveyed by Kao, Anschel, and Eicher.[9] Estimates of disguised unemployment in the early literature are based on what Kao, Anschel, and Eicher call the "indirect method" of measurement. Labor requirements for production of the current level of agricultural output and labor available from the agrarian population are estimated; the difference between labor available and labor required is called "disguised unemployment." One fallacy underlying this method is that agricultural work in all countries is highly seasonal. Substantial parts of the agricultural labor force may be unemployed in agriculture during a part of the year without being redundant. The critical test is whether the agricultural labor force is fully employed during peak periods of demand for labor such as planting and harvesting. Only if labor is redundant during periods of peak demand could the agricultural labor force be reduced without reducing agricultural output. A second fallacy underlying the indirect method is that all members of the agricultural population older than some minimum age, usually fifteen, are treated as members of the labor force and that younger members of the population are not treated as members of the labor force. All of the studies of the 1930's and early 1940's are based on the indirect method of measurement. Examples are provided by the work of Buck on China and of Warriner, Rosenstein-Rodan, and Mandelbaum on southeastern Europe.[10] More recent examples may be found in the work of Warriner on Egypt, Mellor and Stevens on Thailand, and Rosenstein-Rodan on southern Italy.[11]

Warriner has subsequently withdrawn from her position on disguised unemployment in Egypt,[12] noting that her earlier estimate was based on a fallacious set of assumptions. Kenadjian has corrected Rosenstein-Rodan's estimate of disguised unemployment for southern Italy to take into account seasonal demands for labor. By this single adjustment the estimate of dis-

[9] C. H. C. Kao, K. R. Anschel, and C. K. Eicher, "Disguised Unemployment in Agriculture: A Survey," in C. K. Eicher and L. W. Witt (eds.), *Agriculture in Economic Development*, pp. 129–43.

[10] J. L. Buck, *Chinese Farm Economy* (Chicago, 1930); P. N. Rosenstein-Rodan, "Problems of Industrialization of Eastern and South-Eastern Europe," *Economic Journal*, LIII (1943), 202–11; K. Mandelbaum, *The Industrialization of Backward Areas* (Oxford, 1945); D. Warriner, *Economics of Peasant Farming* (London, 1939).

[11] D. Warriner, *Land and Poverty in the Middle East* (London, 1948); J. W. Mellor and R. D. Stevens, "The Average and Marginal Product of Farm Labor in Underdeveloped Economies," *Journal of Farm Economics*, XXXVIII (1956), 780–91; P. N. Rosenstein-Rodan, "Disguised Unemployment and Underemployment in Agriculture," *Monthly Bulletin of Agricultural Economics and Statistics*, VI (1957), 1–7.

[12] D. Warriner, "Land Reform and Economic Development," in *Fiftieth Anniversary Commemoration Lectures* (Cairo, 1955), p. 26.

guised unemployment is reduced from 10 to 12 per cent of the agricultural labor force to less than 5 per cent.[13] Pepelasis and Yotopoulos have attempted to measure disguised unemployment in Greece from 1953 to 1960, taking into account the seasonal pattern of demand for labor. Their conclusion is the following: "From the eight years of our series, [disguised unemployment] existed only in 1953 and 1954 to a degree of 3.4 and 2.3 [per cent] respectively. The other years of the period are marked by a seasonal shortage of labor."[14] A corrected version of Buck's estimate of disguised unemployment has been presented by Hsieh: "The conclusion that in the majority of the localities . . . there was at the seasonal peak a shortage of male labour, which had to be reinforced by a large number of female workers, probably applies not only to many other areas of China but also to other Asian countries. Field investigations of several other localities in China and the rural districts of Bengal in India reveal a similar situation. Considering the extremely intensive input of labour in their farm operations, this is not unexpected."[15] We conclude that estimates of disguised unemployment based on the so-called indirect method of measurement always overestimate the amount of disguised unemployment. When these estimates are corrected to take into account the seasonality of demands for agricultural labor, the situation in southeastern Europe, Egypt, China, and Southeast Asia appears to be one of labor shortage rather than labor surplus.

Almost all of the evidence for the existence of disguised unemployment is based on the indirect method of measurement. However, attempts have been made to test for the existence of disguised unemployment by examining historical instances in which substantial parts of the agricultural labor force have been withdrawn in a short period of time. This type of test is always subject to the criticism that one cannot generalize from isolated historical examples. Nonetheless, the evidence is worth reviewing. One class of examples consists of studies of agricultural production after labor is withdrawn for a public works project. Two such examples are summarized by Schultz: "In Peru a modest road was recently built down the east slopes of the Andes to Tingo Maria, using some labor from farms along the way mostly within walking distances; agricultural production in the area dropped promptly because of the withdrawal of this labor from agricul-

---

[13] B. Kenadjian, "Disguised Unemployment in Underdeveloped Countries," *Zeitschrift für Nationalökonomie*, IX (1961), 216–23.

[14] Quoted in Kao, Anschel, and Eicher, "Disguised Unemployment," p. 140.

[15] H. Oshima, "Underemployment in Backward Economies: An Empirical Comment," *Journal of Political Economy*, LXVI (1958), 259–63; Oshima cites C. Hsieh, "The Nature and Extent of Underemployment in Asia," *International Labor Review*, LV (1952), 703–25; the passage quoted is from pp. 716–7.

ture. In Belo Horizonte, Brazil, an upsurge in construction in the city drew workers to it from the nearby countryside, and this curtailed agricultural production."[16]

Another class of examples consists of studies of the effects of famines and epidemics. Schultz has studied in detail the effects of the influenza epidemic of 1918–19 in India on agricultural production. He summarizes the results:

> The agricultural labor force in India may have been reduced by about 8 per cent as a consequence of the 1918–19 epidemic. The area sown to crops was reduced sharply the year of the influenza, falling from 265 million in 1916–17 to 228 million in 1918–19. This drop, however, is confounded by some adverse weather and by the many millions of people who became ill and who were therefore incapacitated for a part of the crop year. For reasons already presented, 1919–20 is the appropriate year to use in this analysis. The area sown in 1919–20 was, however, 10 million acres below, or 3.8 per cent less than that of the base year 1916–7. In general, the provinces of India with the highest death rates attributed to the epidemic also had the largest percentage declines in acreage sown to crops. It would be hard to find any support in these data for the doctrine that a part of the labor force in agriculture in India at the time of the epidemic has a marginal productivity of zero.[17]

A third type of evidence used to test for the existence of disguised unemployment consists of anthropological studies of peasant agriculture. Eighteen studies by anthropologists and economists are cited by Oshima in support of the following position:

> Despite the limitations of the empirical material, there is no denying the general picture that emerges for Asia. The labor requirement during busy seasons exceeds the male, adult population so that female and juvenile labor must be recruited into the labor force. And, from the description found in the books cited, no part of this larger labor requirement seems redundant, given the existing technology and organization. A withdrawal of portions of the labor force may be expected to reduce total output (in

[16] Theodore Schultz, "The Role of the Government in Promoting Economic Growth," in Leonard D. White (ed.), *The State of the Social Sciences* (Chicago, 1956), p. 375; see also Schultz, *Transforming Traditional Agriculture*, (New Haven), 1964, p. 62.

[17] Schultz, *Transforming*, pp. 66–67. Amartya K. Sen has pointed out to me that the estimates of changes in working-age population used by Schultz are too high, since only deaths between 1917–18 and 1918–19 are recorded as changes in the labor force. The natural increase of the population from 1916–17 and 1919–20, the base dates for the measurement of acreage sown, are ignored. Taking 8.35 per cent per decade as the rate of natural increase, Schultz's estimates of changes in the agriculture labor force should be reduced by 2.4 per cent. Making these changes, Sen obtains an estimate of the labor coefficient of .412 $\pm$ .252. Sen's estimate is closer to the a priori value of .4 given by Schultz than Schultz's own estimate of .349 $\pm$ .152. Both results support the conclusion cited in the text.

the sense that insufficient plowing, inadequate planting, and untimely harvesting will diminish the size of the final crop).[18]

The studies reviewed by Oshima refer to India, China, and Southeast Asia. Schultz gives a detailed summary of two exceptionally complete anthropological studies, that of Panajachel, Guatemala, by Sol Tax and that of Senapur, India, by W. David Hopper. Schultz concludes "that no part of the labor force working in agriculture in these communities has a marginal productivity of zero."[19]

Evidence from anthropological studies is subject to the same criticism as the examination of historical instances of rapid withdrawal of agricultural labor, namely, that one cannot generalize from particular examples. However, the consistency of the evidence from indirect estimates of disguised unemployment for the entire agricultural labor force of countries such as Greece, southern Italy, Egypt, and China, with the evidence from both historical and anthropological studies, leads to the conclusion that disguised unemployment simply does not exist for a wide range of historical and geographical situations where it has been alleged to exist. Lewis admits that disguised unemployment is not typical of Africa and Latin America. This is consistent with the historical and anthropological evidence for Brazil, Mexico, and Peru cited by Schultz. Lewis claims that disguised unemployment exists in southeastern Europe, Egypt, and Asia. But this is inconsistent with the evidence from indirect measurement in the case of southeastern Europe, Egypt, and China and with both historical and anthropological evidence in the case of India, China, and Southeast Asia. We may conclude, with Kao, Anschel, and Eicher that

it is an understatement to say that the development literature in [the early 1950's] was optimistic about development through the transfer of redundant agricultural labor to other occupations. We have shown that the empirical studies supporting this optimism were often poorly conceived. In addition, we have noted that by considering temporary rather than permanent labor transfers and by allowing some reorganization of production, various writers have arrived at a high percentage of disguised unemployment. To date, there is little reliable empirical evidence to support the existence of more than token—5 per cent—disguised unemployment in underdeveloped countries. . . .[20]

III. Evidence: Indirect Implications

We have reviewed the evidence for and against the existence of disguised unemployment. The indirect evidence suggests that the conditions govern-

[18] Oshima, "Underemployment," p. 261.
[19] Schultz, *Transforming*, p. 52.
[20] Kao, Anschel, and Eicher, "Disguised Unemployment," p. 141.

ing the supply of labor in southeastern Europe and Asia are no different from those in Latin America and Africa to which Lewis refers. This evidence does not demonstrate that disguised unemployment never exists in any historical or geographical circumstances, but only that the scope of applicability of the classical approach to the development of a dual economy is severely limited. More specifically, the classical assumptions do not apply to Latin America, Africa, southeastern Europe, India, China, or the remainder of Southeast Asia. Thus far we have reviewed direct evidence for most of Asia except for Japan, for which it is possible to check out the indirect implications of the classical and neoclassical approaches for historical trends in economic development. Japan is the only Asian country for which long-term data exist for trends in agricultural and nonagricultural labor force, agricultural and nonagricultural output, and capital formation. Furthermore, Japanese historical development has been cited in support of the classical approach by Fei and Ranis and by Johnston.[21] Fei and Ranis state that: "Continuous capital shallowing in Japanese industry between 1888 and the end of World War I is evidence that Japan made maximum use of her abundant factor, surplus agricultural labor."[22] They continue: "The empirical evidence on Japan . . . indicates clearly that . . . a change of regime from capital shallowing to capital deepening occurred at about the end of World War I. Moreover, we have convincing evidence that Japan's unlimited supply of labor condition came to an end at just about that time. . . . The virtual constancy before and rapid rise of the real wage after approximately 1918 is rather startling. We thus have rather conclusive evidence in corroboration of our theoretical framework."[23] Since the Japanese data are the only empirical support Fei and Ranis offer for their assumption of an unlimited labor supply at a constant real wage, Japanese economic development up to 1918 provides an important test case for the classical approach to the theory of development of a dual economy.

We first consider the indirect implications of the classical approach for the agricultural sector. For this sector Fei and Ranis assume that there is an institutionally fixed real wage, equal to the initial average productivity of labor.[24] Ohkawa and Rosovsky provide data from which real labor income per capita in agriculture for the period 1878–1917 may be estimated. The share of rents in agricultural income fluctuates during this period, be-

---

[21] Fei and Ranis, *Labor Surplus Economy*, pp. 134, 263–64; B. F. Johnston, "Agricultural Development and Economic Transformation: A Comparative Study of the Japanese Experience," *Food Research Institute Studies*, III (1962), 223–75.

[22] *Ibid.*, p. 132.

[23] *Ibid.*, pp. 263–64.

[24] *Ibid.*, p. 22.

ginning at an average level of 59 per cent in 1878–87 and ending at an average level of 58 per cent in 1908–17.[25] Labor income may be estimated by deducting the share of rents from real income per capita. This results in the series for labor income presented in Table 1. Total real income per capita

Table 1. Real Labor
Income per Capita in Japanese
Agriculture, Five-Year Averages, 1878–1917

1878–82	18.0
1883–87	18.1
1888–92	18.2
1893–97	21.1
1898–1902	27.0
1903–7	31.3
1908–12	39.4
1913–17	42.0

SOURCE: Computed from K. Ohkawa and H. Rosovsky, "The Role of Agriculture in Modern Japanese Economic Development," in C. K. Eicher and L. W. Witt (eds.), *Agriculture in Economic Development*, pp. 129–43.

is 100.0 in 1913–17.[26] We conclude that for the period 1878–1917, the assumption of a constant real wage rate in the agricultural sector is inconsistent with the evidence. The hypothesis of a constant real wage rate in the agricultural sector where disguised unemployment exists is the most important assumption underlying the classical approach to the theory of development of a dual economy. The classical approach stands or falls on this hypothesis.

A second implication of the classical approach for the behavior of the agricultural sector is that the agricultural labor force must decline absolutely as redundant labor leaves the land and later as disguised unemployment is eliminated. This decline must include all of the redundant labor force together with that part of the labor force with marginal productivity less than the real wage rate. The typical pattern of economic development in Europe is a constant or moderately rising agricultural labor force until just before or just after the relative importance of nonagricultural population surpasses that of agricultural population. Subsequently, the agricul-

[25] K. Ohkawa and H. Rosovsky, "The Role of Agriculture in Modern Japanese Economic Development," in C. K. Eicher and L. W. Witt (eds.), *Agriculture in Economic Development*, p. 52.
[26] *Ibid.*, p. 55.

tural labor force begins to fall.[27] In short, absolute reductions in the size of the agricultural labor force occur after industrialization is well under way rather than during its early stages. This pattern also characterizes Japan. The agricultural labor force is essentially constant from 1878–82 to 1903–7, falling slightly from an average level of 15,573,000 to 15,184,000 over this period of twenty-five years. From 1903–7 to 1913–17 the agricultural labor force falls from an average level of 15,184 thousand to an average of 14,613 thousand. The total decline over the thirty-five-year period is 7 per cent.[28] Since Fei and Ranis date the end of the surplus labor period at 1918, we may conclude that 7 per cent can serve as an upper bound for the percentage of the labor force that could be classified as redundant at any time during the period 1878–1917. A second useful comparison may be made between the number of farm households in 1884, a total of 5,437 thousand, and the number in 1920, 5,573 thousand, a slight increase.[29] The movement of labor from the rural areas to the advanced sector did not involve the transfer of a reserve army of the disguised unemployed. The process is described by Ohkawa and Rosovsky: "During the early period of industrialization necessary increases in the labor force did indeed come from the rural areas. But laborers were usually young and left single. There was only very little movement in terms of family units, and no formation of an agricultural proletariat. Thus, a fairly typical Asian type of agriculture remained in existence and was utilized to promote impressive increases in productivity, while Western technology was making rapid progress in manufacturing."[30] The Japanese pattern may be regarded as similar to that of many European countries, including countries of northwestern Europe, where the period preceding the predominance of the nonagricultural labor force in the total labor force is characterized by a stable agricultural labor force, rising or declining at very moderate rates throughout the period of initial industrialization. This pattern is inconsistent with the hypothesis of redundant labor or of disguised unemployment. However, the pattern is entirely consistent with the neoclassical theory of the development of a dual economy. We may conclude with Ohkawa and Minami that "in the light of Japanese experience with the initial phase of economic development, traditional agriculture based on household production grew at a considerable

---

[27] F. Dovring, "The Share of Agriculture in a Growing Population," *Bull. Agr. Econ. Stat.*, VIII (1959), 1–11. For a study of the development of agricultural population during the English industrial revolution revealing a similar pattern, see J. D. Chambers, "Enclosure and Labour Supply in the Industrial Revolution," *Economic History Review*, V (1953), 319–43. I am indebted to Henry Rosovsky for this reference.

[28] Ohkawa and Rosovsky, "Role of Agriculture," p. 46.

[29] *Ibid.*, p. 49.

[30] *Ibid.*, p. 48.

rate in terms of both output and productivity; technological progress had taken place and the level of living and wage rates increased to a certain extent. These responses occurred together with the increase in population. In view of this, it seems that the features of models of the Lewis type are too rigorous to be applied to such historical realities."[31]

We have discussed the empirical validity of the implications of the classical approach to the theory of development of a dual economy for the agricultural sector. These implications—the constancy of the real wage rate, measured in agricultural goods, and the absolute decline of the agricultural labor force during the phase of disguised unemployment—are directly contradicted by the evidence we have reviewed. In particular, the interpretation of Japanese economic development prior to 1917 by Fei and Ranis is inconsistent with the evidence on real labor income in agriculture. The pattern of development of the agricultural labor force up to 1917 is inconsistent with the existence of substantial surplus labor in the agricultural sector during the initial period of industrialization. The development of the agricultural labor force follows the pattern of most European countries and is fully consistent with the neoclassical approach to the development of a dual economy. At this point we turn to the development of the advanced or nonagricultural sector of the Japanese economy during the period preceding 1917. As we have already pointed out, the implications of the classical approach for the advanced sector depend on the historical development of the terms of trade between agriculture and industry. Data on the terms of trade are presented by Ohkawa and Rosovsky.[32] These data are consistent with the assumption that the terms of trade are essentially constant throughout the period before 1917. Accordingly, the implications of the classical approach on this assumption may be confronted with data on the development of the nonagricultural sector of the Japanese economy for this period.

The first implication of the classical approach for the advanced sector is that labor productivity remains constant during the phase of disguised unemployment. The corresponding implication of the neoclassical approach is that labor productivity is always rising. Real income per member of the labor force in secondary and tertiary industry for the period 1878–1917 are given by Ohkawa[33] (see Table 2). The data show an increase in labor productivity from 1878–82 to 1913–17 of 239 per cent in secondary industry and 213 per cent in tertiary industry. These increases in productivity are

[31] K. Ohkawa and R. Minami, "The Phase of Unlimited Supplies of Labor," *Hitotsubashi Journal of Economics*, VI (1964), 1–15; the quotation given here may be found on p. 8.

[32] Ohkawa and Rosovsky, "Role of Agriculture," p. 48, Table 4.

[33] K. Ohkawa, *The Growth Rate of the Japanese Economy Since 1878* (Tokyo, 1957), p. 34.

Table 2. Real Income per
Capita in Japanese Industry,
Five-Year Averages, 1878–1917

	Secondary Industry	Tertiary Industry
1878–82	137	156
1883–87	173	199
1888–92	189	197
1893–97	217	227
1898–1902	268	261
1903–7	237	261
1908–12	266	313
1913–17	327	333

SOURCE: K. Ohkawa, *The Growth Rate of the Japanese Economy Since 1878* (Tokyo, 1957), p. 34.

inconsistent with the implication of the classical theory that labor productivity remains constant throughout the phase of disguised unemployment. Increases in labor productivity are a direct implication of the neoclassical approach. We conclude that the data on labor productivity provide very powerful support for the neoclassical theory.

A second implication of the classical approach for the advanced sector is that the rates of growth of output and employment increase over time. The corresponding implication of the neoclassical approach is that rates of growth of both variables decline over time. Rates of growth of real income and occupied population in secondary and tertiary industry for the period 1878–1917 are presented in Table 3. The rate of growth of real income has a substantial downward trend for this period, which is inconsistent with the implications of the classical approach. The rate of growth of the nonagricultural labor force shows a high initial value but declines monotonically as development proceeds. This trend is also inconsistent with the implications of the classical approach. We conclude that data on the rates of growth of output and employment provide additional support for the neoclassical theory. It should be pointed out that for the period subsequent to 1918, the date at which disguised unemployment disappears, according to Fei and Ranis, there is an increase in the rates of growth in the secondary and tertiary sectors. This is evidence neither for nor against the classical as opposed to the neoclassical approach, since the implications of these approaches are identical for periods in which there is no disguised unemployment.

A third implication of the classical approach for the advanced sector is

Table 3. Rates of Growth
of Output, Employment, and Capital in
Japanese Industry, Five-Year Averages, 1878–1917

	Output	Employment	Capital
1878–82			
to	10.1	5.4	—
1883–87			
to	4.4	4.4	4.7
1888–92			
to	6.3	3.8	5.2
1893–97			
to	6.7	3.4	5.7
1898–1902			
to	1.9	3.0	4.6
1903–7			
to	5.8	2.6	6.5
1908–12			
to	5.2	2.4	5.8
1913–17			

Source: Rates of growth of output and employment computed from *Ibid.*, pp. 20, 34; rate of growth of capital computed from S. Ishiwata, "Estimation of Capital Stocks in Prewar Japan (1868–1940)," p. 12.

that the capital-output ratio falls throughout the phase of disguised unemployment and that the rate of growth of capital increases over time. The corresponding implications of the neoclassical approach are based on asymptotic results; the capital-output ratio eventually becomes constant since the rate of growth of output and the rate of growth of capital tend to the same limit. Data on net capital stock for the period 1883–1917 are given by Ishiwata.[34] Rates of growth computed from these data are presented in Table 3. There is essentially no trend in the rate of growth of capital during this period. We conclude that data on the rate of growth of capital stock are inconsistent with the implications of the classical approach. The capital-output ratio for the advanced sector may be computed from the data on capital given by Ishiwata and the data on real income given by Ohkawa. The resulting capital-output ratios are presented in Table 4, along with the capital-output ratio for the advanced sector computed by Ishiwata from an alternative set of data on real income.[35] For the period as a whole, both series of capital-output ratios show a substantial increasing trend. For

[34] S. Ishiwata, "Estimation of Capital Stocks in Prewar Japan (1868–1940)" (Unpublished Paper D27, Institute of Economic Research, Hitotsubashi University, Tokyo, in Japanese), p. 12.
[35] *Ibid.*, p. 15.

Table 4. Capital-Output Ratio in
Japanese Industry, Five-Year Averages, 1883–1917

	Ohkawa Real Income	Ishiwata Real Income
1883–87	1.96	1.56
1888–92	1.99	1.51
1893–97	1.88	1.53
1898–1902	1.80	1.52
1803–7	2.03	1.72
1908–12	2.10	1.82
1913–17	2.24	1.79

SOURCE: Computed from K. Ohkawa, p. 34, and
S. Ishiwata, *Estimation*, p. 15

Ishiwata's series of capital-output ratios the trend is especially strong. We conclude that the implication of the classical approach of "capital-shallowing" throughout the period prior to 1917 is inconsistent with the evidence. The data on capital-output ratios provide additional support for the neoclassical theory.

IV. SUMMARY AND CONCLUSION

We have considered implications of the classical and neoclassical approaches to the development of a dual economy for both agricultural and nonagricultural sectors. The assumption of a constant real wage rate in the agricultural sector made in the classical approach is inconsistent with the evidence presented by Ohkawa and Rosovsky. Real labor income per capita in agriculture more than doubles during the period 1878–1917. The implication of the classical approach that the agricultural labor force must decline absolutely as redundant labor leaves the land is also inconsistent with the evidence. Data on the occupied population in agriculture show a decline from 1878–1917 of only 7 per cent; data on the number of farm households show a 2.5 per cent increase. The Japanese pattern is similar to that of many European countries where the agricultural labor force is essentially stable throughout the period of initial industrialization.

Implications of the classical approach for the nonagricultural sector are also inconsistent with the evidence. First, the implication that labor productivity remains constant is inconsistent with the data presented by Ohkawa; these data show an increase in labor productivity over the period 1878–1917 of 239 per cent in secondary industry and 213 per cent in tertiary industry. Secondly, the implication that rates of growth of output and employment increase over time is inconsistent with evidence on the growth of real income and employment in the nonagricultural sector presented by Ohkawa. Finally, the implications that the rate of growth of capital increases over time and that the capital-output ratio falls is inconsistent with the data of Ishiwata on capital stock for the period 1883–1917. The rate of growth of capital stock shows no trend over this period; the capital-output ratio actually rises substantially over the period 1883–1917.

The evidence on Japanese economic development from 1878–1917 supports the neoclassical rather than the classical approach to the theory of development of a dual economy. The basic assumptions of the classical approach are inconsistent with the evidence. The implications of the classical approach are also inconsistent with the evidence while the implications of the neoclassical approach are strongly supported. Our knowledge of Japanese economic development corroborates the evidence we have reviewed for and against the existence of disguised unemployment in Latin America, Africa, southeastern Europe, India, China, and Southeast Asia. We conclude that the neoclassical theory of the development of a dual economy is strongly supported by the empirical evidence and that the classical approach must be rejected.

COMMENT

STEPHEN A. MARGLIN, HARVARD UNIVERSITY

The notion of surplus labor is a popular one among development economists and has far-reaching implications for development policy. If the market wage in the advanced, industrial sector does not reflect the social cost of putting another man to work, then the whole fabric of market prices becomes irrelevant for social decisions. The scope for *laissez-faire* in development policy is thereby severely diminished and the need for "accounting prices" for factors and outputs established.

The "classical" surplus-labor hypothesis stands or falls on the premise that no invisible hand guarantees full employment. Instead, the classical theory assumes exogenous determination of the industrial wage rate and posits a wage too high to permit full employment in an enterprise economy in which employers hire additional workers until the marginal productivity falls to the wage. Exogenous determination of the industrial wage rate is the root cause of the gap between the wage and the social opportunity cost of adding to industrial employment:

the social opportunity cost is the productivity of the wholly unemployed worker or the productivity of the partially unemployed agriculturalist, depending on which pool of workers is the relevant one for industry. In contrast to the classical wage hypothesis, the neoclassical hypothesis is that full employment is guaranteed by the invisible hand of a flexible wage rate, with an assist by government (if necessary) to ensure adequate aggregate demand. The neoclassical hypothesis permits of no gap between the industrial wage and the social opportunity cost of industrial employment. Hence accounting prices and market prices are identical.[1]

In view of the differences between the policy implications of the classical and neoclassical wage assumptions, any attempt to test whether or not surplus labor exists is welcome (especially an attempt by as talented an economist as Dale Jorgenson). But Jorgenson's essay does not establish that the existence of surplus labor is inconsistent with the evidence he has amassed. Why not? The essay, together with its companion,[2] appears to be a model for hypothesis testers. Not only does Jorgenson examine direct evidence, he also tests the surplus-labor hypothesis indirectly by deriving implications of the "classical" labor-surplus model which he shows to be inconsistent with Japanese experience. And what's more, he shows the same Japanese evidence to be consistent with the implication of a corresponding neoclassical model.

The rub is that the implications of the "classical model" turn out on close examination to be implications of assumptions Jorgenson (and others) have gratuitously built into the model, not implications of the classical *theory*. For example, Jorgenson reflects the classical assumption of exogenous determination of the industrial wage by a constant wage rate[3] and goes on to assert that a consequence of the constancy of the industrial wage rate is that industrial output and employment grow at the same rate. In fact, this is so only if one adds to the classical assumption of a constant wage rate the assumption that production is governed by the Cobb-Douglas function:

(1) $$X = e^{\lambda t}K^{\alpha}M^{1-\alpha}.$$

In equation (1) X represents output, K the capital stock, and M employment; λ is the rate of technological progress, t represents time, and α is the elasticity of output with respect to capital. If, instead of restricting oneself to Cobb-Douglas

[1] But the neoclassical model Jorgenson offers as an alternative to the classical model in the companion piece to his present essay posits a gap between industrial and agricultural wages. This is for policy purposes (namely, for determination of accounting prices) equivalent to the assumption of surplus labor, at least in an open economy!

[2] Dale Jorgenson, "Subsistence Agriculture and Economic Growth," paper presented to the Conference on Subsistence and Peasant Economics, Honolulu, Hawaii, March 5, 1965.

[3] This, it should be noted, is not the only way of reflecting exogenous wage determination; for policy purposes it would not matter if the industrial wage rate were rising (possibly in response to technological progress) or falling, so long as it remained in excess of the marginal productivity of labor in alternative employment. But no matter. Most, if not all, surplus labor theorists have employed the convenient simplification of a constant wage rate, so it would be inappropriate to blame Jorgenson for this assumption.

functions, one assumes more general constant-returns-to-scale production relationships:

(2) $$X = e^{\lambda t}F(K, M)$$

or

(3) $$X = F(K, e^{\lambda t}M),$$

then a constant wage implies that the difference between the rate of growth of output and the rate of growth of employment is equal to the product of the rate of technological growth and the amount by which the elasticity of substitution, σ,

$$\sigma = \frac{F_1 F_2}{F F_{12}},$$

differs from unity.[4] Symbolically,

(4) $$\frac{\dot{X}}{X} - \frac{\dot{M}}{M} = \lambda(1 - \sigma).$$

Equation (4) assumes (as does Jorgenson's classical model) that profit maximization on the part of industrial employers keeps employment at the level for which the marginal productivity of labor is equal to the wage.[5]

In the Cobb-Douglas case we have $\sigma = 1$, so the right-hand side of equation (4) vanishes; this is the basis of Jorgenson's assertion that equal rates of growth of output and employment are implied by the classical model. But if, for example, the production function is of the constant-elasticity-of-substitution variety conceived by Robert Solow[6] and brought forth by Solow along with Kenneth Arrow, Hollis Chenery, and Bagicha Minhas,[7] the classical assumption of a constant wage is perfectly consistent with the existence of different rates of growth of output and employment. In particular, if σ is less than unity, the classical constancy of the wage rate is as consistent as the neoclassical wage assumption with the Japanese data Jorgenson cites in Table 2. In short, one could as well use these data to "prove" that the elasticity of substitution is less than unity under the assumption that the classical wage postulate holds as to "prove" that the classical wage postulate does not hold under the assumption that the elasticity of substitution is unity.

Take next the implication for the capital-output ratio which Jorgenson derives from classical and neoclassical assumptions. According to the classical model, the capital-output ratio can be expected to fall during the course of development;

[4] Subscripts 1 and 2 indicate differentiation with respect to K and M respectively. Dots indicate differentiation with respect to time.

[5] The appendix contains a proof of equation (4).

[6] R. M. Solow, "A Contribution to the Theory of Economic Growth," *Quarterly Journal of Economics*, LXX (February, 1956), 65.

[7] K. Arrow, H. B. Chenery, B. Minhas, and R. M. Solow, "Capital-Labor Substitution and Economic Efficiency," *Review of Economics and Statistics*, XLIII (August, 1961), 225.

according to the neoclassical model, it should remain constant. In fact, the Japanese data of Table 4 show a slightly rising capital-output ratio. This is damaging evidence for the constant wage hypothesis if one believes the one-sector model of industry adequate to represent the relevant facts of growth. However, the experience of American industry, with apparently different rates of technological progress, profits, and wages in different sectors, suggests that the one-sector model may be woefully inadequate.[8]

The fall in the rates of growth of output and employment in Japanese industry (see Table 3 of Jorgenson's essay) also casts doubt on the adequacy of the classical model which Jorgenson tests and finds wanting. But I do not equate the surplus-labor hypothesis with this model and therefore am relatively unmoved by his findings.

What of the direct evidence Jorgenson cites to demonstrate the fallacy of the surplus-labor hypothesis? Jorgenson points to shortages of labor at harvest time as evidence that the marginal productivity of labor in agriculture is not zero. But surely this is beside the point; the relevant question for policy purposes is whether or not the industrial wage reflects the product foregone by adding another man to the ranks of the employed in industry. Even if the agricultural wage reflects the marginal productivity of agricultural labor and the agricultural daily wage is equal to the industrial daily wage, the long slack season that characterizes agriculture in many parts of the world means that the annual industrial wage does not measure the product foregone in agriculture by transferring a worker from agriculture to industry.[9] For me, and I trust for most theorists who try to reflect surplus labor in their models, the assumption of zero marginal productivity in agriculture is metaphorical. This assumption is designed to reflect a belief that the industrial wage in countries like India is not an accurate measure of the social opportunity cost of increasing industrial employment (II Corinthians, Chapter 3, 6).

Thus Theodore Schultz's epidemic is not to the point. Indeed I think Schultz's epidemic does not even prove the (irrelevant) contention that withdrawal of workers from agriculture by industry necessarily reduces agricultural output. No defender of the surplus-labor doctrine has to my knowledge been so rash as to claim that *any* withdrawal whatsoever of labor would leave agricultural output unchanged. The argument is usually qualified by the assumption of a selective

[8] Until Kenneth Arrow pointed out my error, I thought the following simple two-sector model—which assumes no differences in rates of technological progress, profits, and wages—adequate to prove the irrelevance of the one-sector model. Suppose sector 1 has a higher capital-output ratio than sector 2. Then if sector 1 grows sufficiently more rapidly than sector 2, each sector's capital-output ratio might fall, but the change in the composition of aggregate output might cause the over-all capital-output ratio to rise. Arrow pointed out to me that I was implicitly positing constant relative prices, which under competitive assumption and equal rates of technological progress is inconsistent with a changing composition of output.

[9] In Bengal, to which Jorgenson refers, the slack season is three to four months; very little agricultural employment exists between the December rice harvest and the April planting for lack of water.

withdrawal from families whose numbers are large relative to the size of their holdings, a selective process which the economic incentive of an industrial wage high relative to the opportunities for income within agriculture facilitates, but which—as Amartya K. Sen has pointed out[10]—an influenza epidemic does not. Furthermore, surplus-labor theorists generally assume at least a minimal reorganization of the labor effort of the peasant family upon the withdrawal of one or more of its members to the industrial sector.[11] Surely the *mutatis mutandis* change in output reflects what we mean by "marginal productivity" more closely than does a *ceteris paribus* change in output defined so narrowly that it excludes reorganization.[12]

What of the Japanese data showing a secular rise in real per-capita labor income in the agricultural sector? This growth is perfectly consistent with a constant *daily* wage if the growth in agricultural output sufficiently increased the number of days in the year each worker was employed. If agricultural production was increased through additions to the irrigated or double-cropped acreage, or indeed through any means at all which required a more even application of labor throughout the year, then the growth of labor income would be evidence only that surplus labor was absorbed in agriculture as well as in industry during the process of development. This seems to me entirely plausible. But let me emphasize that constancy neither of the agricultural nor of the industrial wage rate is necessary; it is the gap between the industrial wage and the social opportunity cost that counts.

I suppose my basic disagreement with Jorgenson stems from his view of even simple highly aggregative economic models as contestants, with oblivion the penalty for those which are inconsistent with observed data and survival the reward of the more fit. I rather view simple models as a means of distilling one's assumptions to an essence sufficiently tractable that one can derive and examine their policy implications. To *test* the assumptions one must go beyond simple aggregative models. The evidence, both direct and indirect, just does not refute the essence of the surplus-labor hypothesis, however inconsistent it may be with the particular classical model Jorgenson attacks. Jorgenson's test of the classical surplus-labor hypothesis seems to me of a piece with testing modern assumptions

[10] Amartya K. Sen, "Peasants and Dualism with or without Surplus Labor," Working Paper No. 65 of the Committee on Econometrics and Mathematical Economics, University of California at Berkeley (cited with the author's permission).

[11] See R. Nurkse, *Problems of Capital Formation in Underdeveloped Countries* (New York, 1960), p. 33.

[12] See W. A. Lewis, "Economic Development with Unlimited Supplies of Labor," *Manchester School*, XXII (1954), 151. Also Sen, "Peasants." Despite the weakness of his argument, Schultz's conclusion that the marginal productivity of agricultural labor is positive is probably correct: even the *mutatis mutandis* marginal productivity is unlikely to be literally zero in view of seasonal harvesting requirements. But it is likely to be well below both the annual agricultural wage rate and the industrial wage rate, and this would be sufficient to guarantee a gap between the industrial wage and the social opportunity cost of industrial employment, even under the unlikely assumption of equal annual wage rates in agriculture and industry.

about income determination by the degree to which observed data accords with the elementary macroeconomic models we present in freshman courses. This is not to deny that Jorgenson scores points against the specific classical model of the dual economy which he analyzes, but he does not shed much light on the question of surplus labor.

APPENDIX

In this appendix we prove the following theorem:

Theorem. Let production be governed by a twice-differentiable first degree homogeneous (constant-returns-to-scale) relationship of the form

$$(2) \qquad X = e^{\lambda t}F(K, M)$$

or of the form

$$(3) \qquad X = F(K, e^{\lambda t}M)$$

in which X represents output, K capital stock, M employment, t time, and λ the (constant) rate of Hicks-neutral (2) or Harrod-neutral (3) technological progress. Let the wage rate, w, be fixed exogenously and remain constant over time. Suppose that profit maximization results in equality between the marginal productivity of labor and the wage rate:

$$(5) \qquad F_2 e^{\lambda t} = w \, .$$

Then the difference between the rates of growth of output and employment is equal to the product of the rate of technological change and the amount by which the elasticity of substitution,

$$\sigma = \frac{F_1 F_2}{F F_{12}} \, ,$$

differs from unity. Symbolically,

$$(4) \qquad \frac{\dot{X}}{X} - \frac{\dot{M}}{M} = \lambda(1 - \sigma)$$

Proof. Consider the Harrod-neutral case (3). (The proof for the Hicks-neutral case (2) is exactly parallel.) Differentiate (5) with respect to time:

$$\dot{F}_2 e^{\lambda t} + \lambda F_2 e^{\lambda t} = 0$$

or

$$(6) \qquad \dot{F}_2 = -\lambda F_2$$

But the time derivative of F_2 is identically the following:

$$(7) \qquad \dot{F}_2 \equiv F_{21}\dot{K} + F_{22}(\dot{M}e^{\lambda t} + \lambda M e^{\lambda t}) \, .$$

By virtue of the first degree homogeneity of F,

$$F_{22} \equiv -F_{12} \frac{K}{M} e^{\lambda t}.$$

Thus substituting the above expression into (7) and collecting terms, we have

(8) $$\dot{F}_2 \equiv F_{21} K \left[\frac{\dot{K}}{K} - \frac{\dot{M}}{M} - \lambda \right].$$

Now we substitute the equivalent for $\dot{F}_2$ derived in (6). After rearranging terms, (8) becomes

(9) $$\frac{\dot{K}}{K} - \frac{\dot{M}}{M} = \lambda - \frac{\lambda F_2}{K F_{21}}.$$

Next we differentiate (3) with respect to time and divide the result through by X to obtain

(10) $$\frac{\dot{X}}{X} = F_1 \frac{K}{X} \frac{\dot{K}}{K} + \frac{F_2 M e^{\lambda t}}{X} \left(\frac{\dot{M}}{M} + \lambda \right).$$

By virtue of constant returns to scale, we have

$$\frac{F_1 K}{X} + \frac{F_2 M e^{\lambda t}}{X} = 1.$$

Thus (10) can be rewritten

$$\frac{\dot{X}}{X} = F_1 \frac{K}{X} \frac{\dot{K}}{K} + \left(1 - \frac{F_1 K}{X} \right) \left(\frac{\dot{M}}{M} + \lambda \right),$$

which upon transposition becomes

(11) $$\frac{\dot{X}}{X} - \frac{\dot{M}}{M} = F_1 \frac{K}{X} \left(\frac{\dot{K}}{K} - \frac{\dot{M}}{M} \right) + \left(1 - \frac{F_1 K}{X} \right) \lambda.$$

Now we substitute into (11) the result obtained from the constant wage assumption, (9); we have

$$\frac{\dot{X}}{X} - \frac{\dot{M}}{M} = -F_1 \frac{K}{X} \frac{\lambda}{K} \frac{F_2}{F_{21}} + \lambda$$

or

$$\frac{\dot{X}}{X} - \frac{\dot{M}}{M} = \lambda \left(1 - \frac{F_1 F_2}{F F_{21}} \right) \equiv \lambda (1 - \sigma).$$

Thus the proof is complete.

3. MAXIMUM-SPEED DEVELOPMENT THROUGH AUSTERITY *

JOHN C. H. FEI, CORNELL UNIVERSITY
ALPHA C. CHIANG, THE UNIVERSITY OF CONNECTICUT

The major aim of the typical underdeveloped country is to achieve a maximum per capita consumption at some point in the future. With regard to the present consumption standard, however, various underdeveloped countries may pursue widely divergent policies, depending on the nature of their sociopolitical structure. In countries where incentives are important or pressures for economic welfare strong, for example, per capita consumption may be allowed to rise immediately, thereby forfeiting a certain amount of future consumption. In socialist countries, on the other hand, increases in per capita consumption may be withheld in favor of capital accumulation and, presumably, future consumption.

This paper is concerned with the case of an underdeveloped country which is practically unrestrained by sociopolitical pressures for the immediate elevation of its consumption standard. Being pressure-free, such an economy can effectively pursue a policy of maximizing the rate of growth of capital over an indefinite period of time, during which its per capita consumption standard can be set, not for the sake of consumption itself, but in keeping with the objective of maximum capital growth. We may refer to such a country as an MSD (maximum-speed development) economy and cite Communist China as an outstanding example.

The "rules of growth" for an MSD economy obviously entail a certain degree of austerity, since consumption and capital investment compete for the use of scarce resources. Yet, the MSD concept does not necessarily imply that the consumption standard should be depressed to, and held at,

* The authors have benefited from the valuable comments of Irma Adelman, Alan Manne, Gustav Ranis, and Anthony Tang in the writing of the present version of the paper. Chiang wishes also to acknowledge the support of the National Science Foundation as well as the hospitality of the Cowles Foundation for Research in Economics at Yale University, which he enjoyed during the incipient stage of this study.

the minimum (bare subsistence) level, because too low a consumption standard will impair incentives and reduce the physical efficiency of labor, which will in turn contribute to a decrease in output and possibly also to a reduction in the rate of growth of capital. The appropriate policy for the MSD economy is, rather, to set the consumption standard at an *optimum* level—neither too low so as not to depress labor productivity, nor too high, so as not to dissipate resources. In other words, consumption standards must be set at a level which will maximize the rate of growth of capital. In this context the consumption standard emerges as a *policy tool* rather than an economic end in itself.

In this analysis, we shall consider the real wage rate to be the basic policy instrument for the control of labor effort in the MSD economy. On the assumption that a typical worker is not able to save, the consumption standard may be identified with the real wage rate. We shall therefore speak of "the optimum consumption standard" and "the optimum real wage rate" and even "the optimum degree of austerity" as if they are perfect synonyms.

The fact that labor effort is assumed to be subject to control via the real wage rate makes it imperative for us to draw a clear distinction between *labor in natural units* (L) and *labor in efficiency units* (E). Roughly speaking, L will represent the number of workers, whereas E will refer to the total productive effort put forth by the labor force. These two variables are, of course, closely related. If we let θ denote the productive effort exerted by a typical worker, we can write $E = L\theta$, where θ would be some function of the real wage rate, $\theta = \theta(w)$. This last function, $\theta(w)$, which holds the clue to the possibility of regulating labor effort through wage policy, is a key behavioral assumption of this paper. We shall refer to it as the *effort function*.

The operational significance of the distinction between L and E can be brought out most clearly in the formulation of the production function. Since a given labor force can exert a varying amount of productive effort depending on the real wage rate, output (Q) will be dependent, not upon L, but upon E. That is, the production function should be written in the form of $Q = f(K, E)$ instead of $Q = f(K, L)$, where K denotes the stock of capital. Note that, in our production function, even if the quantities of K and L are fixed, the efficiency labor, E, and thus the output, Q, can still vary according to the wage rate, w. The central problem of the static-analysis portion of our paper will be to determine how the wage rate should be set in order to maximize the rate of growth of capital.

To study the comparative-static aspect of the industrialization process— which will presumably be characterized by continual capital-deepening, or increases in the capital-labor ratio K/L—the population growth rate must be considered in conjunction with the capital growth rate. In this part of the analysis, it will be shown that an MSD economy will in general go through several well-defined stages of growth, each of which can be identified by certain observable structural characteristics. We shall also explore the impact of industrialization upon the key variables of the MSD economy, including its consumption standard.

Lastly, we shall consider a problem of long-run nature—the dynamic equilibrium of the MSD economy, with particular emphasis on its welfare implications. Since the long-run equilibrium consumption standard under an MSD program would fall short of the highest attainable level under a consumption-oriented growth policy, we conclude that a "rational" MSD economy should at some point undergo a fundamental institutional transformation from an accumulation-oriented economy to an economy with a consumption orientation. The appropriate timing of such a transformation will also be suggested in our analysis.

I. THE MODEL

Assumptions

Our analysis is based on the following set of assumptions:

1. The economy is closed and consists of a single production sector. The amount of output (Q) depends on two factors of production, capital (K) and efficiency labor (E). In terms of these inputs, the production function is subject to the usual conditions of constant returns to scale (*CRTS*), positive marginal products, and diminishing returns.

2. The amount of efficiency labor (E) which is actually devoted to production is equal to L times θ, where L is the labor force, and θ is the productive-effort coefficient, defined as the amount of efficiency labor produced by a typical worker per unit of time.

3. The productive-effort coefficient (θ) is a function of the consumption standard which is assumed to be identical with the real wage rate (w).

4. The labor force (L), assumed to be fully employed at all times and identical with the size of population, grows at a constant rate (λ).

5. The increment in capital stock (investment) is equal to the difference between the total output (Q) and the total consumption (wL).

These assumptions give rise to the following equations:

(1) $Q = f(K, E), f_K > 0, f_E > 0, f_{KK} < 0, f_{EE} < 0$,
    and *CRTS*   (the production function)

(2) $E = \theta L$ (the supply of efficiency labor)

(3) $\theta = \theta(w)$ (the effort function)

(4) $\eta_L = \lambda$ (the rate of population growth)

(5) $\eta_K = \dfrac{Q - wL}{K}$ (the rate of growth of capital) .

In (1), $f_E \equiv MPP_E$ stands for the marginal product of efficiency labor, and f_{EE} denotes the rate of change of f_E when E itself changes, f_K and f_{KK} have analogous meanings relative to the stock of capital. In (4) and (5), the symbol $\eta_x \equiv (dx/dt)/x$ means the rate of growth of the variable x.

Since it will frequently be convenient to express the variables Q and K on a per-unit-of-natural-labor or per-unit-of-efficiency-labor basis, we shall employ the superscripts $*$ and $\vartriangle$ to denote these per-unit variables:

(6a) $K^* \equiv K/L$,

(6b) $Q^* \equiv Q/L$,

(6c) $K^\vartriangle \equiv K/E$,

(6d) $Q^\vartriangle \equiv Q/E$,

and thus

(6e) $K^* = K^\vartriangle\theta$ (or, $K^\vartriangle = K^*/\theta$)   (follows from [6a], [6c]) .

Then the rate of growth of capital can be alternatively expressed as

(5′) $\eta_K = \dfrac{Q^\vartriangle - w/\theta}{K^\vartriangle}$ (by [5], [2], [6c], [6d]) .

To see the nature of the essential interrelationships between the variables, let us suppose that we are given the capital stock, K_t, and the labor force, L_t, at time t. If we also have an exogenously determined real wage, w_t, we can immediately find the productive-effort coefficient, θ_t (by [3]), and consequently the total efficiency labor, E_t (by [2]). The total output Q_t (by [1]), the total consumption requirement w_tL_t, and the rate of growth of capital at time t (by [5]) also follow. The last-mentioned information will in turn enable us to find K_{t+1}, the capital stock at the next point in time. Since the labor force, L_{t+1}, can also be inferred, from (4), it is evident that the growth process will be completely determined once the consumption standard at each point of time is specified. This paper will investigate the process of growth under the special restriction that the level of real wages will at all times be chosen so as to maximize the rate of capital growth. This is the analytical interpretation of the maximum-speed (or optimum-austerity) concept referred to in the introduction.

To pave the way for the derivation of the optimization conditions, we must first discuss in more detail the production function (1) and the effort function (3), the two major analytical foundation stones of our model.

The Production Function

By the assumption of *CRTS*, our production function has the property (see Appendix, I) that the amount of capital per unit of efficiency labor (K^Δ) uniquely determines the average product of efficiency labor (Q^Δ), as well as the marginal product of efficiency labor (f_E) and the marginal product of capital (f_K). This fact is illustrated in Figures 1b and 1c, which are vertically aligned with each other, and both of which have K^Δ measured on the horizontal axis.

The two positively sloped curves in Figure 1b represent Q^Δ and f_E, and the negatively sloped curve in Figure 1c represents f_K. The precise relationships which these three curves bear to one another are discussed in Appendix, I; here we shall merely state that, because of the law of diminishing returns: Q^Δ increases at a decreasing rate; f_K measures the slope of Q^Δ and must therefore be downward-sloping; and f_E is increasing, but must lie below Q^Δ.

A related production concept is the elasticity of MPP_E with respect to E:

$$(7) \qquad \epsilon_{EE} \equiv -\frac{\partial f_E}{\partial E}\frac{E}{f_E} = \frac{df_E}{dK^\Delta}\frac{K^\Delta}{f_E} > 0 \, .$$

This elasticity, which (as initially defined) describes the extent of diminishing returns to efficiency labor, is seen to be equal in magnitude to the elasticity of the f_E curve in Figure 1b (see Appendix, I) and must be positive.

The Effort Function

To facilitate the analysis, we shall give the effort function a specific form and postulate it to be an S-shaped curve as in Figure 1d. This curve describes the pattern of response of a typical worker to changes in consumption standard; it represents the typical worker's supply curve of efficiency labor as a function of the real wage rate. For analytical purposes, we may divide the horizontal axis into four distinct regions, $\Omega_1 \ldots \Omega_4$, with points R, S, T on the curve as end points.

In the first region, Ω_1, the effort curve coincides with the w-axis, indicating that when consumption standard is below a certain minimum level, R

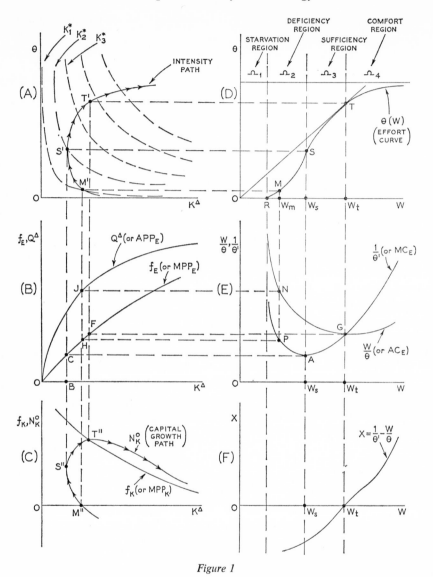

Figure 1

(which is prescribed by such factors as the minimum required caloric intake), the productive-effort coefficient, θ, of the typical worker will be nil. For this reason, Ω_1 may be called the "starvation region."

In Ω_2, which we shall refer to as the "deficiency region," θ becomes positive. However, since consumption standard at R is exceedingly low, successive equal increments in w will tend to result in increasing increments in θ. The segment RS of the effort curve is thus convex from below.

As w increases further, we reach the "sufficiency region," Ω_3, where the consumption standard is sufficiently high to set in motion the operation of a "law of diminishing marginal productive effort." This manifests itself in the fact that in Ω_3 the effort curve is concave.

At point T, the radius vector OT is tangent to the effort curve and therefore the elasticity of effort,

$$(8) \qquad \epsilon_\theta \equiv \frac{d\theta}{dw}\frac{w}{\theta} > 0$$

is equal to unity. To the right of point T (i.e., in Ω_4), however, this elasticity is less than one, and increments in consumption will bring about less-than-proportionate increments in productive effort. This abated enthusiasm in worker response is because w has now reached a quite comfortable level; we shall therefore refer to Ω_4 as the "comfort region." Inasmuch as there exists for a typical worker an absolute upper bound in productive effort, irrespective of how high the level of consumption becomes, the effort curve will tend to approach a horizontal asymptote for high values of real wages.

Since this S-shape of the effort curve conforms closely to the generally accepted pattern of relationship between input and output, we submit that it is a reasonable assumption. In fact, in the context of development economics, various writers have employed an assumption regarding the shape of the wage-productivity relationship strikingly similar to ours.[1]

On the basis of the effort function, $\theta = \theta(w)$, we can define the concepts of average and marginal real cost of efficiency labor as follows:

$$(9) \qquad AC_E \equiv \frac{w}{\theta},$$

$$(10) \qquad MC_E \equiv \frac{dw}{d\theta} = \frac{1}{\theta'(w)}.$$

---

[1] A functional relationship between wage and labor productivity has previously been applied by Leibenstein [2] and Wonnacott [7] to the study of the problem of disguised unemployment. However, the postulated shape of the relationship in their treatment differs from ours in that both of them neglect the possibility that successive wage rate increments may at first bring forth increasing increments in productive effort, as we assume in Figure 1d, in the "deficiency region." Their treatment may thus be considered as a special case of our postulation.

Note that, with the curvature as postulated in our effort function, it is possible to augment the total efficiency labor without cost by the practice of wage discrimination. For instance, while a uniform wage rate of w_m paid to two workers will generate efficiency labor equal to twice the distance of $w_m M$ (Figure 1d), a differential wage—paying $w_m + \delta$ to one worker and $w_m - \delta$ to the other—can yield a net gain in E because the higher-paid worker will add more effort than the lower-paid worker will reduce. However, we will rule out wage discrimination altogether in the subsequent analysis.

These concepts, both functions of *w*, can be represented by the two U-shaped curves in Figure 1e, which is vertically aligned with Figure 1d. These curves and the effort curve are governed by the familiar total-average-marginal relationships. For example, in Ω_2 and Ω_3 the average cost curve declines, with its minimum value occurring at point G which lies directly below point T of Figure 1d. The marginal cost curve, on the other hand, reaches a minimum at point A which lies directly below point S and crosses the average cost curve at the latter's minimum point.

Two other concepts related to the effort function, which are important in the ensuing analysis, can be introduced here. The first is the difference between MC_E and AC_E:

(11)
$$x \equiv \frac{1}{\theta'} - \frac{w}{\theta} = MC_E - AC_E,$$

which can be measured by the vertical gap between the two curves in Figure 1e. The second is the elasticity of the MC_E with respect to *w:*

(12)
$$\overset{\epsilon}{MC} \equiv \frac{d(1/\theta')}{dw} \frac{w}{(1/\theta')} = \frac{-\theta''w}{\theta'},$$

where θ' and θ'' are respectively the first and second derivatives of the effort function $\theta(w)$. Both of these are functions of *w*. And, the function *x*, in particular, is represented by the curve in Figure 1f.

II. Static Equilibrium in the MSD Economy

The Determination of the Optimum Values of the Variables

At any point in time, with *K* and *L* given, the rate of growth of capital will be maximized when the real wage rate is set at a level such that the following condition is fulfilled (see Appendix, II):

(13) $f_E = \dfrac{1}{\theta'}$ or $MPP_E = MC_E$ (See [1] and [10]).

The economic interpretation of this condition is simple: at the margin, the transformation of efficiency labor into output (MPP_E) should be equal to the transformation of output into efficiency labor (MC_E).

When condition (13)—which specifies the optimum real wage rate—is added to equations (1) to (5), the MSD system becomes completely determined, once the values of *K* and *L* are known. However, in view of the assumption of *CRTS*, the mere knowledge of the capital-labor *ratio*, *K**, will be sufficient for this purpose. This can be shown by means of the six aligned diagrams of Figure 1.

Let us first look at Figure 1a, in which the horizontal (vertical) axis, representing K^Δ (θ), is lined up with that of Figure 1b (1d). A family of rectangular hyperbolas, indexed by K_1^*, K_2^*, etc., have been drawn, each representing a specific value of $K^*(=K^\Delta\theta)$ (see [6e]). When K^* is fixed, a downward movement along the (appropriate) hyperbola will increase the value of K^Δ and decrease the value of θ. The variation in K^Δ will in turn alter the level of MPP_E (Figure 1b); the change in θ will, on the other hand, affect the value of w (Figure 1d) and hence the value of MC_E (Figure 1e). Condition (13) states that, given the value of K^*, we must choose the combination of (K^Δ, θ) such that the MPP_E will just be equal to MC_E. This choice will determine the equilibrium values, not only of w, but also of every other variable.

When K^* happens to be at the level of K_2^*, for instance, the optimum combination of K^Δ and θ is at the point S′ because only this combination will bring about the equality of MPP_E (distance BC in Figure 1b) and MC_E (distance w_sA in Figure 1e). Thus, given the capital-labor ratio, K_2^*, the *equilibrium* position (the equilibrium values of MPP_E, MC_E, θ, K^Δ, and w) will be shown by the rectangle S′SAC which links the four diagrams a, b, d, and e to one another. This rectangle can also help to mark off the equilibrium values of Q^Δ (in Figure 1b) and AC_E (in Figure 1e). Indeed, by extending the two vertical sides of the rectangle S′SAC downward into Figures 1c and 1f respectively, we can obtain the optimum values of f_K (in Figure 1c) and x (in Figure 1f) as well. This "rectangle extension" construction thus serves to tie all the six parts of Figure 1 together and to demonstrate the simultaneous determination—by a given capital-labor ratio—of the values of all the variables mentioned above as the rate of growth of capital is maximized. These will be referred to as the "optimum" values and denoted by a superscript o whenever clarity demands it.

The Maximum Growth Rate of Capital

The optimum (maximum) value of the growth rate of capital itself, η_K^0, can be shown to be (see Appendix, II)

(14) $$\eta_K^0 = f_K + \frac{x}{K^\Delta}.$$

This equation can be given an economic interpretation as follows. Let us first imagine, as a reference case, a competitive economy where the real wage per unit of efficiency labor is MPP_E, which is then equated to MC_E

by condition (13) of our model. When competition does not prevail (as is the case of our model), on the contrary, the actual wage per unit of efficiency labor is equal to w/θ or AC_E. Thus, $x = MC_E - AC_E$ will gauge the amount by which the actual wage falls short of the competitive wage and may thus be taken as a measure of "exploitation"[2] per unit of efficiency labor. It then follows that the exploitation per worker will be equal to $x\theta$, and similarly the total exploitation in the economy will amount to xE.

Upon this interpretation of variable x, (14) implies that the optimized growth of capital is dependent on two sources of finance. The first source is f_K, the marginal product of capital; the second is $x/K^\Delta = xE/K$, which signifies the total exploitation of labor per unit of capital. As the latter can be either positive, negative, or nil, η_K^ϱ can be either greater than, less than, or equal to f_K. From Figure 1f, we see that when the optimum wage is w_t, x will be zero; in this case, η_K^ϱ will be equal to f_K. When the optimum wage is less than w_t, however, $x < 0$, and labor will be "subsidized"—paid a wage exceeding the marginal product; in this case, η_K^ϱ will be less than f_K. This latter case is exemplified by the situation where the capital-labor ratio is K_2^* and for which the corresponding equilibrium rectangle is S'SAC. The optimum wage is $w_s < w_t$ (Figure 1e), so the value of η_K^ϱ, represented by the point S'' in Figure 1c, must lie below the f_K curve.

The Second-Order Condition for Maximum

Of course, to assure us of a *maximum* in η_K, a second-order condition will need to be fulfilled in addition to (13). This condition is (see Appendix, II):

(15) $\qquad \epsilon_\theta \, \epsilon_{EE} + \epsilon_{MC} > 0 \qquad$ (refer to [8], [7], and [12]) .

The expression $\epsilon_\theta \, \epsilon_{EE}$ is easily seen to be the elasticity of MPP_E with respect to w.[3] Hence, condition (15) involves essentially a comparison between the elasticities of MC_E and MPP_E, both with respect to w.

---

[2] The usage of the term "exploitation" here is in the sense of Pigou ([4], p. 551), not Marx. The former defines exploitation as the (negative) deviation of actual wage from the marginal product of labor, but the latter takes any net return to capital as evidence of exploitation.

[3] This follows from the chain rule of elasticity. Using Δ (in lieu of d) in defining the elasticities, we have

$$\epsilon_\theta \, \epsilon_{EE} = \frac{\Delta\theta/\theta}{\Delta w/w} \cdot \frac{-\Delta MPP_E/MPP_E}{\Delta E/E} = \frac{-\Delta MPP_E/MPP_E}{\Delta w/w},$$

since $\Delta\theta/\theta = \Delta\theta L/\theta L = \Delta E/E$ for any given L.

The term $\epsilon_\theta \, \epsilon_{EE}$ is positive by definition, but ϵ_{MC} can take either sign. In regions Ω_3 and Ω_4 (Figure 1e), we have $\epsilon_{MC} > 0$, and thus condition (15) is always satisfied. However, in Ω_2, ϵ_{MC} is negative, and hence the satisfaction of condition (15) cannot be directly inferred from the postulated shape of the effort curve. In what follows, we shall assume that the growth rate of capital can always be maximized and that (15) is always satisfied. This condition will prove to be of use in the comparative-static analysis below.

III. Comparative Statics: The Impact of Industrialization

The analysis in the last section pertains to the optimization conditions at a given time, at which, we recall, a fixed capital-labor ratio will determine the optimum values of all the variables in our model. During the process of industrialization, K^* is expected to rise; capital-deepening is expected to take place. To see the impact of industrialization, we must therefore ask: How will the optimum values of these variables change in response to increases in the capital-labor ratio? The answer will have an obvious significance for policy guidance during the industrialization process.

Industrialization and the Optimum Wage Rate

Let us first investigate the impact of changes in K^* on the optimum wage w^0. The crucial policy question here is: As industrialization proceeds, should the real wage be changed or held constant? The answer will depend on the algebraic sign of the elasticity of optimum wage with respect to K^* which can be expressed as (see Appendix, III):

$$(16) \qquad \epsilon_w \equiv \frac{dw}{dK^*} \frac{K^*}{w} = \frac{\epsilon_{EE}}{\epsilon_\theta \epsilon_{EE} + \epsilon_{MC}}.$$

By virtue of (7) and (15), the sign of ϵ_w must always be positive. Thus it may be concluded that the optimizing behavior dictates a continually rising real wage and that we may expect to observe in a country such as Communist China a gradual improvement in the standard of living as industrialization proceeds. This phenomenon, however, does not signify any compromising of the austerity policy, but is only a natural symptom of the continued observance of the rule of maximum-speed development.

A corollary of this result is that, in view of the postulated shape of the effort curve in Figure 1d, the productive-effort coefficient of the typical worker will also rise continually during industrialization. Similarly, we can state on the basis of Figures 1e and 1f that, during industrialization, the optimum values of both AC_E and MC_E will first go through a declining phase and then an increasing phase and that labor subsidization, which characterizes the early stages of development, must eventually give way to labor exploitation as the real wage rises into the comfort region.

Industrialization and the Intensity of Capital Utilization

For given values of K and L, a larger θ implies a more intensive use of the capital stock; we may thus take the variable $1/K^\Delta = E/K = \theta L/K$ as a measure of the intensity of capital utilization. A decrease (increase) in K^Δ may be referred to as "capital-stretching" ("capital-easing")—to distinguish from "capital-deepening" and "capital-shallowing," which relate to changes in K^*.

As capital deepens, will there be capital-stretching or capital-easing? Our analytical result can be stated in terms of the following expression for the elasticity of $K^{\Delta 0}$ with respect to K^* (see Appendix, III):

$$(17) \quad \epsilon_{K^\Delta} \equiv \frac{dK^\Delta}{dK^*} \frac{K^*}{K^\Delta} = \frac{\epsilon_{MC}}{\epsilon_\theta \epsilon_{EE} + \epsilon_{MC}} \gtreqless 0 \text{ as } \epsilon_{MC} \gtreqless 0 \quad \text{(by [15])}.$$

As long as the (increasing) optimum wage lies within the deficiency region (where $\epsilon_{MC} < 0$), capital-stretching will occur, but after the optimum wage rises into the sufficiency and comfort regions, capital-easing will take place.

This result is helpful in explaining a seemingly paradoxical situation which may occur during the early phase of the industrialization process in a country such as Communist China. On the one hand, capital goods may become more "extensively" utilized, as the typical worker gains more of them. Yet, at the same time, there may be a tendency for more and more *in*tensive utilization of capital, as may be observed from speed-up on the assembly line and lengthening of the work day. Actually, when the conceptual distinction between K^Δ and K^* is kept in mind, we see that this situation (capital-stretching occurring concomitantly with capital-deepening) is precisely what *must* occur in the early phase of development of an MSD economy, just as capital-deepening must be accompanied by capital-easing in the later phase of industrialization.

The change in the intensity of capital utilization is depicted graphically on the "intensity path" in Figure 1a. This path is the locus of the upper-left corners of all the equilibrium rectangles such as S'SAC and T'TGF. On that intensity path, as we go in the direction of the arrowheads, ascending to higher hyperbolas, $K^{\Delta 0}$ is seen to decline till the point S' is reached, and thenceforth, it will increase along with K^*. This point S', it may be noted, is the counterpart of the border point S of Figure 1d.

Given this intensity path, we can conclude corollarily from Figures 1b and 1c that, as K^* increases, $APP_E^{0'}$ and MPP_E^0 will at first decrease, but will later increase, in both cases along with $K^{\Delta 0}$. Similarly, MPP_K^0 will increase at first as K^* increases, but will later decline.

Industrialization and the Growth Rate of Capital

Finally, let us consider the effect of industrialization upon the optimum value of the rate of growth of capital. The results to be presented here are based on equation (14) and are summarized graphically in the "capital growth path" in Figure 1c. This path is simply the locus of "rectangle extension" points such as S". During the process of capital-deepening, η_K^0 will move on this path in the direction of the arrowheads and will pass through three significant points M", S", and T".

Point M", where the optimum capital growth rate is zero, is derived from the rectangle M'MPH whose distinguishing feature is that it satisfies the equation $APP_E = AC_E$,[4] signifying that the entire output is being consumed, leaving nothing for investment. This particular equilibrium rectangle thus specifies the critical (minimum) level of K^* (K_1^* in our case), such that capital accumulation can take place only if the initial capital-labor ratio exceeds that level.

The point S" is, on the other hand, associated with the rectangle S'SAC. As explained earlier, this equilibrium position marks off the capital-stretching phase from the capital-easing phase of growth. For this reason, of all the points on the capital growth path, the point S" must take on the minimum value of K^{Δ}. Moreover, since S" relates to the wage level w_s, at which x is negative (Figure 1f), this point must lie below the f_K curve, in view of the relationship in (14).

Now consider the rectangle T'TGF, which is associated with the wage level w_t. At this wage level, x is zero (Figure 1f), and thus (14) reduces to the form $\eta_K^0 = f_K$. Hence, the extension of this equilibrium rectangle must lead to the intersection point between the capital growth path and the f_K curve, which we have labelled as T".

---

[4] This is seen from the fact that the two points J and N in Figures 1b and 1e are situated on the same horizontal line. In general, this equality can occur only in the deficiency and sufficiency regions. According to (14), $\eta_K^0 = 0$ only if $f_K = -x/K^{\Delta}$. Since f_K is always positive, this last equation requires x to be negative, which is possible only in the deficiency and sufficiency regions. In the following, we shall assume that it always occurs in the deficiency region Ω_2.

This intersection point is also the maximum point on the capital growth path, because, as can be verified (see Appendix, III),

(18a) $$\frac{d\eta_K^0}{dK^*} = \frac{-x\theta}{K^{*2}} \gtreqless 0 \qquad \text{when } x \lesseqgtr 0,$$

or alternatively,

(18b) $$\frac{d\eta_K^0}{dK^*} = \frac{f_K - \eta_K^0}{K^*} \gtreqless 0 \qquad \text{when } f_K \gtreqless \eta_K^0.$$

These equations show that the optimum value of the rate of growth of capital reaches a maximum when $x = 0$ or when $f_K = \eta_K^0$, or at point T''. In fact, they also show that the capital growth path must be rising (declining) when it lies below (above) the f_K curve. Even though η_K^0 will fall after point T'', however, it will never go below the f_K curve because the x/K^Δ term in (14) will thereafter always remain positive.

It is now evident that, even in an MSD economy where a constant effort is made to maximize the capital growth rate, the growth rate still must eventually fall. In the long run, it seems, the force of the law of diminishing returns will inevitably dominate and ultimately will restrict the capacity for economic growth, if it is not duly offset by the countervailing force of technological improvement.

The Stages of Growth

From the above analysis, a stages-of-growth thesis naturally emerges. These stages of growth, discernible on the η_K^0 path, are closely related to the distinct regions of real wage, $\Omega_1 \ldots \Omega_4$, which characterize our effort curve. We may delineate four such stages, each with its own observable distinguishing features.

First, let us recall that, with the postulated effort curve, the observance of the optimization rules will give rise to an *intensity path* (Figure 1a), with demarcation points (M', S', T'), and a *capital growth path* (Figure 1c), with demarcation points (M'', S'', T''), which correspond to the points (M, S, T) on the effort curve. During the process of capital-deepening, the optimum-austerity policy has been shown to lead to a continual increase of the real wage (such as from w_m to w_s, w_t, etc., Figure 1d). Consequently the economy must successively go through all of these demarcation points, which serve to mark off the various stages of growth referred to above.

The point M' in Figure 1a relates to a critical minimum level of capital-labor ratio, and therefore its counterpart in Figure 1c, point M'', serves to indicate the transition from the *de*cumulation stage to the incipient *a*ccumulation stage. Clearly, unless the country manages to attain an initial capital-labor ratio above K_1^*, even the optimal level of output will prove inadequate to support the consumption requirements of the labor force, and there can be no capital accumulation. After this critical resource bottleneck is surmounted, however, the economy enters into a stage of growth which is related to the segment MS on the effort curve in the deficiency region Ω_2. In this second stage, the rate of growth of capital is positive and increasing. Furthermore, since productive effort is now "increasingly responsive" to increments in real wage, we can expect to observe capital-stretching, the unique characteristic of this stage of growth. It should be pointed out, however, that the passing of the hurdle at point M" is a necessary, but not sufficient, condition for capital accumulation—we have yet to take into account the important factor of the growth of population, as will be done in the next section.

When the rising real wage reaches the end of the deficiency region, we encounter the turning point S. From here on, the economy enters into a new, third, stage of growth which ranges over the sufficiency region (segment ST on the effort curve). In this stage, the productive effort of the typical worker becomes "decreasingly responsive" to wage increases, thus forcing the MC_E to rise (Figure 1e). As a result, the economy will experience capital-easing for the first time. By the same token, the rate of growth of capital, while still increasing, will tend to slow down toward the end of this stage.

Further increases in K^* and further improvement in the consumption standard will lead into the final (fourth) stage of growth, which is affiliated with the comfort region. Inasmuch as the productive effort is now inelastic with respect to the real wage ($MC_E > AC_E$), it will no longer prove worthwhile to "subsidize" labor. The optimum wage policy will then necessarily involve labor exploitation, and consequently, the rate of growth of capital will exceed the marginal product of capital. Nevertheless, despite the exploitation of labor, the capital growth rate will start to decline in this final stage because the adverse effect of the law of diminishing returns to capital (declining f_K) on the capital growth rate will inevitably come to dominate the uplifting effect of the exploitation of labor.

IV. DYNAMICS: THE INTERPLAY OF CAPITAL GROWTH AND LABOR GROWTH

Dynamic Equilibrium

In the preceding section, we took the capital-labor ratio K^* as a parameter and analyzed the effects of changes in K^* upon the optimum values of real wage and other variables. Now, the process of determination of K^* itself must be examined, and for this purpose, we shall for the first time use the population (labor) growth rate, λ, in (4).

It may be observed that K^* will increase ($\eta_{K^*} > 0$) if and only if the growth of capital outruns the growth of population (i. e., if and only if $\eta_K^0 > \lambda$). For illustration, let us reproduce the η_K^0 curve of Figure 1c as the solid curve in Figure 2c, where we now add a horizontal line η_L, the height of which represents a given population growth rate, λ. Let the latter line intersect the capital growth path at the pair of points (H, J), thereby dividing the η_K^0 path into three segments. On the segment HT′J, the condition $\eta_K^0 > \lambda$ is fulfilled and hence capital-deepening will take place. On the other two segments, however, capital-shallowing will occur. The arrowheads on the curve thus serve to indicate the direction of change of the capital growth rate.

We are now in a position to explain the dynamics of the MSD economy. In general, the points (H, J) which specify the two critical values of capital-

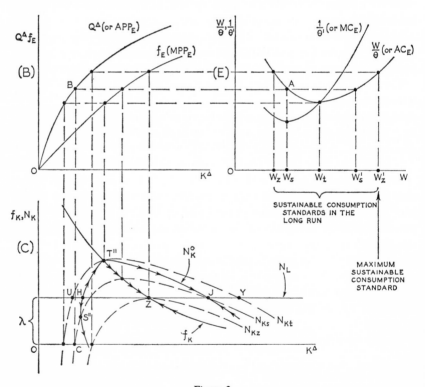

Figure 2

labor ratio $K_H^* < K_J^*$, will be instrumental in distinguishing three types of dynamic behavior, depending upon the magnitude of the initial capital-labor ratio $K^*(0)$. First, a country with very meager initial capital endowment $(K^*(0) < K_H^*)$ will necessarily experience a continuous process of capital-shallowing. The economic interpretation of this case is that the country is in the unenviable position of having been caught in the Malthusian trap. Secondly, a country with a moderate initial capital-labor ratio $(K_H^* < K^*(0) < K_J^*)$ will, on the other hand, undergo continuous capital-deepening as it succeeds in taking off into sustained growth. In such a case, the country will in general travel through the last three stages of growth described in the preceding section.[5] Furthermore, we see that in this case the economy will in the long run move ever closer to an equilibrium state (Von Neumann state) at J, in which the K^* will become stationary, and hence all the significant economic variables in the system will also take on stationary values. Finally, if the country is abundantly endowed with capital resource initially $(K^*(0) > K_J^*)$, it will experience continuous capital-shallowing and will also arrive at the Von Neumann state at J in the long run.

In the very special cases in which $K^*(0)$ happens to be precisely equal to K_H^* or K_J^*, the country will, of course, already be in a long-run equilibrium; but while the equilibrium at J is stable, the one at H is unstable.

The upshot is that the only long-run equilibrium point which is truly relevant to a successful growth process is the one located at point J. What does this point imply in the way of consumer welfare?

The Long-Run Equilibrium Consumption Standard

The MSD economy is one in which the rapidity of development is the chief economic goal, and the consumption standard, rather than an end in itself, serves merely as a policy tool for regulating the efficiency-labor input. Nevertheless, it is relevant and important to ask: How does the long-run equilibrium consumption standard (as determined by the Von Neumann state at J) compare to what is attainable under alternative types of growth policy? In other words, how would the people living under an accumulation-oriented economy fare in the long run with regard to consumption, as compared with people living in a consumption-oriented economy?

To answer this question let us first determine the set of all feasible con-

[5] In the case shown in Figure 2c, the economy will only go through the last two stages of growth. If the population growth rate is low enough so that point S″ lies above the η_L line, however, the country will go through the last three stages of growth.

sumption standards which can be sustained in the long run in an economy with a given population growth rate, a given production function, and a given effort function. For analytical purposes, let us consider as a reference case a country which adopts a constant real wage $\bar{w}$, rather than the (variable) optimum wage of the MSD economy. We shall refer to such an economy as a CPCS (constant per capita consumption) economy. With a fixed effort curve, the constant wage $\bar{w}$ implies a constant productive-effort coefficient θ. Thus the rate of growth of capital becomes

$$(5'') \qquad \eta_K = \frac{Q^\Delta - \bar{w}/\bar{\theta}}{K^\Delta},$$

which is a function of K^Δ.

For every level of $\bar{w}$, there exists one corresponding η_K path, such as one of the (broken) inverse-U-shaped curves in Figure 2c. Each of such CPCS η_K paths possesses the following properties. First, we see from $(5'')$ that $\eta_K \gtreqless 0$ if and only if $Q^\Delta \gtreqless \bar{w}/\bar{\theta}$ (or $APP_E \gtreqless AC_E$). Thus, supposing (for example) that $\bar{w}$ is at the level of w_s (Figure 2e), the auxiliary line w_sABC which links the three diagrams will give us the point C on the horizontal axis of Figure 2c, such that to its left (right), the corresponding capital growth path η_{Ks} must lie below (above) the horizontal axis, because APP_E is by construction less (greater) than AC_E. Secondly, each of these paths is upward (downward) sloping when it lies below (above) the f_K curve, which implies that the η_K path attains its peak value when it crosses the f_K curve.[6] Moreover, the said peak value of η_K must occur at the level of K^Δ where MPP_E is just equal to the fixed value of AC_E (see footnote 6). For example, the point of intersection between line AB (relating to wage w_s) and the f_E curve must lie directly above the peak point of η_{Ks}.

In Figure 2c, we have drawn a system of these η_K curves ($\eta_{Kt}, \eta_{Ks}, \ldots$),

[6] This property can be seen from a direct differentiation of $(5'')$:

$$\frac{d\eta_K}{dK^\Delta} = \frac{1}{K^{\Delta 2}}\left[f_K K^\Delta - (Q^\Delta - \bar{w}/\bar{\theta})\right] = \frac{f_K - \eta_K}{K^\Delta}.$$

It is interesting to note the similarity between this equation and (18b). Though alike in form, however, their meanings are widely different, because (18b) relates to the MSD economy, but the equation in this footnote pertains to the CPCS economy.

Note that, in view of (A2b), we can also write

$$\frac{d\eta_K}{dK^\Delta} = \frac{1}{K^{\Delta 2}}\left(\bar{w}/\bar{\theta} - f_E\right).$$

Consequently, at the peak of each η_K curve, where $d\eta_K/dK^\Delta = 0$, we must have $\bar{w}/\bar{\theta} = f_E$, or $AC_E = MPP_E$.

which correspond to alternative values of $\overline{w}$ (w_t, w_s, . . .) in Figure 2e.[7] Notice that in view of the U-shape of the AC_E curve, two values of real wage (the pair w_s and w'_s) will give rise to the same η_K curve (η_{Ks}). The only exception is the wage level w_t (affiliated with the minimum point of AC_E), which alone gives rise to the η_{Kt} curve, the highest among all the CPCS η_K curves. As the constant wage deviates from w_t in either direction, the corresponding η_K curve will shift downward from η_{Kt} to η_{Ks}, η_{Kz}, . . . ; and sooner or later we will arrive at an η_K curve which is tangent to the η_L curve; in our example, this happens to be the η_{Kz} path, which is associated with the wage levels w_z and w'_z. Further deviations of wage, beyond w_z and w'_z, will result in an η_K curve (not drawn) which lies entirely below the η_L curve, and which is thus incapable of producing a dynamic equilibrium or Von Neumann state, since capital-shallowing will continue indefinitely. This means that a wage below w_z or above w'_z is not sustainable in the long run, and that the set of equilibrium-yielding CPCS η_K curves will be bounded from above by the η_{Kt} curve, corresponding to the wage w_t, and bounded from below by the η_{Kz} curve, to which the population growth curve η_L is tangent.

In Figure 2c, all the possible Von Neumann states for the CPCS economy are shown on the segment UY of the η_L curve. Since these are derived from nothing more than a given production function, a given effort function, and a given population growth rate, the range of sustainable long-run consumption standards (w_z to w'_z) of the CPCS economy should also apply to *all* economies which have these same given functions. Each of these Von Neumann states implies a constant level of perpetual per-capita consumption stream, but, among them, only the one at point Z yields the maximum consumption stream w'_z. Thus, point Z may be taken as the ideal Von Neumann state for a consumption-oriented economy.[8]

Now let us examine the growth path of the MSD economy (solid curve in Figure 2c) in relation to the (broken) CPCS η_K curves. We note that on the segment lying below (above) the f_K curve, the η_K^0 path intersects successively higher (lower) CPCS η_K curves, with point T'' as the common maximum point of η_K^0 and η_{Kt}. This is because in the MSD economy, increases in the capital-labor ratio will lead to monotonic increases in the real wage,

---

[7] The η_K curves in Figure 2c can be used for the analysis of the dynamic aspect of the CPCS economy per se. Since we are not primarily interested in the CPCS economy here, this diagram will only be used in analyzing the MSD economy. For a detailed discussion of the CPCS economy, see Fei [1].

[8] Phelps [3] has proved the existence of a Von Neumann state with a maximum consumption standard on the basis of a given production function and population growth rate. Our result here is a generalization of his conclusion to the case in which an additional economic relation, namely, the effort function, is taken into account.

which implies, in the context of a CPCS economy, successive shifts from lower η_K curves to higher ones up to η_{Kt} (before the wage reaches the level of w_t), followed by similar shifts in the reverse direction (after the wage exceeds w_t).[9]

In order to compare the long-run equilibrium consumption standard of the MSD economy with the maximum feasible one, we recall that the MSD Von Neumann state is at point J. Since point J must lie to the right of point Z, one cannot escape the conclusion that if the maximum-speed or optimum-austerity policy is consistently and persistently followed, consumer welfare can never attain its maximum feasible level in the long run. Referring to Figure 2e, we see that the long-run consumption standard in our example will be w'_s, which is less than w'_z.

The Relaxation Phenomenon

For the sake of hastening the process of development, sacrifices in consumption may be a necessary and justifiable price for the country to pay. However, it is quite another matter to have such sacrifices built into an economy as a permanent feature of economic life. Our conclusion, that the process of growth in the MSD economy cannot lead to the maximum feasible consumption standard in the long run, underscores the basic irrationality of a policy of perpetual austerity under which the maximization of the capital growth rate remains forever the primary economic goal. Therefore the analysis seems to suggest that if the MSD economy is a rational one, it must sooner or later undergo a fundamental transformation of its policy from one of accumulation-orientation to that of consumption-orientation.

This transformation, which may be referred to as the "relaxation phenomenon," does not have to take the form of a sharp turnabout. It may very well come gradually or even imperceptibly. Assuming that Soviet Russia has been growing more or less in accordance with the optimum-austerity rule, we suggest that, judging from her experiences in recent years, the relaxation phenomenon is now perhaps under way in that country. By the same token, we may expect a similar phenomenon to take place in Communist China or any other MSD economy in a later phase of its economic growth.

Aside from suggesting the reasonableness of the relaxation phenomenon,

---

[9] Since the η_{Kt} curve (the highest broken curve) reaches a maximum point at T'' on the f_K curve, it follows that the (solid) η_K^0 curve must also reach a maximum at that point. An alternative proof of this property is given in the Appendix (A12e).

our analysis also provides a clue to the suitable timing of its occurrence. Let us suppose that the MSD economy has already arrived at the point T″ on the η_K^0 path in Figure 2c, which, we recall, indicates the highest attainable growth rate of capital. From there on, the growth rate must begin to decline, and this tendency can immediately be taken as a signal for the ushering in of a relaxation policy. If no relaxation is introduced and the economy adheres to the η_K^0 path, excessive capital-deepening will result. If, on the other hand, it now adopts the new policy of always investing an amount equal to $f_K K$ (the total "competitive" profit), the capital growth rate will be equal to f_K, and the f_K curve (below point T″) will in effect become the new relevant capital growth curve. In that case, the economy will be able to move along the f_K curve toward the (stable) long-run equilibrium point Z. Obviously, the growth of capital along the f_K curve will necessarily be lower than along the MSD path η_K^0 because, as can be seen from (14), to switch from η_K^0 to f_K as a growth path is to relinquish exploitation as a source of finance. But this is precisely what makes possible the prevention of excessive capital-deepening and the attainment of the maximum sustainable consumption standard w_z'.

V. Concluding Remarks

In the preceding pages we have analyzed the growth process of an MSD economy in substantial detail. We have derived the conditions for maximizing the rate of growth of capital, delineated the stages of growth which such an economy is likely to pass through, and, finally, compared the long-run equilibrium consumption potential of the MSD economy against the maximum sustainable consumption stream that can be attained in an economy.

But our analysis has by no means covered every major aspect of the MSD economy. We have ignored any possible effect of real-wage changes on the rate of population growth such as was envisaged by the classical economists. However, no real difficulty will be encountered in attempting to incorporate this effect into the analysis. If the population growth rate is functionally dependent on the real wage rate, then in view of the upward adjustment of the optimum wage during the process of industrialization, the η_L line of Figure 2c will become a *curve* instead. But the basic analysis of the interplay of population growth and capital growth can still be analyzed in essentially the same way. It may happen, of course, that the rise in the real wage rate would so stimulate population growth as to cause the η_L curve to lie entirely above the η_K^0 path. In such a situation, capital-deepening would become absolutely impossible, and the only way out, aside from direct population control, would be an upward shift either in the production function (through improved technology) or in the effort curve (through devices like propaganda appeal to patriotism), both of which would serve to raise the η_K^0 path.[10]

Another omission in our paper is the lack of explicit reference to technological change. This is due mainly to our desire to focus attention on the role of the effort function in the growth process and to avoid as many complicating factors as possible. However, our model does contain an element of the labor-embodied variety of technological progress, if only in an implicit way. For our production function is formulated in terms of efficiency labor rather than natural labor, and thus the output can vary, as real wage varies, even though K and L remain fixed. If it is assumed that the variable w includes in it educational expenditures, part of the increase in output, when w increases, will be ascribable to the improvement in the quality of labor, or to labor-embodied technological improvement (cf. Schultz [6]). In this sense, our model can be interpreted to contain an *endogenous* theory of this particular type of technological progress, even though no exogenous technological change is considered.

Finally, to conclude, we wish to say a word about the scope of applicability of our model. In the course of the analysis, we have made explicit citation only of certain socialistic countries as examples of an MSD economy. The fact remains that our model is equally applicable to nonsocialistic systems, so long as they aim at the maximization of the capital growth rate through the control of productive effort by a wage policy. In particular, it may be noted that these last-mentioned requirements for the applicability of the model happen also to be central to the Marxian view of the development of a *capitalistic* economy. When we consider the Marxian assertion that "Any concession which the capitalist makes to the worker is the concession which the farmer makes to his beasts—to feed them better that they may work the more" ([5], p. 3), we see that it conforms precisely to the idea of the effort function. At the same time, the fact that Marx visualizes the capitalist class as incurably obsessed with capital accumulation ([5], p. 54) is clearly a parallel of the MSD notion. Thus, the conclusions of our paper should, we believe, be of interest to students of Marxian and orthodox theories of growth alike.

---

[10] Since we are dealing with a closed economy, any role which foreign aid can play in overcoming the difficulty of the situation falls outside the scope of this paper.

APPENDIX

I. *The Production Function*

Under the assumption of *CRTS*, the production function $Q = f(K, E)$ can be written in the forms:

(A1a) $$Q = Ef(K^\Delta, 1) = Eg(K^\Delta),$$

or

(A1b) $$Q^\Delta = g(K^\Delta), \quad g'(K^\Delta) > 0, g''(K^\Delta) < 0$$

from which we can obtain the following expressions for MPP_K and MPP_E respectively:

(A2a) $\quad f_K \equiv \dfrac{\partial Q}{\partial K} = Eg'(K^\Delta)\dfrac{\partial K^\Delta}{\partial K} = g'(K^\Delta) \qquad$ (by [A1a]),

(A2b) $\quad f_E \equiv \dfrac{\partial Q}{\partial E} = g(K^\Delta) + Eg'(K^\Delta)\dfrac{\partial K^\Delta}{\partial E} = Q^\Delta - f_K K^\Delta \qquad$ (by [A1b], [A2a]).

These results reveal that Q^Δ, f_K and f_E are all functions of K^Δ as shown by the curves in Figures 1b and 1c.

The elasticity of MPP_E with respect to E is

(A3)
$$
\begin{aligned}
\epsilon_{EE} &\equiv \frac{-\partial f_E}{\partial E}\frac{E}{f_E} = -\left(\frac{df_E}{dK^\Delta}\frac{\partial K^\Delta}{\partial E}\right)\left(\frac{E}{f_E}\right) \\
&= -\frac{df_E}{dK^\Delta}\left(\frac{-K}{E^2}\right)\left(\frac{E}{f_E}\right) = \frac{df_E}{dK^\Delta}\frac{K^\Delta}{f_E}.
\end{aligned}
$$

The expression on the right of the last equal sign is the elasticity of the f_E curve in Figure 1b. This proves (7) in the text.

II. *The Optimum Conditions*

From (5′) in the text, the rate of growth of capital is

(A4)
$$
\begin{aligned}
\eta_K &= \frac{Q^\Delta - w/\theta}{K^\Delta} = \frac{g(K^*/\theta) - w/\theta}{K^*/\theta} \\
&= \frac{\theta g(K^*/\theta) - w}{K^*} \qquad \text{(by [A1b], [6e])}.
\end{aligned}
$$

Since θ is a function of w, the maximized value of η_K for a given value of K^* can be found by differentiating (A4) with respect to w and setting the derivative to zero:

(A5)
$$\frac{d\eta_K}{dw} = \frac{1}{K^*}\left[\theta'g\left(\frac{K^*}{\theta}\right) + \theta g'\left(\frac{K^*}{\theta}\right)\frac{d}{dw}\left(\frac{K^*}{\theta}\right) - 1\right]$$

$$= \frac{1}{K^*}\left[\theta'g(K^\Delta) + \theta g'(K^\Delta)\left(\frac{-K^*\theta'}{\theta^2}\right) - 1\right] \quad \text{(by [6e])}$$

$$= \frac{\theta'}{K^*}\left[Q^\Delta - f_K K^\Delta - \frac{1}{\theta'}\right] \quad \text{(by [A1b], [A2a], [6e])}$$

$$= 0$$

when

(A6a)
$$Q^\Delta - f_K K^\Delta - 1/\theta' = 0,$$

or

(A6b)
$$f_E - 1/\theta' = 0 \quad \text{(by [A2b])}.$$

Result (A6b) yields the necessary condition for maximization, (13) in the text. And, by substituting (A6a) in (A4), we can obtain the maximum value of η_K as

(A7)
$$\overset{0}{\eta_K} = \frac{f_K K^\Delta + 1/\theta' - w/\theta}{K^\Delta} = f_K + \frac{x}{K^\Delta} \quad \text{(by [11])},$$

which proves (14) in the text.

To find the second-order condition for maximum, we differentiate (A5) with respect to w:

(A8)
$$\frac{d^2\eta_K}{dw^2} = \frac{d}{dw}\left[\frac{\theta'}{K^*}\left(Q^\Delta - f_K K^\Delta - \frac{1}{\theta'}\right)\right]$$

$$= \frac{1}{K^*}\frac{d}{dw}\left[\theta'\left(f_E - \frac{1}{\theta'}\right)\right] \quad \text{(by [A2b])}$$

$$= \frac{1}{K^*}\frac{d}{dw}\theta'f_E = \frac{1}{K^*}\left[\theta'\frac{df_E}{dK^\Delta}\frac{dK^\Delta}{dw} + \theta''f_E\right]$$

$$= \frac{1}{K^*}\left[\theta'\left(\frac{\epsilon_{EE}f_E}{K^\Delta}\right)\left(\frac{-K^\Delta\theta'}{\theta}\right) + \theta''f_E\right] \quad \text{(by [A3], [6e])}$$

$$= \frac{1}{K^*}\left[\frac{-\theta'\epsilon_{EE}}{\theta} + \frac{\theta''}{\theta'}\right] \quad \text{(by [A6b])}$$

$$= \frac{-1}{K^*w}\left[\epsilon_\theta\epsilon_{EE} + \epsilon_{MC}\right] \quad \text{(by [8], [12])}.$$

For a maximum, this derivative must be negative, so the second-order condition is

(A9)
$$\epsilon_\theta\epsilon_{EE} + \epsilon_{MC} > 0,$$

which proves (15) in the text.

III. *The Effects of Industrialization*

The first-order condition (A6b) may be written as an implicit function: $f_E - 1/\theta' = \Psi(K^*, w) = 0$. To see the direction of change of the optimum wage when K^* changes, we seek to evaluate the derivative

(A10a)
$$\frac{dw}{dK^*} = -\frac{\partial\Psi}{\partial K^*} \bigg/ \frac{\partial\Psi}{\partial w}.$$

Since the partial derivatives are

(A10b) $\quad \dfrac{\partial\Psi}{\partial K^*} = \dfrac{\partial\Psi}{\partial K^\Delta}\dfrac{\partial K^\Delta}{\partial K^*} = \dfrac{\epsilon_{EE}f_E}{K^\Delta}\left(\dfrac{1}{\theta}\right) = \dfrac{\epsilon_{EE}}{K^*\theta'}$ $\quad$ (by [A3], [6e], [A6b]) ;

(A10c)
$$\frac{\partial\Psi}{\partial w} = \left(\frac{\partial\Psi}{\partial w}\right)_{K^\Delta} + \frac{\partial\Psi}{\partial K^\Delta}\frac{\partial K^\Delta}{\partial w} = \frac{\theta''}{(\theta')^2} + \left(\frac{\epsilon_{EE}f_E}{K^\Delta}\right)\left(\frac{-K^*\theta'}{\theta^2}\right) \quad \text{(by [A3])}$$
$$= \frac{\theta''}{(\theta')^2} - \frac{\epsilon_{EE}}{\theta} \quad \text{(by [6e], [A6b])} ,$$

we have:

(A10d)
$$\frac{dw}{dK^*} = \frac{\epsilon_{EE}}{K^*\theta'[\epsilon_{EE}/\theta - \theta''/(\theta')^2]}$$
$$= \frac{\epsilon_{EE}}{(K^*/w)\,(\epsilon_\theta\epsilon_{EE} + \epsilon_{MC})} \quad \text{(by [8], [12])} .$$

This gives us the elasticity of optimum wage with respect to K^*:

(A11) $\qquad \epsilon_w \equiv \dfrac{dw}{dK^*}\dfrac{K^*}{w} = \dfrac{\epsilon_{EE}}{\epsilon_\theta\epsilon_{EE} + \epsilon_{MC}} > 0 \qquad \text{(by [A9])} ,$

which proves (16) in the text.

To deduce the effects of industrialization on the optimum values of some of the other variables, we compute:

(A12a) $\qquad \dfrac{d\theta}{dK^*} = \dfrac{d\theta}{dw}\dfrac{dw}{dK^*} = \theta'\left(\dfrac{w\epsilon_w}{K^*}\right) \qquad \text{(by [A11])} ,$

(A12b) $\qquad \dfrac{dx}{dK^*} = \dfrac{d}{dw}\left(\dfrac{1}{\theta'} - \dfrac{w}{\theta}\right)\dfrac{dw}{dK^*} = \left[\dfrac{-\theta''}{(\theta')^2} - \dfrac{1-\epsilon_\theta}{\theta}\right]\dfrac{dw}{dK^*}$
$$= \left(\frac{\epsilon_{MC}}{\epsilon_\theta\theta} - \frac{\theta'x}{\theta}\right)\left(\frac{w\epsilon_w}{K^*}\right) \qquad \text{(by [12], [8], [11])} ,$$

(A12c) $\dfrac{dK^\Delta}{dK^*} = \dfrac{d}{dK^*}\dfrac{K^*}{\theta} = \dfrac{1}{\theta} - \dfrac{1}{\theta^2}K^*\dfrac{d\theta}{dK^*}$

$\qquad\qquad = \dfrac{1}{\theta} - \dfrac{1}{\theta^2}\theta'w\epsilon_w$ (by [A12a])

$\qquad\qquad = \dfrac{1}{\theta}(1 - \epsilon_\theta\epsilon_w) = \dfrac{1}{\theta}\left(\dfrac{\epsilon_{MC}}{\epsilon_\theta\epsilon_{EE} + \epsilon_{MC}}\right)$ (by [A11]) .

This last derivative immediately leads to the elasticity expression in (17) in the text. The effect of industrialization on f_K is

(A12d) $\dfrac{df_K}{dK^*} = \dfrac{df_K}{dK^\Delta}K^\Delta\left(\dfrac{dK^\Delta}{dK^*}\right)/K^\Delta$

$\qquad\qquad = -\dfrac{d}{dK^\Delta}(Q^\Delta - f_K K^\Delta)\left(\dfrac{dK^\Delta}{dK^*}\right)/K^\Delta = \dfrac{-df_E}{dK^\Delta}\left(\dfrac{dK^\Delta}{dK^*}\right)/K^\Delta$

$\qquad\qquad\qquad\qquad\qquad\qquad\qquad\qquad\qquad\qquad\qquad\qquad$(by [A2b])

$\qquad\qquad = \dfrac{-\epsilon_{EE}}{K^{\Delta 2}\theta'}\dfrac{1}{\theta}\left(\dfrac{\epsilon_{MC}}{\epsilon_\theta\epsilon_{EE} + \epsilon_{MC}}\right)$ (by [A3], [A6b], [A12c])

$\qquad\qquad = \dfrac{-\theta\epsilon_{MC}\epsilon_w}{K^{*2}\theta'} = \dfrac{-w\epsilon_{MC}\epsilon_w}{\epsilon_\theta K^{*2}}$ (by [6e], [A11], [8]) .

Thus, finally, we can derive

(A12e) $\dfrac{d\eta_K^0}{dK^*} = \dfrac{d}{dK^*}\left(f_K + \dfrac{x\theta}{K^*}\right)$ (by [A7], [6e])

$\qquad\qquad = \dfrac{df_K}{dK^*} + \dfrac{1}{K^*}\left(\theta\dfrac{dx}{dK^*} + x\dfrac{d\theta}{dK^*}\right) - \dfrac{x\theta}{K^{*2}}$

$\qquad\qquad = \dfrac{df_K}{dK^*} + \dfrac{1}{K^*}\left(\dfrac{\epsilon_{MC}w\epsilon_w}{\epsilon_\theta K^*}\right) - \dfrac{x\theta}{K^{*2}}$ (by [A12b], [A12a])

$\qquad\qquad = \dfrac{-x\theta}{K^{*2}}$ (by [A12d])

$\qquad\qquad = \dfrac{1}{K^*}\left(\dfrac{-x}{K^\Delta}\right) = \dfrac{1}{K^*}(f_K - \eta_K^0)$ (by [6e], [A7]) ,

which proves (18a) and (18b) in the text.

R E F E R E N C E S

1. Fei, John C. H. "Per Capita Consumption and Growth," *Quarterly Journal of Economics*, LXXIX (February, 1965), 52–72.
2. Leibenstein, Harvey. "The Theory of Underemployment in Backward Economies," *Journal of Political Economy*, LXV (April, 1957), 91–103.

3. Phelps, E. S. "The Golden Rule of Accumulation," *American Economic Review*, LI (September, 1961), 638–43.
4. Pigou, A. C. *The Economics of Welfare*. 4th ed. London: Macmillan, 1932.
5. Robinson, Joan. *An Essay on Marxian Economics*. London: Macmillan, 1949.
6. Schultz, Theodore. "Investment in Human Capital," *Am. Econ. Rev.*, LI (March, 1961), 1–17.
7. Wonnacott, Paul. "Disguised and Overt Unemployment in Underdeveloped Economies," *Quart. Jour. Econ.*, LXXVI (May, 1962), 279–97.

COMMENT

ANTHONY M. TANG, VANDERBILT UNIVERSITY

This will be a three-part discussion of the Fei-Chiang paper. The first two parts shall take up the question of relevance of the model. The third part explores further implications of the work.

I. EMPIRICAL RELEVANCE OF THE BEHAVIORAL ASSUMPTIONS OF THE MODEL

Professors Fei and Chiang's MSD system has as a goal the maximization of the rate of growth of capital (hence, income) over some period of time. This is reminiscent of the work by Galenson and Leibenstein,[1] who, however, regarded consumption as a leakage to be minimized through judicious choice of investment projects with a view of maximizing subsequent reinvestment. The present paper treats consumption not as an end in itself but as an indirect input whose ultimate effect upon output is felt through its effect on the efficiency of labor. Labor is taken to be homogeneous except that its efficiency attribute can be influenced by varying real wage. Under given resources and state of arts, therefore, some real wage maximizes savings and investment. What that wage will be depends upon the shape of the effort curve. The efficiency wage policy, understood in this sense, is analyzed on three levels, static, comparative static, and dynamic.

The solution of the efficient wage is subject to (1) the constraint that there be full employment and (2) the restrictive assumption that the labor supply is perfectly inelastic. In fact, for simplicity, the paper takes labor measured in natural units to be identical with total population. The full-employment constraint is reasonable, although it does lead to a lowered rate of growth in the "subsidization" phase where workers are paid in excess of their marginal product. It is reasonable because without it the resulting excess supply of labor in that phase

[1] "Investment Criteria, Productivity and Economic Development," *Quarterly Journal of Economics*, LXX (August, 1955), 343–70.

must be liquidated (say, through starvation)—in order to avoid private or public income transfers from the employed to the unemployed—if the strict MSD solution is to be realized.

The assumption of a zero-elasticity labor supply, however, tends to undermine the relevance of the model—a model which is most particularly addressed to command economies of the Soviet type. In Communist China and throughout a large part of the Soviet history, labor mobilization appears to have been a crucial element. The details of implementation need not concern us. What is noteworthy is that in the Soviet Union, mainly under Stalin, real wage fell after 1928 while real consumption per capita rose (after initial setbacks during the early chaotic collectivization drive).[2] This is at variance with the model's dynamic path characterized by increases in the optimum real wage. The Soviet experience clearly implies rises in the labor force participation rate. Once the amount of labor offered (L) is allowed to vary, labor in efficiency unit (E) is no longer uniquely determined by the efficiency coefficient (θ) alone. It is now the product of L and θ, both being functions of real wage, w. If, as is plausible, one supposes that L is negatively inclined in the lower and upper reaches, then Professors Fei and Chiang would be confronted with a second-order condition for the MSD system even "nastier" than they have found.

Professors Fei and Chiang now will also have to recognize that θ is a function of both real wage and real consumption per capita. Real wage presumably bears on incentive while consumption affects work capacity through some physiological relationship. Under the assumption of $L = P$, wage and consumption level move together, so that either stands for the other. Without the assumption, the two can move in a disparate manner. If L is elastic in the lower, negatively inclined reaches, a fall in real wage will be accompanied by an increase in consumption, total and per capita, as well as by a rise in L. Whether this constitutes a cheaper way of "buying" a given increase in E (or indeed whether E, as a resultant of three separate influences, will increase) than the alternative of paying some appropriately higher wage is an empirical question. However, it is perhaps suggestive that in the known classic command economies, the historical development appears to have been at variance with the implications of the Fei-Chiang model.

The backward bend in L's upper reaches will raise further questions about the second-order condition and about the dynamic path of w. In closing this section, one might also relate the model to the early history of Western industrialization. The model would have us believe that the optimum wage from a profit maximization standpoint would probably have been higher than the bare subsistence level, to be followed by steady rises. Yet, we know that for prolonged periods during the English Industrial Revolution real wages (in hourly terms) remained at a miserable level, made livable for the worker and his family only by exceedingly long hours and by widespread participation of women and children in the work

[2] See, for example, Janet G. Chapman, "Consumption," in A. Bergson and S. Kuznets (eds.), *Economic Trends in the Soviet Union* (Cambridge, Mass., 1963).

force. Also, the presence of a large "reserve army" in towns whose ranks had been swelled by the rural exodus under the Enclosure Act need not have prevented employers from paying an optimum wage that leads to excess supply of labor. For, contrary to Leibenstein's belief,[3] competition among workers would not have caused wages to fall so long as it pays employers to insist on the higher optimum wage.

Leibenstein's pioneering work and the comments and replies that followed have made it fairly clear that in a capitalistic system the practice of the individual employer's paying a wage optimum from his profit standpoint and in accordance with wage-efficiency consideration is full of pitfalls. If we assume for simplicity identical production function among firms, the common optimum wage is certain to lead to excess supply during the Fei-Chiang "subsidization" phase, that is, during the underdevelopment phase. In the absence of any extermination plan for the unemployed, income sharing between them and the employed will take place, causing the employer to receive fewer efficiency labor units than expected on the basis of the wage paid. This outcome might well lead the economy to the "conventional" equilibrium which abstracts from the relationship between wage and labor's efficiency attributes. The latter equilibrium would be close to the bare subsistence wage under conditions of severe underdevelopment. This may explain the apparent discrepancy between the Fei-Chiang model and the early Western experiences. If so, their concluding statement that "our model is equally applicable to nonsocialistic systems, so long as they aim at the maximization of the capital growth rate through the control of productive effort by a wage policy" would be subject to qualifications. The question to be asked pertains to the second half of the statement: how to implement an efficient wage policy in a capitalist setting? In fact, if we recognize different production functions among establishments, industries, and sectors, the implementation becomes staggering to behold even (perhaps, especially) for a command economy, since a single wage can no longer satisfy the optimal conditions of the diverse productive units. In principle, there may be as many efficient wages as there are productive units.

II. EMPIRICAL RELEVANCE OF THE OBJECTIVE FUNCTION

Professors Fei and Chiang take the maximization of per capita income in some future year as the goal of the MSD system. Where the MSD system is approximated, it appears to be more realistic to take the maximization of the industrial base as the goal. To decision makers in the Soviet-type economies, this is ideologically appealing and consistent with the desire for rapid structural change, modernization, and enlargement of the country's power base. One interesting element, now well known, that emerges from the Soviet economic literature (then respectable) of the 1920's and more recently from Mahalanobis' writing is the

[3] Harvey Leibenstein, "The Theory of Underemployment in Backward Economies," *Journal of Political Economy*, LXV (August, 1957), 91–103.

notion that growth, especially when conceived in the sense just mentioned, is limited by the capacity of the capital goods sector and not by society's propensity to save.[4] Yet, the central theme of the paper under discussion has to do with maximizing savings through an optimum wage policy.

It is precisely the Soviet preoccupation with industrialization (particularly the growth of the heavy industry) that moved Bergson to remark that "steel is the final good and bread an intermediate product."[5] Under conditions of relative autarchy, how much more steel can be produced next year in order to produce still more steel is in part, at least, determined by how much steel is being produced this year. Whether the capacity constraint, rather than some other critical areas, turned out to be the effective bottleneck is an empirical question. Although solid evidence is hard to come by, there is now some suggestive indication that the capacity of the capital goods sector had indeed been the effective constraint. Savings or, more particularly, savings of the critical agricultural sector (the agricultural surplus) apparently had not been the limiting factor to Soviet industrialization.[6] If this is the case, the notion of an optimum wage policy would lose much of its substance in the planning of some MSD systems. Industrialization in the Communist MSD system in China, on the other hand, appears to have shown signs of being constrained by a faltering agricultural surplus. Here, the savings aspect is crucial and the notion of an optimum wage policy for agriculture becomes relevant. To proceed along these lines, the single-sector model will have to be modified to include at least two sectors.

III. IMPLICATIONS OF THE MODEL

In this section, we shall attempt to explore further the analysis of the paper. As indicated earlier, the "subsidization" and "exploitation" phases appear in the model because of the requirement that the entire labor force be employed. Maximization of the growth rate is accomplished through the solution of a single efficient wage subject to that constraint. We should like to suggest that this growth rate is not the true maximum. A higher rate is possible.

Suppose the economy is operating in the "subsidization" phase. Let the efficient wage be determined without the full-employment constraint. Here, the analytical elements may be borrowed from Leibenstein's work cited earlier. For each w, a particular grade of labor in efficiency terms can be had. Therefore, to each w, there is a corresponding *MPP* function (with quantity of labor in natural unit). Without the full-employment constraint, the optimum employment under each set of w and *MPP* function will be at the point where wage is equal to labor's marginal product. Now, find the particular set of w and *MPP* function

---

[4] See, for example, Evsey Domar, *Essays in the Theory of Economic Growth* (London, 1957), for an analysis of the work by the Soviet economist, Fel'dman, found in the chapter entitled, "A Soviet Model of Growth."

[5] As attributed to Bergson in P. J. D. Wiles, *The Political Economy of Communism* (Cambridge, Mass., 1962), p. 283.

[6] See my recent paper, "Policy and Performance in Agriculture," read before the Conference on Economic Trends in Communist China, Carmel, California, October 21–24, 1965 (conference volume forthcoming).

which yields the largest surplus. This gives us the efficient wage, w^*, at which there is an excess supply of labor so long as we are in the Fei-Chiang "subsidization" phase.

Let us now begin a second round solution to deal with the excess supply. The same procedure applies here and leads to the solution of w^{**}. The process continues until the excess supply disappears. Employment now consists of L^* amount of labor employed at w^*, L^{**} at w^{**}, and so forth. It can be shown that discrimination in a MSD system leads to a higher growth rate than the one solved by Fei and Chiang without sacrificing the sensible full-employment constraint. Whether in a command economy wage discrimination is practicable is a question we are not prepared to answer at this point. A plausible suggestion is that wage discrimination can always be "justified" on the basis of such *nominal* differences as sex, party affiliation, or distinction between primary and secondary wage-earners. If the planner resorts to these nominal differences for justification, the number of rounds of wage solution will be limited. However, the resulting growth rate would be higher in any case than that obtained by Fei and Chiang.

A final thought is that consideration of the Fei-Chiang effort function may throw a quite different light on the economics of discrimination. In terms of Becker's pathbreaking work,[7] discrimination in employment by employers serves to gratify the latter's tastes. They are said to incur a psychic cost in employing persons against whom discriminatory tastes are directed. Thus, they are willing to pay a higher wage to hire persons against whom there is no feeling of discrimination. In this light, employers incur an added money cost in practicing discrimination.

Once the wage-efficiency relationship is introduced, wage discrimination "justified" on grounds of race, sex, or other nominal criteria may turn out to be a rational profit-maximizing scheme. In contrast, Becker's view of discrimination leads to an optimum solution with respect to total returns (including psychic returns or costs), while the solution in money terms is nonoptimum. This is not to suggest that discrimination is not part of an individual's tastes. Rather, it is to suggest that within the Fei-Chiang framework wage discrimination is consistent with profit and that discrimination along lines of certain given and clearly discernible attributes may constitute nominal grounds to make wage discrimination possible.

Lastly, it may be noted that the introduction of wage discrimination into the model under discussion also makes the framework more general. Thus extended, the model becomes fully applicable to all economic systems, whether market- or command-directed.

We would like to make clear that the above discussion represents not so much a critical comment as it does a plea to Professors Fei and Chiang to continue to devote their unusual talent to an interesting area of inquiry. Their present work constitutes an important first step and should prove to be rewarding reading matter to any student of economic development.

[7] Gary S. Becker, *The Economics of Discrimination* (Chicago, 1957).

4. APPLICATIONS OF THE THEORY
OF STOCHASTIC PROCESSES
TO ECONOMIC DEVELOPMENT

G E R H A R D   T I N T N E R , UNIVERSITY OF SOUTHERN CALIFORNIA
J . K . S E N G U P T A , INDIAN INSTITUTE OF MANAGEMENT
E . J . T H O M A S , UNIVERSITY OF KERALA*

I. A STOCHASTIC THEORY OF ECONOMIC
DEVELOPMENT WITH APPLICATIONS
to BRITISH INDUSTRY

Modern theoretical writings on economic development (Domar [14], Baumol [7], Higgins [20]) appear defective because they result in development laws which are exponential functions and, with the significant exception of Haavelmo [19], they neglect stochastic influences. The following theory is a combination of the ideas of Rosenstein-Rodan [36] and Rostow [37] with those of Haavelmo.

Let us assume that, in the short run, the economic order can be represented by a system of linear stochastic difference equations (Tintner [52]):

$$(1) \quad \begin{aligned} & a_{10}^{(k)} x_{1t} + a_{11}^{(k)} x_{1t-1} + \ldots + a_{1p_1}^{(k)} x_{1t-p_1} \\ & + a_{20}^{(k)} x_{2t} + a_{21}^{(k)} x_{2t-1} + \ldots + a_{2p_2}^{(k)} x_{2t-p_2} \\ & \cdot \quad \cdot \quad \cdot \quad \cdot \quad \cdot \quad \cdot \quad \cdot \\ & + a_{m0}^{(k)} x_{mt} + a_{m1}^{(k)} x_{mt-1} + \ldots + a_{mp_m}^{(k)} x_{mt-p_m} = u_{kt} \\ & (k = 1, 2, \ldots . m) . \end{aligned}$$

In this formula, the $a_{rs}^{(k)}$ are constants, the x_{rt-s} represent economic variables lagged by s units, and the p_r are the maximum lag of the rth variable. Further, the quantities u_{kt} are stochastic variables. The system (1), however, is only an approximation of economic relations which are probably much more complicated (Klein and Goldberger [24], von Hohenbalken and Tintner [22], Tintner and Davila [53]. As Tinbergen [47] has shown,

* Research supported by the National Science Foundation, Washington, D.C.

it is possible to replace system (1) with a single stochastic linear difference equation of higher order:

(2) $b_0^{(j)} y_t + b_1^{(j)} y_{t-1} + \ldots + b_p^{(j)} y_{t-p} = v_t$.

In formula (2) $b_p^{(j)}$ are constants and the single variable y_t is one variable in system (1), such as national income. The quantity v_t is a random variable. But equation (2) holds only as a rough approximation in the short run. Let us assume that it holds only if:

(3) $c_{jr} \leq y_{t-r} \leq c_{j+1,r}$ $(r = 1, 2, \ldots, p)$

As soon as y_t moves outside the region defined in (3), we must make a new approximation; we must replace the constants $b_k^{(j)}$ by new constants $b_k^{(j-1)}$ or $b_k^{(j+1)}$. A region defined by (3) will be called a regime. In order to make our theory somewhat more realistic, we must consider the characteristic equation of the nonstochastic difference equation corresponding to (2):

(4) $b_0^{(j)} z^p + b_1^{(j)} z^{p-1} + \ldots + b_p^{(j)} = 0$.

It is not to be expected that all moduli of the roots of equation (4) will be less than one. Hence, in statistical estimation, methods developed by T. W. Anderson [3] and M. M. Rao [34] for the explosive case of stochastic difference equations must be applied.

We have used the data of W. Hoffmann [21] for total British industrial production, 1700–1939, excluding building (base: 1913 = 100) in order to verify the theory empirically. Also, for the sake of simplicity, we have replaced the stochastic difference equation (2) by the simpler one (Thomas [46], Tintner and Thomas [57]):

(5) $x_t = a^{(k)} x_{t-1} + u_t$.

This equation is of the first order and represents the short-term exponential trend. Here $a^{(k)}$ is a constant and u_t a random variable. As a first approximation u_t is assumed to follow a normal distribution with mean zero, constant variance, and no autocorrelation. Equation (5) holds only if:

(6) $c_k \leq x_{t-1} \leq c_{k+1}$.

If x_{t-1} falls outside the interval defined in (6), the constant $a^{(k)}$ has to be replaced by another constant $a^{(k-1)}$ or $a^{(k+1)}$.

The method for estimating the switchover points c_k is an adaptation of the method of Quandt [32, 33]. All possible values of c_k are studied, and that value of c_k is chosen which gives maximum likelihood. The constants $a^{(k)}$ are computed by the method of maximum likelihood. The above model may also be considered as a stochastic version of the "simple" theory of business fluctuations (Tintner [49, 50]).

We give in Table 1 the empirical results for a number of regimes (Hoffmann [21], Table 54, Part A, col. 1).

Table 1.

British Economic Development
1700–1939

Number of Regimes	a_k	95% Confidence Limits		Corresponding Year	c_k
		Lower bound	Higher bound		
2	1.030234	1.020258	1.040210	1834	14.20
	1.010767	0.993004	1.028530		
3	1.023861	1.006460	1.041262		
				1791	4.13
	1.029882	1.019080	1.040684		
				1869	40.60
	1.009564	0.987216	1.031912		
4	1.010724	0.989705	1.031743		
				1777	2.47
	1.026710	1.008864	1.044556		
				1820	8.13
	1.030094	1.016952	1.043236		
				1869	40.60
	1.009564	0.987216	1.031912		

It should be remembered that the confidence limits given in Table 1 are only approximate, since only the asymptotic theory is available. Tests also show that the difference between the values of $a^{(k)}$ belonging to neighboring regimes are not significant, showing that the transition is a gradual one. But the tests are only approximate. On the other hand, the variances of the u_t connected with different regimes are different, and the differences between the variances are statistically significant.

The general conclusion from this analysis seems to be that exponential trends resulting from a first-order stochastic difference equation give a reasonably good short-term explanation of the trend of economic development. But more elaborate systems of equations must be used in order to give a complete description and explanation of economic development.

II. Economic Development As A Classical Birth And Death Process

Let x be a measure of economic development, for example, real national income, which is here assumed to be a discontinuous variable (Bharucha-

Reid [8], pp. 86ff, Bartlett [6], pp. 70ff., Rosenblatt [35], pp. 133ff., Feller [15], pp. 371ff., Takacs [45], pp. 43ff., Parzen [30], pp. 378ff.). The following assumptions are made about possible changes in the time interval between t and $t + \Delta t$: the probability of a transition from x to $x + 1$ is $L_x \Delta t + o(\Delta t)$; the probability of a transition from x to $x - 1$ is $M_x \Delta t$ to $o(\Delta t)$; the probability of no change is $1 - (L_x + M_x) \Delta t + o(\Delta t)$. All other transition probabilities are $o(\Delta t)$. Letting $\Delta t \rightarrow 0$, we have the following differential-difference equation for the probability $P_x(t)$ that x will have a given value at time t:

(7) $dP_x(t)/dt = L_{x-1}P_{x-1}(t) - (L_x + M_x) P_x(t) + M_{x+1}P_{x+1}(t)$.

Now specify the transition probabilities involved as follows. Let a and c be positive constants. Then $L_x = ac$, a constant independent of x; $M_x = cx$, a function proportional to x. Our equation now becomes:

(8) $dP_x(t)/dt = ac\, P_{x-1}(t) - (ac + cx) P_x(t) + c(x + 1) P_{x+1}(t)$.

This differential-difference equation is most easily solved by the use of generating functions:

(9)
$$F(s, t) = \sum_{x=0}^{\infty} P_x s^x \, .$$

For the solution it is more convenient to make the transformations:

(10) $u = s - 1, \; G(s, t) = \log F(s, t)$.

Equation (8) can now be rewritten in terms of generating functions:

(11) $\partial G(u, t)/\partial t = -cu\partial G(u, t)/\partial u + acu$.

This partial differential equation of the first order is linear. We have the subsidiary equations:

(12) $dt/1 = du/(L - cu) = dG(u, t)/acu$.

Combining the first two equations in (12) we obtain a first integral:

(13) $K = ue^{-ct}$.

where K is an arbitrary constant. Combining the last two equations in (12) we obtain the integral:

(14) $G(u, t) = au + L$.

where L is an arbitrary constant.

Hence the solution of the system (12) appears in the form:

(15) $$G(u, t) = au + f(ue^{-ct}).$$

In formula (15) $f(ue^{-ct})$ is an arbitrary function which is to be determined by the initial condition, i.e., by $F(s, 0)$, the generating function of the distribution of x at time $t = 0$. If we assume that x at time 0 follows the Poisson distribution with mean $(a - b)$, the log of the generating function $F(s,0)$ can be written as

(16) $$G(u, 0) = (a - b)u.$$

But we have from (15):

(17) $$G(u, 0) = au + f(u) = (a - b)u.$$

Hence we obtain for the function $f(u)$:

(18) $$f(u) = -bu.$$

The solution of the partial differential equation (11) with initial condition (16) is then

(19) $$G(u, t) = (a - be^{-ct})u.$$

But this is log of the generating function of a Poisson distribution with mean value $a - be^{-ct}$. Therefore the solution $P_x(t)$ is the Poisson distribution.

(20) $$P_x(t) = e^{-h(t)}[h(t)]^x/x\ !$$

The mean of this distribution is (Wilks [58], pp. 140ff.):

(21) $$Ex = h(t) = a - b\ e^{-ct}$$

where b is a positive constant of integration. We have:

(22) $$h(0) = a - b, h(\infty) = a$$

so that we obtain an upper asymptote.

The theory is easily generalized to several independent variables (Bharucha-Reid [8], pp. 118ff.). Let $p_{x_1x_2} \ldots {}_{x_n}$ be the joint probability distribution of $x_1, x_2 \ldots x_n$. Then we have:

(23) $$dP_{x_1x_2\ldots x_n}(t)/dt = a_1c_1P_{x_1-1x_2\ldots x_n} + a_2c_2P_{x_1x_2-1x_3\ldots x_n} + \cdots$$
$$+ a_nc_nP_{x_1x_2\ldots x_n-1} - (a_1c_1 + c_1x_1 + a_2c_2 + c_2x_2 + \cdots$$
$$+ a_nc_n + c_nx_n)P_{x_1x_2\ldots x_n} + c_1(x_1 + 1)P_{x_1+1,x_2\ldots x_n} + c_2(x_2$$
$$+ 1)P_{x_1x_2+1,x_3\ldots x_n} + \cdots$$
$$+ c_n(x_n + 1)P_{x_1x_2\ldots x_n+1}$$

The solution of this differential-difference equation is now:

(24)
$$P_{x_1 x_2 \ldots x_n} = \prod_{i=1}^{n} e^{-h_i(t)}[h_i(t)]^{x_i}/x_i \, !$$

and the means are:

(25) $Ex_i = h_i(t) = a_i - b_i e^{-c_i t}$ $(i = 1, 2 \ldots n)$.

Consider now as an empirical illustration the long-run index of total output for Great Britain (1700–1939) constructed by Hoffmann [21], where the latter index is defined as the sum total of indices of output of consumer goods and producer goods industries with 1913 as a base year (Sengupta and Tintner [39]). Denoting the index of total output by y_t and taking yearly values for the whole period (1700–1939), a first-order autoregressive equation fitted on the basis of least squares turns out to be:

(26) $y_t = 2.096751 + 0.997297 \, y_{t-1}$
               (0.415703)   (0.011161)

where the standard errors are specified in parentheses below each coefficient.

The approximate solution of (26) is

(27) $y_t = 775.712541 - 772.882541 \, e^{-0.002703t}$.

The over-all mean of y_t for the whole period is about 99.3731. Using this as a normalizing factor such that $h(t) = y_t/99.3731$, we obtain from (27) an estimate of equation (4) as,

(28) $h(t) = Ex = 7.806061 - 7.777583 \, e^{-0.002703t}$.

Hence the differential-difference equation characterizing the process of British economic development for this period becomes

(29) $dP_x(t)/dt = 0.021100 \, P_{x-1}(t) - (0.021100$
                    $+ 0.002703 \, x) P_x(t) + 0.002703 \, (x+1) \, P_{x+1}(t)$.

This equation has the following interpretation. The probability of x changing from its given value x to $x + 1$ in the interval of time from t to $t + \Delta t$ is approximately $0.021100 \, (\Delta t)$. The probability of x not changing in the same time interval is approximately $(0.978900 - 0.002703x) \, \Delta t$, and the probability of x changing from x to $x - 1$ in the same time interval is about

$0.002703x$ (Δt). Since y_t in (27) has an upper asymptote, it is obvious that $h(\infty) = 7.806061$ and $h(0) = 0.028478$. By following the same method, we may consider some subperiods of the over-all period and the normalized index of total output now is (Sengupta and Tintner [39]):

$$1846-1880: h(t) = Ex = 11.589788 - 11.015400 \; e^{-0.002438t}$$
$$1881-1908: h(t) = Ex = 3.097561 - 2.321098 \; e^{-0.008154t}$$
$$1909-1940: h(t) = Ex = 1.023308 - 0.071103 \; e^{-0.265286t}.$$

The corresponding differential-difference equations for the probability $P_x(t)$ that x will have a given value at time t can be easily derived.

From an analytical standpoint, it may be more interesting to characterize the process of economic development in terms of more than one variable, such as capital stock, population, and total national output. However, the time-series on these three variables are highly serially and temporally interdependent and hence the assumption of mutual independence underlying solution (24) of the multiple differential-difference equation (23) cannot be empirically justified. We may, however, apply the method of principal components. As an illustration we consider the time-series on population (x_{1t}), the value of fixed capital at 1913 prices (x_{2t}), and the index of total output at 1913 prices (x_{3t}) for the period 1870–1940. Since the figures of capital stock constructed by Cairncross [9] are not available prior to 1870, we restrict ourselves to this period. In our calculation of principal components, we use biennial values for the three variables, using intrapolated values for the period 1936–1940 in the time-series of output index constructed by Hoffmann. The series x_{1t}, x_{2t}, x_{3t} along with the standardized series z_{1t}, z_{2t}, z_{3t} are presented in Table 2 of the Appendix.

On the basis of the period 1870–1940, we compute the correlation matrix

$$
\begin{array}{cccc}
 & x_1 & x_2 & x_3 \\
\begin{array}{c} x_1 \\ x_2 \\ x_3 \end{array} &
\left[\begin{array}{ccc}
1.000000 & 0.977828 & 0.731214 \\
 & 1.000000 & 0.932368 \\
 & & 1.000000
\end{array}\right].
\end{array}
$$

The system of linear equations which gives the coefficients of the first and largest principal component is given by

$$
\begin{aligned}
(30) \quad & 1.000000\, k_{11} + 0.977828\, k_{21} + 0.731214\, k_{31} = \lambda k_{11} \\
& 0.977828\, k_{11} + 1.000000\, k_{21} + 0.932368\, k_{31} = \lambda k_{21} \\
& 0.731214\, k_{11} + 0.932368\, k_{21} + 1.000000\, k_{31} = \lambda k_{31}.
\end{aligned}
$$

The three characteristic roots of the corresponding determinantal equation turn out to be

$$\lambda_1 = 2.565710$$
$$\lambda_2 = 0.352538$$
$$\lambda_3 = 0.081785 \ .$$

Since the total variance of the three standardized variables z_{1t}, z_{2t}, z_{3t} is evidently 3, the first principal component explains about 85.5 percent, the second about 11.8 per cent, and the third about 2.7 per cent of the total variance.

Taking the largest and the first principal component (Tintner [48], pp. 102–114, Hotelling [23]), (λ_1), we compute its coefficients from equation (10). The unit normal eigenvector is

$$\begin{bmatrix} k_{11} \\ k_{21} \\ k_{31} \end{bmatrix} = \begin{bmatrix} 0.614647 \\ 0.649990 \\ 0.446902 \end{bmatrix} \ .$$

Imposing the condition $\sum_{i=1}^{3} k_{i1}^2 = \lambda_1$, we get the standardized coefficients as

$$K_{11}^* = 0.984531, K_{21}^* = 1.041143, K_{31}^* = 0.715840 \ .$$

Similarly the standardized eigenvectors corresponding to second (λ_2) and third (λ_3) principal components are obtained. Then we express the standardized variates z_{1t}, z_{2t}, z_{3t} in terms of the principal components, u_{1t}, u_{2t}, u_{3t} as,

(31) $z_{1t} = 0.984531 \, u_{1t} - 0.249248 \, u_{2t} - 0.228515 \, u_{3t}$
         $z_{2t} = 1.041143 \, u_{1t} + 0.063501 \, u_{2t} + 0.134201 \, u_{3t}$
         $z_{3t} = 0.715840 \, u_{1t} + 0.217304 \, u_{2t} + 0.107493 \, u_{3t} \ .$

We obtain the principal components by inversion of the nonsingular coefficient matrix in (31) as,

(32) $$\begin{bmatrix} u_{1t} \\ u_{2t} \\ u_{3t} \end{bmatrix} = \begin{bmatrix} 0.376325 & 0.385237 & 0.319074 \\ 0.267029 & -4.539114 & 6.234596 \\ -3.045979 & 6.610685 & -5.425522 \end{bmatrix} \begin{bmatrix} z_{1t} \\ z_{2t} \\ z_{3t} \end{bmatrix} \ .$$

Now we fit a first-order autoregressive equation to each of the principal components, the solution of which is as follows:

(33)
$$u_{1t} = 8.950987 - 14.2860e^{-0.032971t}$$
$$u_{2t} = -0.4550 + 1.2499e^{-0.2499t}$$
$$u_{3t} = -2.168802 + 15.7010e^{-0.181828t} .$$

The differential-difference equation corresponding to the first principal component (u_1) now reduces to

$$(34) \quad dp_{n_1}(t)/dt = 0.295123p_{u_1-1}(t) - (0.295123 + 0.032971u_1)p_{u_1}(t)$$
$$+ 0.032971(u_1 + 1)p_{u_1+1}(t) .$$

The other components, which are mutually orthogonal by construction, may be used to compute the multiple difference-differential equation given in (23).

III. Conclusions

The tentative application of the theory of stochastic processes to problems of economic development appears promising, but a number of difficulties involved should not be overlooked. It is relatively easy to construct stochastic processes which involve linear or exponential trends. But up to now it has been impossible to derive a nontrivial stochastic process, yielding a logistic trend, which is surely preferable as an approximation to the law of economic development in the long run [52].

The difficulty with Poisson processes and birth and death processes consists in the choice of the unit. This problem has recently been solved in a manner which is not very satisfactory from a statistical point of view [27]. Perhaps it might be best to envisage stochastic processes which are continuous both in time and state variables, like diffusion processes. Some work on this type of processes is now in progress [54].

Apart from the great mathematical and statistical difficulties which beset the application of the theory of stochastic processes in economics, there are also some difficulties of economic interpretation of the results. Perhaps they should be explained as simple stochastic generalizations of deterministic models of economic development. But they at least have the merit of facing squarely the existence of the chance element in economic life and may point the way to more elaborate and at the same time more realistic stochastic models of economic development.

Development Theory and Strategy

APPENDIX: DATA USED IN THE CALCULATIONS

Table 2. Population (in millions), Capital Stock (in 100 million at 1913 prices), and the Index of Total Output (base year 1913), United Kingdom

Year	Population		Capital Stock		Index of Output	
	x_{1t}	z_{1t}	x_{2t}	z_{2t}	x_{3t}	z_{3t}
1870	22.45	-8.165	69.36	-3.785	88.3	-2.522
1872	23.04	-7.716	69.98	-3.655	96.6	-2.203
1874	23.69	-7.222	70.66	-3.513	101.9	-1.999
1876	24.34	-6.728	71.35	-3.368	101.3	-2.022
1878	24.99	-6.234	72.08	-3.215	98.7	-2.122
1880	25.64	-5.740	72.78	-3.068	110.2	-1.680
1882	26.27	-5.261	73.61	-2.894	114.4	-1.519
1884	26.57	-5.033	74.53	-2.701	121.8	-1.234
1886	27.17	-4.577	75.40	-2.519	114.4	-1.519
1888	27.77	-4.120	76.24	-2.343	120.7	-1.276
1890	28.37	-3.664	77.24	-2.133	134.1	-0.761
1892	29.35	-2.919	78.25	-1.922	130.7	-0.892
1894	30.05	-2.387	79.19	-1.725	127.4	-1.019
1896	30.75	-1.855	80.20	-1.513	138.6	-0.588
1898	31.45	-1.323	81.32	1.278	148.6	-0.203
1900	32.15	-0.791	82.51	-1.029	155.1	-0.046
1902	32.88	-0.236	83.72	-0.775	153.5	-0.015
1904	33.58	0.296	84.97	-0.513	145.2	0.011
1906	34.28	0.829	86.27	-0.241	166.5	0.484
1908	34.98	1.361	87.68	0.054	173.4	0.750
1910	35.68	1.893	89.00	0.331	169.2	0.588
1912	36.30	-2.364	90.44	0.633	185.6	1.219
1914	36.75	2.706	92.00	1.169	196.7	1.646
1916	37.20	3.048	93.47	1.268	178.9	0.961
1918	37.65	3.391	94.92	1.572	164.0	0.388
1920	38.10	3.733	96.34	1.869	176.8	0.880
1922	38.57	4.090	97.38	2.087	136.5	-0.669
1924	38.99	4.409	98.90	2.406	175.6	0.834
1926	39.41	4.729	100.16	2.670	180.5	1.023
1928	39.83	5.048	101.85	3.024	202.5	1.869
1930	40.25	5.367	103.61	3.393	208.2	2.088
1932	40.62	5.648	105.00	3.684	185.9	1.230
1934	40.94	5.892	106.68	4.036	202.1	1.853
1936	41.26	6.135	108.61	4.441	201.2	1.819
1938	41.58	6.378	110.51	4.839	209.8	2.149
1940	41.90	6.622	111.01	4.944	216.3	2.399

REFERENCES

1. Aitcheson, J., and Brown, J. A. *The Log-Normal Distribution*. Cambridge: Cambridge University Press, 1957.
2. Alexander, S. S. "Price Movements in Speculative Markets: Trends or Random Walks," *Industrial Management Review*, II (1961), 7–26.

3. Anderson, T. W. "On Asymptotic Distributions of Estimates of Parameters of Stochastic Difference Equations," *Annals of Mathematical Statistics*, XXX (1959), 676–87.
4. Bachelier, L. *Théorie de la spéculation*. Paris: Gautier Villars, 1900.
5. Bailey, N. T. J. *The Elements of Stochastic Processes*. New York: Wiley, 1964.
6. Bartlett, M. S. *An Introduction to Stochastic Processes*. Cambridge: Cambridge University Press, 1955.
7. Baumol, W. J. *Economic Dynamics*. 2nd ed. New York: Macmillan, 1959.
8. Bharucha-Reid, A. T. *Elements of the Theory of Markoff Processes and Their Applications*. New York: McGraw Hill, 1960.
9. Cairncross, A. K. *Home and Foreign Investment 1870–1913*. Cambridge: Cambridge University Press, 1953.
10. Champernowne, G. D. "A Model of Income Distribution," *Economic Journal*, LXIII (1953), 318.
11. Cootner, P. H. (ed.) *The Random Character of Stock Market Prices*. Cambridge, Mass.: M I T Press, 1964.
12. Cowles, A. "A Revision of Previous Conclusions Regarding Stock Market Prices," *Econometrica*, XXVIII (1960), 909–15.
13. Davis, H. T. *The Analysis of Economic Time Series*. Bloomington, Ind.: Principia Press, 1941.
14. Domar, Evsey. *Essays in the Theory of Economic Growth*. London: Oxford University Press, 1957.
15. Feller, W. *An Introduction to Probability Theory and Its Applications*. New York: Wiley, 1950.
16. Fisz, M. *Probability Theory and Mathematical Statistics*. New York: Wiley, 1963.
17. Gibrat, R. *Les inégalités économiques*. Paris, 1931.
18. Granger, G. W. J., and Morgenstern, O. "Spectral Analysis of New York Stock Market Prices," *Kyklos*, XVI (1963), 1–27.
19. Haavelmo, T. *A Study in the Theory of Economic Evolution*. Amsterdam: North Holland, 1954.
20. Higgins, B. *Economic Development*. New York: Norton, 1959.
21. Hoffmann, W. G. *British Industry 1700–1950*. Oxford: Oxford University Press, 1955.
22. Von Hohenbalken, B., and Tintner, G. "Econometric Models of the OEEC Member Countries, the United States and Canada, and Their Application to Economic Policy," *Weltwirtschaftliches Archiv*, LXXXIX (1962), 29–86.
23. Hotelling, H. "Analysis of a Complex of Statistical Variables into Principal Components," *Journal of Educational Psychology*, XXIV (1933), 417.
24. Klein, L. R., and Goldberger, A. S. *An Econometric Model of the United States*. Amsterdam: North Holland, 1957.
25. Mandelbrot, B. "The Variation of Speculative Prices," *Journal of Business*, XXXVI (1963), 394–419.
26. Morishima, M. *Equilibrium, Stability and Growth*. Oxford: Clarendon Press, 1964.
27. Mukherjee, V., Tintner, G., and Narayanan, R. "A Generalized Poisson Process for the Explanation of Economic Development with Applications to Indian Data," *Arthaniti*, VIII (1965), 1–9.
28. Orcutt, G. H., Greenberger, M., Korbel, J., and Rivlin, A. M. *Microanalysis of Socio-Economic Systems*. New York: Harper, 1961.
29. Pareto, V. *Manuel d'économie politique*. 2nd ed. Paris: M. Giard, 1927.
30. Parzen, E. *Stochastic Processes*. San Francisco: Holden-Day, 1962.
31. Prais, S. J., and Houthakker, H. S. *The Analysis of Family Budgets*. Cambridge: Cambridge University Press, 1955.
32. Quandt, R. "The Estimation of Parameters of a Linear Regression System Obeying Two Separate Regimes," *Journal of the American Statistical Association*, LIII (1958), 873.

33. —— "Tests of the Hypothesis that a Linear Regression System Obeys Two Regimes," *Journal of the American Statistical Association*, LV (1960), 324.
34. Rao, M. M. "Consistency and Limit Distributions of Estimators of Parameters in Explosive Stochastic Difference Equations," *Annals of Mathematical Statistics*, XXXII (1961), 195–218.
35. Rosenblatt, M. *Random Processes*. Oxford: Oxford University Press, 1962.
36. Rosenstein-Rodan, P. N. "Problems of Industrialisation of Eastern and Southeastern Europe," *Economic Journal*, LIII (1943), 202.
37. Rostow, W. W. *The Stages of Economic Growth*. Cambridge: Cambridge University Press, 1960.
38. Rutherford, R. S. G. "Income Distributions: A New Model," *Econometrica*, XXIII (1955), 277–94.
39. Sengupta, J. K., and Tintner, G. *An Approach to a Stochastic Theory of Economic Development and Fluctuations. Problems of Economic Dynamics and Planning. Essays in Honour of Michal Kalecki*. Warsaw: Polish Scientific Publishers, 1964.
40. —— "On Some Aspects of Trend in the Aggregative Models of Economic Growth," *Kyklos*, XVI (1963), 47–61.
41. —— "A Stochastic Programming Interpretation of the Domar-type Growth Model," *Arthaniti*, V (1963), 1–11.
42. —— "The Flexibility and Optimality of Domar-type Growth Models," *Metroeconomica*, XVII (1965), 3–16.
43. Sprekle, C. *Warrant Prices as Indicators of Expectations and Preference*. (*Yale Economic Essays*, Vol. I.) New Haven: Yale University Press, 1961, pp. 178–231.
44. Steindl, J. *Random Processes and the Growth of Firms*. New York: Hafner, 1965.
45. Takacs, L. *Stochastic Processes*. New York: Wiley, 1960.
46. Thomas, E. J. "Stochastic Processes Obeying Two or More Separate Regimes." Unpublished M.S. thesis, Iowa State University, 1961.
47. Tinbergen, J. *Statistical Testing of Business Cycle Theories*. (*Business Cycles in the United States of America, 1919–1929*, Vol. II.) Geneva: League of Nations, 1939.
48. Tintner, G. *Econometrics*. New York: Wiley, 1952.
49. —— "A 'Simple' Theory of Business Fluctuations," *Econometrica*, X (1942), 317–20.
50. —— "The 'Simple' Theory of Business Fluctuations: A Tentative Verification," *Review of Economic Statistics*, XXVIII (1944), pp. 148–57.
51. —— "The Logistic Law of Economic Development," *Arthaniti*, IV (1961), 1–4.
52. —— *A Stochastic Theory of Economic Development and Fluctuations*. (*Money, Growth and Methodology and Other Essays in Economics, in Honor of Johan Akerman*, ed. by H. Hegelund.) Lund: CWK Gleerup, 1961.
53. —— and Davila, O. "Applicaciones de la econometría a la planificación," *El Trimestre Economico*, XXXII (1965), 717–23.
54. —— and Patel, R. C. A. "A Log-normal Diffusion Process Applied to the Economic Development of India," *Indian Economic Journal*, XIII (1965), 465–74.
55. —— and Sengupta, J. K., "Some Aspects of the Design and Use of a Generalized Growth Model," *Indian Economic Review*, VI (1962), 1–21.
56. —— and Sengupta, J. K., "Ein verallgmeinerter Geburten und Todesprozess zur Erklaerung der Entwicklung des deutschen Volkseinkommens 1851–1939," *Metrika*, VI (1963), 143–47.
57. —— and Thomas, E. J. "Un modele stochastique de developpement économique avec application a l'industrie anglaise," *Revue d'Économie Politique*, LXXVII (1963), 278–80.
58. Wilks, S. S. *Mathematical Statistics*. New York: Wiley, 1962.

COMMENT

T. KRISHNA KUMAR, UNIVERSITY OF CALIFORNIA, BERKELEY

Most theories of economic development give rise to growth paths that are exponential in nature.

However, such paths cannot hold indefinitely. Professor Tintner has put forward in this paper and in some of his earlier works two approaches to overcome this difficulty. The first approach assumes that the exponential path represents the economy only in the short run and that different exponential paths represent the economy in different phases. The second approach assumes that the growth paths are logistic in nature with an upper asymptote. There are no studies on the theory of economic development that take into account these two valuable suggestions of Professor Tintner.[1]

Professor Tintner begins by assuming that, as a first approximation, the economic system can, in the short run, be represented by a system of linear difference equations and that different sets of difference equations represent the system in different regimes. In this context, it is interesting to investigate the nature of the underlying *structural equations* which give rise to a set of reduced form equations of the type assumed by Professor Tintner. One might expect to find many realistic forms of structural equations giving rise to a reduced form which is a system of linear difference equations.

The concept of a change of regime is also more meaningful in the context of the underlying structural equations than in that of the reduced form. A behavioristic theory of the economy in Rostovian stages would appear to be a necessary complement to Professor Tintner's theory of economic development.[2] A purely empirical approach to the question of determining the switchover points between different regimes has several limitations. In the present study the authors use Quandt's method of estimating the switchover points. This method has two deficiencies: (1) the number of switchover points has to be assumed a priori, and (2) a different formulation of the model may give rise to different switchover points. The authors remark: "Tests also show that the difference between the values of $a^{(k)}$ belonging to different regimes are not significant, showing that the transition is a gradual one. *But the tests are only approximate.*" However, once they obtained the switchover points they could perform an *exact* test to find if the regression equations corresponding to neighboring regimes are the same.[3]

[1] See, however, Tintner's own work, "The Logistic Law of Economic Development," *Arthaniti*, IV (1961), 1–4.

[2] See S. C. Tsiang, "A Model of Economic Growth in Rostovian Stages," *Econometrica*, XXXII (October, 1964), pp. 619–48.

[3] C. R. Rao, *Advanced Statistical Methods in Biometric Research* (New York, 1952), pp. 112–15.

One would also like to know the effects of specification bias upon the switch-over points. For example, what would be the nature of the switchover points if a second order autoregressive model instead of a first order autoregressive model were assumed. The authors fit a first order autoregressive model assuming the error terms to be serially uncorrelated and normally distributed with the same variance. Usually such a simple model cannot be expected to be a reasonably good approximation to reality and it would have been better if the authors had presented a test of no autocorrelation in the error terms.

With respect to the second model, it is very hard to believe that the national income, output, or any other indicator of growth follows a birth-and-death-process. The economic behavior underlying such a model should be discussed explicitly. Otherwise, it is very difficult for the reader to accept the various assumptions made in the text. For example, the assumption that L_x (the probability of transition from x to $x + 1$) is a constant independent of x, while M_x (the probability of transition from x to $x - 1$) is proportional to x requires justification.

Despite these deficiencies, however, Tintner's work on stochastic growth processes is an interesting contribution.

5. AN OPTIMUM FISCAL POLICY IN AN AGGREGATIVE MODEL OF ECONOMIC GROWTH

HIROFUMI UZAWA, UNIVERSITY OF CHICAGO*

In this paper, the problem of optimum fiscal policy is discussed in terms of the techniques of optimum economic growth. The model is a simple extension of the aggregative growth model of the type introduced by Solow [13], Swan [16], and Tobin [17]. It consists of private and public sectors, both employing labor and private capital to produce goods and services. Private goods may be either consumed or accumulated as capital, while public goods are all consumed. The public sector raises revenues by levying income taxes or by issuing money to pay wages and rentals to the labor and capital it hires to produce goods. The private sector decides how much is to be consumed and invested and how to allocate portfolio balances between real capital and money. These decisions are based upon certain behavioristic assumptions and are made in a perfectly competitive institutional setting. It will then be shown that by a proper choice of dynamic fiscal policy, which consists of income tax rates and growth rates of money supply through time, it is possible to achieve an optimal growth path corresponding to any form of social utility function and any rate of discount.

I. INTRODUCTION

In the postwar period, many countries, both advanced and less advanced, have come to regard fiscal policy both as an instrument to achieve short-run goals and to implement long-run objectives, such as economic growth. The theoretical analysis of the dynamic implications of fiscal policy has been recently started, in particular by Gurley [3], Brown [1], Smith [12], Musgrave [10], and others. In this paper, we will examine the

* This work was in part supported by the National Science Foundation under Grant GS-762 to the University of Chicago and in part by the Mathematical Social Science Board Conference on Economic Growth, 1965.

dynamics of fiscal policy in terms of the theory of optimum economic growth developed in the past few years by Koopmans [6], Srinivasan [14], Cass [2], Kurz [7], Stoleru [15], Mirrlees [9], von Weiszaecker [2], and Inagaki [5].

The basic framework of the theory of optimum economic growth originates in Ramsey's classical paper [11], but only recently has the problem of achieving desired economic growth through optimum allocation of scarce resources between consumption and investment become a central issue in economic analysis. The Ramsey theory, however, is based upon an economic structure similar to that of a centrally planned economy in which a central planning bureau is free to allocate the means of production, labor, and capital, in whatever manner it desires. In most countries, the allocation of the means of production is not directly governed by the state authorities. The Ramsey theory nevertheless is applicable to such economies with proper modifications, and the purpose of the paper is to illustrate with a simple model how an optimum growth can be achieved through such limited policy tools, such as income taxes and changes in the money supply.

The basic structure of the model presented below is similar to that of the aggregative dynamic model first introduced by Tobin [17] to discuss the dynamic implications of monetary policies. In the present model, government is engaged in the production of different goods from those produced by private entrepreneurs; for the sake of simplicity they will be referred to as public goods, in contrast to private goods. Each category of goods is composed of homogeneous quantities, which are substitutes for each other. Public goods disappear instantaneously, while private goods may be either consumed or accumulated as capital. Both sectors employ labor and capital, and the production processes are subject to all the neoclassical conditions (constant returns to scale, diminishing marginal rates of substitution, and the like). The public sector pays wages and rentals from the revenues it gets through income taxes and from deficits; the deficits must be met by an increase in the money supply. The policy variables the public sector can control, however, are assumed to be the income tax rate and the rate of change in the money supply. The private sector decides the allocations of output between consumption and investment and the portfolio balance between monetary and real assets.

We shall first examine (by using the methods developed by Hicks [4] and Metzler [8]) the structure of short- and long-run equilibria in such a model when the fiscal policy (the income tax rate and the rate of change in money supply) is exogenously determined and kept constant throughout the period in question. We then postulate a utility function for the representative member of the economy, which is assumed to depend upon the per capita consumption of private goods and the average amount of public goods available at each moment. The structure of capital accumulation which is optimal with respect to the discounted sum of utility levels will be analyzed in terms of mathematical techniques developed by [2 and 19]. Finally, we shall discuss the structure of optimum fiscal policy in detail for the special case in which the average propensity to consume (out of disposable income) is constant and the velocity of money is independent of the rate of interest.

II. THE MODEL

The analysis will be carried out in terms of the aggregative growth model where a number of simplifying, somewhat unrealistic, assumptions will be postulated to make the analysis possible, although some of them could be relaxed without substantially altering the conclusions.

We consider an economic system composed of public and private sectors. The private sector comprises business firms and households; business firms employ labor and either own or rent capital, while households receive wages for the labor they provide and interest and dividends for the capital they rent to business firms. The output produced in the private sector is assumed to be composed of homogenous quantities so that any portion of it may be either instantaneously consumed or accumulated as part of the capital stock. The public sector provides the private sector with different goods and services than those it produces. The goods and services produced in the public sector are assumed to be measurable and distributed uniformly to the private sector without cost. The public sector raises revenues through income taxes and increases in the money supply to pay wages and rentals for the private means of production it employs. It is required to employ labor and capital in such a way that total expenditure is minimized for any level of public goods produced. The public sector has two means of raising revenues—taxation and printing money—but is assumed to be able to control only the rate of income tax and the rate of increase in money supply. Capital accumulation takes place only in the private sector, and public goods are not accumulated.[1]

At each moment of time, t, we take as given the amounts of (private) capital, $K(t)$, and labor, $L(t)$, available in the economy, together with the

---

[1] In another context, I have analyzed the problem of optimum investment in public capital in which all public goods are regarded as social capital to increase productivity of labor and private capital in the private sector; see Uzawa [20].

outstanding amount of money, $M(t)$.[2] The public sector is in principle free to choose any fiscal policy it desires characterized by the income tax rate, $\tau = \tau(t)$, and the rate of increase in money supply, $\theta = \theta(t)$.

The aggregative output, $Y_C(t)$, in the private sector is assumed to depend only on the amounts of capital, $K_C(t)$, and labor, $L_C(t)$, employed:

(1) $$Y_C(t) = F_C(K_C(t), L_C(t)),$$

where F_C is the private sector's productive function. Production processes here are assumed to be subject to constant returns to scale and to a positive, diminishing marginal rate of substitution between capital and labor, ranging from infinity to zero as the capital-labor ratio is increased from zero to infinity. These assumptions are stated in terms of the per capita production function, $f_C(k_C) = F_C(K_C, L_C)/L_C$, $k_C = K_C/L_C$:

(2) $\quad f_C(k_C) > 0, f_C'(k_C) > 0, f_C''(k_C) < 0 \quad$ (for all $k_C > 0$);

(3) $\quad f_C(0) = 0, f_C(\infty) = \infty$;

(4) $\quad f_C'(0) = \infty, f'_C(\infty) = 0$.

Perfect competition prevails in the private sector, so that the real wage, $w(t)$, and the real rental rate, $r(t)$, are equated to the marginal products of labor and capital, respectively:

(5) $$w(t) = \frac{\partial F_C}{\partial L_C}, \qquad r(t) = \frac{\partial F_C}{\partial K_C}.$$

The public sector, on the other hand, employs capital and labor in such a combination that the total cost in terms of market prices is always minimized. Let

(6) $$Y_V(t) = F_V(K_V(t), L_V(t))$$

be the aggregative output in the public sector, where $K_V(t)$ and $L_V(t)$ are respectively the employments of capital and labor. As for the public sector's production function, F_V, it is again assumed that all the neoclassical hypotheses are satisfied, namely, F_V is homogeneous of order one and strictly quasi-concave, with positive marginal products everywhere. In terms of the per capita production function

$$f_V(k_V) = F_V(K_V, L_V)/L_V, k_V = K_V/L_V,$$

these neoclassical hypotheses are stated by:

(7) $\quad f_V(k_V) > 0, f_V'(k_V) > 0, f'_V(k_V) < 0 \quad$ for all $k_V > 0$;

[2] The concept of money being used here is similar to one adapted by Tobin [17]; it includes all the short-term liabilities of the public sector to the private sector.

(8) $f_V(0) = 0, \quad f_V(\infty) = \infty$;

(9) $f'_V(0) = \infty, \quad f'_V(\infty) = 0$.

The cost in the public sector is minimized when the marginal rate of substitution between labor and capital is equated to the wage-rentals ratio, $w(t)/r(t)$, at time t:

(10) $$\frac{\partial F_V/\partial L_V}{\partial F_V/\partial K_V} = \frac{w(t)}{r(t)}.$$

The real gross national income, $Y(t)$, is given by

(11) $$Y(t) = r(t)K(t) + w(t)L(t) .$$

Hence the tax revenue in the public sector is equal to

$$\tau(t)Y(t) = \tau(t)[r(t)K(t) + w(t)L(t)] ,$$

while the total expenditure is given by

$$r(t)K_V(t) + w(t)L_V(t) .$$

Since the deficit in the public sector's budget is met by an increase in money supply, we have the balance-of-the-budget equation:

(12) $$[r(t)K_V(t) + w(t)L_V(t)] - \tau(t)Y(t) = \theta(t)M(t)/p(t) ,$$

where $p(t)$ is the market price of private goods and $\theta(t)$ is the rate at which money increases.

Since the quantities of capital and labor available are $K(t)$ and $L(t)$, we have

(13) $$K_C(t) + K_V(t) = K(t) ,$$

(14) $$L_C(t) + L_V(t) = L(t) .$$

The output of private goods, $Y_C(t)$, is divided between consumption, $C(t)$, and investment, $Z(t)$:

(15) $$C(t) + Z(t) = Y_C(t) .$$

To determine the allocation of private output between consumption and investment, we need to examine the behavior of households and business firms. Households' allocation of the aggregative disposable income between consumption and savings is chiefly governed by the level of the disposable income, total assets held, and the rate of interest, $\rho(t)$. The disposable income in real terms is given by

(16) $$Y^d(t) = (1 - \tau(t))Y(t) ,$$

while the total monetary and nonmonetary assets, $A(t)$, are evaluated as

(17) $$A(t) = K(t) + M(t)/p(t)$$

in real terms.

Let the consumption function be given by $C(\rho, Y^d, A)$ which relates the level of the consumption the private sector wants to maintain with the rate of interest, ρ, the real disposable income, Y^d, and the monetary and non-monetary asset in real terms, A. Then we have

(18) $$C(t) = C(\rho(t), Y^d(t), A(t)) .$$

It is assumed that C is homogeneous of order one with respect to Y^d and A and that the private sector increases the desired level of consumption whenever disposable income, Y^d, or assets, A, are increased or the rate of interest, ρ, is decreased. Namely, we have

(19) $$\frac{\partial C}{\partial \rho} \leqq 0, \ \frac{\partial C}{\partial Y^d} > 0, \ \frac{\partial C}{\partial A} \geqq 0 .$$

As will be more explicitly formulated later, we postulate the existence of a utility function for each member of the society. Each member's utility level is assumed to be related to the amounts of private and public goods available to him, and his intertemporal utility level is determined as the discounted sum of atemporal levels of utilities throughout his time horizon. In terms of the consumption function postulated above, we assume that the level of consumption each member desires to attain is independent of the amount of public goods available, although his utility level may depend upon public as well as upon private goods.

The desired level of investment, on the other hand, is determined by the Keynesian principle of marginal efficiency of investment, as mathematically formulated in [18]. Business firms in the private sector try to increase the level of investment to that at which the supply price of capital is equated with the demand price (defined as the discounted sum of the expected returns). In general, the desired level of investment, $Z(t)$, is determined by the current rate of returns, $r(t)$, the money price, $p(t)$, the rate of interest, $\rho(t)$, and the stock of capital, $K(t)$. If we assume that the elasticities of expected returns are all unity and that the expected returns depend upon the rate at which the current stock of capital is increased, together with the current level of per capita output, the desired level of investment is described by the following relation:

(20) $$\frac{Z(t)}{K(t)} = Z\left(\rho(t), \frac{Y(t)}{K(t)}\right),$$

where the investment function, $Z(\rho, Y/K)$, satisfies the following conditions:

$$(21) \qquad \frac{\partial Z}{\partial \rho} < 0, \frac{\partial Z}{\partial (Y/K)} \geq 0,$$

$$(22) \qquad \phi(0, Y/K) = \infty, \phi(\infty, Y/K) = 0.$$

As for the portfolio balance between the two types of assets existing in the economy, real capital and money, the private sector as a whole wishes to maintain a certain level of real cash balances to meet transaction, precautionary, or speculative requirements. It will be postulated, as in Tobin [17], that the desired level of real cash balance, M/p, is determined by the rate of interest, ρ, the level of disposable income, Y^d, and the amount of real capital, K:

$$(23) \qquad \frac{M/p}{K} = \lambda\left(\rho, \frac{Y^d}{K}\right).$$

The demand-for-money function, λ, is assumed to satisfy the following conditions:

$$(24) \qquad \frac{\partial \lambda}{\partial \rho} < 0,$$

$$(25) \qquad 0 \leq \frac{\partial \log \lambda}{\partial \log (Y^d/K)} \leq 1.$$

At each moment of time, t, we are given the available stock of capital, $K(t)$, the supply of labor, $L(t)$, and the outstanding amount of money, $M(t)$, together with the rate of income tax, $\tau(t)$, and the rate of increase in money supply, $\theta(t)$, both of which are set as part of a fiscal policy. Then the equations described above, (1), (5–6), (10–12), (13–18), and (20), together determine the allocations of capital and labor, $K_C(t)$, $K_V(t)$, and $L_C(t)$, $L_V(t)$, outputs of private and public goods, $Y_C(t)$ and $Y_V(t)$, real wage and rental rates, $w(t)$ and $r(t)$, the money price of private goods, $p(t)$, consumption, $C(t)$, investment, $Z(t)$, and rate of interest, $\rho(t)$. In the next sections, we shall show that all these variables are uniquely determined.

The accumulation of capital is described by

$$(26) \qquad \dot{K}(t) = Z(t) - \mu K(t),$$

where μ is the rate of depreciation, while the growth rate of labor, n, is assumed to be exogenously given:

$$(27) \qquad \dot{L}(t) = nL(t).$$

If the fiscal policy, $(\theta(t), \tau(t))$, is predetermined through time, the differential equation (26) for capital accumulation specifies the time path of capital, $K(t)$, throughout time, t, for any given stock of capital, $K(0)$, initially held in the economy. After we examine the determination of short-run equilibrium in such an economy, the long-run structure will be briefly analyzed for a particular case in which the rates of income tax and increase in money supply are held constant through time:

$$\tau(t) = \tau, \, \theta(t) = \theta \quad \text{for all } t \, .$$

We then analyze the problem of optimum fiscal policy by introducing a social welfare criterion, which will be expressed as a maximization of a discounted sum of instantaneous utility levels.

III. ANALYSIS OF THE SHORT-RUN EQUILIBRIUM

To analyze the workings of the model, we first reduce the model introduced above to one involving per capita quantities only. In defining the following notation, for the sake of simplicity, the time suffix, t, will be omitted:

$$k = K/L \quad \text{the aggregate capital-labor ratio.}$$
$$y_j = Y_j/K \quad \text{the output of good } j \text{ per unit of capital } (j = C, V).$$
$$l_j = L_j/L \quad \text{the labor allocation to sector } j(j = C, V).$$
$$k_j = K_j/L_j \quad \text{the capital-labor ratio in sector } j(j = C, V).$$
$$y = Y/K \quad \text{the real national income per unit of capital.}$$
$$y^d = Y^d/K \quad \text{the real disposable income per unit of capital.}$$
$$c = C/K \quad \text{the level of consumption per unit of capital.}$$
$$z = Z/K \quad \text{the investment-capital ratio.}$$
$$m = M/pK \quad \text{the real cash balance per unit of capital.}$$
$$a = A/K \quad \text{the assets in real terms per unit of capital.}$$
$$\omega = w/r \quad \text{the wage-rental ratio.}$$

The marginal productivity conditions in both sectors (5) and (10) are then reduced to the following familiar equations:

$$(28) \qquad \omega = \frac{f_j(k_j)}{f'_j(k_j)} - k_j \quad (j = C, V) \, ,$$

which are solved to derive the optimum capital-labor function $k_j = k_j(\omega)$ in each sector. As was discussed in detail in [18 and 19] the optimum capital-labor ratio curve, $k_j(\omega)$, is an increasing function of the wage-rental ratio, ω, ranging from 0 to infinity as ω moves from 0 to infinity. For the sake of simplicity, it will be assumed that the optimum capital-labor curves in the two sectors never intersect. Thus the two curves are typically related to each other as illustrated in Figure 1.

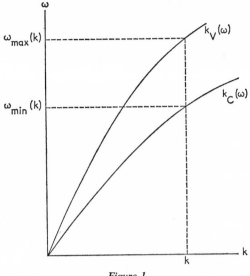

Figure 1

Conditions (13–14) are then solved in terms of l_C and l_V:

$$l_C = \frac{k - k_V}{k_C - k_V},$$

(29)
$$l_V = \frac{k_C - k}{k_C - k_V},$$

where k_C and k_V are respectively optimum capital-labor ratios in the private and public sectors. The output-capital ratios are correspondingly determined:

(30) $y_C = y_C(\omega, k) = f_C(k_C)l_C/k$, $y_V = y_V(\omega, k) = f_V(k_V)l_V/k$

For the rest of the paper, the discussion will be carried on only for the case in which the private sector is always relatively more capital-intensive than the public sector:

(31) $k_V(\omega) < k_C(\omega)$,   for all $\omega > 0$.

For the labor allocations, l_C and l_V, to be positive, the aggregative capital-labor ratio, k, has to lie between the two optimum capital-labor ratios:

(32) $k_V(\omega) < k < k_C(\omega)$.

The relation (31) or (32) may be written as:

(33) $\omega_{\min}(k) < \omega < \omega_{\max}(k)$,

where the critical wage-rental ratios, $\omega_{\min}(k)$ and $\omega_{\max}(k)$, are defined by:

(34) $\omega_{\min}(k) = \omega_C(k),\ \omega_{\max}(k) = \omega_V(k)\,,$

(35) $k_C(\omega_C(k)) = k,\ k_V(\omega_V(k)) = k\,.$

It is easily seen that an increase in the wage-rental ratio, ω, will increase the output of goods whose production is relatively more capital-intensive. Since the private sector is relatively more capital-intensive than the public sector, $y_C(\omega, k)$ is a decreasing function of ω, while $y_V(\omega, k)$ is an increasing function of ω. On the other hand, an increase in k will increase $y_C(\omega, k)$ and decrease $y_V(\omega, k)$. The relationships between the wage-rental ratio and the output of private and public goods are illustrated in Figure 2.

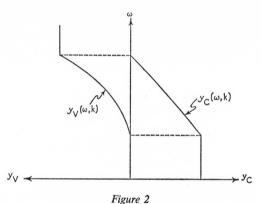

Figure 2

Equations (11–12), (15–18), (20), and (23) are now reduced to:

(36) $y = r(k + \omega)/k$ (national income in real terms per unit of capital)

(37) $r = f_C'(k_C)$ (marginal product of capital)

(38) $y^d = (1 - \tau)y$ (disposable income per unit of capital)

(39) $a = 1 + m$ (assets per unit of capital)

(40) $c = c(\rho, y^d, a)$ (consumption per unit of capital)

(41) $z = z(\rho, y)$ (investment per unit of capital) ;

(42) $c + z = y_C(\omega, k)$ (allocation of private goods between consumption and investment) ;

(43) $$m = \lambda(\rho, y^d) \qquad \text{(portfolio balance)};$$

and

(44) $$\frac{r(k_V + \omega)l_V}{k} - \tau y = \theta m \qquad \text{(balance of the budget)}.$$

To analyze the balance-of-the-budget equation (44), let us first introduce the imputed price, p, of public goods:

(45) $$p = f_C'(k_C)/f_V'(k_V),$$

where

$$k_C = k_C(\omega) \text{ and } k_V = k_V(\omega).$$

The imputed price of public goods is solely determined by the wage-rental ratio, ω; it may be denoted by $p(\omega)$. Differentiating (45) logarithmically and taking into account the derivative of (28), we get:

(46) $$\frac{1}{p(\omega)} \frac{d\,p(\omega)}{d\omega} = \frac{1}{k_V(\omega) + \omega} - \frac{1}{k_C(\omega) + \omega} > 0.$$

Since we have

(47) $$y = y_C + p y_V = [r l_C(k_C + \omega) + r l_V(k_V + \omega)]/k,$$

the balance-of-the-budget equation (44) may be rewritten as:

(48) $$\theta m = (1 - \tau)y(\omega, k) - y_C(\omega, k),$$

where

(49) $$y(\omega, k) = f_C'(k_C)\left(1 + \frac{\omega}{k}\right),$$

(50) $$y_C(\omega, k) = \frac{f_C(k_C)}{k_C - k_V}\left(1 - \frac{k_V}{k}\right),$$

(51) $$y_V(\omega, k) = \frac{f_C(k_C)}{k_C - k_V}\left(\frac{k_C}{k} - 1\right).$$

For fixed values of k and τ, the right-hand side of (48) is an increasing function of the wage-rentals ratio. Therefore, for a positive rate of increase in the money supply, θ, the real cash balance, m, satisfying (48) is also given by a curve with a positive slope, as indicated by the *FF* curve in Figure 3. In other words, any point on the FF curve represents a combination of the wage-rental ratio, ω, and the real cash balance (per unit of capital), m, at which the budget in the public sector is in balance for a given fiscal policy (τ, θ). The FF curve shifts to the left when the tax rate, τ, the growth rate in money supply, θ, or the capital-labor ratio, k, is increased.

The real cash balance-capital ratio, m, on the other hand, must be related to the disposable real income per unit of capital ratio, y^d, in such a manner that the private sector's portfolio is in balance, so that equation (43) is satisfied. For a given value of the interest rate, ρ, the function $\lambda (\rho, y^d)$

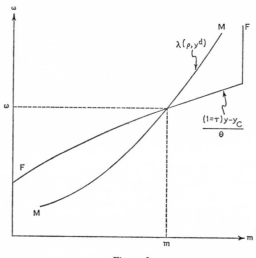

Figure 3

is an increasing function of y^d, with an elasticity not greater than unity. The real cash balance, m, satisfying (43), therefore, is depicted again by a curve with a positive slope, such as the MM curve in Figure 3. Since the elasticity of λ with respect to y^d is not greater than unity, the MM curve has a slope steeper than the FF curve at the point (ω, m) where these two curves intersect.

Since an increase in the rate of interest, ρ, shifts the MM curve to the left, the equilibrium wage-rental ratio, ω, and the real cash balance, m, both are decreased whenever the rate of interest, ρ, is increased. In Figure 4, below, the FM curve represents all the combinations of the rates of interest and wage-rental ratios at which the public budget and the private sector's portfolios are in equilibrium. An increase in the tax rate, τ, a higher growth rate in money supply, θ, or an increase in the capital-labor ratio, k, will easily be seen to result in a shift to the left of the FM curve in Figure 4.

To see the conditions under which the goods-and-services market in the private sector is in equilibrium, let us rewrite the equilibrium condition (42) as follows:

(52) $$z(\rho, y) = y_C(\omega, k) - c(\rho, y^d, 1 + m).$$

For any given level of the rate of interest, ρ, the investment function, $z(\rho, y)$, is by assumption an increasing function of y, while the income-capital ratio, y, defined by (36) is an increasing function of the wage-rental ratio. To see the latter, differentiate (36) and (37) logarithmically and rearrange the result to get:

(53) $$\frac{1}{y} \frac{dy}{d\omega} = \frac{1}{k + \omega} - \frac{1}{k_C + \omega}$$

which is always positive because of the capital-intensity hypothesis we have made.

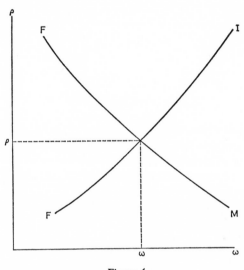

Figure 4

The left-hand side of equation (52) is therefore an increasing function of ω, which is described by the II curve in Figure 5. The right-hand side of equation (52), on the other hand, is a decreasing function of ω. In Figure 5, the SS curve represents the $y_C - c$ function for given levels of the rate of interest and real cash balance. The wage-rental ratio at which the II curve intersects with the SS curve equilibrates the goods-and-service market for given levels of the rate of interest, ρ, and real cash balances, m.

An increase in real cash balances is assumed to increase the desired level of consumption, c, thus shifting the SS curve to the left. Hence, the equilibrium wage-rental ratio is decreased as m is increased. In other words, the greater the real cash balances, the smaller must the wage-rental ratio be for the goods-and-services market to be in equilibrium, because an increase in assets would induce the private sector to increase the desired level of consumption. The relationships between the wage-rental ratio and real cash balance for which the goods-and-services market is in equilibrium are described by the IS curve in Figure 6.

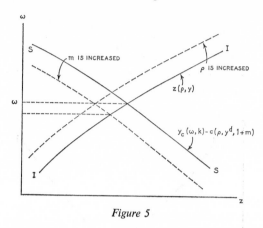

Figure 5

The intersection of the IS curve with the FF curve represents the combination of the wage-rental ratio and the real cash balance at which the public budget and the goods-and-service market are both in equilibrium for a given level of interest rate. An increase in the rate of interest will decrease the desired levels of both investment, $z(\rho, y)$, and consumption, $c(\rho, y^d, 1 + m)$, thus shifting the IS curve upward. Therefore, an increase in the rate of interest will result in increases in both the wage-rental ratio

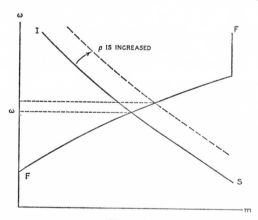

Figure 6

and the real cash balance for which the goods-and-services market is in equilibrium.

The combinations of the rates of interest and wage-rental ratios at which the public sector and the goods-and-services market are in equilibrium are represented by the FI curve in Figure 4. It has a positive slope, while the FM curve previously derived has a negative slope. Therefore, these two curves have a unique intersection (if one exists). The pair of interest rate, ρ, and wage-rental ratio, ω, at which the FI and FM curves intersect, together with the corresponding real cash balance, m, gives the solution to the system of short-run equilibrium conditions (36–44).

IV. Constant Average Propensity to Consume and the Quantity Theory of Money

We have seen under fairly general conditions that the short-run equilibrium is uniquely determined at each moment of time, t. The process of capital accumulation is simply described by the following differential equation:

$$(54) \qquad \frac{\dot{k}}{k} = z - n - \mu,$$

where $z = z(\rho, y)$ is the equilibrium rate of investment per unit of capital, n and μ are respectively the growth rate of labor and the rate of depreciation.

The characteristics of such a dynamic system with respect to the existence and stability of long-run equilibrium may be analyzed with the aid of the techniques developed in the previous section. Here, however, we are interested in a particular case in which the average propensity to consume γ is always constant and the velocity of money, λ, is independent of the rate of interest.

The equilibrium conditions (41–44) then are reduced to the following system of equations:

$$(55) \qquad \theta m = (1 - \tau)y - y_C,$$

$$(56) \qquad z(\rho, y) = y_C - \gamma(1 - \tau)y,$$

$$(57) \qquad m = \lambda(1 - \tau)y,$$

which are further simplified to:

$$(58) \qquad y_C = (1 - s)y,$$

$$(59) \qquad z = \beta y_C,$$

where

(60) $$s = 1 - (1 - \tau)(1 - \lambda\theta),$$

(61) $$\beta = 1 - \frac{\gamma}{1 - \lambda\theta}.$$

In order for the short-run equilibrium solution to be meaningful, it is necessary and sufficient that τ and θ must satisfy the following conditions:

(62) $$\theta < \frac{1 - \gamma}{\lambda},$$

(63) $$\frac{s - \lambda\theta}{1 - \lambda\theta} \leq \tau \leq 1.$$

The dynamic equation (54) may be written as

(64) $$\frac{\dot{k}}{k} = \alpha f'_c(k_c) \frac{k + \omega}{k} - n - \mu,$$

where ω is the equilibrium wage-rental ratio, $\omega = \omega(k)$, and

(65) $$\alpha = (1 - \tau)(1 - \lambda\theta - \gamma).$$

If the rates of income tax, τ, and of increase in money supply, θ, remain constant through time, the mathematical structure of the dynamic system becomes identical with the one introduced in [18], and the stability analysis presented there applies to the present case. In particular, we can show that if the parameters satisfy conditions (62–63), a long-run (quasi-) stationary state exists and the dynamic system defined by (64) is globally stable.

V. Optimum Fiscal Policies

In the model of fiscal policy introduced above, we have analyzed the dynamic implications of a fiscal policy defined in terms of an exogenously determined income tax rate and a growth rate in the money supply. If the public sector is free to choose any fiscal policy it desires but is also interested in achieving that allocation of private means of production which would maximize certain welfare criteria, the problem of optimum fiscal policy becomes to choose at each moment a combination of income tax rate and rate of money supply increase such that an optimum rate of investment is attained through time. We shall show that the techniques of optimum economic growth recently developed by Koopmans [6], Mirrlees [9], Srinivasan [14], Inagaki [5], von Weiszaecker [21], Cass [2], Kurz [7], and others are readily applicable to the formulation and analysis of the problem of optimum fiscal policy.

As before, the economy we are concerned with produces two types of goods, private and public. Public goods are regarded as consumption goods, while private goods can either be consumed instantaneously or accumulated as capital. For the sake of simplicity, the utility function of the representative member of the society depends upon the amount of private goods to be consumed and upon the average quantity of public goods available at each moment. Public goods are assumed to be distributed equally among the members of the society. Let $u(c, x)$ be the utility function where c and x stand respectively for the quantities of per capita consumption of private and public goods (in this and next few sections notation is slightly different from that in the previous sections). It will be assumed that the social welfare function is represented as the discounted sum of instantaneous utilities through time:

$$(66) \qquad \int_0^\infty u(c, x) \, e^{-\delta t} \, dt$$

where δ is the rate by which future utilities are compared with the present utilities with a proper modification when the population is not stationary.

A *dynamic fiscal policy* is defined here as a piece-wise continuous time-path $(\tau(t), \theta(t))$ of income tax rates, $\tau(t)$, and growth rates of money supply, $\theta(t)$. With the structure of the economy introduced in the previous sections, any dynamic fiscal policy uniquely determines the time-paths of capital accumulation, the allocations of capital and labor between the private and public sectors, the allocation of private goods between consumption and investment, and the market prices of output and factors of productions. In particular, the time-paths of output of public goods and the consumption of private goods are uniquely determined for a given dynamic fiscal policy $(\tau(t), \theta(t))$.

A dynamic fiscal policy then is defined as *optimal* if, for a feasible path of capital accumulation, it results in that time-path of consumption patterns $(c(t), x(t))$ which maximizes the social utility functional (66).

Instead of solving the problem as presented here, which poses serious mathematical difficulties, we shall first reformulate the problem of optimum fiscal policy in a somewhat different manner which can be analyzed by standard techniques of optimum economic growth. Then we shall show that the solution to the latter problem may be used to find an optimum fiscal policy in the sense of the previous definition.

VI. Optimum Economic Growth

To reformulate the problem of optimum fiscal policy, suppose that the public sector can determine not only the fiscal policy but also the allocations of capital and labor between sectors and the division of private goods between consumption and investment. The public sector then seeks for the feasible time-paths of factor and output allocations at which the utility functional (66) is maximized. Such time-paths will be called *optimum paths of economic growth*. The problem is more precisely defined as follows:

Find a time-path of $(K_C(t), K_V(t), L_C(t), L_V(t), C(t), Z(t), X(t))$ *for which the utility functional*

$$(67) \qquad \int_0^\infty u\left[\frac{C(t)}{L(t)}, \frac{X(t)}{L(t)}\right] e^{-\delta t} dt$$

is maximized subject to the constraints:

$$(68) \qquad C(t) + Z(t) \leqq F_C(K_C(t), L_C(t)),$$

$$(69) \qquad X(t) \leqq F_V(K_V(t), L_V(t)),$$

$$(70) \qquad K_C(t) + K_V(t) \leqq K(t),$$

$$(71) \qquad L_C(t) + L_V(t) \leqq L(t),$$

$$(72) \qquad K(t) = Z(t) - \mu K(t)$$

$$(73) \qquad L(t) = nL(t),$$

with given initial capital $K(0)$ and labor $L(0)$ where all variables are non-negative.

If we use small letters to indicate the quantities per capita and omit the time suffix, the problem of optimum economic growth is reduced to the following:

Maximize

$$(74) \qquad \int_0^\infty u(c, x) e^{-\delta t} dt$$

subject to the constraints:

$$(75) \qquad c + z = f_C(k_C)l_C,$$

$$(76) \qquad x = f_V(k_V)l_V,$$

$$(77) \qquad k_C l_C + k_V l_V = k,$$

$$(78) \qquad l_C + l_V = 1,$$

$$(79) \qquad \dot{k} = z - (n + \mu)k,$$

with given initial capital-labor ratio, $k(0)$, where all variables are non-negative.

The utility function, $u(c, x)$, is assumed to satisfy the following conditions:

(80)
$$u(c, x)$$

is continuously twice-differentiable and has positive marginal utilities u_c and u_x for all positive c and x; $u(c, x)$ is strictly concave in the sense that the Hessian matrix

(81)
$$\begin{pmatrix} u_{cc} & u_{cx} \\ u_{cx} & u_{xx} \end{pmatrix}$$

is negative definite for all values of c and x.

Private and public goods are substitutes, in the sense that an increase in one of the two goods does not increase the marginal utility of the other, namely,

(82)
$$u_{cx} \leqq 0 .$$

Private goods are not inferior; the income-consumption curve has a positive slope.

These conditions are summarized as:

(83)
$$u_c > 0 , \, u_x > 0$$

(84)
$$u_{cc} < 0 , \, u_{xx} < 0 , \, u_{cx} \leqq 0$$

(85)
$$\Delta = u_{cc}u_{xx} - u_{cx}^2 > 0$$

(86)
$$\frac{u_{xx}}{u_x} - \frac{u_{cx}}{u_c} < 0, \, \frac{u_{cc}}{u_c} - \frac{u_{xc}}{u_x} < 0 .$$

It may be noted that the optimum solution, if it exists, is always uniquely determined, because of the strict concavity of the utility function, $u(c, x)$, and the production functions, $f_C(k_C)$ and $f_V(k_V)$.

The problem now is solved by using a procedure similar to one developed in [19]. Let us introduce the auxiliary variables, $q_C(t)$, $q_V(t)$, $r(t)$, $w(t)$, and $q(t)$, corresponding to constraints (75), (76), (77), (78), (79), respectively, and form the Lagrangian:

(87)
$$\int_0^\infty \{u(c, x) + q(z - (n + \mu)k) + q_C(f_C(k_C)l_C - z - c)$$
$$+ q_V(f_V(k_V) \, l_V - x) + r(k - k_C l_C - k_V l_V)$$
$$+ w(1 - l_C - l_V)\} \, e^{-\delta t} \, dt .$$

The variables $q_C(t)$ and $q_V(t)$ may be interpreted as the imputed prices of private and public goods at time t, while $q(t)$ is the imputed price of investment. The variables $r(t)$ and $w(t)$ are the rental of capital and the wage rate at time t (all measured in terms of private goods).

The problem of optimum growth will be completely solved once we find the time-paths of these imputed prices. We can show the following:

Lemma. Let $c(t)$, $x(t)$, $z(t)$, $k(t)$, $k_C(t)$, $k_V(t)$, $l_C(t)l_V(t)$ give a feasible solution and let $q(t)$, $q_C(t)$, $q_V(t)$, $r(t)$, $w(t)$ be time-paths of imputed prices for which the following conditions are satisfied:

(88) $q(t)$, $q_C(t)$, $q_V(t)$ are continuous positive and bounded functions of time t;

(89) $r(t)$ and $w(t)$ are piece-wise continuous functions of time t;

(90) At each moment of time t, $(c(t)$, $x(t)$, $z(t)$, $k_C(t)$, $k_V(t)$, $l_C(t)$, $l_V(t))$ maximizes

$$u(c, x) + q(t)z + q_C(t)(f_C(k_C)l_C - z - c) + q_V(t)(f_V(k_V)l_V - x) \\ + r(t)(k(t) - k_C l_C - k_V l_V) + w(t)(1 - l_C - l_V)$$

without any constraints (except for nonnegativity),

(91) $$\dot{q}(t) = (n + \mu + \delta)q(t) - r(t).$$

Then the feasible path $c(t)$, $x(t)$, $z(t)$, $k(t)$ is an optimum.

Since the Lagrangian is concave with respect to c, x, z, $k_C l_C$, $k_V l_V$, l_C, l_V, condition (90) is reduced to the following set of first order conditions:

(92) $$\begin{cases} u_c(c(t), x(t)) = q_C(t) \\ u_x(c(t), x(t)) = q_V(t) \, ; \end{cases}$$

(93) $$z(t) = 0 \qquad \text{if } q(t) < q_C(t),$$

(94) $$\frac{w(t)}{r(t)} (\equiv \omega(t)) = \frac{f_j(k_j(t))}{f_j'(k_j(t))} - k_j(t), j = C, V,$$

(95) $$r(t) = q_C(t)f_C'(k_C(t)) = q_V(t)f_V'(k_V(t)).$$

Let us now introduce

(96) $$p = \frac{q_V}{q_C},$$

(97) $$p(\omega) = \frac{f_C'(k_C(\omega))}{f_V'(k_V(\omega))}.$$

Then conditions (92–95) together with the feasibility conditions (75–79) yield (omitting time-suffix t):

$$(98) \qquad \begin{cases} \dot{k} = z - (n + \mu)k \\ \dot{q} = (n + \mu + \delta)q - r, \end{cases}$$

where

$$(99) \qquad \begin{cases} u_c(c, x) = q_C \\ u_x(c, x) = pq_C, \end{cases}$$

$$(100) \qquad q \leqq q_C,$$

with equality if $z > 0$,

$$(101) \qquad p = p(\omega),$$

$$(102) \qquad c + z = y_C(\omega, k) \equiv f_C(k_C(\omega)) \frac{k - k_V(\omega)}{k_C(\omega) - k_V(\omega)},$$

$$(103) \qquad x = y_V(\omega, k) \equiv f_V(k_V(k_V(\omega)) \frac{k_C(\omega) - k}{k_V(\omega) - k_V(\omega)},$$

and

$$(104) \qquad r = q_C f'_C(k_C(\omega)).$$

Since a one-to-one correspondence exists between p and ω through $p = p(\omega)$, $y_C(\omega, k)$ and $y_V(\omega, k)$ are often written as $y_C(p, k)$ and $y_V(p, k)$.

The pair of equations (99) uniquely determines (c, x) for given (p, q_C). We may use the notation:

$$(105) \qquad c = c(p, q_C), \ x = x(p, q_C).$$

Differentiating (94), we get

$$(106) \qquad \begin{pmatrix} u_{cc} & u_{cx} \\ u_{xc} & u_{xx} \end{pmatrix} \begin{pmatrix} dc \\ dx \end{pmatrix} = \begin{pmatrix} dq_C \\ pdq_C + q_C dp \end{pmatrix}.$$

Hence,

$$(107) \qquad \begin{pmatrix} dc \\ dx \end{pmatrix} = \frac{1}{\Delta} \begin{pmatrix} u_{xx} & -u_{cx} \\ -u_{xc} & u_{cc} \end{pmatrix} \begin{pmatrix} dq_C \\ pdq_C + q_C dp \end{pmatrix},$$

where

$$(108) \qquad \Delta = det \begin{pmatrix} u_{cc} & u_{cx} \\ u_{xc} & u_{xx} \end{pmatrix} = u_{cc} u_{xx} - u_{cx}^2 > 0.$$

We have from (107) that

$$(109) \qquad \frac{\partial c}{\partial q_C} = \frac{u_{xx} - pu_{cx}}{\Delta} < 0, \quad \frac{\partial c}{\partial p} = \frac{-q_C u_{cx}}{\Delta} = 0,$$

(110) $$\frac{\partial x}{\partial q_C} = \frac{-u_{xc} + pu_{cc}}{\Delta} < 0 , \quad \frac{\partial x}{\partial p} = \frac{q_C u_{cc}}{\Delta} > 0 .$$

On the other hand, we have

(111) $$\frac{\partial y_C}{\partial p} < 0 , \quad \frac{\partial y_C}{\partial k} > 0 ,$$

(112) $$\frac{\partial y_V}{\partial p} > 0 , \quad \frac{\partial Y_V}{\partial k} < 0 .$$

Now let us consider the equation

(113) $$x(p, q_C) = y_V(p, k) .$$

Since $x(p, q_C)$ is a decreasing function of p and $y_C(p, k)$ is a nondecreasing function of p, equation (113) has a unique solution, p, for any given pair of q_C and k, as described in Figure 7. We may simply write

$$p = p(q_C, k) .$$

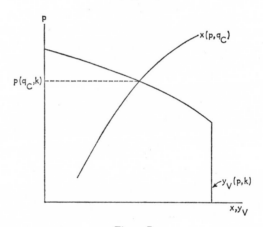

Figure 7

Let us first examine the phase in which the rate of investment, $z(t)$, is always positive. Then the inequality (100) is satisfied by an equality, and we have

(114) $$\begin{cases} \dot{k} = y_C(p, k) - c(p, q) - (n + \mu)k \\ \frac{\dot{q}}{q} = (n + \mu + \delta) - f_C'(k_C) , \end{cases}$$

where $p = p(q, k)$.

The rate of change in the imputed price, q, of investment is zero if and only if

$$(115) \qquad p(q, k) = p^*$$

where p^* is the relative price for which

$$(116) \qquad f_C'(k_C(p^*)) = n + \mu + \delta .$$

We then have

$$(117) \qquad \left(\frac{dq}{dk}\right)_{\dot{q}=0} = \left(\frac{dq}{dk}\right)_{p=p^*} = \frac{\partial y_V/\partial k}{\partial x/\partial q} > 0 .$$

The $\dot{q} = 0$ curve thus has a positive slope everywhere, and it can be seen from (112) and (115) that the rate of change in the imputed price, q, is positive (negative) if (q, k) lies (below) above the $\dot{q} = 0$ curve.

On the other hand, the slope of the $\dot{k} = 0$ curve is given by

$$(118) \qquad \left(\frac{dq}{dk}\right)_{\dot{k}=0} = \frac{\dfrac{\partial c}{\partial q} - \left(\dfrac{\partial y_C}{\partial p} - \dfrac{\partial c}{\partial p}\right)\dfrac{\partial p}{\partial q}}{\dfrac{\partial y_C}{\partial p} - \dfrac{\partial c}{\partial p}\dfrac{\partial p}{\partial k} + \dfrac{\partial y_C}{\partial k} - n - \mu} .$$

The sign of $\left(\dfrac{dq}{dk}\right)_{\dot{k}=0}$ is in general indeterminate, but it is negative at $p = p^*$, as is seen from (109), (111), and the following inequality:

$$(119) \qquad \frac{\partial y_C}{\partial k} = \frac{f_C(k_C)}{k_C - k_V} = f'_C(k_C)\frac{k_C + \omega}{k_C - k_V} > n + \mu$$

$$\text{if } f'_C(k_C) = n + \mu + \delta .$$

The typical structure of solution paths to the pair of differential equations (114) is illustrated in Figure 8, where the stationary point (q^*, k^*) is characterized by

$$(120) \qquad \begin{cases} p(q^*, k^*) = p^* \\ y_C(p^*, k^*) = c(p^*, k^*) + (n + \mu)k^* . \end{cases}$$

Since the stationary point (q^*, k^*) becomes a saddle-point, there are two branches of solution paths which converge to the point (q^*, k^*). Hence, for any capital-labor ratio, k^0, there exists an imputed price, $q^0 = q^0(k^0)$, such that the solution path going through (q^0, k^0) converges (q^*, k^*). The function $q^0 = q^0(k)$ is a decreasing function of k.

Since $p = p(q, k)$ is continuously differentiable, we can transform the system of differential equation (114) into one involving p and k. The struc-

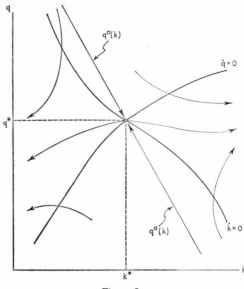

Figure 8

ture of the solution path of the corresponding system is typically described in Figure 9.

It can again be shown that, for every capital-labor ratio, k^0, there exists a unique price ratio, $p^0 = p^0(k^0)$, such that the path going through (p^0, k^0) converges to (p^*, k^*). Such a curve, $p = p^0(k)$, has a negative slope.

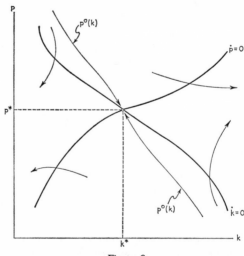

Figure 9

In the discussion above, we have ignored the constraint that z must be nonnegative. The boundary of the domain on the (q, k) plane in which the resulting z is nonnegative is characterized by

(121)
$$\begin{cases} c(p, q) = y_C(p, k) \\ x(p, q) = y_V(p, k) . \end{cases}$$

Hence, we have

(122)
$$\left(\frac{dq}{dk}\right)_{z=0} = \frac{\dfrac{\partial y_C}{\partial k}\left(\dfrac{\partial x}{\partial p} - \dfrac{\partial y_V}{\partial p}\right) - \dfrac{\partial y_V}{\partial k}\left(\dfrac{\partial c}{\partial p} - \dfrac{\partial y_C}{\partial p}\right)}{\dfrac{\partial c}{\partial q}\left(\dfrac{\partial x}{\partial p} - \dfrac{\partial y_V}{\partial p}\right) - \dfrac{\partial x}{\partial q}\left(\dfrac{\partial c}{\partial p} - \dfrac{\partial y_C}{\partial p}\right)} > 0 .$$

Such a boundary is denoted by $q = q(k)$ and the corresponding boundary in the (p, k) plane by $p = p(k)$. The stationary state (q, k) lies above the boundary.

If (q, k) lies below the curve $q = q(k)$, the optimum level of investment is zero. In this case (100) is satisfied with a strict inequality and we have

(123)
$$\begin{cases} \dot{k} = -(n + \mu)k \\ \dfrac{\dot{q}}{q} = n + \mu + \delta - f_C'(k_C) , \end{cases}$$

where $k_C = k_C(p), p = p(k, q)$.

There is a uniquely determined solution path to (123) such that it coincides with the $q^0(k)$ curve at the $q(k)$ curve (Figure 10). The $q^0(k)$ curve, as introduced above, then is modified so that below the $q(k)$ curve it satisfies the system (123). The $p^0(k)$ curve will be correspondingly adjusted.

It is easily shown that, for any initial capital-labor ratio, k_0, the optimum path is obtained by choosing the initial imputed price at the level $q_0 = q^0(k_0)$ and by allocating labor, capital, and private goods between consumption and investment so that (92–95) are satisfied at each moment of time, t.

The imputed relative price of public goods with respect to private goods is accordingly determined by $p_0 = p(q, k_0)$, and the allocations of labor and capital are also uniquely determined, together with the division of output between consumption and investment. The optimum relative share, $1 - s^0(k)$, of the private output in the gross national product and the proportion of total private output to be invested, $\beta^0(k)$, are uniquely determined as well:

(124)
$$1 - s^0(k) = y_C(p^0(k), k)/y(p^0(k), k) ,$$

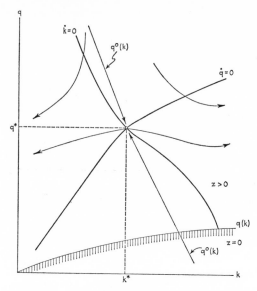

Figure 10

(125) $$\beta^0(k) = 1 - c(p^0(k), q^0(k))/y_c(p^0(k), k).$$

On the other hand, the path of optimum growth is uniquely determined by equating s and β with $s^0(k)$ and $\beta^0(k)$.

It is now possible, under some conditions, to achieve optimum growth by choosing an appropriate dynamic fiscal policy $(\tau(t), \theta(t))$. In particular, if the average propensity to save out of disposable income, γ, and the velocity of money, λ, are both constant, then the optimum rates, τ^0 and θ^0, of income tax and of increase in the money supply are determined by the following relations:

(126) $$1 - s^0(k) = (1 - \tau^0(\lambda))(1 - \lambda\theta^0(\lambda)),$$

(127) $$\beta^0(k) = 1 - \frac{\gamma}{1 - \lambda\theta^0(k)}.$$

Hence,

(128) $$\theta^0(k) = \frac{1 - \dfrac{\gamma}{1 - \beta^0(k)}}{\lambda}$$

(129) $$\tau^0(k) = 1 - \frac{1 - s^0(k)}{1 - \lambda\theta^0(k)} = 1 - \frac{1}{\gamma}(1 - s^0(k)(1 - \beta^0(k))).$$

REFERENCES

1. Brown, E. C. "Fiscal Policy in a Growing Economy: A Further Word," *Journal of Political Economy*, LXIV (1956), 170–72.
2. Cass, D. "Optimum Economic Growth in an Aggregative Model of Capital Accumulation," *Review of Economic Studies*, XXXII (1965), 233–240.
3. Gurley, J. G. "Fiscal Policy in a Growing Economy," *Jour. Pol. Econ.*, LXI (1953), 523–35.
4. Hicks, J. R. "Mr. Keynes and the 'Classical'; A Suggested Interpretation," *Econometrica*, V (1937), 147–59.
5. Inagaki, M. "A General Proof of Existence in Optimum Savings." Unpublished manuscript, 1964.
6. Koopmans, T. C. "On the Concept of Optimal Economic Growth." Cowles Foundation Discussion Paper, 1963.
7. Kurz, M. "Optimal Paths of Capital Accumulation under the Minimum Time Objective," *Econometrica*, XXXIII (1965), 42–66.
8. Metzler, L. A. "Wealth, Saving, and the Rate of Interest," *Jour. Pol. Econ.*, LIX (1951), 93–115.
9. Mirrlees, J. A. "Optimal Planning for a Dynamic Economy." Unpublished manuscript.
10. Musgrave, R. A. *The Theory of Public Finance: A Study of Public Economy.* New York: McGraw-Hill, 1959, especially pp. 472–500.
11. Ramsey, F. P. "A Mathematical Theory of Savings," *Economic Journal*, XXXVIII (1928), 543–59.
12. Smith, W. L. "Professor Gurley on Fiscal Policy in a Growing Economy," *Jour. Pol. Econ.*, LXII (1954), 440–41.
13. Solow, R. M. "A Contribution to the Theory of Economic Growth," *Quarterly Journal of Economics*, XXXII (1956), 65–95.
14. Srinivasan, T. N. "Optimal Saving in a Two-Sector Growth Model," *Econometrica*, XXXII (1964), 358–73.
15. Stoleru, G. "An Optimal Policy for Economic Growth," *Econometrica*, XXXIII (1965), 321–48.
16. Swan, T. W. "Economic Growth and Capital Accumulation," *Economic Record*, LXVI (1956), 358–73.
17. Tobin, J. "An Aggregative Dynamic Model," *Jour. Pol. Econ.*, LXIII (1955), 103–15.
18. Uzawa, H. "On a Two-Sector Model of Economic Growth, II," *Rev. Econ. Stud.*, XXX (1963), 105–18.
19. —— "Optimal Growth in a Two-Sector Model of Capital Accumulation," *Rev. Econ. Stud.*, XXXI (1964), 1–24.
20. —— "Optimum Investment in Social Capital." Paper presented at a NSF-Purdue Conference on Quantitative Methods in Economics, 1963.
21. Von Weizsaecker, C. C. "Existence of Optimal Programs of Accumulation for an Infinite Time Horizon," *Rev. Econ. Stud.*, XXXII (1965), 85–104.

COMMENT

DANIEL MCFADDEN, UNIVERSITY OF CALIFORNIA, BERKELEY

Professor Uzawa's excellent paper brings the powerful analytic tools of neoclassical growth theory to bear on the question of aggregate fiscal policy for optimal development. His conclusions are potentially of great use in examining the broad issues of aggregate planning. Perhaps more important, the paper marks the beginning of a convergence of growth theory and development theory. This merger will result in the addition of the mathematical techniques of growth theory to the development economist's bag of tools and an increase in the practicality and applicability of growth models.

Before discussing Professor Uzawa's conclusions and their implications, it will be useful to review the model he has used. I will give a free translation of his model which I think has some advantages in simplicity and added generality.

I. VARIABLES

In his analysis, Professor Uzawa has worked with variables expressed in "per unit of capital stock" terms. However, the optimal growth portions of the paper are handled more naturally with "per man" variables, and empirical data are more commonly collected in "per man" terms. For these reasons, I will choose the "per man" alternative. I will put primes on variables to indicate that they are now in "per man in the population" rather than "per unit of capital" terms.

k = aggregate capital per man (in population).
y'_c = output of private goods per man.
y'_v = output of public goods per man.
p = imputed price of public goods, measured in units of private goods.
y' = real national income per man (private goods are taken as numéraire, so that all real quantities are measured in units of private goods).
$y^{d'}$ = real disposable income per man.
ρ = money interest rate.
m' = real cash balances per man.
c' = real consumption of private goods per man.
z' = real investment of private goods per man.
a' = real value of assets per man.
θ = rate of increase of real money supply (money supply = net liabilities of public sector to private sector).
τ = income tax rate on national income.

We have a total of thirteen variables, among which k is predetermined, θ and τ are instrument variables, and the remaining ten are endogenous.

II. RELATIONS

Professor Uzawa takes the wage-rental ratio as his "key" variable in analyzing the model and works explicitly with the production functions and factor markets. We take an alternative approach in which the output of public goods per man is our "key" variable, the production frontier is explicit, and all factor markets are implicit. This alternative has the advantage of not requiring the "no factor intensity reversal" condition assumed by Professor Uzawa.

Two goods are produced in the model: public goods which are consumed and private goods which are either consumed or accumulated as capital stock (capital can then be measured in units of private goods).

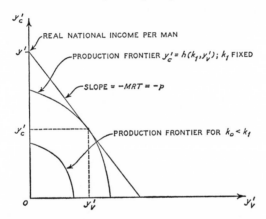

Figure 1. Production Frontier

The relation between capital per man and per capita outputs of public and private goods is given by a production frontier illustrated in Figure 1 and having a formula:

(1) $$y'_c = h(k, y_v).$$

Under the assumptions Professor Uzawa has placed on the production functions, the frontier h is concave in (k, y'_v), strictly increasing in k, and strictly decreasing in y'_v. Further, the function is *strictly* concave except for k values at which a factor intensity reversal occurs, resulting in y'_c depending linearly no y'_v.

The imputed price of public goods is given by the marginal rate of transformation of the production frontier:

(2) $$p = -h_2(k, y_v) \qquad \text{(Notation: } h_2 = \partial h / \partial y'_v).$$

From (1) and (2), we can now define real national income:

(3) $y' = y'_c + py'_v = h(k, y'_v) - y'_v h_2(k, y'_v)$.

Equation (3) defines y' as a function $y' = g(k, y'_v)$. From Figure 1, g is non-decreasing in y'_v and increasing except at a factor reversal. The sign of $\partial g/\partial k$ is not generally determinate. However, if the private sector is more capital-intensive than the public sector, then g is strictly increasing in k.

The balance-of-the-budget equation for the public sector is

(4) $\theta m' = py_v - \tau y' = (1 - \tau)y' - y'_c$,

and states that the public sector meets a deficit in its budget by increasing the real money supply.

Balance in the private sector requires

(5) $y'_c = c' + z'$.

Real assets per man equal capital stock held per man plus real cash balances held per man,

(6) $a' = k + m'$.

Disposable income is related to national income by

(7) $y^{d'} = (1 - \tau)y'$.

Consumption of private goods per man is given by a consumption function,

(8) $c' = C(\rho, y^{d'}, a')$,

where $0 \geqq C_1[= \partial C/\partial \rho]$; $0 < C_2$; $0 \leqq C_3$; and C is concave in $y^{d'}$ and a' with $C(\rho, 0, 0) = 0$.[1]

[1] Professor Uzawa assumes further that C is linear homogeneous in the last two variables. Our assumption implies nonincreasing average propensities to consume.

Investment per man is given by an investment function,

(9) $z' = Z'(\rho, y', k)$

where $0 > Z'_1[= \partial Z'/\partial \rho]$; $0 \leqq Z'_2$, and the elasticity of z' with respect to k is no greater than one ($\partial \log Z'/\partial \log k \leqq 1$). This class of investment functions includes the one used by Professor Uzawa, which in terms of our variables takes the form $z' = kZ(\rho, y'/k)$.

The portfolio balance of assets is determined by a liquidity preference function,

(10) $m' = \lambda'(\rho, y^{d'}, k)$

where $0 > \lambda'_1[= \partial \lambda'/\partial \rho]$, and the elasticities of m' with respect to $y^{d'}$ and k lie between zero and one ($0 \leqq \partial \log \lambda'/\partial \log y^{d'} \leqq 1$ and $0 \leqq \partial \log \lambda'/\partial \log k \leqq 1$). This class of liquidity preference functions includes the one used by Professor Uzawa, which in terms of our variables takes the form $m' = k\lambda(\rho, y^{d'}/k)$.

III. ANALYSIS

The system (1)–(10) of ten equations in k, τ, θ, and the ten endogenous variables can be simplified considerably by elimination of variables. Using equation (1), substitute h for y_c in the remaining equations. Substituting (2) into (3) yields

(11) $$y' = g(k, y'_v) \equiv h(k, y'_v) - y'_v h_2(k, y'_v) .$$

Using (7), eliminate $y^{d'}$ from the rest of the equations. Then, using (10), eliminate m' from equations (4) and (6). The public sector balance equation (4) becomes

(12) $$\theta\lambda'(\rho, (1 - \tau)y', k) = (1 - \tau)y' - h(k, y'_v) .$$

Substituting (6) into (8), and then (8) and (9) into (5) yields the private sector balance equation:

(13) $$h(k, y'_v) - C'(\rho, (1 - \tau)y', k + \lambda'(\rho, (1 - \tau)y', k)) = Z'(\rho, y', k) .$$

Equations (11)–(13) give three equations in the three endogenous variables, ρ, y', and y_v. Substituting $y' = g(k, y'_v)$ in (11) into (12), one can solve for ρ as a function $\rho = \rho'(y'_v; k, \theta, \tau)$ of y_v and the variables (k, θ, τ). Substituting this solution into (12) and differentiating,

(14) $$\theta\lambda'_1 \frac{\partial\rho'}{\partial y'_v} = [(1 - \tau) - (1 - \tau)\theta\lambda'_2]\frac{\partial g}{\partial y'_v} - h_2 .$$

Now, the term in square brackets in (14) is nonnegative: $0 \leq \partial \log \lambda'/\partial \log y^{d'} \leq 1$ implies $\lambda'_2 \leq \lambda'/y^{d'}$, giving $[1 - \theta\lambda'_2] \geq [1 - \theta\lambda'/y^{d'}] = h/(1 - \tau)y'$ by (12). Since $h_2 < 0$, $\theta\lambda'_1 \partial\rho'/\partial y'_v$ is positive, implying $\partial\rho'/\partial y'_v$ negative. Further differentiation shows that ρ' is *increasing* in θ and *increasing* in τ. In general, $\partial\rho'/\partial k$ is not determinant in sign. However, if the private sector is *less* capital-intensive than the public sector, then p falls when k rises, implying $\partial g/\partial k \leq \partial h/\partial k$ and $\delta\rho'/\delta k'$ *positive*. These conclusions are illustrated in Figure 2.

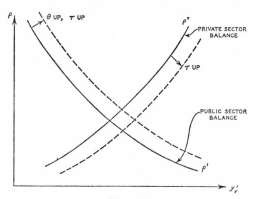

Figure 2

Next substitute $y' = g(k, y'_v)$ in (11) into (13). The left- and right-hand sides of (13) are plotted in Figure 3. The right-hand side is a strictly decreasing function of y'_v, is strictly increasing in ρ and τ, and is independent of θ. The left-hand side is strictly decreasing in ρ, nondecreasing in y'_v, and independent of θ and τ.

The solution of (13) in Figure 3 defines ρ as a function $\rho = \rho''(y'_v; k, \tau)$ which is strictly increasing in y'_v and strictly decreasing in τ.

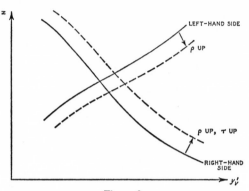

Figure 3

The function ρ'' is graphed in Figure 2. The curves ρ' and ρ'' in Figure 2 can intersect at most once, and hence, with equation (11), give a *unique* solution for y', y'_v, and ρ in terms of k, θ, and τ. Hence, the original system (1)–(10) has a unique solution, provided it exists.

Let $y'_v = \hat{y}'_v(k, \theta, \tau)$; $y' = \hat{y}'(k, \theta, \tau)$; and $\rho = \hat{\rho}(k, \theta, \tau)$ denote the solutions derived from (11)–(13) above. Then, from Figure 2, we see that y'_v is an *increasing* function of both policy instruments θ and τ. Since, from (11), y' is strictly increasing in y'_v except at factor intensity reversals, it follows that $\hat{y}'$ is also *increasing* in the policy instruments. We now examine $\rho = \hat{\rho}(k, \theta, \tau)$. From Figure 2, $\hat{\rho}$ is an *increasing* function of θ. A more involved argument will show that $\hat{\rho}$ is an *increasing* function of τ. An implication of the concavity of the consumption function in $(y^{d'}, a')$ is

(15) $C(\rho, y^{d'}, a') - C(\rho, 0, 0) \geqq C_2(\rho, y^{d'}, a')y^{d'} + C_3(\rho, y^{d'}, a')a'$

or

$$1 \geqq \epsilon(c'; y^{d'}) + \epsilon(c', a'),$$

where $\epsilon(f, x)$ is the elasticity of f with respect to x. That is, the sum of the elasticities of consumption with respect to disposable income and real assets cannot exceed one. Now, differentiating the system (11)–(13) yields

$$\begin{bmatrix} -g_2 & 1 & 0 \\ h_2 & (1-\tau)[\theta\lambda'_2 - 1] & \theta\lambda'_1 \\ -h_2 & (1-\tau)[C_2 + C_3\lambda'_2] + Z'_2 & C_1 + C_3\lambda'_1 + Z'_1 \end{bmatrix} \begin{bmatrix} dy'_v \\ dy' \\ d\rho \end{bmatrix} = \begin{bmatrix} 0 \\ y(\theta\lambda'_2 - 1) \\ y(C_2 + C_3\lambda'_2) \end{bmatrix} d\tau .$$

The determinant of this matrix is negative, and the numerator in the Cramer's rule solution for $\partial \rho / \partial \tau$ is

(16) $\qquad$ numerator $= g_2 Z_2' y [\theta \lambda_2' - 1] - h_2 y (C_2 + C_3 \lambda_2 + \theta \lambda_2' - 1)$.

From (14), $\theta \lambda_2' - 1 \leq -h/y^{a'}$. Further, $\lambda_2 \leq \dfrac{\lambda'}{y^{a'}} \leq \dfrac{a'}{y^{a'}}$ and (15) yields $C_2 + C_3 \lambda_2' \leq$ $[C_2 y^{a'} + C_3 a']/y^{a'} \leq C/y^{a'} < h/y^{a'}$. Hence, both terms of the numerator in (16) are negative.

In general, the impact of the policy instruments θ and τ on the equilibrium investment level $\hat{z}'$ is not determinant. However, let us now assume, as Professor Uzawa does, that the liquidity preference function and consumption are perfectly interest inelastic (i.e., $\lambda_1' = 0$ and $C_1 = 0$). Then $z' = \hat{z}'(k, \theta, \tau)$ can be shown to be a strictly *decreasing* function of θ and a strictly *increasing* function of τ.

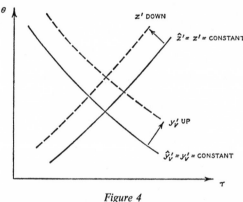

Figure 4

As illustrated in Figure 4, the values of the policy instruments θ and τ are then uniquely determined as functions of the predetermined capital stock k and a planner's desired levels of the target variables z' and y_v': $\theta = \hat{\theta}(k, y_v', z')$ and $\tau = \tau(k, y_v', z')$, where $\hat{\theta}$ is *increasing* in y_v' and *decreasing* in z'; and $\hat{\tau}$ is *increasing* in y_v' and in z'.

The problem of atemporal and/or intertemporal maximization of a planner's preference function (social utility function) by choice of the mix of public and private goods and of the rate of investment can now be analyzed directly in terms of the target variables y_v' and z', with the $\hat{\theta}$ and $\hat{\tau}$ functions specifying the appropriate fiscal policy for any set of targets.

IV. CONCLUSIONS

Professor Uzawa's result illustrates the common proposition that policy analysis can be couched directly in terms of target variables (public goods/man, investment/man) provided their number does not exceed the number of independent instrument variables (rate of increase of real money supply, income tax rate). A corollary to this observation is that additional flexibility in policy could be obtained by expanding the model to include additional instrument variables. A first step might be the introduction of government bonds, allowing the government some freedom in the control of the interest rate via its portfolio decision on the mix of new issues of interest-bearing and non-interest-bearing debt. This step should give a somewhat closer approximation to the financial instruments actually available to governments. At the next level of complexity, it would be desirable to include in the model a foreign trade sector, with foreign debt and the exchange rate as instruments, and additional domestic instrument variables: differential tax rates on wage and non-wage income, direct transfers to the private sector, direct government investment, and private investment credits. The gain in flexibility in choice of instruments in a more complex model would be partially offset by the addition of new target variables, including possibly income distribution, foreign debt and exchange reserves, employment levels (if the current condition of competitive factor markets is relaxed), and the rate of inflation.

Finally, Professor Uzawa's paper suggests (and leaves open) a number of interesting questions. What is the impact of government policy changes in the presence of a more complex expectations structure than the "rain today, rain tomorrow" expectations implicit in the current model? What is the behavior of the economy when the current assumptions of perfectly clearing markets are relaxed (particularly, the labor market)? What are the qualitative characteristics of optimal fiscal and monetary policies? In the steady state growth of the Golden Age, what are the levels of the savings rate, the income tax rate, the rate of inflation, and the rate of increase of the money supply? How do these values compare with current ranges of political feasibility?

PART II
DEVELOPMENT PLANNING AND PROGRAMMING

6. OPTIMAL PATTERNS OF GROWTH AND AID: THE CASE OF PAKISTAN*

HOLLIS B. CHENERY, HARVARD UNIVERSITY
ARTHUR MacEWAN, HARVARD UNIVERSITY

One of the principal means for poor countries to accelerate their development is by using external resources to supply additional imports and to finance a higher level of investment. While this policy offers substantial benefits, it also requires that the structure of the economy be adapted to accommodate the expected resource inflow over a substantial period of time. For this reason, the extent of reliance on external capital—public and private—becomes one of the critical elements of development strategy.

There has been relatively little theoretical study of the benefits and costs of using a controlled inflow of resources to promote development. Formal growth models typically either ignore this variable or take it as fixed. In the formulation of development programs by planning organizations, the projected inflow of aid and private capital is determined largely on a historical and political basis rather than through a systematic evaluation of alternatives. This is true in Pakistan as well as in most countries receiving foreign assistance.

This paper explores the properties of optimal growth strategies in which the total amount and time pattern of the resource inflow can be varied within limits. The problem is studied both from the point of view of the borrowing country trying to make the best use of its domestic and foreign resources and from that of the lender trying to assess the productivity of additional amounts of public assistance in different recipient countries.

* Our research has been supported by the Center for International Affairs at Harvard University and by the Agency for International Development. Neither has any responsibility for the analysis or conclusions presented here.

The linear programming model used in this study was suggested by Robert Dorfman, who took the lead in its initial formulation. It is derived from the projection model used in Chenery and Strout [5]. We are indebted to Robert Dorfman, Alan Strout, and Joel Bergsman for helpful comments.

These different viewpoints are reflected in alternative forms of the objective function which is maximized to determine the optimal policy.

While the formulation of the problem is designed to bring out its general features, the resulting programming model is applied to the planning situation described in the Pakistan Perspective Plan for 1965–85. Apart from the variables affecting the inflow of external capital—which is taken as given in the Pakistan Plan—we have taken most of our other assumptions from the Plan in order to isolate the effects of variation in external resources. Generalization of the results to other countries will be attempted in a subsequent paper.

I. The Analytical Framework

Growth Models and Planning Models

The problem of optimal growth paths over time has been studied only under assumptions which are rather far from those describing the policy choices facing underdeveloped countries. The main weaknesses of existing growth models are that they (1) assume closed economies, (2) focus mainly on the allocation of resources between investment goods and consumer goods production, (3) ignore some of the central constraints on policy, and (4) study long-run equilibrium conditions rather than developments over a relevant planning period.[1] There is therefore little carryover to the problem at hand of the specific results so far achieved by formal analysis. The principal contribution of formal models is to show the importance of formulating an explicit welfare function and of relating alternative strategies to both the parameters in this function and the restrictions placed on the system.

The analytical framework used here is largely derived from detailed empirical models of open economies which are dependent on external assistance.[2] These studies utilize models in which import choices and alternative levels of external capital are explicitly considered. Multisectoral analyses are used in most of them to derive relations among capital inflow, import requirements, savings rates, investment allocation, and over-all growth for the planning period considered. In these disaggregated open models, the balance-of-payments limit replaces the capacity to produce

[1] Despite these differences, we have gotten considerable insight into the present problem from Goodwin [6], Uzawa [13], and Stoleru [11].

[2] Primarily the studies of Chenery and Kretschmer [3] of Southern Italy, Sandee [10] and Bergsman and Manne [2] of India, Chenery and Bruno [4] of Israel, Adelman and Chenery [1] of Greece, Manne [9] of Mexico, and Tims [12] of Pakistan.

investment goods as a general factor limiting growth. The inflow of external capital plays the dual role of raising both this specific resource limit and the savings limit on the rate of investment.

While most of the planning models cited above include some elements of optimization for a five- or ten-year period, they do not consider the pattern of capital inflow over a long enough period to show the welfare implications of alternative strategies of aid and growth. However, they do suggest that there are some common characteristics of optimal patterns of aid and growth. The model developed for the present analysis is designed to explore this possibility more systematically. It tries to relate the features of optimal growth patterns to the development policies and objectives of aid recipients and the assistance policies of the donors.

The Empirical Background

Pakistan has been chosen for this study because it receives substantial external aid and it has an explicitly formulated twenty-year plan for future growth. It is also broadly representative of the initial conditions from which many poor countries are attempting to start a process of accelerated growth. The typical features most relevant to the present analysis, taken from a comparative analysis of thirty-one underdeveloped countries [5], are summarized below. Compared to the medians of this sample, Pakistan starts from a generally less favorable position of per capita income, savings and investment rates, and previous growth of GNP, but the improvement in its development performance in recent years has been significantly better than the average.[3]

The following observations provide a basis for both the design of the model in Section II and the range of values for the policy variables over which it will be tested in Section III.

1. External resources—three-quarters of which are classified as public assistance—normally finance 20 to 30 per cent of both investment and imports in underdeveloped countries and a higher proportion of the increases in these elements in typical cases of rapid development.

2. There is substantial evidence of a limit to the ability of developing countries to transform large increases in external resources into productive investment. The most convenient measure of this absorptive capacity limit is the rate of increase in investment which a country can achieve on a sustained basis. Rates of 15 to 20 per cent per year have

---

[3] The initial conditions and measures of recent performance in Pakistan are given in Section III.

been observed in a number of countries, but there has been no case of a higher value over any substantial period.

3. Shortages of imported investment goods and raw materials provide a limit to growth in a number of countries. In contrast, while the capacity to produce the nonimportable components of investment is a potential bottleneck, it is more easily avoided and rarely observed.

4. Gross marginal savings rates are significantly above the initial average rates of about 12 per cent of GNP in the thirty-one country sample; they reach 30 per cent in the upper quartile of countries. However, there are no observed cases of marginal rates approaching 50 per cent or more which are implied by most theoretical analyses of the "optimal" rate of saving.[4]

5. The availability of external capital permits an economy to grow at the limit corresponding to its ability to increase its capital stock rather than at the lower rate implied by its ability to increase domestic savings. A period of accelerating growth in which investment, savings, and external assistance all increase is therefore to be expected; it is observed in a number of countries.

6. Under present institutional arrangements for the transfer of resources from advanced to developing countries, the amount available is rationed among claimants whose total demands substantially exceed the supply. Since supply conditions vary greatly among recipients, however, different formulations of the restriction on external capital may be appropriate for different countries.

Elements of a Two-Sector Model of an Open Economy

These empirical observations require a substantial reformulation of conventional aggregate growth models. It remains to be seen whether some of the qualitative results of two-sector closed-economy analysis can be carried over to the open-economy case. However, with the addition of the choice of the capital inflow over time, the optimizing problem can be put in similar terms. In both cases, we are primarily interested in the general behavior of the principal variables which describe a growth pattern or development strategy over time. The empirical studies summarized above suggest the following characteristics for a two-sector model of an open economy.

Sector breakdown. The basis for disaggregating the economy is crucial

[4] See, for example, Goodwin [6] and Stoleru [11], who have derived illustrative paths of optimal savings for underdeveloped countries from a variety of assumed welfare functions.

because of the limits which it imposes on the possibilities for future growth and of the way in which it reflects the role of the capital inflow. Disaggregation into two sectors should show the capacity of an open economy to transform domestic resources into foreign exchange, which can then be used to fill the gaps between the composition of demand and the composition of supply. Although the foreign exchange bottleneck cannot be identified with a particular industrial category, the need to allocate capital and labor to increasing its supply is quite similar to the allocation of resources to the production of investment goods in a closed economy. In our model, a category of "trade-improving" production will be identified, which produces either increased exports or substitutes for goods presently imported. Whether the corresponding commodity is cotton, steel, or machinery is irrelevant.[5]

A two-sector model which embodies this distinction could be derived from solutions to an interindustry model in which the input structure and composition of final demand is fixed. In this way, the inputs of capital and imported goods required for an expansion of output with the existing economic structure could be determined. Possibilities for import substitution or introduction of new exports could then be described by additional activities as in [3]; the possibilities of transforming capital and labor into foreign exchange ("trade improvement") could be determined by an optimizing procedure. In a multisectoral analysis the result would be a rise in the incremental capital cost as the output of the trade improvement sector rises, reflecting the operation of the principle of comparative advantage. (For Pakistan, we will represent this input function by a constant incremental capital coefficient, since we cannot estimate the function directly.)

Scarce Factors. Instead of capital and labor, the scarce factors relevant to our analysis are capital and foreign exchange. The rationing of external capital means that its supply must either be taken as given or valued at an opportunity cost reflecting its scarcity. The transformation of unskilled into skilled labor can be treated as part of the investment process, however, and total labor supply is not likely to be a limiting factor within the period relevant for the analysis.[6]

Policy Objectives and Restrictions. Within the limitations of two-sector analysis, it is desirable to incorporate restrictions which reflect both the limited flexibility of economic systems and the political limits to feasible

[5] A similar conceptual problem arises in identifying investment goods in a two-sector model, which can only be solved empirically by means of an interindustry analysis.

[6] The unemployment rate in Pakistan is estimated in the Pakistan Plan [7] at 20 per cent and the growth of population at 2.6 per cent. In countries having less unemployment, a more explicit treatment of the potential labor limitations might be needed, as in Chenery and Bruno [4].

policy changes. For example, any significant reduction in per capita consumption (which occurs in many so-called "optimal" growth paths) should probably be ruled out as politically infeasible. The introduction of such constraints makes the conclusions more realistic, although the results are less susceptible to generalization in the form of simple decision rules.

II. The Model

The problem of determining an optimum pattern of aid and growth over time will now be stated in linear programming form. The objective is to maximize a social welfare function, incorporating benefits (consumption) and costs (capital inflow) for each period of time. The constraints are the policy goals and the definitional, structural, and behavioral relationships for each time period. Variables and parameters are defined below. The variable and parameter values used in the basic solution are given in Tables 1 and 2 in Section III.

Variables:

V = gross national product.
V^1 = production for import substitution and export expansion.
V^0 = all other production.
I = total gross investment.
I^1 = investment in import substitution and export expansion.
I^0 = all other investment.
S = gross savings.
F = net capital inflow.
M = demand for traditional imports.
E = traditional exports.[7]
C = consumption.

Parameters:

γ = cost of foreign capital exogenously specified.
i = rate of discount.
ρ = postplan growth rate.
r = rate of discount on postplan consumption.
δ = weight on postplan consumption.
η = weight for terminal year income incorporating discount procedure for future consumption.
e = exogenous rate of growth of traditional exports.

[7] Traditional imports and traditional exports mean imports which would be required and exports which could be sold were the structure of the economy to remain unchanged from the base year.

k_1 = capital-output ratio for import substitution and export expansion.

k_0 = capital-output ratio for other production.

α = marginal savings rate.

m_0 = marginal import rate on income.

m_1 = marginal import rate on investment.

β = maximum feasible rate of growth of investment.

p = minimum allowable rate of growth of consumption.

T = terminal year of the plan.

$T - n$ = year in which aid must cease.

The Welfare Function

We wish to maximize the general welfare function

$$W = \sum_{t=1}^{T} \frac{C_t}{(1+i)^t} + \eta V_T - \gamma \sum_{t=1}^{T} \frac{F_t}{(1+i)^t}$$

where

$$\eta = \delta(1 - \alpha) \sum_{t=1}^{\infty} \frac{(1+\rho)^t}{(1+r)^{T+t}}.$$

This function has three parts: (1) the discounted sum of consumption prior to the terminal year of the plan; (2) an indicator of the discounted value of consumption in all years posterior to the plan, with a variable weight;[8] (3) the discounted sum of total capital inflow with a weight, γ, representing the price of foreign capital, which varies according to the supply conditions for the country concerned.

By varying γ and certain policy constraints, it is possible to simulate a wide range of supply conditions. If no policy constraints affecting supply conditions were added, the supply of foreign capital would be assumed to be infinitely elastic at the price γ.

This assumption of infinite elasticity is modified in the two alternative forms of the model in order to yield a more realistic statement of the scarcity of foreign capital:

1. In the "Basic Solution" defined below we have imposed the condition that foreign aid must terminate in a given year $(T - n)$ prior to the

---

[8] We put a weight, δ, on postplan consumption and use a weight of unity for the present value of plan period consumption so that the numéraire of the shadow prices which the solution yields will be the value of consumption in year 1.

terminal year of the analysis (T).[9] In this case the supply of foreign capital remains perfectly elastic at the price γ prior to $(T - n)$, but for years after $(T - n)$ the economy must be self-sufficient.

2. In a second alternative form[10] we assume that the total quantity of discounted aid received during the plan cannot exceed a given amount.

The results obtained by solving the model using these different specifications of the supply conditions are discussed in Section III.

The question arises as to whether the welfare function is formulated from the point of view of a recipient or a donor. The answer is that it can represent views of either recipients or donors, as well as a variety of views within each group. Different welfare assumptions are represented by the values given to the parameters in the objective function. For example, a country having a high preference for improvement of living standards during the period of the plan, compared to concern for living standards in the distant future, would give a relatively low weight to post-terminal consumption. This view implies a low value of δ or a plan discount rate (i) that is low relative to the postplan discount rate (r). The higher rate in later periods can also reflect a judgment as to the diminishing marginal utility of added consumption.

A second example is the donor or planning authority which desires the recipient country to become self-sufficient by the end of the plan period. In this case conditions in the short run are not of primary concern, though certain minimum standards must be met. This view can be represented in the basic model by a high value of δ. The donor would not view supply conditions as given, but would use the model to help in establishing supply conditions.

Our treatment of postplan consumption in the welfare function assumes that after period T the economy will proceed along a path of self-sustaining growth and that a constant portion $(1 - \alpha)$ of income will be consumed. An estimate of the self-sustaining rate of growth (ρ) can thus be determined.[11]

Our use of discount rates in the welfare function is based upon the standard time preference arguments. We allow for a higher discount rate in later years, which can be justified in terms of diminishing marginal utility

---

[9] See inequality (14) below.

[10] See inequality (16) below.

[11] As t becomes large, the average savings rate approaches the marginal savings rate, and the aggregate capital-output ratio approaches a (constant) weighted average of the two sectoral capital-output ratios in inequalities (7 and 8). The ratio of the average savings rate to the aggregate capital output ratio yields the long-run rate of self-sustaining growth.

of rising per capita income. As time passes there is a corresponding rise in per capita consumption and the marginal utility of consumption declines.[12] (The discontinuity of year T is chosen for convenience but does not significantly affect the conclusions.)

Definitional Equations

GNP is the sum of the net output of the two sectors: regular production and production for trade improvement.

$$(1) \qquad V_t = V_t^0 + V_t^1.$$

Gross investment is similarly the sum of investment in the two sectors:

$$(2) \qquad I_t = I_t^0 + I_t^1.$$

Investment is equal to domestic savings plus net foreign capital:

$$(3) \qquad I_t = S_t + F_t.$$

The trade gap is determined by the excess of the demand for "traditional" imports over the sales of "traditional" exports, less the output of the trade improvement sector.[13] It must be filled by a net flow of external resources, F_t.

$$(4) \qquad F_t = (M_t - E_t) - V_t^1.$$

This definition of the trade gap leads to a formulation of the national income equality which shows trade improving production as a reduction in the trade gap:

$$(5) \qquad V_t = C_t + I_t + E_t - M_t + V_t^1.$$

Traditional exports are assumed to grow at an exogenously determined rate:

$$(6) \qquad E_t = E_0 (1 + e)^t.$$

These exports can be produced at the capital-output ratio of regular production.

Structural and Behavorial Constraints

Since labor is assumed to be in surplus, production in each sector is limited only by capital in that sector and by the supply of imports. The

[12] This argument is made by Goodwin [6] in determining the optimal savings rate.
[13] As explained above "traditional" imports and exports mean imports which would be required and exports which could be sold if the structure of the economy were to remain unchanged from the base year.

structure of the economy in the base year is the basis for defining the limit to regular production:

$$(7) \qquad V_t^0 \leq V_0 + 1/k_0 \sum_0^{t-1} I_\tau^0 .$$

Production for trade improvement requires a higher capital-output ratio, and, by definition, investment in this sector begins only after the plan has commenced:

$$(8) \qquad V_t^1 \leq 1/k_1 \sum_1^{t-1} I_\tau^1 .$$

The aggregate capital-output ratio is a weighted average of the capital-output ratios of the two sectors. It changes over time as the distribution of investment between the two sectors changes. In the period of self-sustaining growth the proportion of trade improvement investment asymptotically approaches a limit of about 25 per cent of total investment. In the basic solution of the model, the economy is forced to self-sustaining growth after $t = 20$.

Maximum savings in any year is a function of base year savings and the increase of income since the base year:

$$(9) \qquad S_t \leq S_0 + \alpha(V_t - V_0) .$$

As V_t becomes large the average savings rate will approach the marginal savings rate, α. The marginal savings rate can be viewed as partially a behavioral constraint and partially an instrument of policy. Within certain limits the government could institute policies which would affect α. However, within the model presented here the marginal savings rate is taken as given.

The requirement for goods traditionally imported is a function of base year imports and the increases from the base year in income and investment.

$$(10) \qquad M_t \geq M_0 + m_0 (V_t - V_0) + m_1 (I_t - I_0) .$$

Although the marginal import rates can be affected by policy decisions, within the present model they are taken as technical parameters. The relatively high value of the marginal import rate on investment (m_1) produces some of the pressure of rapid growth upon the trade gap.

The observed limits to the ability of an underdeveloped country to absorb increases in the supply of capital are incorporated in the model by placing an upper limit (β) on the rate of growth of investment:

(11) $$I_t \leq (1 + \beta) I_{t-1} \, .$$

While an underdeveloped country may be able to raise its absorptive capacity in time, it is in the early years of the plan—when little could be done to raise the absorptive capacity—that the upper bound on growth of investment is of greatest importance.[14]

It is also necessary for technical reasons to place a lower bound on the growth of investment. To prevent unrealistic declines in investment—which the model would otherwise yield—we have included the following constraint:

(12) $$I_t \geq I_{t-1} \, .$$

Policy Constraints

The welfare function largely defines the policy goals of the nation. However, certain goals can only be formulated in terms of absolute targets and must therefore be stated as constraints of the model. One such goal is the undesirability of allowing per capita consumption to decline. This can be prevented by the inclusion of a constraint requiring total consumption to grow at least as rapidly as population:

(13) $$C_t \geq C_{t-1} (1 + p) \, .$$

Another policy goal which it is necessary to formulate as a constraint is the requirement that capital inflow be terminated by some predetermined year:

(14) $$F_t \leq 0 \text{ for } t = T - n, T \, .$$

The significance of this modification of the aid supply condition was pointed out above in the discussion of the welfare function.

Alternative Forms of the Model

As formulated above, the model allows the foreign assistance supply conditions to be specified in two forms: either as the price of foreign capital (γ) or as the terminal date for capital inflow ($T - n$). An alteration of the

---

[14] The absolute limit on absorptive capacity is somewhat arbitrary. It implies that no further investment can take place because of shortages of complementary inputs. It would probably be more realistic to assume that above this limit further investment can be carried out but only at higher capital-output ratios and with longer time lags. It would be possible to incorporate this more realistic assumption into our linear model by using step functions.

model allows a third method of specifying supply conditions. In this third form we place an upper limit on the total quantity of aid received over the plan and specify neither a price of foreign aid nor a termination date. That is, we add the constraint

$$(15) \qquad \sum_{t=1}^{T} \frac{F_t}{(1 + i)^t} \leq \bar{F}.$$

The three forms of the model will be discussed in Section III. It will be shown that equivalent results can be obtained from each form. For example, if a price is specified, a termination date and a total quantity of aid will be endogenously determined. We can therefore summarize the three forms of the model as follows:

	Price (γ)	Termination date $(T - n)$	Total aid $(\bar{F})$
Form 1	specified	determined	determined
Form 2	determined	specified	determined
Form 3	determined	determined	specified

It is, of course, possible to combine two of these forms although only one of them will turn out to be effective. This was done in the basic solution (see below) where both a minimum price of aid and a maximum termination date were specified. The solution then determines which limit is controlling.

Limitation of the Pattern of Aid

As explained below, foreign assistance is typically rationed on an annual basis by the donors. To reflect this supply limitation in our model, we will compute a set of solutions in which capital inflow cannot exceed a given ratio to GNP. This results in adding the following limit to the model:

$$(16) \qquad F_t \leq q V_t.$$

In the experiments discussed below $q = .05$.

Other Limits. In developing the basic model, alternative forms of some of the structural relationships were employed. The most important of these was the use of separate upper and lower bounds on the rate of growth of investment in each sector. This procedure is based on the rationale that regular production and trade improvement are actually two distinct types of investment. Trade improvement requires the construction of new plants and the development of new industries. While this assumption prevents the rapid shifting between one form of investment and another, it does not significantly alter the qualitative form of the results. It was therefore omitted from the final form of the model.

III. Growth Alternatives for Pakistan

The Pakistan Planning Commission has made two twenty-year projections or "perspective plans" as a basis for its Third Five-Year Plan for 1965–70 [7, 8]. In both these projections the net inflow of external resources is assumed to decline steadily and to approach zero by 1985. Little reason is given for this assumption apart from the desire to become independent of foreign assistance. Its effect on other objectives of the plan, such as the terminal year income, is not discussed.

In order to isolate the effects of varying amounts of external assistance, we start from the planning situation described by the objectives and constraints of the Pakistan Plan. The Plan document and other analyses of the Pakistan economy are used to determine plausible values for the parameters in our model and possible variations in them. We have made no attempt, however, to incorporate all of the economic and political considerations that affect the preparation of a development program. Our results are not designed as a critique of the Plan but to suggest the possibilities for more effective development strategies if assistance policies could be modified.

Our procedure is as follows. We first determine an optimum solution to the model in its original form based on welfare objectives and performance characteristics similar to those in the Pakistan Plan. This basic solution provides a point of departure for several sets of experiments. The first is designed to show the welfare effects of supplying assistance under conditions that more closely approximate present arrangements. The second set of experiments shows the effects of development performance on aid requirements. In both cases, we have assumed a range of values for the external capital inflow to show the increases in consumption and income made possible by increasing aid. Taken together, these experiments bring out the interrelations between development strategy and foreign assistance policy and suggest the advantages of greater coordination between the two.

The Basic Solution for Pakistan

The development of the model described in Section II required a period of experimentation. It was necessary to determine a satisfactory form of the model in which (1) the postulated objective function led to a rate of growth of national output similar to that taken as the objective of the

Pakistan long-term plan and (2) implausible fluctuations in consumption and investment were eliminated. The end product of these experiments is contained in relations (1)–(14) above. The result of maximizing the welfare function subject to these fourteen constraints (for each time period) will be called the basic solution.

The initial conditions and structural parameters assumed in the basic solution are given in Tables 1 and 2, which also present the corresponding

Table 1. Base Year Data (Rs. million 1965)

		Model Values		Pakistan Plan Values	
		Base Year 1962	$t = 3$ 1965	Version 1 1965	Version 2 1965
F_0	Foreign aid	1,183	1,956	2,750	3,690
S_0	Savings	3,381	4,620	4,200	4,710
I_0	Investment	4,564	6,586	6,950	8,400
M_0	Imports	3,743	4,920	5,700	6,990
E_0	Exports	2,559	2,954	2,950	3,050
V_0	National income	37,380	42,539	44,000	45,540
C_0	Consumption	33,999	37,919	39,800	40,830

Sources: Version 1: Government of Pakistan, *Outline of the Third Five-Year Plan* (1965–70), 1964.

Version 2: Government of Pakistan, *The Third Five-Year Plan* (1965–70), 1965.

Model values are averages derived from a time trend for the years 1957–62, which were thought to be more representative than the actual data for 1962.

values from the two versions of the Pakistan Perspective Plan[15] wherever they are available. The welfare function parameter values used in the basic solution are given below.

Nonstructural Parameters in the Basic Solution:

$i = .08$ (rate of discount during plan period).

$r = .10$ (rate of discount on postplan consumption).

$\rho = .073$ (postplan rate of growth).

$\gamma = 2$ (cost of foreign capital).

$\eta = 3.4$ (defined in the text).

$\delta = 1$ (relative valuation of postplan consumption).

$T = 23$ (terminal year of plan).

$T - n = 20$ (year in which aid must cease).

The growth of national output in the basic solution is shown in Figure 1 and Table 3 to be approximately midway between the two versions of the

[15] We started from the preliminary version of the Pakistan five-year plan for 1965–70 [7] and twenty-year perspective (Version 1 in Table 1) and made some revisions after the final plan (Version 2) became available [8].

perspective plan and therefore adequately representative of Pakistan's objectives. The time paths of the other variables in the basic solution are shown in Figures 2–5 and Tables 4 and 5. Since the solution to the model does not distinguish between that part of trade-improving investment which is import substitution and that part which is export expansion, we

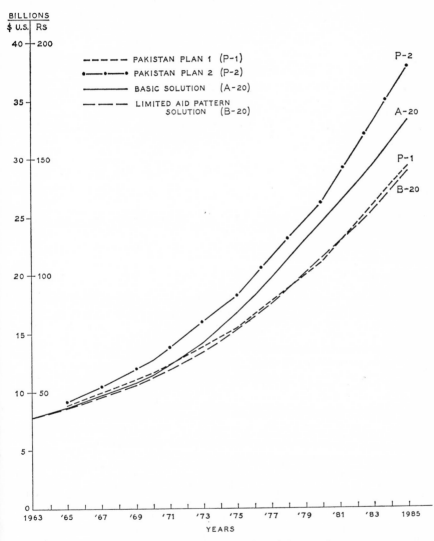

Figure 1. Growth of GNP in Pakistan's Perspective Plans and in Two Solutions to Model

Development Planning and Programming

Table 2. Value of Structural Parameters

	Model 1965–85	Pakistan Plan 1965–85		Pakistan Plan 1965–70		Pakistan Plan 1970–75		Pakistan Plan 1975–80		Pakistan Plan 1980–85	
		Version 1	Version 2	Version 1	Version 2	Version 1	Version 2	Version 1	Version 2	Version 1	Version 2
α Marginal savings rate	.24	.286	.25	.23	.22	.26	.25	.30	.28	.31	.25
m_0 Marginal import rate on income	.10	.072	.06	na	.12	na	.09	na	.06	na	.04
m_1 Marginal import rate on investment	.35	na	na	na	na	na	na	na	na	na	na
k_0 Incremental capital-output ratio, regular production	3.0	3.6	2.9	3.5	2.9	3.5	2.9	3.6	2.9	3.7	3.0
k_1 Incremental capital-output ratio, trade improvement	4.5	na	na	na	na	na	na	na	na	na	na
p Rate of population growth, in per cent	2.5	—	2.6	2.6	2.7	2.7	2.8	2.6	2.6	2.2	2.1
β Maximum rate of growth of investment	.13	na	na	na	na	na	na	na	na	na	na
e Rate of growth of exports, in per cent	4.9	6.0	7.9	6.0	9.5	6.0	8.7	6.0	8.6	6.0	4.9

SOURCES: Version 1: Government of Pakistan, *Outline of the Third Five-Year Plan.* Version 2: Government of Pakistan, *Third Five-Year Plan.*
Model: m_0, m_1, and k_0 were estimated from time trends for 1957–62; e and α were modified to reflect improved performance in 1963 and 1964.

have made an arbitrary distribution of trade improvement output for illustrative purposes.[16]

The Basic Pattern of Investment and Capital Inflow. An examination of the binding constraints and their shadow prices shows that the twenty-three year period of the basic solution can be divided into three subperiods or "regimes." Each regime may be identified by the set of constraints bind-

---

[16] Trade improvement production was allocated to export expansion so long as the rate of growth of exports did not exceed 6 per cent, which was the export forecast in Version 1. When this level was reached, the remainder was allocated to import substitution.

Table 3. Growth Rates and Significant Ratios for the Basic
Solution of the Model and the Two Versions of the Pakistan Plan

Years	Plan	*Per cent Rate of Growth*	V_n/V_0	I_n/V_n	S_n/V_n	F_n/V_n	I_n^1/I_n
		Basic Solution					
1965–70	III	5.9	1.33	.21	.14	.07	.05
1970–75	IV	7.7	1.45	.27	.17	.10	.07
1975–80	V	8.0	1.47	.23	.19	.03	.39
1980–85	VI	6.3	1.36	.21	.21	0	.21
		Pakistan Plan, Version 1					
1965–70	III	5.4	1.30	.19	.13	.06	
1970–75	IV	5.9	1.33	.20	.16	.04	
1975–80	V	6.7	1.38	.22	.20	.02	
1980–85	VI	6.8	1.39	.24	.23	.01	
		Pakistan Plan, Version 2					
1965–70	III	6.7	1.38	.20	.14	.07	
1970–75	IV	7.3	1.43	.21	.17	.04	
1975–80	V	7.5	1.44	.22	.20	.02	
1980–85	VI	7.5	1.44	.23	.22	.01	

SOURCE: Same as Table 1. In this table the subscript n refers to the final year of the particular plan and the subscript 0 refers to the first year of the particular plan.

ing it. Since some are binding throughout (the limits on capacity, savings, and trade) the regimes can be described in terms of those that change.
This gives the following combinations in the basic solution:

Regime	Description	Distinguishing Constraint	Period
I	Maximum investment and growth	Upper bound on rate of growth of investment (11)	1963–76
II	Trade improvement	Lower bound on rate of growth of investment (12)	1977–81
III	Balanced growth	No foreign capital (14)	1982–85

In the first regime[17] the economy grows at the maximum rate permitted by the absorptive capacity limit on total investment, with only a small fraction allotted to import substitution. Since investment rises more rapidly than domestic savings, the capital inflow increases steadily in this

[17] This regime corresponds to Phase I of Chenery and Strout [5].

Table 4. Variable Values in the Basic Solution (1965 Rs. Billions)

Plan Year	Net Capital Inflow (F)	Gross National Product (V)	Regular Production (V⁰)	Trade Improvement Production (V¹)	Total Gross Investment (I)	Regular Investment (I⁰)	Trade Improvement Investment (I¹)	Savings (S)	Consumption (C)	Imports^a	Exports^a	Traditional Imports (M)	Traditional Exports (E)
1963	1.41	38.9	38.90	0	5.16	5.08	.08	3.74	35.15	4.10	2.68	4.10	2.68
1964	1.67	40.6	40.59	.02	5.83	5.71	.11	4.16	36.45	4.51	2.84	4.51	2.82
1965	1.97	42.5	42.43	.04	6.58	6.41	.17	4.62	37.92	4.96	2.99	4.96	2.95
1966	2.30	44.7	44.63	.08	7.44	7.20	.24	5.14	39.57	5.47	3.17	5.48	3.10
1967	2.68	47.2	47.03	.13	8.41	8.09	.32	5.73	41.43	6.04	3.36	6.06	3.25
1968	3.11	49.9	49.72	.20	9.50	9.09	.41	6.39	43.53	6.67	3.56	6.72	3.41
1969	3.59	53.0	52.75	.30	10.74	10.22	.51	7.14	45.90	7.36	3.77	7.47	3.58
1970	4.15	56.6	56.15	.41	12.13	11.50	.63	7.99	48.58	8.15	4.00	8.31	3.75
1971	4.77	60.5	59.98	.55	13.71	12.94	.77	8.94	51.59	9.01	4.24	9.26	3.94
1972	5.48	65.0	64.29	.72	15.49	14.56	.93	10.01	55.00	9.97	4.49	10.33	4.13
1973	6.28	70.1	69.14	.93	17.51	16.39	1.12	11.23	58.84	11.00	4.72	11.54	4.33
1974	7.18	75.8	74.59	1.17	19.78	18.45	1.33	12.60	63.18	12.19	5.00	12.90	4.54
1975	8.21	82.2	80.74	1.47	22.35	20.78	1.57	14.14	68.07	13.51	5.30	14.45	4.22
1976	9.37	89.5	87.66	1.82	25.26	20.06	5.20	15.89	73.60	14.99	5.62	16.19	5.00
1977	9.44	97.3	94.34	2.97	27.20	16.34	10.87	17.77	79.55	15.39	5.96	17.65	5.25
1978	7.55	105.2	99.78	5.39	27.20	16.38	10.82	19.65	85.52	13.87	6.32	18.44	5.50
1979	5.67	113.0	105.23	7.79	27.20	16.43	10.77	21.54	91.49	12.37	6.70	19.23	5.77
1980	3.78	120.9	110.70	10.13	27.20	16.49	10.72	23.43	97.47	10.88	7.10	19.96	6.05
1981	1.89	128.8	116.20	12.56	27.20	16.54	10.66	25.31	103.45	9.42	7.53	20.80	6.35
1982	0	136.6	121.70	14.93	27.20	21.68	5.53	27.20	109.43	7.98	7.98	21.59	6.66
1983	0	145.1	128.92	16.15	29.23	23.26	5.98	29.23	115.85	8.46	8.46	23.14	6.99
1984	0	154.2	136.67	17.48	31.40	24.95	6.46	31.41	122.74	8.97	8.97	24.81	7.33
1985	0	163.9	144.98	18.91	33.75	26.78	6.97	33.75	130.15	9.50	9.50	26.59	7.68

^a Trade improvement production was allocated to export expansion so long as the rate of growth of exports did not exceed 6 per cent which was the export forecast in Version 1. When the 6 per cent level was reached, the remainder was allocated to import substitution.

Table 5. Shadow Prices in the Basic Solution

Plan Year	Savings Constraint	Foreign Trade Constraint	Production Capacity Constraint	Absorptive Capacity Constraint	Minimum Growth of Investment Constraint	Aid Termination Constraint	Incremental Value of Consumption
1963		.93	.83	89.22			.93
1964	.40	.45	.91	75.43			.86
1965	.37	.42	.84	63.64			.79
1966	.35	.39	.78	53.36			.74
1967	.32	.36	.72	44.41			.68
1968	.30	.33	.67	36.61			.63
1969	.27	.31	.62	29.85			.58
1970	.25	.29	.57	23.98			.54
1971	.23	.27	.53	18.88			.50
1972	.22	.25	.49	14.47			.46
1973	.20	.23	.45	10.65			.43
1974	.19	.21	.42	7.36			40
1975	.17	.19	.39	4.53			.37
1976	.16	.18	.36	2.09			.34
1977	.15	.17	.33				.32
1978	.14	.15	.31		2.02		.29
1979	.13	.14	.29		3.98		.27
1980	.12	.13	.27		5.88		.25
1981	.11	.12	.25		7.72		.23
1982	10.18	1.27	2.53		9.52	11.22	.21
1983	.93	.20	.40			.93	.20
1984	.83	.18	.36			.83	.18
1985	.74	1.61	2.33			.71	.17

regime. The limit on external assistance—whether defined by its total or by the period over which it is available—causes the economy to shift to regime II in 1977. In this regime total investment ceases to grow and trade-improving investment (I^1) rises to the proportion of the total needed to close the trade gap by the terminal year. As a result, the rate of growth of GNP slows down from its maximum of 8 per cent in 1975 to the rate which can be sustained by domestic savings in 1982 of about 6.3 per cent.

Regime III starts in the year in which aid is required to end. It is characterized by a proportion between trade-improving and total investment of about 1:4, which is just sufficient to prevent imports from outrunning exports. We have arbitrarily attributed enough of this investment to increased exports to achieve the steady growth of 6 per cent assumed in the first Pakistan plan; the rest reduces import needs.

The sharp transitions from one regime to another result from the use of a two-sector model with linear restrictions. This pattern of rising and then

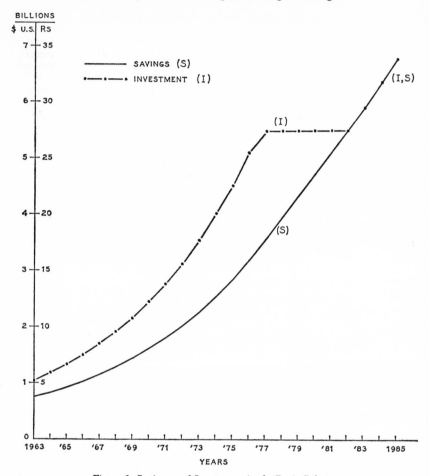

Figure 2. Savings and Investment in the Basic Solution

falling aid is a logical consequence of the high value of early increases in investment, income, and savings for future growth. If the restriction on the rate of increase in investment were not imposed, the peaking of aid in the early years would be even more pronounced.

So long as the requirement that aid be terminated by the twentieth year (1982) is maintained, the basic solution is highly insensitive to variation in the relative valuation of plan and postplan period consumption. With a price of foreign capital (γ) of 2 and the value of plan period consumption as unity, the basic solution is the same for all values of the weight on terminal year income (η) greater than one. Even when consumption during the plan is given no weight at all, the basic solution is not altered so long as the weight on terminal year income is greater than 1.2.

The composition of investment over time is a consequence of the high productivity of aid in the early years. In order to absorb it, a gap has to be opened between imports and exports and then closed as rapidly as the rise in savings permits. Since the economy may not be sufficiently flexible to

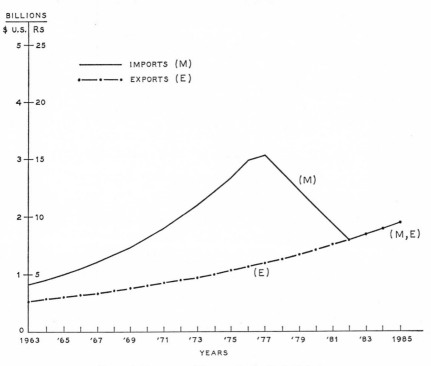

Figure 3. Exports and Imports in the Basic Solution

carry out this rapid structural change, observed growth paths—as shown in [5]—are likely to reflect a slower decrease in aid and a longer period of transition than the optimizing solution would suggest.

The Marginal Value of Aid. The basic solution can also be described as the solution to either of the other two forms of the model suggested above. Having determined the optimal amount of external capital corresponding to a twenty-year terminal period, we can take this amount as given in the third form of the model. In the latter case, we do not specify a unit cost of the capital inflow, but determine its value as a result of the solution.

When the optimal solution is recalculated on these assumptions, the

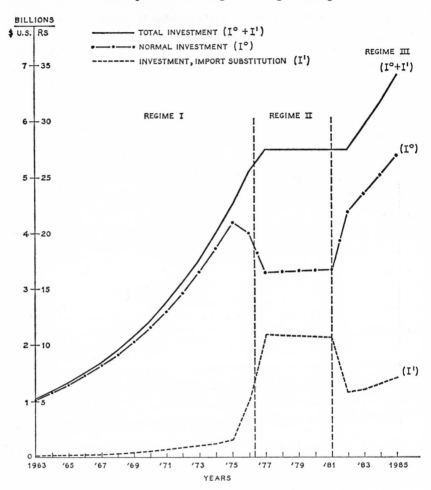

Figure 4. Composition of Investment in the Basic Solution

quantity solution is the same in all respects as that previously determined. The price solution differs in that the value of an additional unit of external capital is determined to be 7.4 instead of the 2.0 assumed initially. With this opportunity cost, the given amount of aid is distributed over time as shown in Figure 5 and reaches zero in twenty years without this condition being required in the model.[18] The reasons for this pattern have been given

---

[18] The cost of imposing this restriction would therefore be zero, whereas it was 11.2 in the first formulation for $F_{21} = 0$. Otherwise the shadow prices in the two formulations are the same.

above. In the basic solution with a specified terminal date (and undervalued external capital) the economy utilizes the maximum amount of aid consistent with the absorptive capacity constraint in regime I and the composition of investment required by regime II. The same solution will result for any preassigned unit value of foreign capital less than its true opportunity cost of 7.4.

This analysis of the basic solution shows that it could also be produced from the original form of the model if we assume initially a value of γ of 7.4. If Pakistan were offered unlimited amounts of capital at this (dis-

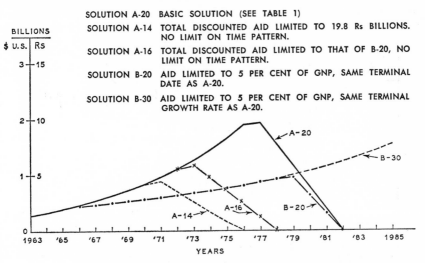

Figure 5. *Optimal Patterns of Aid: Varying Aid Conditions*

counted) cost, its optimal development strategy would be to utilize this capital only over the next twenty years under the conditions specified in the model.[19]

Variations in the Supply of External Capital

At the present time there is no coherent policy governing the total supply of external capital to underdeveloped countries. The procedures followed by the multilateral and bilateral lending institutions contain elements of three different allocation principles: (1) offers of loans at specified rates; (2) rationing of assistance among countries on subjective criteria of need, performance, and political importance; (3) planning of aid against a given

---

[19] This statement is unrealistic in assuming constant supply and performance conditions over time.

terminal date. We now impose restrictions on the model to show the effect of alternative supply conditions on the optimal growth pattern and the social welfare.

Variation in Total Supply. We first determine the effects of varying the total capital inflow, assuming that its intertemporal distribution is unrestricted. A systematic variation in total supply can be specified with any of the three forms of the model by either (1) varying the parameter, γ, in

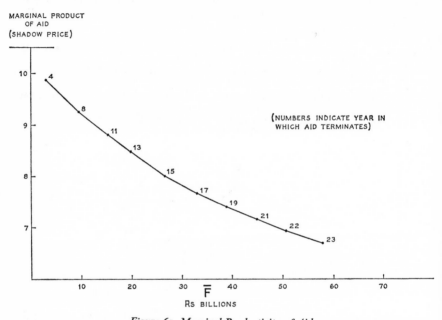

Figure 6a. Marginal Productivity of Aid

the original welfare function; (2) varying the total discounted amount of aid supplied; or (3) varying the terminal date with no limitation on price or quantity. Our analysis of the basic solution shows that the set of solutions will be equivalent whichever approach is followed.

The results of varying total discounted aid are shown in Figure 6a for values of $\bar{F}$ ranging from 10 to 150 per cent of the amount in the basic solution. The corresponding variation in the value of aid (γ) is from 9.7 to 6.7 and in the terminal year from four to twenty-three years.

The decline in the marginal productivity or value of aid results from the fact that as its quantity is increased, the use of external resources for investment purposes has to be postponed because of the limitation on absorptive capacity. This postponement reduces the amount of additional consumption and saving achieved per unit of additional aid during the plan period. On the other hand, since the value of future aid is discounted at 8 per cent, a dollar of aid today is equal in present value to $4.5 twenty years from now. For this reason, there is no decline in the marginal productivity of total discounted aid as measured by its effect on the terminal year income although there would be a decline with a lower discount rate.

The two components of the welfare function are given separately in Table 6 and Figure 6b to show these two effects. For any aid total, the

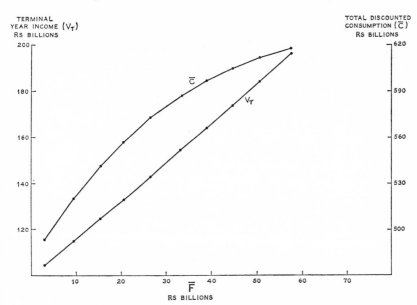

Figure 6b. Components of Total Welfare

marginal product in Figure 6a is equal to the sum of the marginal effects of aid on total consumption and terminal income with V_T given its appropriate weight.

The development sequence represented by the three regimes of the basic solution is unaffected by changes in the total amount of aid. As the total is reduced, the length of each of the first two regimes is shortened as indicated in Table 6. The effect on the optimal time path of aid is shown in Figure 5. Solution A-14 shows the effect of reducing the total aid by 50 per cent from the basic solution and consequently shortening the period of aid from twenty to fourteen years.

It is significant for assistance strategy that the optimal paths of all the variables are unaffected in regime I by an earlier termination date. Therefore a change in the total aid anticipated need not affect planning during this period.

Table 6. Effects of Varying Aid Supply ᵃ (Rs. Billions 1965)

Solution	Aid Measures			Benefit Measures			Characteristics of Development Patterns				
	Total Aid Discounted	Shadow Price of Discounted Aid	Total Aid Undiscounted	Discounted Plan Consumption	Terminal Year Income	Plan Rate of Growth of Income	Peak Year of Aid	Terminal Year of Aid	Regime I	Regime II	Regime III
1. Variation of total aid supply											
A–9	9.5	9.3	12.9	520.7	114.9	5.0%	1966	1970	1963–66	1968–71	1972–85
A–12	15.3	8.8	23.6	541.3	124.3	5.4%	1969	1973	1963–68	1970–73	1974–85
A–14	19.8	8.4	33.4	556.0	131.7	5.6%	1971	1975	1963–71	1973–75	1976–85
A–16	25.8	8.0	48.6	571.4	141.7	6.0%	1973	1977	1963–73	1975–77	1978–85
A–20	38.9	7.4	90.5	597.8	163.9	6.6%	1977	1981	1963–75	1977–81	1982–85
A–24	57.4	6.7	172.1	618.1	196.1	7.5%	1981	1985	1963–80	1982–85	—
A–20*	38.9	—	90.5	—	275.0	6.6%	1977	1981	1963–75	1977–81	1982–92
2. Variation of total supply with annual aid limited to 5 per cent of GNP											
B–20	25.8	—	56.8	562.8	142.1	6.0%	1979	1981	1963–78	1979–81	1982–85
B–30	40.3	—	150.5	—	275.0	6.6%	1988	1991	1963–87	1988–91	1992–
3. Variation of total supply and variation of performance											
C–13	12.9	7.3	19.8	520.3	98.3	4.3%	1968	1975	1963–67	1968–75	1976–85
C–20	30.6	7.0	60.6	570.8	120.5	5.2%	1973	1981	1963–72	1973–81	1982–85
D–11	16.5	9.1	23.9	547.5	125.8	5.4%	1968	1972	1963–65	1968–72	1973–85
D–20	83.0	7.6	190.6	725.3	234.4	8.3%	1974	1981	1963–75	1976–81	1982–85

ᵃThe solutions to the model are designated by a letter and a number. The letter indicates the form of the model and the number indicates the year in which self-sustaining growth begins.

A = solutions using the parameters and form of the basic model.
B = solutions in which the annual capital inflow is limited to 5 per cent of GNP.
C = solutions in which the marginal savings rate (α) is .16. Otherwise the same as A.
D = solutions in which the limit on the rate of growth of investment (β) is .20. Otherwise the same as A.

Example: A-20 is the basic solution.

Annual Rationing of Aid. The procedures by which public capital is currently supplied to developing countries result in a system of rationing in which there tends to be an absolute ceiling on the amount of aid furnished to any country in any one year. This ceiling can be represented in our model by limiting the annual inflow to a predetermined fraction of GNP. We will analyze the effects of such a limit in Pakistan by assuming a maximum of 5 per cent of GNP, which is approximately the average capital inflow in the past several years.

Solution B-20 in Table 6 and Figure 5 shows the effect of imposing this limitation in addition to the requirement of aid termination in twenty years. The growth rate of the economy is reduced by 10 per cent and total capital inflow by about a third. The loss in welfare is significantly greater than would be the case if the same amount of aid were optimally distributed.

The effect of annual rationing with a given growth target is shown by solution B-30, which determines the amount of aid needed to achieve the same growth target as the basic solution with aid limited to 5 per cent of GNP. The result is to prolong the date of aid termination to 1992,[20] to increase total aid, and to reduce total consumption as shown in Table 6. It is only for discount rates of greater than 9 per cent that there is any gain to the aid donors from this form of rationing. On an undiscounted basis the total aid required to achieve the given growth target is 65 per cent greater than with the optimum pattern.[21]

Variation in Development Performance

The most significant measures of a country's development policies in the present model are the marginal rate of savings (α), the absorptive capacity for investment (β), and the efficiency of use of capital ($1/k$). Since their effect on growth in closed models is well known, we are primarily interested in how they affect the productivity of aid and the amounts needed to obtain a given objective.

Figure 7 shows the variation in the marginal productivity of aid under the assumptions of a marginal savings rate of .16 instead of .24 (curve *C*) and of an absorptive capacity of .20 instead of .13 (curve *D*). Other assumptions of the basic solution are unchanged. These curves can be compared to the productivity of the basic solution (curve *A*). The time path of aid for a terminal year of twenty is similarly compared to the basic solution in Figure 8.[22]

[20] Solution A-20* shows the basic solution projected to 1992.
[21] In the optimal pattern, aid reaches a peak of 10.5 per cent of GNP in the fourteenth year.
[22] Table 6 gives other characteristics of the solutions.

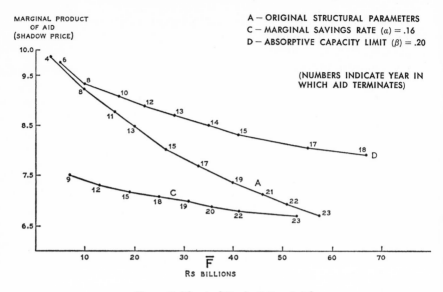

Figure 7. Marginal Productivity of Aid

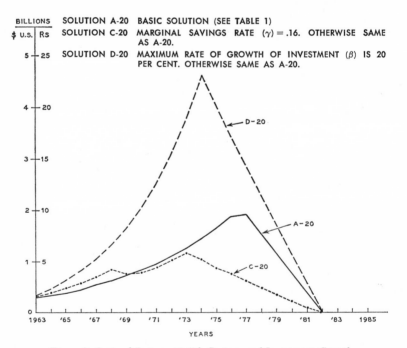

Figure 8. Optimal Pattern of Aid: Savings and Investment Growth

Higher absorptive capacity raises the marginal productivity by an increasing amount as the total aid is increased. At the level of the basic solution, the same growth target could be achieved with about 10 per cent less aid. Alternatively, a growth rate of 8.3 per cent could be achieved for the plan period compared to the 6.6 per cent of the basic solution. Even with the doubling of aid that this increase would require, its marginal productivity would remain higher than in the basic solution.

A fall in the marginal savings rate from .24 to .16 would lower the marginal productivity most substantially at low levels of aid. For a given terminal year (solution C-20) the lower savings performance reduces the terminal year income by about 25 per cent with only a small reduction in total discounted aid. It is clear that the ability of a country to save and reinvest a substantial proportion of its increases in income is one of the most important reasons why external assistance can be highly productive.[23]

Finally, we can make a brief comment on the most significant difference between our analysis and the Pakistan Perspective Plan. As shown in Figure 1, our solution B-20 (with aid limited to 5 per cent of GNP) closely parallels the growth of GNP in the more conservative preliminary version of the perspective plan. This solution requires about 50 per cent more external capital than the preliminary plan mainly because of our assumption that trade improvement will require substantially more capital than is indicated by the marginal coefficient of 3.0 that has been experienced recently. Since the problems of closing the balance-of-payments gap are not explicitly analyzed in the perspective plan, we cannot explore this difference further.

IV. DEVELOPMENT AND ASSISTANCE STRATEGY

Although our experimentation with this model has not proceeded far enough to test the generality of our results, several aspects of development strategy seem to apply under a wide variety of assumptions. The first is the high productivity of early increases in investment and consequently of the external resources which make them possible. Our optimum investment patterns bear a striking resemblance to those of Goodwin [6], even though the savings rate necessary to sustain them is held within realistic limits by the availability of external resources. The main function of aid is thus to permit an economy to grow at a rate determined by its ability to invest rather than by its initial ability to increase savings.

For aid donors interested in achieving either self-sustaining growth or a given growth target, the assistance provided will be considerably more

---

[23] Estimates of the productivity of assistance over shorter periods are given in references 1, 4, and 5.

effective if it permits the recipient to follow this optimum strategy of rapid growth in the early years, which permits a shorter period of assistance for any given target.

There is a strong indication that the optimal growth strategy while investment is rising in regime I is not dependent on the total aid to be provided. In our example, Pakistan's optimum policy until 1969 would be the same either with the aid expected in the basic solution or with half that much. This suggests the possibility of conditional planning by donors and recipients in which the aid of subsequent years could depend on initial performance without distorting investment decisions in the earlier years. The implications of this conclusion need to be tested in more realistic models.

Finally, the possibility of measuring the productivity of assistance from an analysis of a country's development possibilities suggests a line of improvement in the procedure for intercountry allocation of aid. The marginal productivity curves of Figures 6 and 7 can be interpreted as demand curves for external capital, which could be helpful in rationing any given amount of foreign assistance. The use of such measures would focus attention on the aspects of both donor and recipient performance that are most important to successful development.

References

1. Adelman, I., and Chenery, H. B. "Foreign Aid and Economic Development: The Case of Greece," *Review of Economics and Statistics*, XLVIII (February, 1966), 1–19.
2. Bergsman, J., and Manne, A. S. "An Almost Consistent Intertemporal Model for India's Fourth and Fifth Plans," this volume, pp. 239–61.
3. Chenery, H. B., and Kretschmer, K. "Resource Allocation for Economic Development," *Econometrica*, XXIV (October, 1956), 365–400.
4. Chenery, H. B., and Bruno, M. "Development Alternatives in an Open Economy: The Case of Israel," *Economic Journal*, LXXII (March, 1962), 79–103.
5. Chenery, H. B., and Strout, A. M. "Foreign Assistance and Economic Development," *American Economic Review* (forthcoming).
6. Goodwin, R. M. "The Optimal Growth Path for an Underdeveloped Economy," *Economic Journal*, LXXI (December, 1956), 75–89.
7. Government of Pakistan. *Outline of the Third Five Year Plan (1965–70)*. Karachi, 1964.
8. ———. *The Third Five Year Plan (1965–70)*. Karachi, 1965.
9. Manne, A. S. "Key Sectors of the Mexican Economy, 1962–72," this volume, pp. 263–89.
10. Sandee, J. *A Long Term Planning Model of India*. New York: United Nations, 1959.
11. Stoleru, G. "An Optimal Policy for Economic Growth," *Econometrica*, XXXIII (April, 1965), 321–48.
12. Tims, W. *Growth Model for the Pakistan Economy: Macro-economic Projections for Pakistan's Third Plan*. Karachi: Planning Commission, 1965.
13. Uzawa, H. "Optimal Growth in a Two-Sector Model of Capital Accumulation," *Review of Economic Studies*, LXXXV (January, 1964), 1–24.

COMMENT

MAX MILLIKAN, MASSACHUSETTS INSTITUTE OF TECHNOLOGY

Since I am not an accomplished professional model builder, I shall leave critique of the technical model design to others and concentrate my attention on the implications for aid policy suggested by the model.

The principal practical conclusion that appears to emerge from this analysis is that aid will be much more productive in generating self-sustaining economic growth if it is heavily concentrated in the early years of a development program rather than spread out more evenly over a longer period. This is not a very surprising conclusion in this kind of a linear model since the engine of increased domestic savings is assumed to be the gap between the marginal and average savings rates, and the more rapidly income can be expanded in the early stages, the more effectively this engine operates. The authors are clearly aware of the numerous respects in which their conclusion is a consequence of certain of the assumptions made to simplify the model. I should like to comment on one or two of these and add a couple of others of my own.

The model greatly simplifies the decision as to how much aid to offer in the early years by postulating a sharp discontinuous limit, beta, to the maximum feasible rate of growth of investment. The capital output ratio is in effect assumed to be constant for all values of $\frac{I}{V}$ up to beta and then goes in effect to infinity for rates in investment above this. If the world were like this, and if one could discover the critical parameter data, aid would always be economized by providing enough to insure that investment proceeded at the absorptive ceiling in the early years. In fact of course, as the authors recognize, absorptive capacity is not that sharply bounded. The model would gain greatly in realism if k, the capital output ratio, could be made an explicitly increasing function of the rate of investment. In such a model the rising capital costs of successive increments of output would have to be balanced against the increased savings which such additional increments would generate.

The generality of the authors' conclusion is perhaps suggested by the fact that I have searched diligently for modifications of their assumptions which would invalidate the basic conclusion that aid should be heavily concentrated in the early years. Only one such family of modifications has occurred to me. This is the not wholly unrealistic possibility that three of the basic parameters—k the capital output ratio, beta the absorptive capacity ceiling, and alpha the marginal propensity to save—might be direct functions of the amount of aid supplied.

On the one hand, for example, aid might be accompanied by technical assistance which would have the effect of lowering the capital output ratio. In this event, the qualitative conclusions of the model, far from being vitiated, would in fact be reinforced. On the other hand, it is possible that with large amounts of capital coming on a grant basis from an aid agency, the incentives on the recipients to utilize this aid effectively, i.e., to keep the capital output ratio down, might be lower the larger the quantity of aid. In this event, some stretch-out of the aid period might increase its productivity.

It is difficult to see how aid could have an effect upon beta other than to raise it, thus reinforcing the qualitative conclusions of the model.

With respect to alpha, however, the position is more uncertain. It is the expressed intention of most aid donors to attempt to employ their offer of aid as an incentive to persuade the recipient to raise its marginal rate of saving above what it would otherwise be. To the extent this is successful the qualitative conclusions of the model are in fact substantially reinforced. It is frequently alleged, however, that whatever the intentions of the donor the incentive effects of the availability of aid are in fact perverse, so that recipients, being reasonably confident they can rely on outside sources of funds for a considerable portion of their investment needs, are a good deal less vigorous in taking the tax, fiscal, and other measures necessary to raise the marginal rate of saving. To the extent that higher aid levels have in fact the effect of depressing the marginal rate of saving, it is no longer clear that the most effective aid policy is to concentrate aid in the early years to the extent permitted by absorptive capacity.

In conclusion, let me say that the difficulty I have had in thinking of situations in which the authors' qualitative conclusions would not hold is testimony to the importance of their results.

7. MACROECONOMIC GROWTH AND DEVELOPMENT MODELS OF THE PERUVIAN ECONOMY*

E R I K   T H O R B E C K E , IOWA STATE UNIVERSITY (AMES)
A P O S T O L O S   C O N D O S , IOWA STATE UNIVERSITY (AMES)

I. PURPOSE AND SCOPE OF STUDY

The main purpose of this paper is to formulate and construct three alternative macroeconomic models. These models are used to describe quantitatively the growth of the Peruvian economy from 1950 to 1964, to project the future path of the major macroeconomic variables, and to check the internal consistency of projections and intended policies in the public investment program prepared by the Peruvian National Planning Institute (INP) [3]. Finally, certain policy recommendations are derived which might be useful in the formulation of a development plan.

The third model presented below, Model C, incorporates the public sector and a number of policy variables available to the government. The introduction of the policy instruments makes it possible to follow through the impact of alternative values of the variables on such target variables as the level of income and the balance of payments. Model C can be considered as a modest preliminary step toward a more complete medium-term development planning model.

II. STATISTICAL SOURCES, COVERAGE, AND QUALITY OF DATA

There are two basic sources of national income statistics in Peru: the Central Bank [1] and the National Planning Institute [2, 3, 4]. The Central Bank was responsible for the preparation and publication of the national income account until 1962 when the National Planning Institute (INP) was created to undertake research and to advise the government in planning.

*Much of the research on this paper was done during the authors' tenure in Peru as advisors to the National Planning Institute, intermittently, after September, 1963.

181

The Central Bank had used one or two price deflators, but the INP derived the national income accounts at constant prices with the help of a number of sectoral deflators. The use of these two entirely different deflating procedures created for the major macroeconomic variables two sets of mutually inconsistent time series covering the period from 1950 to the present. The quality of the Central Bank statistics at current prices seems relatively good, but the time series expressed at constant prices are unreliable because of the very rough deflating procedure used.[1] Thus the INP figures are used exclusively.

The INP has published annual statistical data covering the period from 1950 to the present for the major macroeconomic variables expressed in constant 1960 prices. The amount of sectoral information is very limited. Time series are available for output (value added) in an eleven-sector breakdown. However, no such breakdown exists for investment, the only division being between public and private investment on the one hand and between gross investment in machinery and equipment and in construction on the other. Not too much reliance should be placed on the investment data since they are derived indirectly from capital goods import statistics rather than estimated directly.

Unfortunately, the INP does not provide any data on functional income shares, such as wages and salaries, profits, interest, and rent. Such information is of fundamental importance due to the very unequal income distribution in Peru and the desirability of establishing a more equal income distribution as a target of economic policy. The lack of income distribution data and reliable employment statistics limited the construction of a medium-term development planning model. Finally, only a limited amount of input-output and regional information is available.

The underlying statistical information for 1950–64 for the macroeconomic variables appearing in the three models constructed below is given in Table 3. The data are expressed in millions of 1960 soles.[2]

III. Brief Review of the Structure and Development of the Peruvian Economy Since 1950

From 1950 to 1964 the Peruvian gross domestic income (GDI) grew at a cumulative annual rate of 5.5 per cent, while population grew at an

---

[1] The Central Bank is presently making a serious effort to improve the quality of its data, particularly the real data. An important contribution could be made to development planning by improving the quality of the data and expanding the coverage to the sectoral and regional levels. Obviously, it will take a few years before the new information becomes available.

[2] The rate of exchange remained practically constant since 1959 at about 26.80 soles = $1.

annual rate of approximately 2.8 per cent. Three subperiods can be distinguished: one of moderate growth between 1950 and 1956 with an annual growth rate of 5.5 per cent; one of stagnation from 1956 to 1959, during which the growth rate declined to below 1 per cent annually; and one of accelerated growth from 1959 to 1964 with a rate of 8.5 per cent.

It is very clear—and will be abundantly illustrated in the subsequent models—that the growth of the Peruvian economy was export-propelled. Peru has both a diversified pattern of exports[3] and a high dependence on exports, as indicated by the high ratio of exports to GDI. A measure of the importance of the export sector is the sum of the value of exports and the so-called terms-of-trade effects. The latter term (Z) is defined as the product of the terms-of-trade index minus one and the value of exports at constant 1960 prices.[4]

The sum of exports (E) and the terms-of-trade effects (Z) measured at constant (1960) prices reflects the purchasing power of exports. The ratio of $(E + Z)$ to GDI increased from 19.6 to 23.3 per cent from 1950 to 1956, declined subsequently to 20.4 per cent in 1958, then rose substantially, reaching 27.4 per cent in 1964.

There appears to be very little doubt that the high rate of growth of the Peruvian economy after 1959 was very largely caused by the tremendous rise in the value of exports and the improvements in terms of trade.[5] The rate of growth of $(E + Z)$ went up from a moderate 4.5 per cent annually between 1950 and 1959 to about 14 per cent between 1959 and 1964, which suggests that the acceleration in the growth rate of national income after 1959 was occasioned by the export sector.

The main impact of exports has been on aggregate income. The contribution of exports to a more equal income distribution has been either marginal or negative and the contribution to employment creation is small because of the high capital-intensive nature of the major export commodities. For instance, the total labor force employed in the mining, fish meal, and sugar industries is relatively very small. A substantial share of the ex-

---

[3] Half of the exports by value are accounted for by cotton, copper, and fish meal and the other half are divided between sugar, lead, wool, silver, zinc, petroleum, iron ore, coffee, and others.

[4] The terms-of-trade effect (Z) is defined as follows:

$$Z_t = \left(\frac{P_{X_t}}{P_{X_0}} \div \frac{P_{M_t}}{P_{M_0}} \right) P_{X_0} Q_{E_t}$$

where P_X and P_M refer to the unit value of exports and imports, respectively, and Q_X to the volume of exports. The further subscripts 0 and t refer to Year 0 (base year) and Year t. Since 1960 is used as the base year, the terms-of-trade effects equal zero in 1960 $(Z_{60} = 0)$ and deviations are measured either positively or negatively from the 1960 level.

[5] See Columns 21 and 22, Table 3.

port earnings in the above industries is reinvested and, thus, spent abroad to import the necessary capital goods.[6]

The structure of the Peruvian economy is essentially dualistic, with an advanced export sector concentrated primarily on the coast and a backward traditional sector in the "Sierra." However, a rigid regional breakdown between the coastal region and the Sierra would miss the pockets of traditional, essentially barter subsectors around the coastal cities (mainly Lima) as well as the highly advanced mining centers in the Sierra. In some respects the economy of Peru can be better studied with a "dual-dual economy" model.

The rate of inflation has been relatively moderate over the period under consideration, at least by Latin American standards. The rate of exchange has been kept fixed since 1959. However, inflationary forces have been evident since the latter part of 1963, and the present rate is about 20 per cent annually. Notwithstanding these inflationary pressures, the balance of payments continued to show strength until the latter part of 1965. This unusual situation appears to reflect the tremendous strength of the Peruvian export commodities in world markets and the low labor-capital and labor-output ratio in many export industries. This latter effect results in a low labor-to-total-cost ratio which tends partially to insulate the export industries from wage increases due to inflation.

The public sector has become relatively more important in the economy. The government's share of GDI (X^g) increased from 9.2 per cent in 1950 to 15.8 per cent in 1963, the main increase occurring after 1960. It is relevant that of the two components of X^g, government investment (I^g) and public consumption (C^g), the former fluctuated considerably with no visible upward trend until 1960, then it rose steeply (see Columns 3, 7, and 11, Table 3).

It would appear, in summary, that the major macroeconomic characteristic of the Peruvian economy over the period under consideration is a relatively high aggregate growth rate, which was essentially generated by a very dynamic export sector, particularly after 1959. At the same time the effects of the export sector on other macroeconomic policy objectives, such as income distribution and level of employment, appear to have been small.

IV. ALTERNATIVE MACROECONOMIC MODELS

Three alternative macroeconomic models were specified and are presented below. The list of variables and the symbols appearing in these

[6] The capital equipment requirements cannot be satisfied from within because of the absence of a capital-goods-producing sector.

models is given in the Appendix. Each model is presented first as an estimated model and second in reduced form expressing the endogenous variables as functions of the exogenous predetermined variables exclusively.

For the estimated equations the sample consists of yearly observations for the period 1950 to 1963 (in some cases including 1964). Two different estimation procedures were used for those equations containing more than one endogenous variable, namely, ordinary and two-stage least squares.[7] The estimates appearing in the specified models are the ordinary least squares estimates, whereas the two-stage least squares estimates are given in the Appendix. With one exception, the differences between single-stage and two-stage least squares estimates were relatively small, hence the reason for using the ordinary least squares estimates in the models.

As usual, the standard errors of the coefficients are listed in parentheses below each coefficient, and R^2 denotes the value of the coefficient of multiple determination adjusted for degrees of freedom. The Durbin-Watson (DW) test, measuring serial correlation in the residuals, is also given.[8]

Table 1 was prepared as a test of the descriptive validity of the models, showing side by side the values actually observed during the sample period and the predicted values of the endogenous variables obtained from the reduced form after substituting for the values of the exogenous (predetermined) variables.

The models appear to describe relatively well the paths of the major macroeconomic variables over the period under consideration.

Models A and B are relatively simple and straightforward and only of a limited interest from a policy standpoint since they contain only a very limited number of variables which could be considered as instrument variables under the control of the government. Model C, on the other hand, incorporates a few instrument variables and is, therefore, of somewhat greater relevance from a policy standpoint.

Consequently, Models A and B are described cursorily and explored mainly to illustrate their possible use in checking the internal consistency of macroeconomic projections. Model C, in contrast, will be analyzed in more detail and used to follow through the impact of changes in the set of (1) noncontrolled exogenous variables (such as exports and the terms of

---

[7] The procedure used to derive two-stage least squares estimates is based on Johnston [5, pp. 258–59].

[8] With the sample size used here and a single independent variable, a value of DW below .81 indicates significant autocorrelations at the 1 per cent level of significance; a value of DW above 1.07 indicates serial independence, while a value of DW between .81 and 1.07 yields inconclusive results. For equations with two independent variables the corresponding limits for DW are .70 and 1.25 respectively. Finally, for equations with three independent variables, the relevant values of DW are .59 and 1.46.

Table 1. Actual and Estimated Values of the Most Important
Endogenous Variables, 1951–64 (subscripts refer to model in which variable appears)
(in millions of soles at 1960 prices)

Year	1 X	2 $\hat{X}_A$	3 $\hat{X}_B$	4 $\hat{X}_C$	5 C^p	6 $\hat{C}_B^p$	7 $\hat{C}_C^p$	8 C^v	9 $\hat{C}_B^v$	10 C	11 $\hat{C}_C$	12 I^v
1951	39,604	40,502	40,154		28,651	29,393	29,753	2,481	2,605			2,261
1952	40,046	41,308	41,984	40,768	28,084	30,439	30,476	2,593	2,869	30,677	32,240	2,426
1953	42,201	41,968	42,346	42,042	29,668	30,647	31,079	2,698	2,909	32,366	33,329	1,649
1954	44,158	43,151	43,440	43,100	31,440	31,269	32,865	3,286	3,045	34,726	34,133	3,161
1955	45,651	46,114	46,967	46,224	32,803	33,276	34,202	3,125	3,679	35,927	36,405	2,842
1956	47,135	49,784	49,842	48,556	33,524	34,928	34,531	3,168	4,156	36,693	37,678	2,854
1957	48,941	50,337	50,750	49,141	35,175	35,446	32,843	3,894	4,347	39,068	38,287	1,919
1958	47,638	46,191	46,738	46,185	35,435	33,156	33,398	3,928	3,656	39,363	36,572	1,016
1959	49,007	46,271	45,528	47,164	36,593	32,464	37,878	4,458	3,474	41,051	37,598	1,095
1960	55,650	54,157	54,426	55,005	37,308	36,830	41,979	5,383	4,729	42,691	43,082	1,752
1961	60,444	61,797	60,954	62,160	40,318	41,277	43,818	6,001	6,004	46,319	48,398	2,741
1962	65,008	66,244	66,137	65,389	43,057	44,239	44,792	6,379	6,853	49,436	50,316	3,188
1963	68,492	67,266	68,325	67,105	45,681	43,164		7,608	6,571	53,289	51,771	

Table 1. continued

Year	13 $\hat{I}_C^y$	14 I^p	15 $\hat{I}_{A,B}^p$	16 $\hat{I}_C^p$	17 M	18 $\hat{M}_C$	19 T^d	20 $\hat{T}_B^d$	21 $\hat{T}_C^d$	22 T^i	23 $\hat{T}_B^i$	24 $\hat{T}_C^i$
1951		7,092	7,198									
1952	2,526	8,112	8,392	8,061	9,052	9,902	1,602	1,604	1,637	2,723	2,809	2,810
1953	2,587	8,998	7,786	7,576	9,991	9,974	1,660	1,675	1,751	2,823	3,021	2,996
1954	1,540	7,640	7,873	7,678	9,062	9,466	1,634	1,771	1,845	2,779	3,048	3,150
1955	3,452	7,261	8,453	8,211	10,350	11,919	1,974	1,868	2,126	3,356	3,143	3,608
1956	3,205	9,726	8,737	8,482	13,096	11,818	2,083	2,182	2,335	3,413	3,726	3,948
1957	2,796	10,628	9,705	9,352	14,535	12,239	2,126	2,441	3,387	3,440	4,142	4,033
1958	1,830	8,835	9,613	9,276	12,180	11,208	2,255	2,523	2,123	4,338	4,334	3,620
1959	926	6,618	8,243	8,093	10,202	9,403	2,081	2,163	2,210	3,917	3,716	3,746
1960	1,043	9,605	8,542	8,420	11,427	11,243	2,249	2,055	2,933	4,087	3,567	4,890
1961	1,922	10,804	10,634	10,363	13,990	14,175	3,257	2,739	3,557	4,764	4,663	5,943
1962	2,799	11,918	11,644	11,328	15,770	15,765	3,353	3,438	3,845	5,448	5,775	6,410
1963	3,066	12,104	12,354	11,985	17,028	16,667	3,713	3,902	3,999	6,313	6,517	6,658
1964		12,747	12,907				4,212	3,741		7,180	6,281	

trade) and (2) controlled exogenous variables (such as tax rates and the net inflow of foreign public investment) on the set of endogenous variables, including such ones as gross domestic income, consumption, and other potential target variables. The major limitations and weaknesses of this type of model will be brought out and suggestions made about the kinds of changes needed to convert it to a development planning model which could be used to formulate a medium term (five-year) plan.

Model A

The endogenous variables appearing in Model A are: gross domestic income (X), disposable income (X^D), total gross investment (I), indirect

Model A

1. Estimated Model

   a. Stochastic (Behavioral) Equations $\qquad$ R^2 $\quad$ F $\quad$ $D.W.$

   $C^p = 5195 + 0.6275X^D$ $\qquad$ .97 $\quad$ 417 $\quad$ 1.009
   $\qquad$ (1463) $\quad$ (.0307)

   $C^g = -448 + 0.704T$ $\qquad$ .97 $\quad$ 527 $\quad$ 1.25
   $\qquad$ (209) $\quad$ (.030)

   $I^p = 2361 + 0.6044E_{-1} + 0.968Z_{-1}$ $\qquad$ .81 $\quad$ 24 $\quad$ 2.32
   $\qquad$ (1301) $\quad$ (.0967) $\qquad$ (.374)

   $M = -3078 + 0.1816(C^p + C^g) + 0.6898I$ $\quad$ .96 $\quad$ 186 $\quad$ .84
   $\qquad$ (841) $\quad$ (.034) $\qquad\qquad$ (.097)

   $T = -5170 + 0.235X$ $\qquad$ .98 $\quad$ 1,108 $\quad$ 2.10
   $\qquad$ (355) $\quad$ (.007)

   b. Identities

   $X = C^p + C^g + I^p + I^g + E + Z - M$
   $X^d = X - T^d$
   $I = I^p + I^g$
   $T^i = T - T^d$

2. Reduced Form Matrix

	$E + Z$	I^g	E_{-1}	Z_{-1}	T	Constant
X	2.853	.885	.535	.857	-1.465	13,446
C^p	1.7903	.555	.335	.537	-1.567	13,632
C^g	.4742	.1471	.0889	.142	$-.243$	$-1,859$
I^p	0	0	.604	.968	0	2,362
M	.411	.817	.494	.791	$-.325$	689
T	.672	.208	.126	.202	$-.345$	$-2,001$

taxes (T^i), private consumption (C^p), public consumption (C^g), private investment (I^p), imports (M), and total tax receipts (T). The model consists of four identities, defining X, X^D, I, and T^i respectively, and five behavioral relationships defining the remaining endogenous variables.

It should be noted that Gross Domestic Income (X) was used in all the models instead of Gross National Product or Gross National Income. The main reason for the adoption of GDI hinges on the relative importance of the terms-of-trade effects (Z), which permits the study of a potentially important factor in the growth of the Peruvian economy.[9]

In the behavioral equations, private consumption (C^p) is expressed as a function of disposable income (X^D), government consumption (C^g) as a function of total tax receipts (T), and total taxes as a function of Gross Domestic Product (X). As could be expected, the coefficients appearing in these three functions are highly significant. In addition, the total value of imports (M) is regressed on total consumption and total investment (I). It is interesting to note that the marginal propensity to import investment goods is considerably higher than that to import consumption goods, the corresponding parameters being respectively .69 and .18. The high magnitude of the former coefficient is, of course, explained by the almost total absence of a domestic capital-goods-producing sector.[10]

A fairly good fit was obtained by regressing private investment (I^p) on exports lagged one year and on the terms-of-trade effects lagged one year. A number of alternative forms were tried without success for the private investment function, the major limitations being the lack of a sectoral breakdown for investment and the fairly arbitrary way in which depreciation was derived to obtain net investment.

Model A does not include an aggregate production function. This is, of course, a major limitation of this and the other models. A number of

[9] The difference between Gross National Income and Gross Domestic Income consists of the net transfers abroad on account of services which are subtracted from the latter to obtain the former. Since these net transfers were relatively small—fluctuating between a fraction of 1 per cent and 2 per cent of X over the period under consideration —it makes very little difference whether GNI or GDI is selected. The identities relating these concepts are: GDI = GNP + Z + Net Transfers and GNI = GDI − Net Transfers.

[10] An element of "forced correlation" is introduced by regressing M on I since the latter was estimated indirectly on the basis of the imports of capital goods in the preparation of the national income accounts. This illustrates one of the problems, and possible pitfalls, which a model builder faces in a developing country. He ought to be well-acquainted with the procedures used to derive and generate national income data, so as to be able to recognize those apparently—and necessarily—highly significant quantitative relationships or regressions which describe the (synthetic) methods used to generate national income statistics rather than describing the underlying economic reality. It is, of course, true that in an ideal case the latter two situations should overlap completely.

attempts were made at deriving significant relationships between investment and its components, on the one hand, and output, on the other, without any success. Likewise, no significant relationship could be derived between X and the stock of capital (K). However, as expected, X was highly and significantly correlated with exports and the terms of trade.[11]

There appears to be strong evidence that private investment, particularly in the mining and fish meal industries (which together accounted for 61 per cent of the total value of exports in 1964), lagged behind world demand for these products. The tremendous growth of the fish meal industry which catapulted Peru to become the leading fish-exporting country in the world is a case in point. Fish meal exports grew from around $1 million in 1955 to $109 million in 1964 (at 1960 prices).

The implication of the private investment function selected here is obvious: I^p is determined completely exogenously through the changes occurring in the export sector. This appears to be a reasonable hypothesis in the case of Peru, given (1) the relative importance of the export sector (the ratio of $E + Z$ to X having increased from about 20 to over 27 per cent from 1950 to 1964); (2) the very highly capital-intensive nature of the export sector; and (3) the virtual absence of a domestic capital-goods-producing sector.

One of the difficulties in the establishment of a significant relation between investment and output is the highly erratic behavior of both private and public investment over the period under consideration. The wide fluctuations in private investment can be explained partially by the discrete nature of certain types of investment such as in mining, where the investment over time, instead of being continuous, shows substantial jumps and by the different gestation periods for investment between industries. However, the absence of sectoral investment and capital stock figures precluded the estimation of sectoral production functions.[12]

Model A approximates fairly well the movements in X over the sample period, as Table 1 indicates, but does not perform very well in terms of the other endogenous variables. Since the sample size is relatively small, any sudden annual changes in one or two observations affect negatively the

[11] The following regressions were obtained:

$$X = 23223 + 2.68E_{-1} - 1.04(I_{-1} - M^c_{-1}) \qquad R^2 = .96$$
$$X = 21334 + 2.80E_{-1} - .52I \qquad R^2 = .97 \, .$$

Using longer lags with respect to I failed to change the negative sign attached to the I parameter.

[12] The output-capital ratio measured as the increments to Gross Domestic Product over Gross Investment increased substantially from .17 between 1951 and 1956 to .25 between 1957 and 1962. This development and the extremely volatile nature of the annual incremental output-capital ratio are discussed in [6].

predictive performance of the model. This can be seen, for example, by comparing the computed value of GDI ($\hat{X}$) to the observed value of X in 1959. In that year, X was considerably underestimated because of the sudden change in public investment between 1958 and 1959 and in the terms of trade between the 1957 and 1958 (Z_{-1}).

As an illustration, this model was used to check the internal consistency of the projections made by the INP. The export tax and public investment projections made by the INP for 1970 were plugged into the reduced form to obtain the resulting set of endogenous variables. The export projections were based on a very detailed study of exports yielding an over-all growth rate of about 7 per cent annually between 1964 and 1970. The values resulting from the INP studies were plugged into the reduced form: $\bar{E}_{70} = 26,591$ and $\bar{Z}_{70} = 2,659$. The INP made so-called "policy projections" (*proyección con intencionalidad*) such that $\bar{I}^q_{70} = 7,979$ and $\bar{T}^d_{70} = 6,472$ (see [3]). Solving the reduced form, one obtains the following values for the endogenous variables: $\hat{\bar{X}}_{70} = 110,159$; $\hat{\bar{M}}_{70} = 31,375$; and $\hat{\bar{T}}_{70} = 20,743$.[13]

The computed value of GDI for 1970 ($\hat{X}$) implies a growth rate of slightly less than 7 per cent per annum between 1964 and 1970. The computed values of the set of endogenous variables for 1970 show that, on the assumption that the underlying structure given by the model remains the same, a balance-of-payments deficit would result from the given set of exogenous variables (i.e., $\hat{\bar{M}}_{70} = 31,375$ and $\bar{E}_{70} + \bar{Z}_{70} = 29,250$) and that the projected tax receipts made by the INP appear optimistic.

Assuming that the model holds over the planning period, corrections could be made or introduced in the set of instruments (T^d and I^q) and through a set of converging iterations a set of consistent projections obtained.[14]

Some of the limitations of Model A, such as the lack of a production function and the extent to which it can be used for planning purposes, are discussed under Model C.

Model B

Model B is an extension of Model A. It contains the same equations for public consumption, private consumption, and private investment, but

[13] Symbols with a bar indicate projections determined exogenously (from INP sources), and symbols with a bar and a circumflex denote computed values of endogenous variables after substituting the projected values of the exogenous variables (policy instruments and other data) in the reduced form.

[14] Given the relatively poor predictive validity of this model over the sample period, the above exercises should only be taken to illustrate the possible use of such a model.

Model B

1. Estimated Model
   a. Stochastic (Behavioral) Equations

		R^2	F	$D.W.$
$C^p = 5195 + 0.627X^D$		.97	417	1.009
$(1463)\ \ (0.030)$				
$C^g = -448 + 0.704T$		.97	527	1.25
$(209)\ \ \ (.030)$				
$I^p = 2361 + 0.604E_{-1} + 0.968Z_{-1}$		.81	24	2.32
$(1301)\ \ (0.096)\ \ \ \ \ (0.374)$				
$M^c = 3347 + 0.040C - 23.743U$		.81	24	1.15
$(2597)\ \ (0.026)\ \ \ \ (15.505)$				
$M^i = 0.443I^p + 0.389I^g$		.99	737	1.11
$(0.050)\ \ \ \ (0.205)$				
$M^{rmfs} = -1480 + 0.120X$		.93	185	.64
$(443)\ \ (0.008)$				
$T^d = -2020 + 0.089X$		.97	571	1.97
$(187)\ \ (0.003)$				
$T^i = -4192 + 0.209C^p_* + 0.626M^c$		.97	215	1.44
$(489)\ \ (0.026)\ \ \ \ (0.211)$				

   b. Identities
   $$X = C^p + C^g + I^p + I^g + E + Z - M$$
   $$X^D = X - T^d$$
   $$C = C^p + C^g$$
   $$I = I^p + I^g$$
   $$T = T^i + T^d$$
   $$C^p_* = C^p - M^c$$

2. Reduced Form Matrix

	E_{-1}	Z_{-1}	$(E+Z)$	I^g	U	Constant
C^p	.4554	.7294	1.3528	.8265	22.9095	10,464
C^g	.1243	.1991	.3694	.2257	−.8012	−1,754
M^i	.2677	.4288	0	.389	0	1,045
M^c	.0233	.0374	.0693	.0423	−22.8522	3,698
M^{rmfs}	.0959	.1535	.2848	.1740	4.8319	−608
I^p	.6044	.9680	0	0	0	2,361
T^d	.0714	.1144	.2121	.1296	3.5998	−1,393
T^i	.105	.168	.311	.190	−4.741	−402
X	.7973	1.2768	2.3680	1.4468	40.1657	7,006

breaks down imports into three categories: imports of consumption goods (M^c), investment goods (M^i), raw materials, fuels, and services (M^{rmfs}), and total taxes into direct (T^d) and indirect taxes (T^i). M^c is given as a function of total consumption and the ratio of the price index of M^c to the domestic price index of consumer goods (U). M^i is regressed on public investment (I^g), I^p, and M^{rmfs}, and direct taxes are regressed on X. Finally, indirect taxes are regressed on private consumption minus imports of consumption goods (C_*^p) and on M^c independently.

If the same values of the predetermined variables as in Model A are plugged into the reduced form, values of $\hat{X} = 114,442$ and of $\hat{M} = 32,556$ (the sum of the three types of imports) result. Here again the inference is that the above high value of $\hat{X}$ is not feasible since it would violate balance-of-payments equilibrium, the sum of imports ($M^r + M^c + M^{rmfs}$) exceeding $E + Z$ by about 3 billion soles.

Model C, which follows, is better than the two previous ones because of the larger number of potential instruments incorporated in it and because of its better predictive performance over the sample period (see Table 1).[15]

Model C

The model includes the following variables, which are listed below in terms of both endogenous and exogenous variables. The exogenous variables are further subdivided into potential policy instruments and other data.

1. Endogenous variables:
$$X, C^p, I^p, M, T^d, T^i, X^p, X^g, X^D, C, I^g, I \, .$$

2. Exogenous variables:
   a. potential instruments: $t_0^i, t_0^d, s^g, F, R \, .$
   b. other data: $\dfrac{\Delta M_{-1}^{rmf}}{\Delta K_{-1}}, E_{-1}, Z_{-1}, E, Z \, .$

Five behavioral relationships appear in the model: two tax functions and one function each to explain imports, consumption, and private investment. Both direct and indirect taxes are given as a function of GDI; imports are expressed as a function of C and I (as in Model A), and private consumption is regressed on Disposable Income. The equation describing private investment contains exports and the terms-of-trade effect, both lagged one year, and a variable which reflects capacity considerations. This

---

[15] It should be noted that the parameters of the regression for M^c estimated by the two-stage least-squares in Model B, as well as their statistical significance, were substantially different than when estimated by the ordinary least squares (see Appendix C).

last variable is the ratio of the annual change in imports of raw materials and fuels to the annual change in the stock of capital (net investment), both lagged one year $\left(\text{i.e.,} \dfrac{\Delta M_{-1}^{rmf}}{\Delta K_{-1}} = \dfrac{M_{-1}^{rmf} - M_{-2}^{rmf}}{K_{-1} - K_{-2}}\right)$. The economic rationale underlying the use of this last variable is that a high value of this ratio will tend to indicate excess capacity, whereas a low value would normally imply a high level of capacity utilization. A number of other proxy variables for capacity were tried without success, such as introducing as explanatory variable for I^p the above ratio in elasticity form, the stock of capital, and so forth.

Model C

1. Structural Model

   a. Stochastic Equations

$$C^p = c_0^p + c^p X^D$$

$$I^p = i_0^p + i_1^p \frac{\Delta M_{-1}^{rmf}}{\Delta K_{-1}} + i_2^p E_{-1} + i_3^p Z_{-1}$$

$$M = m_0 + m^c C + m^i I$$

$$T^d = t_0^d + t^d X$$

$$T^i = t_0^i + t^i X$$

   b. Identities

$$X = C^p + I^p + X^g + E + Z - M$$

$$X^p = C^p + I^p + E + Z - M$$

$$X^g = T^i + T^d + F + R \qquad (R = D + H - Tr - S)$$

$$X^D = X - T^d$$

$$C = C^p + X^g - I^g$$

$$I^g(=S^g) = s^g X^g + (1 - s^g) F$$

$$I = I^p + I^g$$

2. Estimated Model

   a. Stochastic Equations

		R^2	F	$D.W.$
(1)	$C^p = 5195 + 0.627 X^D$	.97	417	1.009
	$\quad\;\;(1463)\quad(.030)$			
(2)	$I^p = 2585 + 40.6503 \dfrac{\Delta M_{-1}^{rmf}}{\Delta K_{-1}}$			
	$\quad\;\;(1402)\quad(31.275)$			
	$\qquad\qquad\quad + .5673 E_{-1} + .8433 Z_{-1}$	.82	14	2.64
	$\qquad\qquad\quad\;\;(.1065)\qquad(.3937)$			

(3) $M = -3078 + 0.181C + 0.689I$ .96   186   .84
        (841)   (.034)   (.097)

(4) $T^d = -2020 + 0.089X$ .97   571   1.97
        (187)   (.003)

(5) $T^i = -3150 + 0.136X$ .98   594   1.85
        (301)   (.006)

b. Identities

(6) $X = C^p + I^p + X^g + E + Z - M$
(7) $X^p = C^p + I^p + E + Z - M$
(8) $X^g = T^i + T^d + F + R$ $(R = D + H - Tr - S)$
(9) $X^D = X - T^d$
(10) $C = C^p + X^g - I^g$
(11) $I^g(= S^g) = s^g X^g + (1 - s^g)F$
(12) $I = I^p + I^g$

3. Reduced Form Matrix for 1962 ($s^g_{62} = .259$)

	Constant	F	R	$\dfrac{\Delta M^{rmf}_{-1}}{\Delta K_{-1}}$	E_{-1}	Z_{-1}	$E + Z$
X	15,166	.8386	1.8580	34.087	.4758	.7072	2.7034
X^D	16,261	.7631	1.6912	31.027	.4330	.6436	2.4609
I	2,170	1.0510	.3518	42.731	.5962	.8862	.1649
C	13,942	.6255	2.1270	29.591	.3549	.5277	2.0170
M	947	.8379	.6403	34.072	.4751	.7065	.4785
X^P	16,756	−.3592	.3975	26.045	.2852	.5403	2.0656
C^P	15,121	.4787	1.0613	19.470	.2716	.4038	1.5442
T^d	−647	.0751	.1665	3.057	.0424	.0632	.2424
T^i	−936	.1224	.2716	4.982	.0694	.1032	.3952
I^g	−412	1.0510	.3518	2.081	.0289	.0429	.1649
I^P	2,585	0	0	40.650	.5673	.8433	0

An examination of the identities appearing in Model C reveals that the public sector has been explicitly incorporated. Gross Domestic Income is broken down into a private part (X^p) and a public part (X^g)[16] Public income is defined first from the revenue side and second from the expenditure side. Public income on the revenue side, given the accounting breakdown prevailing in Peru, consists of indirect taxes, direct taxes, net public foreign

---

[16] Implicit in the second identity (see equation 7 of Model C) is the assumption that the foreign-trade sector is entirely in the hands of the private sector.

4. Reduced Form Matrix Expressed in Terms of s^a[17]

	Constant	F	R
X	$\dfrac{4{,}938 + 2{,}593s^a}{A}$	$\dfrac{.3102}{A}$	$\dfrac{.8190 - .5088s^a}{A}$
X^D	$2{,}020 + \left[\dfrac{4{,}504 + 2{,}360s^a}{A}\right]$	$\dfrac{.2823}{A}$	$\dfrac{.7455 - .4631s^a}{A}$
I	$2{,}585 - 5{,}170s^a + \left[\dfrac{611(s^a)^2 + 1{,}164s^a}{A}\right]$	$1 + \left[\dfrac{.0731s^a}{A}\right]$	$s^a + s^a\left[\dfrac{.1932 - .1200s^a}{A}\right]$
C	$1{,}292 + 5{,}170s^a + \left[\dfrac{3{,}985 + 928s^a - 611(s^a)^2}{A}\right]$	$\dfrac{.2503 - .0731s^a}{A}$	$1 - s^a + \left[\dfrac{.6610 - .6038s^a + .1200(s^a)^2}{A}\right]$
M	$-1{,}061 - 2{,}593s^a + \left[\dfrac{720 + 971s^a + 311(s^a)^2}{A}\right]$	$.6898 + \left[\dfrac{.0452 + .0372s^a}{A}\right]$	$.181 + .5088s^a + \left[\dfrac{.1194 + .0241s^a - .0611(s^a)^2}{A}\right]$
X^P	$10{,}108 + 2{,}593s^a + \left[\dfrac{2{,}100 + 509s^a - 311(s^a)^2}{A}\right]$	$-.6898 + \left[\dfrac{.1319 - .0372s^a}{A}\right]$	$-\left[.181 + .5088s^a\right] + \left[\dfrac{.3483 - .3146s^a + .0611(s^a)^2}{A}\right]$
C^P	$6{,}462 + \left[\dfrac{2{,}820 + 1{,}481s^a}{A}\right]$	$\dfrac{.1771}{A}$	$\dfrac{.4678 - .2906s^a}{A}$
T^d	$-2{,}020 + \left[\dfrac{448 + 232s^a}{A}\right]$	$\dfrac{.0278}{A}$	$\dfrac{.0734 - .0456s^a}{A}$
T^i	$-3{,}150 + \left[\dfrac{721 + 379s^a}{A}\right]$	$\dfrac{.0453}{A}$	$\dfrac{.1197 - .0743s^a}{A}$
I^v	$-5{,}170s^a + \left[\dfrac{1{,}164s^a + 611(s^a)}{A}\right]$	$1 + \dfrac{.0731s^a}{A}$	$s^a + s^a\left[\dfrac{.1932 - .1200s^a}{A}\right]$
I^P	$2{,}585$	0	0

[17] $A = .3388 + .1201s^a$

$\dfrac{\Delta M^{rmf}_{-1}}{\Delta K_{-1}}$	E_{-1}	Z_{-1}	$E+Z$
$\dfrac{12.609}{A}$	$\dfrac{.1760}{A}$	$\dfrac{.2616}{A}$	$\dfrac{1}{A}$
$\dfrac{11.477}{A}$	$\dfrac{.1602}{A}$	$\dfrac{.2381}{A}$	$\dfrac{.9103}{A}$
$40.6503 + \left[\dfrac{2.974s^a}{A}\right]$	$.5673 + \left[\dfrac{.0415s^a}{A}\right]$	$.8433 + \left[\dfrac{.0617s^a}{A}\right]$	$\dfrac{.2359s^a}{A}$
$\dfrac{10.176 - 2.974s^a}{A}$	$\dfrac{.1420 - .0415s^a}{A}$	$\dfrac{.2111 - .0617s^a}{A}$	$\dfrac{.8071 - .2359s^a}{A}$
$28.0403 + \left[\dfrac{1.839 + 1.514s^a}{A}\right]$	$.3913 + \left[\dfrac{.0256 + .0211s^a}{A}\right]$	$.5817 + \left[\dfrac{.0381 + .0314s^a}{A}\right]$	$\dfrac{.1459 + .1201s^a}{A}$
$12.6098 + \left[\dfrac{5.362 - 1.514s^a}{A}\right]$	$.1706 + \left[\dfrac{.0478 - .0211s^a}{A}\right]$	$.2616 + \left[\dfrac{.1112 - .0314s^a}{A}\right]$	$\dfrac{.4253 - .1201s^a}{A} +$
$\dfrac{7.202}{A}$	$\dfrac{.1005}{A}$	$\dfrac{.1494}{A}$	$\dfrac{.5712}{A}$
$\dfrac{1.131}{A}$	$\dfrac{.0157}{A}$	$\dfrac{.0234}{A}$	$\dfrac{.0897}{A}$
$\dfrac{1.843}{A}$	$\dfrac{.0257}{A}$	$\dfrac{.0382}{A}$	$\dfrac{.1462}{A}$
$\dfrac{2.974s^a}{A}$	$\dfrac{.0415s^a}{A}$	$\dfrac{.0617s^a}{A}$	$\dfrac{.2359s^a}{A}$
40.6503	$.5673$	433	0

investment (F), and a composite term (R) to be defined below.[18] Public expenditures are broken down into public investment (I^g) and public consumption, which appears as an implicit variable in the model, as can be seen from the tenth equation, $X^g = I^g + C - C^p$.

The significance of the eleventh relationship is that there are two sources of public investment: a foreign source which is given by F and a domestic source which can be expressed as the proportion of public income from domestic sources, $s^g(X^g - F)$. In symbols, $I^g = s^g(X^g - F) + F$, equivalent to the eleventh equation in model C, s^g is a parameter which can be controlled by the government within certain limits. Since s^g is equal to $\dfrac{I^g - F}{X^g - F}$, it follows that, from the standpoint of the policymaker, s^g and F are to some extent substitutable instruments. Indeed, if a relatively high amount of net public foreign capital can be attracted from abroad in any one year the proportion of domestic public resources to be devoted to public investment can be reduced.[19] Therefore, the above identity can be considered a policy relationship in the *ex ante* sense.

The strong balance-of-payments position of Peru means that its public foreign indebtedness capacity is considerable. The results of a study of Peru's servicing capacity indicated that the balance of payments and the government budget could support a substantial increase in the new inflow of foreign public loans. Consequently, the INP recommended that the government embark on a "big push" policy with respect to public investment. The underlying idea was to concentrate public investment over a three-to-four-year period starting in 1965 and investing as much as was consistent with the foreign indebtedness capacity, projected government revenues, and capital absorption capacity which is essentially a function of the stock of implementable projects (see [3] and [6] and Table 2, showing the intended values of F).

---

[18] F is equal to $E_x - A_x - i_x$ where E_x is the new inflow of foreign public investment; A_x and i_x are respectively the amortization and the interest payment on the foreign public debt. $R = D + H - Tr - S$, where D stands for net domestic public borrowing ($D = E_i - A_i - i_i$, where E_i represents the new public domestic borrowing and A_i and i_i the amortization and interest payment on the domestic public debt, respectively). H represents the net revenues of public enterprises; Tr are the transfers, and S consists of the government surplus (the excess of total public revenues minus total public expenditures). In most years Peru operated close to a balanced budget so that S was not a significant term.

[19] The series for F and s^g are given in Table 3, Columns 27 and 32. F was negative in 9 of the 14 years in the sample period, indicating that in these years amortization and interest payments on the foreign debt exceeded the new public loans from abroad. No apparent correlation can be seen between F and s^g in the two above time series, which reflects to a large extent the erratic nature of public investment as shown by Column 11.

Table 2. Values of Exogenous Variables Used for Projections (based on INP projections [3] and assumptions made in text)
(in millions of soles at 1960 prices)

Year	$\bar{E}$	$\bar{Z}$	$\bar{C}^o$	$\bar{I}^o$	$\bar{X}^o$	$\bar{F}$	$\bar{T}$	$\bar{R}$	$\hat{\bar{X}}$	$\bar{s}_o$
1964	17,692	2,497	8,955	4,788	13,024	1,701	13,669	−3,818	72,728	.237
1965	19,044	2,457	9,403	6,336	16,239	2,200	15,381	−1,342	83,028	.330
1966	20,298	2,618	9,873	7,840	17,713	3,358	16,458	−2,103	87,332	.312
1967	21,687	2,386	10,367	8,033	18,400	2,806	17,610	−2,016	90,516	.335
1968	23,240	2,324	10,885	7,218	18,103	707	18,843	−1,447	93,611	.374
1969	24,848	2,485	11,429	7,362	18,791	−174	20,162	−1,197	98,301	.397
1970	26,591	2,659	12,000	7,979	19,979	−495	21,573	−1,099	103,798	.414

Before examining the reduced form of the model, we should stress that since no explicit production function relating investment to output appears in this model, it follows that the model is demand- (mainly foreign demand-) oriented. Thus, it can only be used for short-term planning and projecting purposes on the assumption that changes in investment (particularly public investment) do not immediately affect the output-capital ratio. Private investment responds to changes in exports and appears only partially interested in the domestic market possibilities.

The reduced form of Model C ought to be explained.[20] In both reduced form matrices 3 and 4 the endogenous variables are given in the first column and the exogenous (predetermined) variables are given in the first (top) row. The coefficients (multipliers) appearing in Matrix 3 refer to 1962. Indeed, since s^g is a policy parameter which varies from year to year, the quantitative reduced form can only be given once s^g is specified. Reduced form Matrix 4 shows the impact multipliers of the set of exogenous variables on the set of endogenous variables, leaving s^g unspecified. Matrix 4 can, thus, be used to compute the impact of different values of s^g, *ceteris paribus*, on the endogenous variables, and, more specifically, on the policy targets contained in the latter set.[21]

Given the specification of the model, it follows that the higher s^g, *ceteribus paribus*, the lower X. In other words: $\dfrac{dX}{ds^g} < 0$. The explanation for this phenomenon lies in the much higher magnitude of the marginal propensity to import investment goods compared to the marginal propensity to import consumption goods (i.e., $m^i = .69$ and $m^c = .18$). Thus, a decision on the part of the policymaker to allocate a higher proportion of his domestic income to public investment results in a higher flow of imports of capital goods on government account which would tend to depress X.[22] An idea of the sensitivity of X to small changes in s^g can be obtained by varying the latter ratio in a given year, assuming everything else to be constant. The computed value for X in 1962, for $s^g = .259$, was 65,389 million soles. For a slightly higher magnitude of s^g ($= .285$), gross domestic income in 1962 comes out to 65,077 million soles.

As a test of the consistency and the feasibility of the macroeconomic projections made by the INP from 1965 to 1970, the values of the instru-

---

[20] This section benefited from comments made by A. Goldberger.

[21] It is clear that Matrix 3 can be obtained from Matrix 4 by substituting the value of s^g in 1962 in the latter and computing the resulting coefficients ($s^g_{62} = .259$).

[22] Incidentally, as was pointed out above, the identities defining private and public GDI imply that the totality of the foreign trade is in the hands of the private sector. Thus, conceptually, the public sector purchases its imports through the private sector.

ment variables and the other exogenous variables presumed by the INP were substituted into the reduced form to obtain the resulting projected Gross Domestic Income ($\hat{X}$) (See Table 2). Projections for $\bar{Z}$ and $\bar{C}^g$ were made by the authors and appear consistent with the INP projections.[23] Computing the set of endogenous variables for the period 1965–70, we realized that the expectations of the INP for the earlier years (1965–66) would violate balance-of-payments equilibrium, $\hat{M}_{65} = 22,942$, whereas $\bar{E}_{65} + \bar{Z}_{65} = 20,189$. The sudden increase in public investment between 1964 and 1965 and in anticipated tax revenues would lead to a pressure which the balance of payments could not stand. As we get closer to 1970 the balance-of-payments gap disappears to be replaced by a "tax gap," $\hat{T}_{70} = 19,316$ whereas $\bar{T} = 21,573$ for 1970. The tax gap could conceivably be corrected through improvements in tax collection as opposed to tax rates.

It appears that one way in which better tax collection with an unchanged tax structure could be introduced into this model would be through a change in the two tax functions intercepts, t_0^i and t_0^d. For instance, if it could be estimated that the total direct tax receipts in any one year could be increased by 2 billion soles, t_0^d would equal -20 as opposed to $-2,020$. In this sense, the effectiveness of better tax enforcement and collection could be measured as the ratio of $\dfrac{dX}{dt_0^d}$. The effect of a change in t_0^d or t_0^i on the set of endogenous variables would appear to be relatively large, as can be seen by calculating the above derivative.

In any case, with the help of the reduced form expressed in algebraic terms the impact of an autonomous tax shift can easily be calculated.

The very large computed increase in GDI ($\bar{X}$) in 1965 (see Table 2) seems to result from overly optimistic expectations by the planning bureau concerning public revenues and possible economies in transfer payments. Implicit in the INP's projections is the assumption of a 7 per cent growth rate for gross domestic product over the period 1964–70. The computed growth rate for X on the basis of the INP's projections and intentions contained in Table 2 results only in a cumulative annual growth rate of about 6 per cent.

In a sense, since Model C is not able to incorporate the effects of invest-

[23] The INP does not provide projections for public transfers and for government consumption as such. It was assumed here that government consumption would increase at an annual rate of 5 per cent, which is consistent with the rate of growth assumed by the INP for current public expenditures on "general services" and health, welfare, and education.

ment (mainly public investment in social overhead facilities) on output, the growth rate resulting from solving the reduced form of Model C can be considered as a lower limit. This would be true as long as the positive effects of public investment on the over-all productivity of capital were consistent with balance-of-payments equilibrium.

If such a model is to be used to make projections and derive desirable values for the public instruments over medium and long-term periods, some allowance has to be made for the effects of public investment on the output-capital ratio. However, it would appear that this model can be applied for short-run purposes without major difficulties.

Two major conclusions can be drawn from the above study. First, macroeconomic models of the type developed here can be used, within limits, to check the internal consistency of development plans and projections. Furthermore, the impact of changes in broad policy instruments— such as tax rates and the ratio of domestic public revenues to be allocated to public investment (s^g)—can be computed on policy targets such as gross

APPENDIX A

Table 3. Macroeconomic Data, 1950–64
(based on INP sources, in millions of soles at 1960 prices)

	1	2	3	4	5	6	7	8
Year	X	X^p	X^g	X^D	C	C^p	C^g	C^p_*
1950	36,004	32,688	3,316	34,691	29,334	26,930	2,384	25,463
1951	39,604	35,248	4,356	38,002	31,132	28,651	2,481	26,621
1952	40,046	35,192	4,854	38,386	30,677	28,084	2,593	26,086
1953	42,201	37,077	5,124	40,567	32,366	29,668	2,698	27,771
1954	44,158	39,223	4,935	42,184	34,726	31,440	3,286	29,672
1955	45,651	39,365	6,286	43,568	35,927	32,803	3,125	30,603
1956	47,135	41,125	6,010	45,009	36,693	33,524	3,168	31,046
1957	48,941	42,193	6,748	46,686	39,068	35,175	3,894	32,282
1958	47,638	41,791	5,847	45,557	39,363	35,435	3,928	32,897
1959	49,007	43,533	5,474	46,758	41,051	36,593	4,458	34,642
1960	55,650	49,172	6,478	52,393	42,691	37,308	5,383	35,000
1961	60,444	52,691	7,753	57,091	46,319	40,318	6,001	37,421
1962	65,008	55,888	9,120	61,295	49,436	43,057	6,379	39,837
1963	68,492	57,696	10,796	64,280	53,289	45,681	7,608	41,892
1964	73,767	60,743	13,024		54,991	46,036	8,955	

domestic income and the balance of payments. Such aggregative models can be helpful in the first stage of the derivation of an optimum economic policy. Further stages would be necessary to disaggregate along sectoral, regional, and policy lines.

Second, the models presented here described relatively well the growth of the Peruvian economy over the sample period (1950–64). The tremendous importance of the export sector as the leading sector in the Peruvian economy was abundantly illustrated by these models. It was shown that the high dependence of the economy on the export sector is both an inducement and an obstacle to the development of Peru. It provides a dynamic element which has permitted a high aggregate growth rate, at least since 1959. On the other hand, the highly capital-intensive nature of most export products and the limited backward linkages have impeded a highly necessary improvement in the income distribution and a rise in the level of employment.

9	10	11	12	13	14	15 $\frac{\Delta M_{-1}^{rmf}}{\Delta K_{-1}}$	16
I	I^p	I^g	K	$I^n = \Delta K$	D^K		M
6,596	5,664	932	109,496	2,153	4,380		6,968
8,967	7,092	1,875	111,649	3,847	4,556		8,719
10,373	8,112	2,261	115,496	4,926	4,780	.167	9,052
11,424	8,998	2,426	120,423	5,680	5,035	.044	9,991
9,289	7,640	1,649	126,103	3,947	5,199	.036	9,062
10,422	7,261	3,161	130,051	4,513	5,400	.017	10,350
12,568	9,726	2,842	134,564	6,710	5,676	.107	13,096
13,482	10,628	2,854	141,275	6,801	5,975	.088	14,535
10,754	8,835	1,919	148,076	4,026	6,160	.041	12,180
7,634	6,618	1,016	152,103	1,953	6,216	−.080	10,202
10,700	9,605	1,095	154,056	3,919	6,389	.034	11,427
12,555	10,804	1,752	157,976	6,842	6,467	.288	13,990
14,659	11,918	2,741	164,819	8,480	6,607	.131	15,770
15,292	12,104	3,188	173,299	9,310	6,749	.044	17,028
16,816	12,747	4,069	182,609	10,792	6,690		18,229

Table 3. continued

	17	18	19	20	21	22	23
	M^c	M^i	M^{rmfa}	M^{rmf}	E	Z	U
1950	1,467	2,650	2,891	1,696	5,447	1,595	112
1951	2,030	3,800	2,869	2,057	5,315	2,910	114
1952	1,998	4,083	2,971	2,230	6,507	1,540	117
1953	1,897	4,738	3,356	2,412	7,211	1,191	119
1954	1,768	3,498	3,796	2,512	7,754	1,451	124
1955	2,200	3,878	4,272	2,936	8,161	1,490	112
1956	2,478	5,899	4,719	3,334	9,011	1,959	108
1957	2,893	6,690	4,952	3,613	9,147	1,779	101
1958	2,538	5,277	4,365	3,067	9,655	47	110
1959	1,951	3,708	4,543	3,206	11,015	−493	109
1960	2,308	4,091	5,028	3,769	13,686	0	100
1961	2,897	5,513	5,580	4,283	15,898	−338	91
1962	3,220	6,395	6,155	4,589	16,936	−252	85
1963	3,789	6,471	6,768	4,661	16,097	842	85
1964					17,692	2,497	

APPENDIX B

List of Symbols and Variables

All variables are expressed in millions of soles at 1960 prices unless indicated otherwise.

X = gross domestic income.
X^p = private gross domestic income.
X^g = government gross domestic income.
X^D = disposable gross domestic income.
Z = terms-of-trade effect.
C = total consumption.
C^p = private consumption.
C^g = public consumption.
C^p_* = total private consumption minus imports of consumption goods ($C^p_* = C^p - M^c$).
I = total gross investment.
I^p = private gross investment.
I^g = public gross investment.
K = stock of capital.
$I^n = \Delta K$ = net investment.
D^K = depreciation.
M = total imports of goods and services.

24	25	26	27	28	29	30	31	32
T	T^i	T^d	F	E_x	A_x	i_x	R	s^g
3,547	2,234	1,313	−201	252	376	77	−30	.322
4,325	2,723	1,602	−188	108	213	83	219	.454
4,483	2,823	1,660	−127	162	201	88	498	.479
4,415	2,779	1,634	108	340	141	91	603	.462
5,330	3,356	1,974	−20	218	131	107	−375	.337
5,496	3,413	2,083	1,026	1,552	370	106	236	.406
5,366	3,440	2,126	−69	645	604	110	513	.479
6,593	4,338	2,255	183	951	655	113	−28	.407
5,998	3,917	2,081	−95	648	631	112	−56	.339
6,336	4,087	2,249	−376	374	606	144	−486	.238
8,021	4,764	3,257	−436	479	739	176	−1,107	.221
8,801	5,448	3,353	−239	1,048	1,103	184	−809	.249
10,028	6,313	3,713	511	1,869	1,185	173	−1,419	.259
11,392	7,180	4,212	1,708	2,890	991	191	−2,304	.163

M^c = imports of consumption goods.

M^i = imports of investment goods.

M^{rmf} = imports of raw materials, fuels, and other.

M^s = imports of services.

$M^{rmfs} = M^{rmf} + M^s$

E = total exports of goods and services.

T = total tax revenues.

T^d = direct taxes.

T^i = indirect taxes.

$\dfrac{\Delta M^{rmf}_{-1}}{\Delta K_{-1}}$ = capacity index. Ratio of annual change in imports of raw materials, fuels and services, lagged one year, to net investment, lagged one year (i.e. $= \dfrac{M^{rmf}_{-1} - M^{rmf}_{-2}}{K_{-1} - K_{-2}}$, see text).

U = ratio of the price index of M^c to the domestic price index of consumer goods.

Additional Public Sector Symbols

F = net inflow of foreign public investment ($F = E_x - A_x - i_x$).

E_x = net inflow of foreign public investment.

A_x = amortization of foreign public investment.

i_x = interest payment on foreign public investment.

R = net revenue (or expenditure) from nontax, nonforeign sources ($R = D + H - Tr - S$).

s^g = ratio of public income from domestic sources allocated to public investment $\left(s^g = \dfrac{I^g - F}{X^g - F}, \text{ see text} \right)$.

APPENDIX C

Least-Squares (L.S.) and Two-Stage Least-Squares (T.S.L.S.) Estimates of Parameters Appearing in Models

Model A

		R^2	F	$D.W.$
L.S.	$C^p = 5,195 + .627\,X^D$ (1,463) (.030)	.97	417	1.009
T.S.L.S.	$C^p = 5,554 + .620\,X^D$ (1,984) (.040)	.96	237	0.90
L.S.	$C^g = -448 + .704\,T$ (209) (.030)	.97	527	1.25
T.S.L.S.	$C^g = -572 + .720\,T$ (250) (.034)	.97	427	1.089
L.S. \ T.S.L.S.	$I^p = 2,361 + .6044\,E_{-1} + .968\,Z_{-1}$ (1,301) (.0967) (.374)	.81	24	2.32
L.S.	$M = -3,078 + .181\,(C^p + C^g) + .689\,I$ (841) (.034) (.097)	.96	186	.84
T.S.L.S.	$M = -3,397 + .173\,(C^p + C^g) + .745\,I$ (1,574) (.046) (.143)	.92	52	0.65
L.S.	$T = -5,170 + .235\,X$ (467) (.007)	.98	1108	2.10
T.S.L.S.	$T = -5,494 + .241\,X$ (433) (.008)	.98	836	2.46

Model B

		R^2	F	$D.W.$
L.S.	$C^p = 5,195 + 0.627\,X^D$ (1,463) (0.030)	.97	417	1.009
T.S.L.S.	$C^p = 5,260 + 0.626\,X^D$ (1,843) (0.037)	.96	271	0.84
L.S.	$C^g = -448 + 0.704\,T$ (209) (0.030)	.97	527	1.25

T.S.L.S.	$C^g = -590 + 0.722\,T$ $\quad\quad\;\;(262)\;\;(0.037)$	.97	373	1.25
L.S. T.S.L.S.	$I^p = 2{,}361 + 0.604\,E_{-1} + 0.968\,Z_{-1}$ $\quad\;\,(1{,}301)\;\;(0.096)\quad\;\;(0.374)$	.81	24	2.32
L.S.	$M^c = 3{,}347 + 0.040\,C - 23.743\,U$ $\quad\quad(2{,}597)\;(0.026)\quad(15.503)$	.81	24	1.15
T.S.L.S.	$M^c = 6{,}531 + .005\,C - 40.467\,U$ $\quad\quad(2{,}730)\;\;(.028)\quad\;(15.749)$	.84	27	1.14
L.S. T.S.L.S.	$M^i = 0.443\,I^p + 0.389\,I^g$ $\quad\quad\;\,(0.050)\quad\;(0.205)$	.99	737	1.11
L.S.	$M^{rmfs} = -1{,}480 + 0.120\,X$ $\quad\quad\quad\;(443)\quad(.008)$	.93	185	.64
T.S.L.S.	$M^{rmfs} = -1{,}251 + .090\,X$ $\quad\quad\quad\;(378)\;\;(.007)$	.93	148	.75
L.S.	$T^d = -2{,}020 + 0.089\,X$ $\quad\quad(187)\;\;(0.003)$	.97	571	1.97
T.S.L.S.	$T^d = -2{,}091 + 0.090\,X$ $\quad\quad(241)\;\;(0.004)$	.97	368	2.42
L.S.	$T^i = -4{,}192 + 0.209\,C_*^p + 0.626\,M^c$ $\quad\quad(489)\;\;(0.026)\quad\;\;(0.211)$	.97	215	1.44
T.S.L.S.	$T^i = -4{,}262 + 0.205\,C_*^p + 0.706\,M^c$ $\quad\quad(559)\;\;(.028)\quad\quad\;(.239)$	.96	160	2.49

Model C

L.S.	$C^p = 5{,}195 + 0.627\,X^D$ $\quad\;\;(1{,}463)\;\;(0.030)$	.97	417	1.009
T.S.L.S.	$C^p = 5{,}509 + 0.621\,X^D$ $\quad\;\;(1{,}910)\;\;(0.038)$	.96	257	0.96
L.S. T.S.L.S.	$I^p = 2{,}585 + 40.6503\,\dfrac{\Delta M_{-1}^{rmf}}{\Delta K_{-1}} + .5673E_{-1}$ $\quad\;\,(1{,}402)\;(31.275)\quad\quad\quad(.1075)$ $\quad\quad + .8433\,Z_{-1}$ $\quad\quad\quad\;(.3937)$	.82	14	2.64
L.S.	$M = -3{,}078 + 0.181\,C + 0.689\,I$ $\quad\quad(841)\;\;(0.034)\quad\;\;(0.097)$	.96	186	.84
T.S.L.S.	$M = -3{,}848 + 0.178\,C + 0.762\,I$ $\quad\;\;(1{,}554)\;(0.044)\quad\;\;(0.135)$	.93	57	0.80
L.S.	$T^d = -2{,}020 + 0.089\,X$ $\quad\quad(187)\;\;(0.003)$	.97	571	1.97
T.S.L.S.	$T^d = -2{,}174 + 0.092\,X$ $\quad\quad(233)\;\;(0.004)$	.97	421	2.20

L.S. $T^i = -3,150 + 0.146\,X$ .98   594   1.85
          (301)   (0.006)
T.S.L.S. $T^i = -3,321 + 0.149\,X$ .97   420   1.86
          (378)   (0.007)

References

1. Banco Central de Reserva del Peru. *Renta nacional del Peru* (annually).
2. Instituto Nacional de Planificación, Dirección de Macroeconomia. "Estadisticas preliminares para la programación del desarrollo económico y social." Unpublished paper, 1965.
3. Instituto Nacional de Planificación. *Programa de inversiones públicas 1964–65.* 2 volumes. Lima: Government Printing Office, 1964.
4. Instituto Nacional de Planificación, Dirección de Planificación del Sector Publico. *Cuadros del sector publico, series históricas.* Lima, 1964.
5. Johnston, J. *Econometric Methods.* New York: McGraw-Hill, 1963.
6. Thorbecke, Erik. "Peru: Determination of the Aggregate and Sectoral Growth Rates for Peru 1960–1970." (International Studies in Economics, Monograph No. 3, Iowa-Peru Program, Iowa State University, 1966.)

COMMENT

ARTHUR S. GOLDBERGER, UNIVERSITY OF WISCONSIN

The Peruvian economy has grown at the rate of 5½ per cent over the period 1950–64, which is somewhat over 2½ per cent per year per capita. This rather satisfactory aggregate performance is, according to Thorbecke and Condos, in good part attributable to the export sector. Peru, it would appear, has a diversified pattern of exports; they constitute about one-fifth of total output. Further, according to Thorbecke and Condos, exports are highly capital-intensive, and capital is highly import-intensive. This is the constellation of circumstances emphasized by the authors.

The models reported in their paper are developed in part to investigate various policy alternatives for raising the Peruvian growth rate. In particular, Model C is offered as a tool for such an investigation.

In view of the constellation just noted, one would expect that an evaluation of Peru's growth possibilities would focus on the issue of comparative advantage: is export expansion an attractive policy in view of the high import content of exports? The specification of Model C is not very conducive to studying this question. First, exports are taken as exogenous, which rules out of the model itself one aspect of the export expansion problem from the start. Second, the private investment demand equation does not do justice to the constellation emphasized in the text. While exports appear as a major determinant of investment, they appear only with a lag. This lag and the treatment of terms-of-trade gains as another major determinant suggest that exports induce investment not because of technological considerations, but rather simply because they are a source of investible earnings. Nor is the implementation of Model C very helpful. The import content of exports is reflected only indirectly—via the investment term in the import demand function. To compute the imports required to expand exports, therefore, requires a solution of the system, in which the investment content of exports interacts with the import content of investment. In view of the lag specified for exports in the investment equation, this interaction extends over time, so that an appropriate solution would involve iterating over several periods. But no such solution is offered by the authors; their reduced-form tables, which provide measures of impact effects only, are not very helpful for this problem. More generally, in a model with important lags, impact effects may be seriously misleading guides to policy.

As a guide to development policy, Model C suffers from another major deficiency. In the model, the only role played by investment expenditures is that of a component of final demand, and their capacity-creating function is simply absent. To be sure, the authors do call attention to this limitation. Still, it remains difficult to see how a model in which investment has no lasting effect can be useful as a tool for studying a government investment program. In this connection, it is disconcerting to find that a policy of increasing the share of government domestic resources which is devoted to investment has the effect of depressing the level of income; still more disconcerting is the authors' casual acceptance of this rather anomalous result.

It is hard to agree with Thorbecke and Condos' conclusion that this model can be applied for short-run purposes without major difficulties.

Finally, some questions may be raised about the accuracy of the constellation mapped by the authors. They attribute the high growth rate of Peru essentially to the export sector. This attribution is repeatedly made, in such terms as "it is very clear," "it will be abundantly illustrated," "there appears to be very little doubt," and indeed "[it] was abundantly illustrated by these models." However, the only piece of evidence actually offered is the simple coincidence of high export growth with high national growth. Second, they call attention to the "almost total absence of a domestic capital goods sector." But the coefficient of investment in the aggregate demand equation implies that, on the margin, almost one-third of investment goods are obtained from domestic rather than foreign sources; while the time series on M^i and I suggest that, on the average, over one-half of investment goods are obtained from domestic rather than foreign sources. Thus Peru must have a substantial domestic capital-goods sector—of which construction activity is presumably a major constituent.

Despite these deficiencies, however, the authors have provided us with an interesting attempt to quantify behaviorial relationships in an underdeveloped economy. Experiments with such models and data improvements are both required before macro models can be built which will provide useful guidelines for policy formulation.

8. THE USE OF A MODIFIED INPUT-OUTPUT SYSTEM FOR AN ECONOMIC PROGRAM IN ZAMBIA

DUDLEY SEERS,

UNITED KINGDOM MINISTRY OF OVERSEAS DEVELOPMENT*

In a paper for the International Association for Research in Income and Wealth Conference at Corfu in 1963,[1] I described an accounting system that had been used by the planning offices in Jamaica and Trinidad. The paper argued the case for disaggregation in an economy dependent on exports of primary products; but it concluded that, partly because of the difficulties of preparing a full input-output matrix, a simplified version is usually preferable.

Since that paper was written, the system advocated has been used by the United Nations Economic Mission to Zambia[2] as a basic framework for its economic policy recommendations, and I will here restate the case in the light of this Zambian experience, with some of its results and problems.[3]

I. THE NEED FOR A MODIFIED INPUT-OUTPUT SYSTEM IN DEVELOPING COUNTRIES

Some degree of disaggregation is essential for any economy of this type because the prime movers consist of a few leading export sectors (often

* I am grateful for comments by Mr. Bjerve, Director of the Statistical Office of Norway, Mr. Eleish of the U.N. Economic Commission for Africa, and Mr. Jolly, formerly Research Fellow at Makerere College, currently Ministry of Overseas Development Fellow at Cambridge, on loan as adviser on manpower planning to the government of Zambia. This paper is, of course, a purely personal contribution, based on work before I took up my present post.

[1] "An Accounting System for Projections in a Specialised Exporter of Primary Products" (unpublished, 1963).

[2] "The Economic Development of Zambia" (Government of Zambia, 1964). The planning office of Tanganyika (as it then was) also made use of the system in drawing up the country's development plan.

[3] The appendixes to this paper have been adapted from the report of the United Nations Mission to Zambia.

only one). To understand such an economy one needs to see the relations between these leading sectors and the remainder; a development plan consists essentially of changing the economic structure and developing new sectors. Aggregative accounting systems are thus of only limited use, and we must look toward Leontief rather than Keynes for our tools of analysis.

Yet the normal procedures of the interindustry operator need to be modified. First, the accounting frame has to be adapted to local circumstances. Because of lack of data, one probably cannot allocate the sales of *all* the economically significant sectors which produce intermediate products to each of the industries which buy them. On the other hand, *more* detail is needed than for developed countries. The payment of various sectors to the government should be broken down to show the main taxes separately because their incidence varies greatly between sectors; export industries and subsistence production may need to be split off from the rest of the agricultural sector; and it may be necessary to allow for the income and consumption of various racial groups because of different patterns of consumer behavior and (possibly) different official employment objectives.

Second, several of the functions describing the development of the matrix may be significantly nonlinear. Thus, export duties, income taxes on foreign companies, and marketing board profits usually increase more rapidly than exports. Moreover, the process of development involves the appearance of new industries and changes in the input coefficients of many already in existence.

Third, in these economies production is rarely determined endogenously. The output of the leading export sector or sectors is largely determined by economic developments elsewhere; it has to be estimated from projections of world demand when there is a fairly competitive world market, or from company plans when the market is highly imperfect. A large fraction of the supply of nearly all other products is imported, often even cement and electricity; so output is usually estimated on the basis of what is physically feasible, imports being shown as a residual.

These modifications are needed in an economy dependent on exports of a few commodities: they would not (particularly the last one) apply with such force to a diversified economy, such as Argentina. But one of the great merits of an input-output system is that it is highly flexible, and its construction and operation can be adapted to the type of economy and the data available.

II. A PRACTICAL EXAMPLE: USES IN ZAMBIA

The methods of constructing and projecting the matrix for Zambia are discussed in the attached Appendix A;[4] one of the projections is also shown, to illustrate the construction of the system. It will be seen that this was a very crude do-it-yourself business. We did not start out with a model for testing. We had four months to carry out a statistical exercise to throw light on the policy issues faced by the Mission.

Some policy issues, such as the future of the copper royalties (under which a large portion of the value of copper exports was lost to the economy) were big issues which needed as much statistical illumination as could be provided. We started by constructing a set of projections on the assumptions that taxes and royalty arrangements remained unchanged. We could then see that if the government's objectives were to be achieved without undue stress on the balance of payments, certain increases in taxes and changes in royalty arrangements would be needed. We estimated that these would ensure a sum of public and private savings sufficient to finance the necessary scale of capital development. We also concluded that in the case of Zambia, if policies recommended in the fiscal field (and in others) were carried out, there would be no *net* need for foreign capital over the next five years; foreign reserves would be built up at the beginning and could be run down later. This naturally had a profound effect on the thinking of the Mission and, I believe, on subsequent government economic policy. The point is not only that a disaggregated system indicates the magnitude of such "gaps" to be filled by policy. Realistic projections cannot be derived *in any other way*, especially in a period of structural change. Mere extrapolation of past trends in global aggregates would be of little value.

Secondly, it helped us grasp quite quickly the economic structure and the method of operation of Zambia. This was partly because we did *not* use a computer. Those who project a matrix by hand get accustomed to the relative magnitudes of the outputs of various sectors and of their factor and material requirements, and they really grasp (in a more profound sense than that of understanding a set of functions) how the structure might be expected to change during the development process. Many problems of economic change are also thrown up in the course of using the system.

The third virtue of this system (or of any that is sufficiently disaggre-

[4] This was prepared for the Mission's report by Mr. Belai Abbai, an Ethiopian economist on the staff of the Economic Commission for Africa, who was the research officer on the mission, in charge of projections work.

gated) is that a strategy can be devised which is internally consistent and which satisfies the main objectives of government policy. The contributions of the members of the Mission and its consultants, about twenty people, can all be integrated more easily with the help of such a framework.[5] Appendix B, an extract from the report, summarizes the main features of the strategy devised for Zambia. It brings out *inter alia* the interaction between development in agriculture and in industry; nobody who has worked with such a system is likely to take sides in the a priori argument, whether, in general, agriculture is more important than industry.[6]

The projections had further uses which may be more novel, at least for developing countries. As Appendix C shows, they threw light on the likely pattern of money flows between the main sectors of the economy, pointing the way toward the basic *financial* strategy needed.[7] They were also used to bring out the manpower needs of the program.[8] Another major conclusion of the Mission was that the shortage of high-level manpower would be the main constraint (and an increasingly serious one) on the country's economic growth. The admittedly crude projections indicated the magnitude of the problem, making it easier for us to show what could be expected in a few years' time and thus to reach and present clearly the policy implications. These included proposals for accelerating educational and training programs, for taking measures to retain and attract expatriates in professional fields, and for avoiding complex direct controls (see Appendix D).

[5] Another way of trying to ensure integration was by arranging meetings at which all those working on this exercise were invited to comment on each draft chapter.

[6] In Trinidad, the projections showed that increases in exports of manufactures were a necessary condition of fast growth; in Zambia increases in exports of minerals and farm products.

[7] The method of extending the projection into the financial field was due to Dr. Petter Bjerve, and the work was carried out by a Swedish associate expert in economics, provided under the United Nations technical assistance program, Mr. Esaieson.

[8] This work was carried out by Mr. Richard Jolly. Following one of the recommendations of the Mission, a Manpower Planning Unit has been set up in Zambia, under Mr. Jolly, to guide manpower and educational policy. This unit has refined the original manpower projections in several ways, though still within the framework of the input-output matrix. In the first place, a major survey of the skilled and educated labor force was undertaken in both the private and public sectors to provide a firmer base for future projections. Secondly, employers were asked about their future needs for manpower in relation to the programs for expansion, thus providing information which can be used to calculate sectoral employment-output ratios. Thirdly, these manpower data have been put on tape, so that future projections can be projected by a computer program. The parameters for their projections are the sectoral growth rates derived from the matrix, and the program forecasts the numbers required in particular occupations for each combination of education and training. The computer makes it possible to run quickly a number of alternative projections, which is particularly useful for coordinating manpower planning with the day-to-day process of planning the economy as a whole.

III. Problems Encountered in Zambia

We encountered a number of problems in Zambia which, to a varying degree, must be faced in all similar exercises for developing countries.

In the first place, those making a set of projections of this kind are tempted to adopt an excessively mechanical approach to development programming, and we may not have completely avoided this trap. Anyone using a matrix should not ignore the social changes involved in development or the political and administrative assumptions. But economists are very prone to do this anyway, and there is a real danger that anyone operating this (or any similar) model will become so absorbed in its manipulation that they will look on it as the core of development strategy, instead of the basis from which the strategy can be derived. To choose a few examples, the following repercussions may be overlooked: investment in housing and health services raises productivity; the adoption of social targets (such as universal primary education) affects public support for development and thus incremental capital-output ratios, as well as the extent of public cooperation in wage and fiscal policy; large programs in certain sectors may raise insoluble problems of project preparation and management, causing labor productivity to decline. Those of us who belonged to the United Nations Mission were uneasily aware that we made many tacit social assumptions, especially in the fields of agriculture and wages policy. Some work was done on these questions (by consultants Mr. Ngrobo and Mr. Vilakazi), but there was no time to explore the social aspects thoroughly.

Another failing of economists, not attributable to use of a matrix but possibly aggravated by it, is the tendency to overlook physical realities, especially those affecting other sectors. In a large, developed economy, one can ignore the effects of any particular project, but this is impossible if a big plant is built in Zambia. One project under consideration for manufacturing fertilizers, for example, will have a different effect if it is built in Livingstone, where there is spare hydroelectric capacity, than if it is built elsewhere; there is also some margin of choice over the type of fertilizers to be produced which would have implications for the extent to which the needs of the mining industry for explosives could be met (and thus affect the import bill).

The Zambian work also suffered from some more basic deficiencies. Many problems were slurred over by jumping from a base-year pattern to one projected for several years later. The pace of development is generally not uniform. Nor does it have the same content throughout; unless certain types of development materialize in the early years, others will lag later. Using widely separate years permits, if it does not encourage, the economist to overlook the phasing of the development process. We also lost a good deal by failing to disaggregate sufficiently. Some of the sectors used, especially in manufacturing, are large and heterogeneous. It may not be true for all the industries in a given sector that production is supply-determined. The failure to allocate inputs in detail meant, moreover, that the projected increases in consumption of various intermediate products did not fully reflect the different rates of growth of different sectors.

Our treatment of fixed-capital investment was perfunctory. For two sectors, mining and industry, an attempt was made to work out the approximate implications of the projected change in output. But elsewhere the methods were very crude. In the case of construction (mainly for the government and housing sectors) our starting point was the maximum rate of expansion in the period. Then we asked: Could the investment be financed? Was the increase in capital approximately what was needed? The limit to construction was admittedly little more than a hunch; it was based on an assessment by our building consultant[9] of how fast the construction industry might be expected to grow, taking into account the shortage of skilled building workers and of engineers and architects capable of preparing and carrying out projects. Some experts criticized us for over-estimating this limit, but preliminary indications are that we may have under-estimated it because contractors are bringing in their own skilled personnel. The uncertainty in the rate at which construction could be expanded is serious, especially for Zambia at present, where neither savings nor foreign exchange is the dominant constraint. Had we felt that fixed investment could be expanded more quickly, we would have proposed a bigger development program.

Some of the statistics we used were very rough. The base itself was weak, especially on imports into various sectors, largely because the only firm trade statistics then available were for the Federation of Rhodesia and Nyasaland as a whole. (A new matrix which has been constructed for 1964 is very much better in this respect because trade returns for Zambia itself are at last available.)

In addition, the coefficients may be wrong. The estimates of future productivity changes were little better than guesses; the data on past trends are not helpful, partly because in many sectors activity has fallen, and partly because the composition of the labor force is changing quite

---

[9] Mr. Turin, then an adviser to the Economic Commission for Africa.

rapidly. We do not place much confidence in the income-elasticities of demand either, though the results do not seem very sensitive to the assumptions made for these coefficients.

Future values of "exogenous" variables are subject to wide error. It is hard to pick a plausible price for copper in view of (1) the political uncertainties in each of the main Southern Hemisphere producers, and (2) the economic uncertainties in each of the main Northern Hemisphere consumers. (The problem is complicated by the unrepresentative nature of the London Metal Exchange quotation.) Similar though less severe uncertainties exist for the volume of copper sales, rail and shipping tariffs, and others. Our assumption of constant domestic prices is a serious weakness; although the copper price could fall to the rather low figure we used, wage changes are irreversible. Parallel increases in wages and import prices would not matter greatly, but wage increases in the past year have already been big enough to imperil our projections, especially of the volume of imports and employment.[10] The output of some sectors is hard to project; the future course of agricultural production is the domain of the sociologist rather than the economist.[11]

These problems reflect inevitable sources of error and inescapable uncertainties about the future when one is dealing with a country at such a low level of economic development. It would be helpful to call in the help of a computer in due course, after turning the system into an explicit model, and to recalculate the projections for 1970 on a number of assumptions (using the new 1964 base); they might well show quite wide differences.

IV. Is an Input-Output Matrix Worth Constructing?

In view of all these difficulties, it is natural to ask whether the input of the man-years of scarce labor that are required, even for a rough set of projections such as we made, was worthwhile, and, in particular, whether the policy recommendations are soundly based.

I agree in general with those who argue that it is dangerous to advocate the use of sophisticated programming methods in developing countries. There is a tragic, though understandable, tendency for young economists

[10] Wage increases have a much more serious effect on employment in a developing country than in one already industrialized. I tried to show how this works in the most obvious case, a petroleum economy, in "The Mechanism of an Open Petroleum Economy," *Social and Economic Studies* (March, 1964).

[11] For example, a central question is whether means can be found for inducing "subsistence farmers" to use fertilizers and better techniques of planting maize.

from developing countries to want to apply the latest techniques without inquiring whether they would be useful and feasible under local conditions, particularly whether the statistics would bear the analysis. In most countries, the result of proposing highly sophisticated systems (more complex than the one we used) is only too often to divert statisticians from more essential tasks and to encourage economists and even planning officials to live in a world so fanciful that "planning" is reduced to a set of functions and real policy issues are bypassed. Unfortunately, such tendencies are encouraged by some of those teaching "development economics."

My own view, which was, I believe, shared by my colleagues who worked with the matrix (see previous footnotes), is that the general pattern of Zambia's future development shows up so strongly that the projection system described was helpful and that the main policy conclusions were sufficiently well based.

An exercise like the one described above is not really one of "forecasting"; projecting a matrix is essentially making a "hypothetical" statement. If the mainly foreign-determined variables (export sales, import prices) behave in certain ways and the output of various goods and services changes and wages have a certain trend, then the objectives of the government carry certain implications.

Some version of this system could be used for central policy advice in almost any developing country. Most countries have fairly complete trade statistics and output figures covering some of the main products. Any input-output table, constructed in this way, acts as a convenient working sheet for gathering statistical information and for devising aggregative accounts for households, savings and investment, and so forth.

Its central uses, however, are to help the economist gain insight into the working of the economy, especially its future potentialities, and to focus attention on the key issues of policy. A forward look for both the government budget and the balance of payments will be needed. Projections of imports, for example, and thus of import duties are greatly improved if allowance is made for the different rates of growth of different types of final and intermediate demand.

More important, this is the only way to assure consistency between expansion programs in various sectors. There is really no other way of assessing whether any industrial or agricultural policy is likely to be supported by sufficient increases in domestic demand, allowing for government objectives in other fields and likely trends in exogenous variables. Even if some of the base-year figures have to be guessed, and very rough coefficients used, a simple matrix should be constructed. Provided the users are not naive, a disaggregated system can only be an improvement on a 'global" one. With further work, some of the weaknesses mentioned above can be made less serious.

* * *

APPENDIX A
(Adapted from Appendix A of the Report of the United Nations Mission to Zambia)

The Design of the Matrix

The basic frame for the projections is an adapted input-output table. It contains fewer input columns than a table of this sort normally does because it only attempts to allocate certain basic inputs (imports, electricity, transport, and distribution) directly to the purchasing sector, while the rest are lumped together in one column. This is done because the statistics do not permit a finer breakdown and the table would have been unwieldy. The table also contains more columns than an input-output table would, in that it identifies the stragetic policy variables, including direct and indirect taxes and nonwage incomes payable at home and abroad; it also distinguishes between imports of intermediate products consumed by a sector and imports of finished products similar to those produced by the same sector. The matrix includes the standard national accounts for households, government revenue and expenditure, saving and investment, and foreign payments.[12]

Two dominant features of Zambia which were considered are that Zambia is a primary exporter of minerals and that it has a nonhomogeneous social structure (Africans and Europeans). The analysis of mineral sales and of the incomes generated by this sector is central to the table; it is possible to trace the implication of a given rise in copper sales for employment incomes, tax receipts, royalties, and dividends arising from the industry. Employment incomes and consumption have been shown separately on the table for Africans and non-Africans; this separation is also appropriate for Zambia, since the consequence of a given rise in incomes for the pattern of consumption is different for the two racial groups. This also makes it possible to use different assumptions about the growth of population and employment for the two groups, which is particularly relevant during the period of transition.

The Base Year, 1961

A table analogous to Table 1 was constructed for 1961 by Mr. Osborn.[13] It shows, in the rows marked 1 to 9 (condensed from 31 rows originally prepared),

---

[12] Naturally the balance of payments shown here treats all other countries as "foreign," including Malawi and Southern Rhodesia.
[13] Of the statistical office of Rhodesia.

Table 1. A Projected Matrix for Zambia, 1970

		Basic Inputs						
(£ million) (at 1965 prices and 1963–64 tax and royalty rates)		Imports	Import Duties	Electricity	Transport	Distribution	Other	Total Inputs
		1	2	3	4	5	6	7
Mining	1	26.3	0.7	11.4	2.1	0.1	6.1	46.7
Agriculture	2	3.3			0.2	0.8	3.7	8.0
Manufacture	3	18.1	0.5	0.7	1.4	0.7	22.7	44.1
Food and beverages	a	5.6	0.3	0.1	0.3		11.0	17.3
Textiles	b	2.5					2.6	5.1
Nonmetallic minerals	c	0.5			0.2		1.8	2.5
Metal manufacturing	d	6.6	0.2	0.3	0.9	0.7	3.6	12.3
Other manufacturing	e	2.9		0.3			3.7	6.9
Construction	4	12.6	0.6		1.6	3.8	14.0	32.6
Electricity and water	5	1.1		1.6	0.1			2.8
Transport and communications	6	1.9				0.1	2.9	4.9
Distribution	7			0.2	7.1		2.4	9.7
Government services	8							
Other services	9			0.1			1.4	1.5
Intermediate products	10			−14.0	−12.5	−5.5	−53.2	−85.2
Rest of world	11	−63.3						−63.3
Government current account	12		−1.8					− 1.8
Households non-African	13							
Households African	14							
Savings and investment	15							

the productive sectors of the economy; below the horizontal line appear the main national income accounts, except for line 10 which shows the supply and use of intermediate products (other than those given separately in columns 1 to 6). Items are shown as positive where they are payments by the accounting entity concerned, negative when they are receipts. Columns 24 to 32 show the origin of the receipts of each productive sector, the total appearing in column 23; the other columns show how the supply is built up between imports (column 20) and domestic output (column 19), the latter being split again into inputs (columns 1 to 7) and value added, divided to show the income created (columns 8 to 18).

One problem arose out of the constitutional change after 1961, the base year. It was solved by including under "Government" not only the receipts and payments of the territorial government and the local authorities, but also the receipts

Value Added

Employee Income		Subsistence	Direct Tax	Mixed		Property Income Payments		Transfers	Savings and Depreciation	Total Value Added
Non-African	African			Non-African	African	Home	Abroad			
8	9	10	11	12	13	14	15	16	17	18
18.6	15.1		30.1				25.4		35.2	124.4
1.2	3.3	30.9		3.8	12.1					51.3
4.4	7.3		5.2	1.7	0.9	0.1	2.1		9.4	31.1
0.9	0.8		1.4			0.1	0.1		3.0	6.3
0.1	1.4		0.6				0.6		0.7	3.4
0.5	1.2		1.2				0.2		2.4	5.5
2.2	2.0		1.5	1.7	0.9				3.3	11.6
0.7	1.9		0.5				1.2			4.3
5.1	11.7		2.0	2.2	2.5		0.9		3.6	28.0
0.5	0.4					1.6	0.3		1.7	4.5
5.2	3.9		2.5	0.6	1.1	0.5	2.3		2.9	19.0
7.2	6.3		1.7	7.5	2.6	0.5	0.1		2.3	28.2
13.4	16.8									30.2
4.7	5.8	7.0	1.2	4.3	1.3				2.0	26.3
							−31.1	+1.0	+ 25.8	− 4.3
			−49.4	− 4.0		−0.9		+2.0	+ 9.2	− 43.1
−60.3			+ 5.4	−16.1		−1.8		−3.0	+ 8.4	− 67.4
	−70.6	−37.9	+ 1.3		−20.5				+ 6.3	−121.4
									−106.8	−106.8

by the federal government of taxes arising in Zambia (and the corresponding payments of federal departments that have now reverted to Zambian control). This made it possible to use the table as a base for projections into the post-federal period.

*   *   *

Mr. Osborn warned us that the table for 1961 was very approximate. All appropriation accounts in the publishing national accounts had been completed at the federal level only; a number of indirect methods using incomplete data, of various degrees of reliability, have been used in estimating transfer flows between sectors. Consumption estimates for the years 1954–62 were only reliably

Table 1. continued

(£ million) (at 1965 prices and 1963–64 tax and royalty rates)		Gross Output	Imports final, CIF	Distribution	Indirect Tax	Total Supply/Demand
		Composition of Supply				
		19	20	21	22	23
Mining	1	171.1	0.1	0.1		171.3
Agriculture	2	59.3	2.0	7.9		69.2
Manufacture	3	75.2	91.1	26.0	8.9	201.2
Food and beverages	a	23.6	25.0	6.2	3.8	58.6
Textiles	b	8.5	14.1	5.3	1.8	29.7
Nonmetallic minerals	c	8.0	0.8			8.8
Metal manufacturing	d	23.9	38.6	10.7	1.8	75.0
Other manufacturing	e	11.2	12.6	3.8	1.5	29.1
Construction	4	60.6			0.2	60.8
Electricity and water	5	7.3	9.1			16.4
Transport and communications	6	23.9	1.1			25.0
Distribution	7	37.9	1.1		0.5	39.5
Government services	8	30.2				30.2
Other services	9	27.8	11.1		1.5	40.4
Intermediate products	10	− 85.2		−34.0		−119.2
Rest of world	11	− 67.6	−115.6			−183.2
Government current account	12	− 44.9			−11.1	− 56.0
Households non-African	13	− 67.4				− 67.4
Households African	14	−121.4				−121.4
Savings and investment	15	−106.8				−106.8

made at the federal level; the estimates of private consumption are either derived from budget survey data or federal estimates broken down to the territorial level, largely on the basis of comparative disposable incomes. Only sketchy information was available for federal government expenditure in Northern Rhodesia. The detail shown in the published Government Estimates and Auditor General Reports was inadequate to provide a reliable commodity analysis of government consumption. Finally, and most serious, trade statistics were not available at the territorial level for the years of federation. There was no great problem in the export side, but all the import figures were derived figures. It was possible to complete the table for 1961 only because satisfactory production data have recently become available through the completion of the census of industrial production for 1961. The table was therefore unique in its construction; usually consumption

				Composition of Demand				
Sales to Other Sectors	Exports	Non-African Consumption	African Subsistence	Other African Consumption	Government Consumption	Government (Capital formation)	Other (Capital formation)	Change in Stocks
24	25	26	27	28	29	30	31	32
− 2.0	−156.6	− 2.0		− 1.0	− 0.2		− 6.5	−3.0
− 10.8	− 15.9	− 3.6	−30.9	− 5.8	− 1.2		− 1.0	
− 32.9	− 2.2	−37.9		−68.6	−13.2	− 3.8	−42.6	
− 1.3		−16.8		−37.6	− 2.9			
− 3.0	− 0.2	− 7.1		−18.3	− 1.1			
− 8.6		− 0.2						
− 13.6	− 0.3	− 7.3		− 5.6	− 1.8	− 3.8	−42.6	
− 6.4	− 1.7	− 6.5		− 7.1	− 7.4			
− 4.4					− 6.5	−26.3	−23.6	
− 12.4		− 2.3			− 1.7			
− 12.0	− 7.4	− 1.0		− 1.1	− 3.0			
− 39.5								
					−30.2			
− 4.7		−21.7	− 7.0	− 7.0				
−119.2	182.1	+ 1.1 +67.4	+37.9	+83.5	+56.0	+30.1	+73.7	+3.0

or production are the derived figures, but here imports into each sector are fundamentally the residuals.

Coefficients Used

Work also proceeded—mainly in the Ministry of Finance, Lusaka—with a view to establishing the basic coefficients to be used in the projections. Accordingly, income and expenditure elasticity coefficients (for Africans and Europeans separately) were computed, using the family budget studies that already exist for Zambia. Estimates of trends in productivity per worker were made, based on the available production census and employment data. The incidence of direct taxation on companies was also computed for mining and other sectors. (Tax receipts had already been classified by the Central Statistical Office, Salisbury, by originating sector; allowance was made for recent changes in tax rates.)

It was assumed as a starting point that input-output ratios and components of total supply remain as in the base year. This assumption was modified when price and wage changes were introduced and when import substitution was expected to take place. When projecting the consumption of electricity by the copper industry, allowance was also made for additional electricity inputs due to the changing composition of copper production, that is, the increase of electrolytic relative to blister copper. Inputs into agriculture were largely treated as a function of the monetary component of agricultural production.

* * *

Assumptions and Procedures: Projections for 1965 (Taxes Assumed Unchanged)

The 1965 matrix was projected in two stages. Stage One involved projections from 1961 to 1965 at 1961 prices. Stage Two involved the introduction of estimated wage and price changes between 1961 and 1965.

* * *

In finalizing the 1965 projections, account was taken of the fact that the faster increase assumed in wages than in import prices causes the volume of imports and consumption to increase. The initial projection of consumption at fixed (1961) prices had thus to be roughly adjusted.

Finally, the test for a normal consumption function for the two racial groups was separately applied; namely, that gross incomes, personal taxes, personal savings, and consumption expenditure bear reasonable relationships to one another, judged by past experience, allowance being made for changes in average earnings.

* * *

Projections for 1970 (Taxes Assumed Unchanged)

The 1965 table was then carried forward to 1970, keeping the same prices, wage rates, and tax rates. In projecting for 1970 considerable care was taken to establish the basic assumptions to be made concerning (1) the level of copper sales and production, (2) the scope for import substitution, and (3) the level of government investment and current expenditure.

The Mission was fortunate in having access to a number of independent studies (projections) concerning the future demand for copper. It also conferred with the authorities concerned regarding the expected changes in the domestic capacity to produce.

*   *   *

The industry experts had assembled a complete inventory of existing projects and their current capacity utilization, as well as a list of additional projects expected to materialize between 1965 and 1970. The first exercise in this case was to estimate the capacity utilization of existing projects by 1965 and the additional projects expected to materialize between 1963 and 1965. Estimates were made of gross output of the additional projects expected to materialize between 1963 and 1965. Then estimates of gross output of the additional projects expected to materialize between 1965 and 1970 were made. The additional gross output by sectors was further broken down into consumption, intermediate sales, investment, and exports. As a result a separate matrix for intermediate sales was constructed, showing the additional output of intermediate sales by producing and consuming sectors. This matrix showed the additional intermediate products to be produced by domestic industry, above 1965 levels (at 1965 prices).

The additional gross output and intermediate sales by sector were added to the 1965 levels. The gross output of commodity sectors being exogeneously determined, the implication for total inputs was traced by first assuming no import replacement. Domestically produced inputs thus projected were then compared with the input-output matrix for intermediate sales, and the balance was used to adjust imports of intermediate sales. Account was also taken of the additional electricity inputs for metal manufacturing, the fertilizer plant, and other manufacturing plants. The relevant total input requirements were accordingly adjusted. These estimates were sufficient to determine the balance of intermediate products in the input-output matrix, and accordingly the gross output of electricity, transport, and distribution.

Total investment (both government and private) was arbitrarily estimated in the first instance on the basis of what it should be to play a leading role in activating the economy and creating big rises in employment; later it was adjusted by reference to the total investment implied in the sector programs. This task was made relatively easy since sector investment requirements were elaborated in some detail, particularly for agriculture, industry, power development, education, and housing. The allocation of investment between the public and the private sector was made after the exercise on sector programs was completed, in the light of programs for which the government would be responsible.[14] The projected increase in government services in real terms reflected primarily the program of increasing the number of teachers.

Employment was estimated on the basis of productivity estimates for each sector. . . . If employment were assumed to be homogeneous, the level of em-

[14] It should be noted that government investment is carried out by government departments and does not include transfers to the private sector (e.g., through the Industrial Development Corporation).

ployment corresponding to given levels of output could be derived by making specific assumptions about changes in productivity. The levels of employment incomes could be regarded as providing an employment index. Total employment (African and non-African together) having been derived from target values of value added and assumed changes in labor productivity, specific assumptions by sector, regarding the increase in non-African employment, are needed to determine the level of African employment separately. Non-African employment is assumed to remain unchanged between 1965 and 1970 for the economy as a whole, but to decline in the mining section, which would be compensated by corresponding increases in the nonmining sectors, particularly in government and manufacturing.

However, the consequent sharp rise in the African share of employment creates an interesting technical problem, because it is impossible to assume that average earnings remain unchanged for any sector's labor force as a whole, and for each race. If wages are unchanged for each given job, the average will rise for Africans (because they advance up the ladder) and also for non-Africans (because their less skilled jobs are lost to Africans); the working assumption was made that the effect of the change in composition was to increase the average earnings for both races in the same proportion, for any sector.

Consumption was estimated for each race separately on the basis of coefficients mentioned above and imports were again obtained as a residual, except for agriculture, where exports were considered to be whatever would not be consumed locally.

What then emerged was that these various developments would cause a big deficit in the balance of payments for 1970, assuming existing royalty arrangements and tax rates. Table 1 brings this out. The policies required to close this gap are discussed in Appendix C.

* * *

Appendix B

Use of the Matrix to Show the Economic Strategy Required (Adapted from the Mission's Report, Chapter I, Paragraph 74 to 84).

For the year 1970, we sketched the sort of economic structure that would satisfy the following conditions:
1. to provide at least 150,000 more jobs than there are in 1964;
2. to imply significant improvements in living standards, more specifically, a rise in average African real consumption per head by at least one quarter;
3. to be compatible with a balance in foreign payments;
4. to contain no excess of purchasing power with inflationary implications;
5. to act as a base for further and faster advances in the 1970's (implying a high rate of investment).

These constitute an economic expression of the government's major political objectives. It should be clearly understood at the outset that while it is a relatively simple exercise to sketch out an economic program, its achievement will require a tremendous effort by the government to mobilize the will and the abilities of the people. The structure projected here for 1970 is therefore not to be considered a forecast, but rather as the sort of economic situation which would meet the requirements indicated above, especially the rise in employment. The methods are described in Appendix A.

* * *

The whole set of projections adds up to a comprehensive program. The rise in copper revenues would finance increased government services (such as education) and government construction; this would expand incomes, leading to higher consumption, which would in turn widen the market for manufactured consumer goods and for foodstuffs, providing a bigger demand for agricultural products; the rising flow of goods would require more transport and provide more work for those engaged in distribution and other services; the general economic boom would stimulate private construction in offices, houses, shops, and the like.

The program is internally consistent. If the industrial expansion were slow, it would be difficult to find markets for the food; if agricultural output lagged, there would be heavier imports of food and agricultural materials than the country could pay for.

The Projected Rise in Demand

Table 2. Gross Domestic
Expenditure at Factor Cost by Type, 1961
(actual), 1965 (projected), and 1970 (projected at 1965 prices)
(£ millions)

	1961 Actual	1965 Projected	1970 Projected
Non-African consumption	52	56	67
African consumption subsistence	26	33	38
African consumption cash	36	51	84
Government consumption	25	37	56
Government investment	9	17	30
Private fixed investment	29	36	74
Change in stocks	+9	−5	+3
Export surplus (goods and services)	25	35	4
Minus indirect taxes	−7	−9	−13
Gross domestic expenditure at factor cost	204	251	343

SOURCE: See Appendix A.

The main objectives of this strategy being the creation of employment, the basic quantitative targets refer to manpower, not to the national income. . . .

However, we will start from conventional categories of national income analysis. Table 2 shows how the increases in demand would be injected in the economy. The impetus would come from government consumption and government investment, which would rise by about 50 and 75 per cent respectively between 1965 and 1970. This would impart an upward momentum to the whole economy, enabling employment (especially African) to grow. Largely because of higher employment, African cash consumption would rise by 65 per cent. Taking subsistence output into account, the total increase in African consumption would be 45 per cent; that is, average levels of living would rise about 25 per cent, allowing for the population increase. Non-African consumption would also rise, mainly due to the fact that the Europeans in Zambia in 1970 will be a more highly skilled and professional body than today. But the proportionate rise could be smaller, so the inequalities in levels of consumption would become less marked (apart from the effect of tax changes which will be considered below). On the assumptions made, investment overseas (the export surplus) will fall sharply.

Private investment should react sharply, however, more than doubling, from levels which will still be relatively low in 1965. Altogether, fixed investment (excluding stocks) would rise from 21 per cent of gross domestic expenditure to 30 per cent, a very high figure by international standards, and providing an excellent point of departure for the 1970's.

The Projected Rise in Output

The necessary output of the different sectors of the economy by 1970, to meet the rise in demand, is indicated in Table 3.

Table 3. Gross Domestic
Product by Sector, 1961 (actual), 1965
(projected), and 1970 (projected at 1965 prices)
(£ millions)

	1961 Actual	1965 Projected	1970 Projected	Per cent change 1965 to 1970
Mining	96	108	124	15
Agriculture[a]				
Commercial	9	10	20	100
Subsistence	21	27	31	15
Manufacturing	10	16	31	97
Construction	9	14	28	100
Distribution	14	17	28	65
Government services	13	20	30	30
Other[b]	32	39	50	28
Gross Domestic Product	204	251	343	37

SOURCE: See Appendix A.
[a] Includes fishing and forestry.
[b] Electricity and water, transport and communications, miscellaneous services.

A rise in demand on the scale indicated would involve a big increase in imports. It would therefore require a big increase in copper exports; output of copper should rise from 680 thousand short tons in 1965 to at least 800 thousand in 1970, or, by at least 18 per cent. Study of the possibilities of commercial agriculture and manufacturing indicates that in both these sectors output could double. Output in subsistence agriculture would rise with the help of extension services, but more slowly—about 1 per cent faster than the population living off agriculture. The increase in construction is necessary to spur the economic expansion and to make it possible. The increase in government service is needed to provide both more teaching and more administration, as will be required in a planned economy. Changes in output in other sectors would be induced by the increases just described.

Altogether the rise in the domestic product of 37 per cent would be equivalent to over 6 per cent a year, about twice as fast as the population is rising (implying a growth of some 3 per cent a year in income per head of the population).

The Projected Rise in Employment

Table 4 and Figure 1 show the effect that this program would have on employment by 1970. Company information is that employment will, if anything, fall

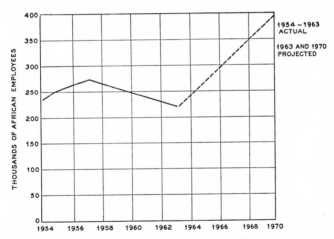

Figure 1. African Employment (Source: Monthly Digest of Statistics and Mission Projections)

in the mines because of mechanization. There will also be small increases in employment in agriculture; much of the increase in commercial output will come from farmers who count as "self-employed" (and are therefore not included in the table). The rises in employment in the other sectors reflect the changes in output discussed above, with allowance for expected improvements in productivity.

Table 4. Employment by Race and Sector, 1961 and 1963 (actual); 1965 and 1970 (projected)[a]
(thousands)

	African				Non-African				Total			
	1961	1963ᵇ	1965 Projected	1970 Projected	1961	1963ᵇ	1965 Projected	1970 Projected	1961	1963ᵇ	1965 Projected	1970 Projected
Mining	42	41	42	42	8	8	8	6	50	49	50	48
Agriculture[a,c]	38	34	39	48	1	1	1	1	39	35	40	49
Manufacturing	19	16	21	36	2	3	3	3	21	19	24	39
Construction	30	24	33	60	2	2	3	3	32	26	36	63
Distribution[d]	15	} 109	22	37	7	} 18	5	5	22	} 127	27	42
Government services	35		59	92	6		7	8	41		66	100
Other	59		60	73	6		6	7	65		66	80
Total	238	224	276	388	32	32	33	33	270	256	309	421

SOURCE: 1961 and 1963, *Monthly Bulletin of Statistics*; 1965 and 1970, Mission projections.
[a] Excludes those working for African employers outside the main towns, estimates in the census report at 41 thousand males in 1963.
ᵇ On the basis of figures for March, June, and September.
[c] Includes forestry and fishing.
[d] Includes finance.

APPENDIX C

Use of the Matrix to Show the Financial Policies Required (Adapted from the Mission's Report, Chapter VIII, Paragraph 121 to 133).*

An attempt has been made to illustrate quantitatively the prospective need for foreign borrowing by means of projections of changes in assets and liabilities over the period. These projections suggest that the development plans for 1964–70

Table 5. Projections for Government Account,
Nation's Capital Account, and Balance of Payments for 1970,
on Alternative Assumptions on Tax Rates and Government Expenditures[a]
(£ million)

	X	Y
Government account		
Net taxation	65	87
Expenditure on goods and services	86	86
Surplus (deficit = −)	−21	1
Fixed gross capital formation	30	30
Gross saving	9	31
Nation's capital account		
Personal saving	15	14
Corporate saving	57	51
Private saving	72	65
Government saving	9	31
Total saving	81	96
Net foreign borrowing	26	11
Gross real investment	107	107
Government gross fixed capital formation	30	30
Increase in stocks	3	3
Private fixed capital formation	74	74
Balance of payments		
Export surplus of goods and services	4	11
Net transfers abroad	30	22
Net foreign borrowing (balance of payments deficit)	26	11

SOURCE: See Appendix A.
   [a] Alternative X: Assuming for taxes and royalties at 1963–64 rate (see Appendix A, Table 1).
Alternative Y: The following changes are assumed:
   1. All mineral royalties transferred to government;
   2. Tax of 5 per cent on export value of copper;
   3. Duties on imports from Southern Rhodesia raised;
   4. Duties and indirect taxes for a number of nonessential goods increased by an average of 30 per cent as compared with present rates;
   5. Personal income tax increased, the effect being to raise the average rate on non-Africans from 6.4 per cent to 11.6 per cent of total income and for Africans from 1.5 per cent to 5.1 per cent.

* Minor changes result from deletion of tables.

may not require much net foreign borrowing, provided that both budget and credit policy are pursued as indicated here. If copper prices rise relatively more than the level of import prices, which is not unlikely, the need for foreign borrowing will be correspondingly smaller.

To illustrate quantitatively the rough order of government expenditure and the level of taxation required by 1970, two alternative projections are presented in Table 5. Alternative X assumes implementation of the development plans suggested for government consumption and government gross capital formation, while tax rates are assumed to be maintained as in 1963. This alternative is identical with the projection presented for 1970 in Appendix A. Alternative Y assumes that government expenditure on goods and services is the same as in alternative X, but that tax rates are increased as indicated in the footnotes to Table 5.

As might be expected, alternative X shows large deficits both on government account and on the balance of payments. Although projections of this kind may have large margins of error, they clearly indicate the need for tax increases. If a policy in line with alternative X were pursued, the result would also be a relatively strong wage and price increase which again would further adversely affect the balance of payments.

Alternative Y is intended to represent an approximate illustration of the level of taxation needed to avoid harmful wage and price increases and to prevent the deficit on the balance of payments from becoming too large. The balance-of-payments deficit of £11 million generated in this alternative appears not to exceed the volume of foreign capital supply possible and the use of exchange reserves justifiable at this stage of development. However, the figures in the table must be conceived as illustrations only. Final decisions on the level of taxation in years to come must, of course, be taken on the basis of all currently available information. The situation will no doubt be rather different from that described in alternative Y; one conclusion can be drawn with certainty, though, that the implementation of development programs requires on the assumptions made a very substantial increase of tax rates.

It will be noted that the entire increase of total saving in alternative Y as compared with alternative X is due to increased government saving, while corporate saving shows a substantial decline, due to the tax on copper exports.

*   *   *

Table 6 shows figures for the government account, the nation's capital account, and the balance of payments for the entire period 1966–70. Figures for 1966 to 1969, which are implied in the totals for 1966–70, have been estimated by interpolation between the projections for 1965 and 1970. Under the assumptions made, a government surplus of £16 million would accumulate in this period, and the balance-of-payments surpluses in the first years would be offset by deficits in the later years. The government's surplus would decline from £6 million in 1965 to £1 million in 1970, and the balance of payments would deteriorate from a surplus of £17 million in 1965 to a deficit of £11 million in 1970. The estimates for 1970 are made at 1965 prices. If copper prices should develop more favorably

Table 6. Projections for Government
Account, Nation's Capital Account, and
Balance of Payments in Total for the Period 1966–70
(£ millions at 1965 prices)

	1965	1970	Total 1966–70
Government account			
Net taxation	60	87	377
Government expenditure on goods and services	54	86	361
Surplus, net lending	6	1	16
Fixed gross capital formation	17	30	122
Gross saving	23	31	138
Nation's capital account			
Personal saving	10	14	60
Corporate saving	32	51	216
Private saving	42	65	276
Government saving	23	31	138
Total gross saving	65	96	414
Net foreign lending	17	−11	—
Gross real investment	48	107	414
Government gross fixed capital formation	17	30	122
Private gross fixed capital formation	36	74	279
Increase in stocks	−5	3	13
Balance of payments			
Export surplus of goods and services	36	11	104
Net transfers abroad	19	22	104
Net foreign lending	17	−11	—

than prices for Zambian imports, which is not unlikely, both the budget surplus and the balance of payments would be correspondingly more favorable. The projections for each of the years within the period (not all included in the table) show that Zambia, under the assumptions made, would have a surplus on its balance of payments until 1968 inclusive, but from then there would be increasing deficits up to 1970 and later. This illustrates the need for accumulating exchange reserves for the purpose of financing deficits on the balance of payments which may emerge in a few years, as a consequence of the development program. Increased government revenues and budget surpluses are the means by which this can be achieved.

Applying the method described above, under the assumptions underlying Tables 5 and 6, projections have been made of total credit supply to the private sector and the increase in private financial assets over the five-year period 1966–70. According to these projections the credit supply to the private sector would have to be not less than £82 million in the period to achieve the speed of development aimed at, and this credit expansion would create an increase of private claims amounting to £66 million. An attempt at allocating the credit supply by lending sectors and the increase in private claims by type of assets suggests that more than half of the total credit supply would come from credit institutions, primarily agricultural credit institutions, commercial banks, and building societies. Moreover, more than half of the increase in private financial assets would take the form of increased deposits.

Furthermore, separate projections for 1970 seem to indicate that the total credit supply in this year, under the assumptions made, would be as much as £28 million and the increase in private claims would be £16 million. As the government surplus would be only £1 million, practically the entire difference is assumed to be obtained by a reduction of exchange reserves and by borrowing abroad.

* * *

To provide the credit expansion needed to implement the development plans it appears that the government would have in 1970 to supply the private sector (credit institutions and the public) with loans at an amount significantly larger than its budget surplus. Thus, while government and the central bank in 1964–65, as we have seen, would have to play an active role to reduce liquidity of the private sectors, they would by 1970 have to do the opposite, supply loans (or buy securities) to increase liquidity. This is due to the fact that under the assumptions made, holdings of foreign assets by the central bank would significantly increase in the former period, whereas in the latter they would not change. . . . The activity of credit institutions would have to be considerably increased, which illustrates the desirability of rationalizing the Zambian credit system to enable it to cope with the expanded tasks imposed upon it by the development program.

Concluding Remarks

The projections made in this Appendix are intended to serve three purposes. In the first place, they demonstrate a method by which broad financial aggregates can be projected to provide the framework within which a detailed financial plan could be prepared by the Ministry of Finance. . . . Second, they serve to illustrate the kind of financial thinking which the Mission believes is essential in development planning—that the single purpose of a financial plan is to show how budget and credit policy can and should be applied to implement the real development plan. Third, it is hoped that the projections express a rough approximation of some of the magnitudes of the main financial transactions discussed in this report.

* * *

APPENDIX D

The Use of the Matrix to Devise the Targets for Manpower and Educational Policy (Adapted from the Mission's Report, Chapter VI, Paragraph 42 to 48)

The development of Zambia's human resources must be guided by manpower needs. . . . Using estimates from various sources for the stocks of high-level manpower in each sector in 1961, rough projections of needs were made for five-year intervals until 1980. For the years 1965 and 1970, these estimates were made on a sectoral basis, increasing the present stocks according to the projected output for each sector (see Appendix A).

*   *   *

In global terms, these projections, rough as they are, indicate beyond doubt that Zambia's need will far outstrip local supplies for many years. Even ignoring the needs of the educational system, the demand for "administrative and professional personnel"[15] is likely to rise from about 3,000 in 1961 to over 4,000 in 1965 and over 6,000 in 1970. Most of these must be graduates or professionally qualified. Second-level manpower, usually with school certificates and some training, will be required in much greater numbers; needs will rise from nearly 11,000 in 1961 to about 15,000 in 1965 and to over 23,000 in 1970. In addition, the educational system itself will absorb many school certificate holders, some as teachers but most as students at the higher levels; the educational plans suggested would require in total about 2,300 school certificate holders in 1965 and 5,500 in 1970. This would raise the gross needs for school certificate holders (or above) from almost 22,000 in 1965 to 39,000 in 1970. The Mission would not claim that these are accurate estimates and repeats its conviction that a thorough manpower survey must be undertaken as soon as possible, nor is education the sole qualification for high-level work. But, as orders of magnitude, these rough estimates establish the dimensions of the educational task facing the country.

It must be the explicit purpose of the educational system, and of other institutions of training, to provide the people of Zambia with the education and skills they need to build and develop the country.

COMMENT

PAUL G. CLARK, WILLIAMS COLLEGE

This is an extremely interesting account of an operational application of an intersectoral approach to development planning problems in a country at an early stage of development. Many points which emerge from the experience are highly suggestive, but I shall limit my discussion to a few points under three headings—the nature of the input-output system employed, the operational uses of the calculations, and the indicated development strategy for Zambia.

[15] Precise definitions of each category of manpower are given in a survey by Taylor and Pearson.

I. Nature of the Input-Output System

The first point is that the accounting system which Seers presents is a mixture of conventional national accounting and conventional input-output flows. It looks "toward Leontief rather than Keynes," but it draws heavily on Stone. In Table 1 the information on intermediate transactions among producing sectors (columns 1–7 and rows 1–9) is a small part of the information presented, and within the intermediate flows about two-fifths are imported (even in 1970) and two-fifths are from unidentified sectors. There is much more detail on the value-added flows and on the other elements in the composition of supply, and it is these flows, particularly for various taxes and for savings and property incomes, which prove to be most significant for policy. Above all, the accounting system highlights the balance-of-payments transactions of the various sectors of the economy—the concentration on a single major export, the heavy use of inter-mediate imports, the extensive reliance on final imports, and the substantial foreign income and capital flows.

The fact that the accounting system departs considerably from a simple input-output framework seems to me clearly appropriate for the circumstances of early-stage underdeveloped economies. An approach distinguishing various producing sectors with diverse input structures is still very revealing, as Seers urges, but the value-added and balance-of-payments transactions rather than the intermediate transactions are most significant for policy.

The other point to note here is that the analysis really relies on the accounting system rather than on an explicit model of endogenous economic relationships. As outlined in Appendix A, the projection methodology estimates most gross outputs exogenously, allocates them among intermediate and final uses, and then derives intermediate imports as residuals. Capital formation is estimated initially to provide the desired stimulus to domestic demand and employment, though constrained by an exogenous estimate of construction capacity and checked later against the capital formation suggested in sector expansion programs. After the other final demands are estimated, exogenously except for consumption, final imports and agricultural exports are derived as residuals.

The usefulness of the accounting system in pulling together a variety of exoge-nous estimates and subjecting them to some endogenous checks and to qualitative judgments about policy adjustments is certainly indicated by Seers' account. But in relation to most of the other contributions at this conference, it should be recognized that the paper does not attempt to develop an explicit model.

II. Operational Uses of the Calculations

The most evident of the operational uses of the Zambia projection was its role in integrating the sectoral analyses of the various specialists. Appendix C pro-vides an impressive illustration of how the general projection provided real measures of the desired effects of taxation policy and credit policy and how in turn the fiscal-monetary analysis devised specific policy actions to induce these real adjustments in the economy. Similarly, Appendix D illustrates nicely how the projection called for a consistent manpower analysis and how subsequent manpower surveys and record systems have been designed to fit into a continuing planning process.

To perform this integrating function effectively, a projection technique must be sufficiently disaggregated to provide each sector specialist with links between his analysis and the general projection. Moreover, this is not just a problem for short-term missions, but a recurring difficulty for planning ministries dealing with operating ministries and independent agencies. The disaggregated system presented here seems well designed to handle this problem.

The most crucial of the uses which Seers describes, of course, was to point up the main policy issues which the government would have to face in the develop-ment process. The paper and its appendices certainly contain many insights about appropriate policies, and these are related consistently to the underlying statistical projection. However, it may be worth stressing, at the risk of restating the obvious, that the policy inferences depend only partly on the "gaps" indicated by the calculations. They also depend on qualitative judgments and preferences. For example, the striking conclusion that Zambia's ambitious development pro-gram can be carried through with no net inflow of foreign capital over the next five years depends partly on the size of the balance-of-payments gap indicated in the projection, assuming unchanged policies, and partly on other considera-tions leading the mission to suggest closing the gap by increases in domestic taxes and changes in royalty arrangements rather than by arranging foreign bor-rowing. I do not wish to criticize this choice, but simply to emphasize that in policy matters quantitative calculations always merge with qualitative judgments and preferences.

III. DEVELOPMENT STRATEGY FOR ZAMBIA

The sectoral pattern of development over the next five years indicated in the Zambia projection can be summarized roughly as follows. Mining, and hence the principal export, is likely to expand only 15 to 20 per cent. Commercial agri-culture and domestic manufacturing can reasonably be expected to double and government services to rise about 50 per cent. Thus the over-all growth of gross domestic product may work out to be 35 to 40 per cent. To support this growth, public investment is projected to expand about 75 per cent, and it is hoped that private investment will approximately double. The ratio of gross investment to GDP would rise from something over 20 per cent to around 30 per cent, and the implied aggregative net capital-output ratio is around 2.8. To stay within the foreign exchange constraint, given the tendency of imports to rise more rapidly than exports (particularly as investment has a relatively high import content), there must be considerable import substitution in food products and manufactured consumer goods and a decline in Zambia's initial balance-of-payments surplus.

I have been struck by this sectoral pattern of development because in a very general way it corresponds to the pattern indicated for the three neighboring East African countries—Kenya, Uganda, and Tanzania—by our research at the East African Institute of Social Research over the past two years. These countries have relied on several agricultural commodities rather than copper as their major exports, but broadly speaking the sectoral adjustments for significantly accelerated growth in the future seem to be similar. In particular, the role of import substitution in manufacturing may be surprising, yet it emerges both as an expanding source of gross product when the traditional export sector is unlikely to grow as fast as the rate considered acceptable for GDP and as an essential device for holding down the balance-of-payments deficit which would otherwise be generated by accelerated growth. Such a sectoral pattern may well be characteristic of other early-stage underdeveloped countries if they are to succeed in growing significantly more rapidly than in the past.

The other feature of the Zambia development strategy on which I would like to comment is the estimated employment effects. As Appendix B indicates, a principal goal of the program was to provide 150,000 more jobs than in 1964—something more than a 50 per cent rise over six years. Since mining employment is not expected to rise, and much of the expansion of commercial agriculture is by self-employed farmers, the additional jobs would have to be mainly in manufacturing and construction and in services and government. The projection suggests that such an expansion of employment is attainable, but the implied trends in gross product per employee (comparing Tables 3 and 4) seem unreasonably low in the light of trends experienced in East Africa—only 4 per cent per year in manufacturing, 2 per cent per year in construction, 1 per cent per year in services, and 0 per cent per year (by definition) in government. Seers comments that wage increases in the past year have imperiled the employment projections, but such wage increases and their adverse employment effects may well be an integral part of the economic process in countries at this early stage of development. Slow growth of employment, even if GDP expands at an acceptable rate, seems to me the great unsolved problem of such economies.

9. AN ALMOST CONSISTENT INTERTEMPORAL MODEL FOR INDIA'S FOURTH AND FIFTH PLANS*

JOEL BERGSMAN, AGENCY FOR INTERNATIONAL DEVELOPMENT
ALAN S. MANNE, STANFORD UNIVERSITY

"There was probably no other person in the whole country who had meditated so much on the question of interest. Margayya's mind was full of it. Night and day he sat and brooded over it. The more he thought of it the more it seemed to him the greatest wonder of creation. It combined in it the mystery of birth and multiplication. Otherwise how could you account for the fact that a hundred rupees in a savings bank became one hundred and twenty in course of time? It was something like the ripening of corn. Every rupee, Margayya felt, contained in it seed of another rupee and that seed in it another seed and so on and on to infinity. It was something like the firmament, endless stars and within each star an endless firmament and within each one further endless. . . . It bordered on mystic perception."—R. K. Narayan, *The Financial Expert*

I. INTRODUCTION

In this paper we present a model intended to quantify some implications of alternative paths of economic growth for India. The model may be regarded as a "requirements analysis." The calculations are begun by postulating aggregate growth and import substitution targets. The im-

* Financial support for this study was provided primarily by the Agency for International Development. Further support was provided from funds made available by the Ford Foundation to the Graduate School of Business, Stanford University. The conclusions and other statements, however, are the sole responsibility of the authors and do not imply agreement or approval by any of the supporting institutions.

The authors gratefully acknowledge helpful suggestions from Richard S. Eckaus, Kenneth M. Kauffman, Louis Lefeber, Wassily Leontief, Pitambar Pant, T. N. Srinivasan, and A. Vaidyanathan. We are also grateful to Anne Bergsman for computer programming, and to James Barr, Peter C. Mayer, and Carmella Ullman for help with computations.

An earlier version of this paper appeared in *The Economic Weekly* (Bombay), November 20, 1965.

plications for production, investment, and the balance of trade are then derived.

The model itself does not specify the particular mix of policy instruments (quantitative controls, fiscal, and monetary measures) that would be best suited to achieve the postulated targets. Moreover, we do not present our personal value judgments with respect to such political decisions as the rate at which consumption is to be increased and the date by which India is to achieve independence from foreign aid.

The analysis is intended to be useful in estimating the absolute levels of foreign exchange needs implied by a specified set of growth and performance assumptions. The principal purpose, however, is to compare the balance-of-trade time paths under alternative strategies for the Fourth and Fifth Plans. For this reason, no constraint has been placed on the magnitude of the balance-of-trade deficit in any year.

Because it takes machines to make machines, there is an immediate additional cost attached to import substitution or export promotion in the capital goods industries. This cost can be measured both in additional import requirements and in additional investment requirements. According to our calculations, the additional foreign exchange costs are more than recovered over the ten-year period considered here.

In our calculations, an accelerated program of capital formation during the Fourth and Fifth Plans implies a sharp immediate rise in the demand for such investment goods as machinery and construction. To the extent that this additional demand can be met through an increase in foreign aid and loans, there is no immediate domestic economic problem. But to the extent that the investment goods are to be provided from domestic sources (for example, construction projects employing manpower in large quantities), a domestic policy problem may exist. An ambitious program for the mobilization of domestic manpower and physical resources also implies an ambitious program for raising taxes, private savings, and the earnings of public enterprises. If the mobilization of savings is less vigorous than is implied by the import substitution and physical output targets, then inflation—whether open or repressed—is a likely consequence.

II. THE MODEL

Model Formulation

In two previous reports, a thirty-sector interindustry model was employed to construct an internally consistent set of output levels, investments, and import requirements for a specific future year. Manne and

Rudra [5] deal with 1970–71, the terminal year of India's Fourth Plan; and Srinivasan, Saluja, and Sabherwal [6] deal with 1975–76, the terminal year of the Fifth Plan. The present project is even more ambitious: tracing out alternative time paths for each of the thirty sectors over each year of the Fourth and Fifth Plans—starting from the expected condition of the economy as of 1965–66.

We believe that investigation of annual time paths is a useful extension of single-period analyses. Our model was designed primarily to explore balance-of-trade time paths under alternative growth and import substitution strategies. With a one-period model, such an analysis is impossible. Also, investment program bottlenecks may be hidden unless year-to-year time phasing is explored (see Chakravarty and Lefeber [1]).

In addition to the time phasing of imports, this model is designed to explore some specific effects of time lags between investment and output. The model calculates the structure of the economy for a target year five or ten years in the future and works out the time paths that would get the economy "from here to there"—from the assumed base year position to the calculated target year position. The model operates as if the demand-supply gap for each commodity is to be filled either by imports (producers' goods), by consumption shortfalls (food and fibers), or by increases in domestic output (services). These "shock absorbers" are assumed to be available for bridging the gap between domestic supplies and total demand. We take the 1965–66 levels of domestic output of each item as a datum, and we suppose that each sector's output expands at a constant growth rate during the Fourth Plan and at another rate during the Fifth. Because of the domestic service sectors, the model is "almost consistent" rather than fully consistent. In the service sectors (notably construction), domestic production could be a bottleneck during years too close to the base year for output to be expanded. See Appendix for details on the mathematical formulation.

Principal Assumptions

The calculations are based upon two alternative time paths of aggregate domestic expenditure. For each time path, three alternative assumptions concerning import substitution targets are considered. Each of the six possible combinations of aggregate growth and import substitution has been explored.

Table 1 indicates the two alternative aggregate growth paths. The figures for induced investment emerged from the calculations themselves. The other three items (exogenous investment, government consumption, and

Table 1. Alternative Projections of Domestic Expenditure Components

	Rupees, Thousand Crores (1959–60 market prices)					Annual Percentage Increase	
	1960–61 (actual)	1965–66 (estimates)	1965–66 (model)	1970–71 (model)	1975–76 (model)	Fourth Plan[a]	Fifth Plan
Case A1							
Induced investment[b]	}2.51	2.15	3.21	4.13	6.12	13.9%	8.2%
Exogenous investment[c]		1.45	1.45	2.45	4.47	11.1	12.8
Government consumption	1.38	2.70	2.70	3.80	5.40	7.1	7.3
Household consumption	12.60	14.70	14.70	19.20	26.70	5.5	6.8
Gross domestic expenditure	16.49	21.00	22.06	29.58	42.69	7.1	7.6
Case A2							
Induced investment[b]		2.15	3.08	4.26	6.12	14.7	7.5
Case A3							
Induced investment[b]		2.15	2.94	4.05	5.91	13.5	7.9
Case B1							
Induced investment[b]	}2.51	2.15	2.68	3.49	5.51	10.2%	9.6%
Exogenous investment[c]		1.45	1.45	2.22	3.94	8.9	12.2
Government consumption	1.38	2.70	2.70	3.80	5.40	7.1	7.3
Household consumption	12.60	14.70	14.70	18.30	23.90	4.5	5.5
Gross domestic expenditure	16.49	21.00	21.53	27.81	38.75	5.8	6.8
Case B2							
Induced investment[b]		2.15	2.56	3.60	5.51	10.9	8.9
Case B3							
Induced investment[b]		2.15	2.43	3.40	5.31	9.4	9.3

a Growth rate based on estimated level for 1965–66.
b Includes inventories.
c Includes replacement investment, together with housing, health, education, roads, etc. See Table 29, Manne and Rudra [5].

household consumption) were determined exogenously prior to running the model.

Case A represents what we believe to be the consensus at the Planning Commission for the Fourth Plan, together with the Perspective Planning Division's proposals for the Fifth Plan. Case B corresponds to a more pessimistic view than is being considered by the Planning Commission—hence slower growth rates of agricultural development and of consumption and a reduction in exogenous investment. Note that the annual percentage increases in household consumption during the Fourth Plan are projected at 5.5 per cent in case A and 4.5 per cent in case B. Since population is increasing at 2.5 per cent per year in both cases, these projections imply per capita increases of 3 and 2 per cent per year respectively.

For each of the two aggregate growth assumptions, three cases are considered with respect to import substitution. These three alternatives differ in the assumed ratios of imports to domestic production for each sector. Table 2 indicates the ratios assumed for the target years of 1970–71 and 1975–76. Case 1 represents the most rapid program. Case 2 is less rapid during the Fourth Plan, but reaches the same position as Case 1 by the end of the Fifth Plan. Case 3 is slower than Case 2 for both Plan periods. Table 2 contains the actual import coefficients for 1960–61, preliminary estimates for 1965–66, and the three alternative assumptions for the future.

The six combinations of assumptions will be identified as Case A1, A2, B1, and so forth.

Principal Results—Import Substitution

We first turn to the results with respect to import substitution. Figure 1 is based upon aggregate projection A and shows the trade deficit corresponding to the three alternative targets for import substitution. Household and government consumption, exogenous investment, and exports are identical for all three curves in Figure 1. The curves represent our estimates of the time paths of the trade deficit corresponding to the three different import substitution strategies—exogenous final demands being held constant. Case 1, the most ambitious import substitution strategy, has the highest deficit in the early years, but achieves the greatest reduction in future deficits. Over the eleven-year period considered, the present cost of the trade deficit for Case 1 is lower than that for Case 2, and that of Case 2 is lower than that for Case 3, discounting at either zero or 10 per cent per year.

Figure 2 shows similar results under aggregate projection B. Regardless

Table 2. Merchandise Imports and Gross Domestic Production

Commodity	Merchandise Imports (Rupees, crores)			Gross Domestic Production		Ratio of Imports to Gross Domestic Production		Case 1		Case 2		Case 3	
	1960–61	1965–66	1965–66	1960–61	1965–66	1960–61	1965–66	1970–71	1975–76	1970–71	1975–76	1970–71	1975–76
	(1)	(2)	(3)	(4)	(5)	(6)	(7)	(8)	(9)	(10)	(11)	(12)	(13)
03 Equipment, electrical	57	106	168	126	246	.452	.431	.150	.100	.200	.100	.375	.250
04 Equipment, transport	69	92	162	201	369	.343	.249	.150	.100	.200	.100	.250	.200
05 Equipment, other	229	429	605	344	660	.666	.650	.250	.200	.450	.200	.525	.350
06 Iron and steel	121	93	67	269	578	.450	.161	.050	.025	.100	.025	.100	.050
09 Other metals	49	63	93	32	62	1.531	1.016	.500	.500	.500	.500	.500	.500
10 Other minerals	10	n.a.	24	45	65	.222	n.a.	.180	.180	.180	.180	.180	.180
23 Petroleum products	}123	}101	97	237	405	n.a.	n.a.	.040	.040	.040	.040	.040	.040
24 Crude petroleum			52	3	23	n.a.	n.a.	a	a	a	a	a	a
27 Chemicals[b]	111	92	21	284	548	.391	.168	.100	.022	.100	.022	.125	.070
Others, excluding food grains	177	326[c]	314										
Total, excluding food grains	946	1302	1603										

SOURCES: Column 1: Manne and Rudra [5], 1959–60 prices.
2: Our estimates of actuals, current prices.
3: Model results, Case A1, 1959–60 prices.
4: Manne and Rudra [5], 1959–60 prices.
5: Our estimates of actuals, 1959–60 prices.
6: Column 1 ÷ Column 4.
7: Column 2 ÷ Column 5.
8–13: Assumptions, cases 1–3.

a Future domestic production of crude petroleum is specified exogenously. Imports are determined residually as the difference between demand and domestic production.
b From 1965–66 onward, total demand for chemicals is probably underestimated by the model because of outdated norms.
c Includes commodity 10, "other minerals."

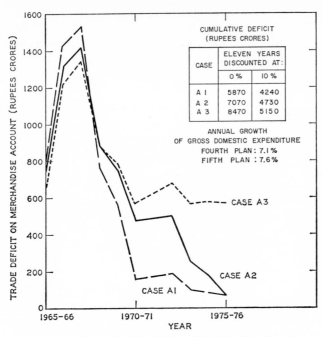

Figure 1. *Alternative Time Paths of Trade Deficit, Case A*

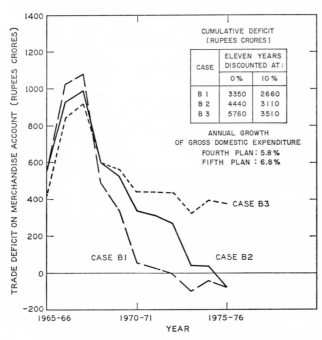

Figure 2. *Alternative Time Paths of Trade Deficit, Case B*

of the aggregate projection considered, our calculations indicate that a rapid import substitution strategy pays off in terms of foreign exchange costs.[1] This payoff holds true over the entire range for which the capital and current input coefficients remain valid.

For those concerned with the over-all balance of payments, Table 3

Table 3. Net and
Gross Foreign Exchange
Requirements, Fourth Plan (Rupees crores)

		Debt Service		
	Balance-of-Trade Deficit	Existing Debt	Fourth Plan Borrowings	Total
	(1)	(2)	(3)	(4)
Case A1	4,440		} 240	5,800
A2	4,840			6,200
A3	4,800			6,160
B1	3,000	} 1,120		4,290
B2	3,380		} 170	4,670
B3	3,360			4,650

SOURCES: Sources are given by column.
1: Results of model. Note that imports of food grains have been excluded.
2: U.S. Agency for International Development.
3: Rough estimates based on average historical lending patterns and terms and column 1.
4: Sum of columns 1, 2, and 3.

indicates both debt service and the balance-of-trade deficit for the six alternative cases. The total would have to be covered by gross foreign aid, foreign private investment, and net exports of other services such as tourism.

Principal Results—Domestic Savings

Cases A and B differ substantially in terms of growth of household consumption: 5.5 per cent per year in A versus 4.5 per cent in B during the Fourth Plan (see Table 4). In order to satisfy the higher consumption demands, gross investment and the trade deficit are both higher in A than in B.

Now assume that just enough foreign financing to cover the trade deficit

[1] In earlier experiments we analyzed a case with a higher aggregate growth rate than Case A. The results with respect to import substitution were similar.

Table 4. Implied Gross
Domestic Savings (Rupees crores)

		1965–66 (estimated)	1970–71	1975–76
Case A1 (consumption grows at 5.5% per year in Fourth Plan)	Gross investment	3,600	6,590	10,600
	Trade deficit	500	160	70
	Implied domestic saving	3,100	6,430	10,530
	Gross domestic expenditure	21,000	29,600	42,700
Case B1 (consumption grows at 4.5% per year in Fourth Plan)	Gross investment	3,600	5,710	9,450
	Trade deficit	500	60	−80
	Implied domestic saving	3,100	5,650	9,530
	Gross domestic expenditure	21,000	27,800	38,700

is always available and that there is a zero deficit in the invisibles account. Gross domestic savings will then be identically equal to the difference between gross investment and that trade deficit. If foreign financing can be adjusted in this way, the implied domestic savings ratios (whether marginal or average) are not significantly different as between Cases A and B. Even though A provides more consumption than B, the foreign financing of the trade deficit would enable India to get along with almost the same savings *ratios* in either case.

If we continue to assume that enough foreign financing will be made available to cover whatever trade deficits are generated, it turns out that the implied domestic savings ratios *are* affected by the import substitution program (see Table 5). The more rapid the import substitution program (i.e., in moving from Case 3 to 2 to 1), the less foreign financing becomes available and the greater the reliance upon domestic savings.

Case A1 (the most ambitious in terms of both aggregate growth and import substitution) would require that domestic savings be stepped up from an average 15 per cent of gross domestic expenditures in 1965–66 to 22 per cent in 1970–71. The implied domestic marginal propensity to save would be 39 per cent during the Fourth Plan. The less ambitious import substitution cases (A2 and A3) would imply marginal savings propensities of 36 and 33 per cent respectively. The less rapid the import substitution program, the lower would be the requirements for domestic savings and

Table 5. Implied Gross Domestic Savings
Ratios (per cent of gross domestic expenditure)

	Marginal Ratios		Average Ratios		
	Fourth Plan	Fifth Plan	1965–66 (estimates)	1970–71	1975–76
Case A1	39	31 ⎤		22	25
A2	36	33 ⎬	15	21	25
A3	33	30 ⎦		20	23
B1	38	35 ⎤		20	25
B2	34	37 ⎬	15	20	25
B3	31	34 ⎦		19	23

for fiscal austerity and the longer would be the continued dependence upon foreign aid.[2]

Construction Bottleneck

Cases A and B both imply an increase in aggregate growth rates from the Third Plan to the Fourth Plan. The rate of increase of gross domestic expenditures would move from 4.9 to 7.1 per cent for Case A and to 5.8 per cent for Case B. This implies an immediate rise in demand for producers' goods—particularly investment goods.[3] Because it takes time to expand the capacity of the Indian economy, much of this sharp increase of demand would have to be satisfied by imports (see Figures 1 and 2, above). Demand for services such as construction, transport, and electric power cannot, however, be met by imports. According to our estimates of growth in demands, present capacities, and time lags, this problem of excess demand would be serious only in the urban and industrial construction sector. The 1965–66 demand for this service implied by our growth assumptions is about 50 per cent higher than our estimate of current supply. We have assumed that this sector's output can be expanded with only a one-year lag. Domestic supply could therefore rise to meet the demand by 1966–67; the required increase in output in one year would be between 50 and 75 per cent.

[2] We have calculated the magnitude of this trade-off for the period 1965–66 through 1975–76. The ratio of reduction in domestic savings to increase in trade deficit, holding consumption and exports constant, can be regarded as the rate of transformation of rupees into foreign exchange through the process of import substitution. For the import substitution programs we have analyzed, roughly two rupees of additional domestic savings would be needed to reduce by one rupee the requirement for foreign aid.

[3] Note that this would make possible a corresponding increase in the employment of construction workers.

The exact magnitude of this problem depends on several assumptions and parameter estimates which are all subject to error. One does not, however, have to believe the precise specifications of our model, or the precise estimates of our parameters, to realize that an acceleration of growth requires a sharp increase in the supply of investment goods and services.

There will be wide differences of opinion as to the feasibility of providing the resource inputs needed for internal consistency within one or another of our six alternative cases. Our model is intended only to quantify the requirements to "get from here to there" under a given set of productivity assumptions. The efficiency implied by our estimates of capital and current input requirements, gestation lags, and others, is not fixed forever. Resource input requirements could be reduced either by reducing targets or by increasing efficiencies.

Other Results

Table 6 contains selected output targets implied by our calculations for Case A1. Note that the growth rates for producers' goods (machinery, steel, petroleum products, and electricity) are all much higher during the Fourth than during the Fifth Plan. The output of consumers' goods, on the other hand, grows more rapidly during the Fifth Plan. These results are reasonably close to the targets shown in Perspective Planning Division (1964). Output levels for all thirty sectors are listed in Table 7.

The Fourth Plan investment allocations proposed in Planning Commission (October, 1964) are shown in Table 8. Also shown are the investment allocations generated in our calculations for Cases A1 and B1. The Planning Commission is evidently counting on a more substantial gain in the productivity of investment than is implied by our capital coefficients.

All of the six basic cases have been premised upon merchandise exports growing from rupees 633 crores in 1960–61 to rupees 1,520 crores in 1975–76—a growth rate of 6 per cent per year. These six basic cases explored alternative import substitution strategies. We have also investigated a variant concerned with export promotion. Starting from the same initial position in 1965–66, this variant is premised upon an aggregate growth of exports at 9 per cent per year, with most of the additional exports concentrated in the engineering industries. Since both the import substitution and the export promotion assumptions are rather arbitrary, a comparison of the absolute trade deficits is not very useful. A more meaningful result is the ratio of reduction in the trade deficit to the additional export revenues. This comes out to about 75 per cent. This means that 25 per cent of the

Table 6. Comparison of Gross Output Targets[a]

Case Al		1965–66	1970–71	1975–76	Per cent growth over five years	
					Fourth Plan	Fifth Plan
05 Equipment, other	(Rs. crores)	660	1,423	2,278	116%	60%
06 Iron and steel	" "	578	1,359	2,254	136	66
15 Food grains	" "	4,642	5,770	7,389	24	28
16 Cotton and other textiles	" "	1,024	1,320	1,943	29	48
23 Petroleum products	" "	405	894	1,497	120	68
29 Electricity		168	427	732	154	72
Perspective Planning Division (1964)						
Machinery	(Rs. crores)	432	1,151	1,928	166	68
Steel ingots	(million tons)	7.8	17.5	29.0	124	66
Food grains	(million tons)	90	122	151	36	24
Cotton fabrics	(million meters)	5,075	6,400	9,500	26	48
Petroleum products	(million tons)	13	27	42	108	55
Electricity generation	(billion kw. hours)	47	95	151	102	59

[a] Sectoral classifications are not strictly comparable between the two sources.

| | Output Levels (Rupees crores, 1959–60 producers' prices) | | | | Annual Growth Rates, Fourth Plan | |
| | | | 1970–71 | | | |
Sector	1960–61	1965–66	Case A1	Case B3	Case A1	Case B3
1. Construction, urban and industrial	1,201.0	1,615.	3,678	3,149	18.0%	14.0%
2. Construction, rural	416.0	[a]	620	536	8.8	8.4
3. Equipment, electrical	126.0	246.	501	371	15.0	8.6
4. Equipment, transport	201.0	369.	716	594	14.0	10.0
5. Equipment, other	343.5	660.	1,423	1,040	17.0	9.5
6. Iron and steel	269.0	578.	1,359	1,070	19.0	13.0
7. Iron ore	7.8	15.	38	33	21.0	17.0
8. Cement	52.6	71.	170	146	19.0	16.0
9. Other metals	32.0	62.	227	174	30.0	23.0
10. Other minerals	45.4	65.	198	175	25.0	22.0
11. Plantations	196.0	232.	276	272	3.5	2.2
12. Leather and leather products	189.0	220.	338	317	9.0	7.6
13. Animal husbandry	1,130.0	1,323.	1,881	1,778	7.3	6.1
14. Food industries	1,323.0	1,550.	1,980	1,903	5.0	4.2
15. Food grains	3,974.3	4,642.	5,770	5,551	4.4	3.6
16. Cotton and other textiles	800.0	1,024.	1,320	1,250	5.2	4.1
17. Jute textiles	130.0	165.	214	206	5.4	4.5
18. Other agriculture	2,097.0	2,427.	3,353	3,194	6.7	5.6
19. Chemical fertilizers	20.7	83.	455	435	41.0	39.0
20. Glass, wooden and nonmetallic mineral products	398.0	507.	1,107	960	17.0	14.0
21. Forestry products	180.0	240.	506	440	16.0	13.0
22. Motor transport	325.0	480.	965[b]	885[b]	15.0	13.0
23. Petroleum products	237.1	405.	894	818	17.0	15.0
24. Crude oil	3.2	23.	71[b]	71[b]	25.0	25.0
25. Rubber products	67.5	102.	162	147	9.7	7.6
26a. Synthetic rubber	—	8.	11	8	6.6	0.0
26b. Plantation and reclaimed rubber	15.5	18.	30[b]	30[b]	11.0	11.0
27. Chemicals	284.0	548.	842	749	9.0	6.4
28. Railways	454.0	513.	884	792	11.5	9.0
29. Electricity	103.4	168.	427	379	20.5	17.7
30. Coal	109.0	152.	246	214	10.0	7.1

[a] Output level for Case A1: Rs. 406 crores; for Case B3: Rs. 357 crores.

[b] Determined exogenously.

Table 8. Size and Pattern of Investment, Fourth Plan

	Planning Commission (1964)	Case A1	Case B1
Net fixed investment:[a]			
Agriculture and irrigation	17%	23%	22%
Power, industry, transport, and communications	64	61	63
Housing, education, health, and other	19	16	15
	100%	100%	100%
Total net investment (Rs. crores)[b]	20,000[c]	26,700[d]	22,800[d]

[a] Sectoral classification not strictly comparable between sources.
[b] Includes Rs. 1,200 crores for increase in stocks; excludes replacement estimated at Rs. 3,000 crores.
[c] 1963–64 prices.
[d] 1959–60 prices.

additional export revenues are offset by imports needed to produce the additional exports.

For each of the thirty sectors, a gestation lag of one or more years has been assumed.[4] One set of calculations was made which was identical to Case A1 except for these lags. The modification consisted of reducing the lags by one year. The most pronounced effect, as might have been anticipated, was a reduction of about 5 per cent in endogenous investment. In a growing economy, a shortened lag has a similar effect to a reduction in the capital-output ratio. The reduction in investment in turn implies a corresponding reduction in machinery imports and in the balance-of-trade deficit.

APPENDIX: MATHEMATICAL FORMULATION

This work has been carried out in two parts. First, a consistent set of output levels, imports, and induced investment was derived for each of two target years. Except for induced investment, these interindustry calculations are similar to those discussed in Manne and Rudra [5] and Srinivasan, Saluja, and Sabherwal [6], and we omit a detailed verbal description here. The target years were the ends of the Fourth and Fifth Plans, 1970–71 and 1975–76. In each case the base year was the last year of the Third Plan, 1965–66.

After calculating these output levels for the target years, the output levels, the input-output coefficients, and the exogenous final demands for the intermediate years (1966–67 through 1969–70 and 1971–72 through 1974–75) were interpolated

[4] All numerical data are available upon request from the authors.

log-linearly. Interindustry demands were then calculated by the input-output method.

In each year, the induced investment demands were generated through an accelerator relationship, that is, through multiplying capital coefficients by *future* output increases. In order to calculate induced investment within the interindustry model of the two target years, 1970–71 and 1975–76, the future output increases were derived from the current *absolute* levels of output by exogenously specified sectoral growth rates for the subsequent five-year plan. An iterative procedure was employed to insure that the output growth rates specified for the Fifth Plan would be consistent with the absolute output levels derived separately for 1970–71 and 1975–76. The computer was programmed to calculate the 1970–71 output levels, then revise the Fifth Plan growth rates, then revise the 1970–71 output levels, and so on. Fewer than ten iterations were required in order to obtain a mutually consistent set of growth rates and output levels.

After calculating the demands and interpolating domestic production levels log-linearly for the first four years of each Plan period, the computer program calculates the implied supply-demand gaps for each item in each year. It is supposed that these gaps will be bridged in one of three ways, depending upon the sector: (1) *imports* of investment and producers' goods in sectors 3–10, 19–21, 23–27, 30; (2) *consumption shortfalls* in the food and fiber sectors, 11–18; (3) *revisions of the domestic output levels* within the five service sectors: 1, 2, 22, 28, and 29. (Revisions *above* the log-linear trend line are not permitted during years for which this would imply additional investment prior to 1965–66.)

As the calculations turned out, the consumption shortfalls were negligible, and so were the revisions of domestic output for the five service sectors. The only service in which a significant gap occurred was urban and industrial construction (sector 1) for the year 1965–66. It is because of this one major gap that our calculations are "almost consistent" rather than fully consistent.

The following characteristics of the computing procedure should be noted:

1. By postulating shock absorbers such as consumption shortfalls and producers' goods imports, the formulation resembles an open-loop simulator rather than a fully consistent model. (In a closed-loop, negative feedback simulator, these gaps would trigger policies designed to reduce their magnitude.)

2. Unlike a recursive dynamic input-output model, this interpolation procedure insures that virtually all domestic output levels for the initial year 1965–66 will match the estimates of initial conditions. The five service sectors are the only ones in which this output matching cannot be guaranteed in advance.

3. Output during the Fourth Plan is assumed to grow along a log-linear trend line. This implies that the short-run accelerator is sufficiently flexible so that these output increases in the first years of the Fourth Plan are *not* constrained by the project starts that were under way during the final years of the Third Plan.

The model has the following variables:

x_j^t = annual rate of domestic production, process j, year t.
y_i^t = annual import rate, item i, year t.
v_i^t = annual rate of investment demand in year t for good i induced by output increase.

The superscripts t on the above three variables take on the value for each year from $t = $ 1965–66 through $t = $ 1975–76.

The model also has the following parameters and exogenous data:

a_{ij} current account interindustry demands on item i per unit output of process j. Some of these norms change over time.

b_{ij} fixed capital account demands on item i per unit increase in output of process j.

c_i^T ratio of imports to domestic production of item i, year T. The superscripts T take on two values: $T = $ 1970–71 and $T = $ 1975–76. Most of the nonzero c_i^T parameters drop from 1970–71 to 1975–76.

J inventory demand per unit increase in activity level (set at zero for service sectors and .25 for others).

q lag in investment demand; varies with sector of destination.

Exogenous data:

x_j^{65} annual rate of domestic production, process j, 1965–66.

$(h,g,e,o,k)_i^t$ annual rate of demand, item i, year t, by households, government, exports, "others," and exogenously specified capital formation.

m^t total value of exogenous imports, year t.

x_{22}^t, x_{24}^t annual rate of domestic production of motor transport and crude petroleum, year t.

r_j annual growth rate of process j, subsequent Plan.

The variables are related through the following equations:

(domestic production) + (imports) = $\begin{pmatrix} \text{interindustry} \\ \text{demand} \end{pmatrix}$

$$x_i^T \quad + \quad y_i^T \quad = \quad \Sigma_j a_{ij} x_j^T$$

$$+ \begin{pmatrix} \text{exogenous} \\ \text{final demand} \end{pmatrix}$$

$$+ (h + g + e + o + k)_i^T$$

$$+ \begin{pmatrix} \text{induced investment demand:} \\ \text{fixed and inventories} \end{pmatrix}$$

$$+ v_i^T + J(x_i^{T+1} - x_i^T) \quad (i = 1, \ldots, 30).$$

Induced fixed investment demand:

$$v_i^T = \Sigma_j b_{ij} r_j x_j^T (1 + r_j)^{q-1} \qquad (i = 1, \ldots, 30).$$

Import levels:

$$y_i^T = c_i^T x_i^T \qquad (i = 1, \ldots, 30).$$

Note that we have eliminated the noncompetitive imports specified in Manne and Rudra [5] and Srinivasan [6].

The investment demands and imports are expressed in terms of the domestic production levels. We are then left with a set of thirty equations, in thirty unknowns x_i^T. It has been our experience that the model is sufficiently well behaved to produce unique, nonnegative values of the x_i^T.

Having calculated the x_j^T for each sector for 1970–71 and 1975–76, we then calculate the annual variables as follows:

x_j^t = log-linear interpolation between x_j^{65} and x_j^0 for $t = 66$ through 69; between x_j^{70} and x_j^{75} for $t = 71$ through 74 ($j \neq 1, 2, 22, 28, 29$).

x_j^t = outputs in the service sectors are set equal to total demand unless this value lies above log-linear trend line during Fourth Plan, and additional investment would be required prior to 1965–66 ($j = 1, 2, 22, 28, 29$).

$$y_i^t = \begin{cases} -x_i^t + \Sigma_j a_{ij} x_j^t + (h + g + e + o + k)_i^t + J(x_i^{t+1} - x_i^t) + v_i^t \\ \qquad\qquad\qquad\qquad\qquad (i = 3\text{–}10, 19\text{–}21, 23\text{–}27, 30) \\ 0 \text{ all other } i. \end{cases}$$

$$v_i^t = \Sigma_j b_{ij}(x_j^{t+q} - x_j^{t+q-1}) \qquad (i = 1, \ldots, 30).$$

In calculating the trade deficit for each year, we include imports of commodities as well as additional exogenous imports. Since the export final demand vector is valued at producers' prices, we allow for trade and transport margin on exports:

$$\begin{pmatrix} \text{trade} \\ \text{deficit} \end{pmatrix} = \begin{array}{c} \text{imports} \\ 17 \text{ sectors} \\ \\ \displaystyle\sum_{\substack{i=3-10, \\ 19-21, \\ 23-27, \\ 30}} y_i \end{array} + \begin{array}{c} \text{exogenous} \\ \text{imports} \\ \\ m^t \end{array} - \begin{array}{c} \text{exports at} \\ \text{producers'} \\ \text{prices} \\ \Sigma_j e_j \end{array} - \begin{pmatrix} \text{margin} \\ \text{on exports} \end{pmatrix}.$$

REFERENCES

1. Chakravarty, S., and Lefeber, L. "An Optimizing Planning Model," *The Economic Weekly* (Bombay), February, 1965.
2. Government of India. *Economic Survey, 1964–65*. New Delhi, February, 1965.
3. Perspective Planning Division. *Notes on Perspective of Development, India, 1960–61 to 1975–76*. New Delhi: Government of India, Planning Commission, April, 1964.

4. Planning Commission. *Memorandum on the Fourth Five Year Plan.* New Delhi: Government of India, October, 1964.
5. Manne, A. S., and Rudra, A. "A Consistency Model of India's Fourth Plan," *Sankhya,* Series B, vol. 27, Parts 1 and 2, 1965.
6. Srinivasan, T. N., Saluja, M. R., and Sabherwal, V. C. "Structure of the Indian Economy: 1975–76." New Delhi: Indian Statistical Institute, Discussion Paper Number 4, April, 1965.

COMMENT

Louis Lefeber, STANFORD UNIVERSITY

In recent years, in developed and developing countries alike, there has been an increasing awareness of the need for improving the methods of economic planning. In particular, politicians and public administrators want detailed prescriptions for a consistent and feasible path toward socially desired goals. The evident public need, coupled with recent advances in growth theory and computational techniques, has motivated a number of economists to search for computable models of economic planning. The Bergsman-Manne paper represents the outcome of such an effort.

The paper was written before the outbreak of India's most recent military engagement with Pakistan and before the information on the current crop failure due to drought in India was available. Hence the computations and the authors' judgment as to feasibility are based on information and expectations which prevailed before these recent emergencies. Clearly, it would be pointless to discuss the relevance of the actual numerical results, and I shall confine my comments primarily to the qualitative aspects of the Bergsman-Manne approach.

Economic plans are political documents and as such they are made up of three components: (1) the statement of the social goals; (2) the projection of those patterns of private and public activities which are required for approaching the social goals; and (3) a design of policies aimed at motivating the private and public decision makers (consumers, investors, and producers) to act in a manner consistent with the projected path. In this sense, the Bergsman-Manne model— as well as any other model I am acquainted with—is *not* a model of an economic plan, since it is not concerned with either the selection of or the relative weights to be given to the social goals or the design of policies. It is designed to find or to describe a path which is consistent with a limited number of exogenously given social objectives. The latter are stated in the form of desired annual rates of growth for household and government consumption and exogenously specified capital formation.

The computations are carried out in two distinct steps. First, the sectoral targets (consistent output levels, endogenous investments, and imports) are computed for the terminal years of the plans under investigation. Then the sectoral output levels in each of the intermediate years are determined on the basis of a log-linear interpolation between the terminal and initial plan years. The resulting sectoral time paths are mechanical extensions of the single-period solutions for the target years. They are best described as trajectories which have neither a recursive structure nor a necessary internal consistency. Thus the authors do not work with a growth model which would ensure an optimal or even a consistent allocation of resources. Nonetheless—with some limitations which I shall discuss below—by literally bridging the resulting supply and demand gaps with what they call "shock-absorbers" (unconstrained imports of producers' goods, consumption shortfalls, and changes in domestic services) they can trace out a consistent and, on the trajectory itself, feasible time path for each of the sectoral outputs. This procedure does not ensure economic feasibility at the beginning of the plan period. Here the assumption is that whatever the required sectoral rates of growth, the necessary initial productive capacities (capital and investment in progress) are available in each sector. In sectors where production lags and investment gestation periods are significant, this assumption may not be readily defensible.[1]

After the derivation of a consistent set of trajectories, the authors (1) compare the computed outputs with the statistical estimates of outputs in the initial year of the period under investigation; (2) compare the domestic savings implications of the alternative computed growth paths with statistical estimates of the economy's current savings; and (3) trace the behavior of the "shock-absorbers" over time with particular reference to determining the foreign exchange requirements of the alternative paths. The information thus obtained can then be used to analyze the feasibility of alternative development paths in terms of their particular savings, foreign exchange, and initial capital requirements.[2] It is in this sense that the authors regard their work as a model for "requirements analysis."

The model was specifically developed in order to analyze the foreign exchange requirements of India's Fourth and Fifth Plans. For this purpose the authors investigate the implications of two alternative aggregate growth paths over the ten-year period beginning in 1965–66. Each of the two alternatives is then considered in combination with three different import-substitution policies. The results of the computations can be briefly summarized as follows: (1) with the exception of the initial induced construction requirements, the different growth paths are found to be feasible in terms of the estimated initial capacities, and (2) the foreign exchange costs (measured in balance-of-trade deficits) of accelerated programs of import substitution are not only recovered over the ten-year planning horizon but are smaller than those of less ambitious programs of substitution.

These are interesting and significant results. However, since there may be a

---

[1] To the extent that multiple shift operations can be introduced, the assumption may be less damaging.

[2] Nonfeasibility in this context does not necessarily mean absolute impossibility in a technical sense; it may just mean social or political lack of desirability.

temptation to look upon planning models as if they could serve primarily *predictive* rather than *normative* purposes, it may be useful to consider some of the qualitative aspects of the relationship between the computational results and the structure of the model. This is all the more important since the computations were not performed in the context of a hypothetical economy but in the very real setting of the Fourth and Fifth Indian Five-Year Plans which are currently in preparation and under technical and political consideration.

In this connection, we must first remember that the Bergsman-Manne log-linear trajectories are arbitrarily determined and do not represent optimal paths with respect to any objective. The necessary implication is that the efficiency of the trajectories may be improved by injecting some optimizing principle. Since in the model the rate of growth of private and public consumption is given—and the focus is on the foreign exchange requirements of alternative import-substitution policies—the minimization of foreign exchange costs of production and investment may provide such a principle. The point is not that optimizing models are necessarily preferable; depending on their specification they may or may not be better approximations of the conditions prevailing in the economy than the Bergsman-Manne model.[3] The point is that the structure of the model was chosen by the authors not because it provides a better description of the economy than some optimizing model—as far as I know, no tests were performed with alternative models—but because of its computational advantage, which is an arbitrary criterion in determining a model's relevance. Thus one must keep in mind that more efficient resource utilization than that in the Bergsman-Manne trajectories could be indicated which would make the attainment of the targets that much easier. The same comments are also relevant to the efficiency of foreign exchange use: the extreme rigidity of fixed import-output ratios does not permit allocation according to real cost advantage. If some endogenous choice were permitted in the framework of an optimizing mechanism, decreases in the implied foreign exchange requirements might be experienced.

Second, the way the technical and demand coefficients are entered may be of importance. We know from the experience of advanced countries that in addition to investment, technological change has a fundamentally important role in bringing about (explaining) economic growth. There is reason to believe that the same must be true—possibly with even greater force—in the case of underdeveloped countries. We might expect this change to manifest itself both in the structure of the input-output tables and in the magnitudes of the capital-output ratios. The Bergsman-Manne computations are based on input-output tables which, save for a shift in the direction of greater reliance on chemical fertilizers in the agricultural sectors, show *no further change* during the period 1970–71 to 1975–76. In addition, the capital coefficients remain constant over the entire ten-year period. These may be correct assumptions, but if they happen not to be, they

---

[3] In a normative context, however, optimizing models are inherently less arbitrary than nonoptimizing ones. But this in itself is insufficient to determine the relevance of any model to an actual economy.

will have strong implications for the computed savings and foreign exchange requirements. And though no one can accuse the authors—and particularly Professor Manne who has already done important work in India on the effects of technical change on the input-output structure—of ignoring technological change, it would be desirable if the paper itself were more explicit about the underlying assumptions and their implications for the computed results.

Similar observations could be made about the demand coefficients. Though in general the computations do not indicate a major consumption shortfall over the entire ten-year period, the paper is termed "an almost consistent" model because insufficient capacity in the construction sector could be a bottleneck in the initial years of the ten-year planning period.[4] In evaluating the significance of this constraint, one has to keep in mind, however, that as much as half of the shortfall in the initial induced investment may correspond to residential house construction. On the one hand, the demand for housing in a country like India can be defined only in the most arbitrary terms, and on the other, the supply of residential construction is relatively easily restricted if that is considered desirable.[5] Hence the initial bottleneck in construction may be less constraining than indicated by the unexplained findings.

When computations with the help of planning models are undertaken with the intention of using them as aids in actual policy decisions, the relevant coefficients must be subjected to scrutiny not only regarding their historical plausibility but also with an eye toward the possibility of changing the norms. The purpose is not to cheat with statistics but to investigate the possibility and desirability of adjusting demand and supply by suitable policy measures.

Of course, every time the norms are adjusted or the constraints are shifted, the implied savings and foreign exchange requirements are correspondingly affected. It is unlikely that the general findings of the paper as to the time profiles of the balance-of-payments deficits would be very much altered by changes in the norms—though the size of the deficits might be significantly affected.[6] Savings would be very sensitive to technological change and also to demand restrictions. It would be important to undertake at least some sensitivity analysis to determine the savings implications of variations in the norms, particularly since the average savings requirements as computed by Bergsman and Manne seem to be excessive.

[4] Though this is semantics, the title of the Bergsman-Manne paper is somewhat misleading. The model itself is consistent. The question is whether the computed trajectories are feasible in terms of the estimated capacities expected to prevail in the initial year. Hence, if the authors are concerned about the nonfeasibility of their trajectories because of the initial construction bottleneck, they would be more accurate if they used the term "almost feasible" rather than "almost consistent."

[5] In fact, historical experience suggests that the supply of housing lags in the initial stages of both capitalistic and socialistic development. Consider the Manchester slums and the Soviet housing squeeze.

[6] The profiles themselves would change, however, in response to introducing an optimizing mechanism combined with some endogenous choice in the import-substitution policies. This is borne out by the results of Chenery and MacEwan, "Optimal Patterns of Growth and Aid: The Case of Pakistan," this volume, pp. 149–78.

But they may be attainable only if the recent average savings trends continue over the coming plan periods. However, the road from 15 to 22 per cent is arduous. At the same time, as a matter of relief, the prohibitive percentages listed as "marginal ratios" cannot be considered to be marginal savings ratios in their generally understood sense. They are the slopes of straight lines which connect points on vertically shifting savings functions and not changes in planned savings (as function of income) with respect to changes in income. The actual marginal rates cannot be determined from the model; a simple geometrical exercise, however, can convince us that if the average savings rates are increased in response to a shift in the savings function, the actual marginal rates must be below the rates computed by the authors.[7]

As mentioned above, the authors do not specify the policy measures needed to implement any one of the alternative programs computed in their "requirements analysis." Nor do they take a position as to the feasibility or the desirability of any of the alternatives. They are correct in pointing out that the parameters and constraints they work with must not be considered as fixed forever. And, indeed, constraints are not immovable and norms can be changed. For instance, in a country like India, agricultural productivity could be increased if the government would intensify its farm program. Then, on the basis of some assumptions about how agricultural productivity would be affected, we could estimate the corresponding changes in the norms used in the computations.

Thus, resource or input requirements can be reduced not only by reducing targets but also—most importantly—by increasing efficiency or by adjusting the composition of demand. In fact, the process of planning does not consist of searching for some path which takes the structure of the economy as constant and which has only the merit that it is historically consistent and feasible. Instead, planning consists of trying to ascertain the benefits and costs of adjusting the

---

[7] For the case of comparing observed savings S_0 and S_1 before and after a shift in the savings function (say in response to a change in tax policy), consider the following geometrical representation. The *MPS* are the slopes of the functions shown in solid lines. The rates computed by the authors correspond to the slope of the straight line defined by the points (Y_0, S_0) and (Y_1, S_1).

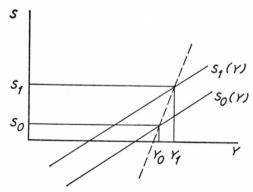

supply and demand relationships so as best to approximate the social objectives of development. And, indeed, this is where the use of planning models is justified: they can be employed to analyze the relationship between certain strategic elements of a plan and to study the consequences of changing the assumptions underlying these elements. But since the analysis can be undertaken only at the cost of abstracting from the majority of objectives and constraints, the results must be interpreted from the point of view of their qualitative rather than quantitative significance.

Before concluding my discussion, I would like to make one further comment about the uses of planning models for choosing growth paths and strategy. The Bergsman-Manne computations provide us with six alternatives to choose from. By subjecting the model structure and the norms to further changes, we could generate any number of other growth paths, many of which might be as plausible or as relevant as the Bergsman-Manne trajectories. Each path implies a different set of policies, and the choice among the alternatives can be made only in terms of some political-economic judgment. Thus, I agree with the authors when they consciously side-step the question of choice. Economic plans represent the reconciliation of a vast number of political and economic constraints with a multitude of frequently contradictory and non-quantifiable social objectives. In a world of imperfect knowledge and uncertainty, the use of planning models is necessarily confined to partial analysis. It would be not only illegitimate from the methodological point of view but also foolhardy to use them for prejudging the strategy of economic development.

10. KEY SECTORS OF THE
MEXICAN ECONOMY, 1962–72

A L A N S. M A N N E, STANFORD UNIVERSITY*

This paper describes a model which is intended to be useful for long-range investment programming within Mexico. The analysis deals with the interdependence between investment decisions in key sectors of the economy. The model is of the "process analysis" type. It includes technological detail with respect to products and alternative processes.

Time is treated in a highly aggregative fashion. The model deals with the changes that might take place during the course of a decade, but there is no detailed analysis of time-phasing within that decade. Capital investment demands are calculated endogenously through the device of a stock-flow conversion factor for the target year of 1972.

The following are the principal features that distinguish this from an earlier programming model constructed at Nacional Financiera:

1. The earlier calculations were based upon a single criterion: satisfying the exogenous demands within a minimum input of foreign exchange to the key sectors. The present model has the flexibility to allow for several alternative criteria: minimization of foreign exchange, minimization of total input costs at conventional prices, and minimization of total input costs at various shadow prices for foreign exchange and capital. For purposes of this sectoral analysis, we found it more reliable to estimate the shadow prices than the absolute quantities available of these scarce inputs.

* This is a report summarizing work done during 1963, sponsored both by Nacional Financiera, S.A., and by the United Nations Technical Assistance program. It is a pleasure to acknowledge indebtedness to each of the following individuals: Dr. Alfredo Navarrete R. who initiated the study; Lic. Ignacio Navarro G. and Victor Navarrete R. who headed the working group; and Lic. Pedro Galicia Estrada, Alfonso García Macías, Emmanuel J. Uren, Tulio Espinosa Cabrera, and Humberto Gaetan Rojo.

2. One of the striking results of the earlier model was the recommendation that Mexico embark upon an extensive program of new industries for the production of capital goods. Because of the small size of the Mexican market, there had been considerable skepticism with respect to this finding. For the present series of calculations, there are twelve categories of equipment that have been examined more closely from this make-or-buy viewpoint. In comparison with plant sizes that are representative of the U.S., the present model predicts that the 1972 Mexican market will be sufficiently large to support nine of these new industries.

3. In the earlier effort, considerable difficulties were experienced in connection with data processing. Through the introduction of various precautionary steps (a "bedsheet" of the entire matrix and automatic analyses of each individual row and column), it is believed that there has been a considerable improvement in the reliability of the numerical results.

I. BACKGROUND

A number of the specific characteristics of this model stem from the fact that it was developed by a group within Nacional Financiera, S.A. This institution, founded in 1934, is Mexico's official industrial development bank—but not an over-all planning agency. Financiera's function consists of obtaining long-term capital from both domestic and foreign sources and of channeling these funds into individual enterprises, both in the public and the private sectors. Much of the bank's day-to-day business concerns evaluating investment project proposals and relating these proposals to over-all criteria of economic efficiency and of social welfare. Ultimately, this is the problem to which the work is addressed—constructing a bridge between evaluation procedures at the micro and at the macro level.

The model deals with the interdependence between investment decisions in certain basic sectors of the economy that are of most immediate concern to Financiera: paper, heavy chemicals, petrochemicals, petroleum, cement, steel, copper, aluminum, foundries, machinery production, electricity, and railroad services. For shorthand, these are labeled "key sectors." The balance of the economy is viewed exogenously—both as a source of inputs and as a market for products. The calculations are intended to examine the implications of alternative rates of growth of Mexico's Gross National Product, particularly insofar as this affects the key sectors' aggregate demands for investment funds and for foreign exchange.

Since the work is directed toward the interdependence of investment decisions and not toward the management of individual projects or enterprises, many details have been suppressed. The time-phasing of construction is completely neglected. There is a high degree of aggregation both in the product-mix and in the process alternatives.

II. AGGREGATIVE RESULTS

The model calculates the interdependence effects of installing new domestic production capacity over the decade 1962–72. The year 1962 is known as the "base" and 1972 as the "target year." The new capacity constructed during the decade, together with imports and with the capacity surviving from the base year, is to be chosen in such a way as to cover the target year's demands for each of the 103 commodities produced by the key sectors. Certain components of demand are regarded as endogenous: the demands of the key sectors for their own products, both on current and on capital account. Other elements of demand are treated exogenously and are predicted on the basis of both secular trends and elasticities with respect to the GNP: household and government demands, plus the current and capital account demands of industries outside the key sectors. Export demands are also regarded as exogenous.[1]

The conditions of the model ensure that the exogenous demands will be satisfied at minimum total input costs. The total costs include domestic and foreign exchange inputs, both on capital and current account. The model is *not* intended to determine the optimal rate of growth of the GNP, but only to explore the resource implications of alternative growth policies. At each growth rate, results are presented with respect to the major bottleneck items: foreign exchange and total investment funds.

Calculations have been performed at three alternative rates: 5.0, 6.0, and 6.5 per cent, compounded annually. The lowest of these corresponds to Mexico's average performance during 1950–62.[2] Mexico's population

---

[1] Within the key sectors, there are only a few of Mexico's traditional export items: crude petroleum, natural gas, and copper. In these cases, it is probable that the country's export potential will continue to be determined primarily by the level of protection adopted by the United States.

There is also the possibility of developing new export lines, e.g., machinery and chemicals to be sold in other parts of Latin America. As of 1963, however, it seemed doubtful that this trade would result in *net* exports for the key sectors.

[2] Evaluating the GNP at 1950 prices and using the official GNP statistics in Banco de México (1963), Mexico's past performance has been as follows:

> 1950–60: 4.9 per cent per annum
> 1951–61: 4.5 per cent per annum
> 1952–62: 4.9 per cent per annum

Postscript added in 1965: The real growth rates experienced in 1963 and 1964 were 6.3 per cent and 10.0 per cent respectively.

growth is approximately 3 per cent per annum. The official goal of the Alliance for Progress is a 2.5 per cent rate of growth of per capita income within Latin America. For these reasons, the three alternative GNP targets cover most of the spectrum of official Mexican thinking on the possibilities for economic growth. The 6.0 per cent and 6.5 per cent figures are regarded, respectively, as optimistic and exceedingly optimistic.

Table 1. General Summary

	Parameters of linear programming calculations			Results of Calculations			
				FFDIV	FFCSTS	ZZXB	ZZXB ÷ FFCSTS
Case identification	Annual percentage rate of growth of GNP, 1962–72	Level of protection (per cent)	Gross rate of return on capital (per cent per year)	Foreign exchange demands 1972[a] (10^6DL)	Total input costs, 1972; capacity constructed during 1962–72[b] (10^9MN)	Total capital requirements, 1962–72 (10^9MN)	Capital-input ratio
1	5.0	0	15	455	26.2	44.7	1.71
2	6.0	0	15	536	30.8	55.2	1.79
3	6.5	0	15	579	33.1	60.8	1.84
4	5.0	∞[c]	15	347	27.6	53.4	1.93
5	6.0	∞[c]	15	403	32.4	65.8	2.03
6	6.5	∞[c]	15	431	34.9	72.6	2.08
7	6.0	20	15	499	32.1	58.0	1.81
8	6.0	0	20	614	33.5	53.0	1.58

[a] Excludes constant amount of foreign exchange required for 1972 operation of plants surviving from 1962.

[b] Inputs for key sectors only; this includes labor, capital charges, foreign exchange, *and* goods and services from non-key sectors.

[c] Criterion for minimization: foreign exchange costs.

In the series of calculations shown in Table 1, there have been no explicit limitations placed on the over-all availability of either foreign exchange or investment funds. Instead, the scarcity of these items is reflected through assigning a high cost coefficient to them. Capital funds are typically priced at a gross rate of 15 per cent per annum, including amortization as well as the net return on capital. The foreign exchange bottleneck is explored via three alternative levels of protection: zero, 20 per cent, and infinity. The zero protection level is based upon an evaluation of foreign exchange at the prevailing 1962 rate of 12.5 MN per DL (pesos per dollar). The 20 per cent level corresponds to an accounting price of 15.0 MN per DL. An infinite level of protection implies that domestic input costs are to be neglected entirely and that the criterion is shifted to one of minimization of foreign exchange costs alone.

Table 1 contains a general summary of the linear programming results for the various growth rates, levels of protection, and gross rate of return on capital. The first six cases are intended to show the interaction between GNP growth policies and the scarcity value imputed to foreign exchange. According to these calculations, there is a significant range of economic substitution possible between imports and domestic production. For example, in moving from zero to infinite protection but holding the growth rate constant at 6.0 per cent, it is possible to reduce the foreign exchange demands from 536 to 403 millions of dollars per year. Note that in order to achieve this saving in foreign exchange, there is an increase in total capital requirements from 55.2 to 65.8 billion pesos over the decade. (The difference in capital requirements is close to 20 per cent at each of the three alternative rates of growth.)

III. AGGREGATIVE RESULTS — ADDITIONAL CASES

In order to avoid calculating and presenting an unmanageable number of parameter combinations, there are just two additional cases shown in Table 1. Both cases 7 and 8 are based upon a 6.0 per cent growth rate. In case 7, with a 20 per cent level of protection, the results are intermediate between those of 2 and 5. The foreign exchange demands are lower than in 2, and the capital requirements are lower than in 5. It is likely that a rate of protection ranging from 20 to 80 per cent would be acceptable within the Mexican government and that the intermediate case 7 coincides more closely with Mexican planners' preferences than do either of the extreme cases.

One check upon the various calculations is to be found in the far right column of Table 1. The quantity FFCSTS refers to the 1972 flow of current and capital costs incurred by plants constructed during the decade 1962–72.[3] Since the total capital requirements, ZZXB, are also estimated on the basis of these new plants, the quantity ZZXB/FFCSTS is an incremental capital-*input* ratio. This aggregate ratio ranges from 1.58 to 2.08 and ap-

---

[3] In order to avoid double-counting, FFCSTS refers only to inputs obtained from outside the key sectors. However, since FFCSTS includes both foreign exchange and domestic materials purchased from outside the key sectors, this quantity is considerably larger than the conventional definition of domestic value added.

Table 2. Foreign Exchange Demands, 1972[a]

	Case 2 Minimum input costs; zero protection	Case 7 Minimum input costs; 20 per cent protection	Case 5 Minimum foreign exchange; infinite protection
Commodity imports (excluding machinery)			
Semi-kraft paper	23	23	0
Caustic soda	5	5	0
Sodium carbonate	29	29	0
Kerosene, diesel oil, jet fuel	57	58	0
Iron ore	52	0	0
Ferrous scrap	4	10	10
Bauxite, trihidrate	1	1	1
Subtotal	171	126	11
Machinery imports			
Turbines and generators	18	18	18
Ships	30	30	30
Locomotives	26	28	29
Subtotal	74	76	77
Miscellaneous current account inputs, complementary to domestic production			
Requirements of machinery sector	162	163	168
Requirements of petroleum, petrochemical, and heavy chemical sectors	86	89	96
Requirements of all other sectors	11	12	14
Subtotal	259	264	278
Miscellaneous capital account inputs, complementary to domestic production			
15 per cent of value of goods and services imported during 1962–72	32	33	37
FFDIV, Grand total	536	499	403

[a] Excludes a constant amount of foreign exchange for 1972 operation of plants surviving from 1962. This table does not purport to be a projection of Mexico's total demand for foreign exchange—only of those amounts required by the key sectors. Assumptions: 6 per cent rate of growth of GNP, 1962–72; 15 per cent rate of return on capital. Figures are in millions of dollars per year.

pears generally consistent with other calculations that have been made for the Mexican economy. *Ceteris paribus*, the capital-input ratio increases with an increase in the economy's growth rate, it increases with the level of protection, and it diminishes when the rate of return on capital is increased from 15 to 20 per cent per annum. All of these directional effects are quite plausible.

Table 1 contains only the aggregate for FFDIV, the 1972 foreign exchange demands of the key sectors. Table 2 shows a detailed breakdown of this total, based upon a 6 per cent rate of growth and a 15 per cent rate of return on capital. The table suggests that the system's import flexibility is confined to a small group of specific commodities: semi-kraft paper, caustic soda, and so forth. As the importance of foreign exchange becomes more and more critical—that is, in moving from case 2 to 7 to 5—these commodity imports are reduced from 171 to 126 to 11 millions of dollars per year. Each of the other three general categories of foreign exchange expenditures increases slightly in order to permit domestic production to serve as a substitute for the commodity imports. The model predicts that the largest single item of foreign exchange expenditure will be the current account requirements that are *complementary* to domestic production of machinery.

IV. ALGEBRAIC FORMULATION

The algebraic formulation resembles others that have been proposed in a similar context by Chenery and Kretschmer [3], Frisch [5], and Sandee [12]. The principal technical difference consists of the treatment of investment demand within the key sectors. Here this source of interindustry demand is treated as an endogenous element. Even though a finite-horizon model is employed, the formulation avoids "edge effects" and contains a built-in rationale for investment activity toward the cutoff date.

The projection of investment demand is based upon choosing a fixed interval between the base and the target year. A decade has been adopted as the time interval. In justification of this choice, some comments will be repeated from a previous report:

A decade seemed preferable to either a much closer or a more distant date. A five-year model would not have permitted us to ignore the lags between investment and output. There would be inadequate lead time to make major changes in the currently projected plant expansions. On the other hand, a 20-year or even more distant time horizon—although more representative of the service life of these investment projects—was rejected because of doubts that our group had the time to make reasonable estimates of technological change over such a long horizon. A decade was adopted as a pragmatic compromise, and not because the more distant future is of negligible interest.[4]

Taking a one-decade interval, and knowing that the rate of growth of capacity and of gross investment in the key sectors will be of the order of magnitude of 5 to 12 per cent compounded annually, investment during the target year can be predicted on the basis of a 15 per cent stock-flow conversion factor. This means that out of the gross accumulated investment over the decade, approximately 15 per cent will take place during the target year. The numerical value of the factor may be determined as follows:

Let e^{rt} = index of gross investment rate at t years after the base date, with annual growth rate r.

Therefore:

e^{10r} = index of gross investment rate at the target date.

Also:

$$\int_{t=0}^{10} e^{rt}\, dt = \frac{e^{10r} - 1}{r} = \text{index of accumulated gross investment over decade.}$$

Therefore:

$$\frac{e^{10r}}{\int_{t=0}^{10} e^{rt}\, dt} = \frac{r}{1 - e^{-10r}} = \text{target year stock-flow conversion factor at growth rate } r \text{ for a decade.}$$

Now if the gross investment rate remains constant for a decade, the amount of investment during the target year will amount to one-tenth the total for the decade. Hence Table 3 shows that as the growth rate r approaches zero, the stock-flow conversion factor takes on the value of 10.0 per cent. The conversion factor is an increasing function of r. Strictly speaking, the factor of 15.0 per cent is applicable for the one growth rate of 8.7 per cent per year. However, it remains a tolerably good approximation at other rates within the broad range of 5.0 to 12.0 per cent.

There are 148 rows and 446 activities in this model. Listed immediately below are the definitions of the major groups of activities—omitting positive and negative unit vectors—together with certain vectors utilized for

[4] A. S. Manne, "Key Sectors of the Mexican Economy, 1960–70," in A. S. Manne and H. M. Markowitz (eds.), *Studies in Process Analysis* (New York, 1963), p. 382.

Table 3.

Growth rate, r, per cent per year	0	5.0	8.7	12.0
Stock-flow conversion factor, $\dfrac{r}{1 - e^{-10r}}$, per cent	10.0	12.7	15.0	17.2

bookkeeping and diagnostic[5] purposes. Also defined below are the parameters that enter into the various restrictions:

Definitions of unknowns

x_j = level of operation of process j, new plants, target year.

y_i = imports of item i, target year.

v_i = demand for investment good i within key sectors, total for the decade.

z_k = key sector demand for input k; these six activities are ZZDA, ZZMA, ZZDB, ZZMB, ZZXB, and ZZTMA.

$FFDIV$ = 1972 foreign exchange demanded by key sectors.

$FFCSTS$ = 1972 total input costs within key sectors.

Definitions of parameters

a_{ij} = current account output $(+)$ or input $(-)$, process j, new plants, target year flows.

b_{ij} = capital coefficient for item i, process j, new plants, total investment over decade.

d_i = capacity of old plants to produce item i during target year, less the current account inputs of i demanded by these plants.

q_i = final demand for i, outside key sectors:

[5] In the course of numerical analysis, it appeared desirable to introduce a group of 103 diagnostic vectors. Each of these had the effect of supplying one or another of the items produced within the key sectors, but at an artificially high cost in terms of foreign exchange. The purpose of these vectors was threefold: (1) They ensured the existence of an initial feasible solution. (2) They guarded against the possibility that a clerical error would result in a gross overstatement of the quantity of an input per unit of output. Two years previously, there had been a combination of two such errors which made it impossible to find any initial solution and made it extremely difficult to trace the cause of the infeasibility. (3) On the basis of a limited amount of experimentation, it was conjectured that these vectors reduced the cumulative errors due to roundoff in the simplex procedure.

$$\begin{pmatrix} \text{demand of} \\ \text{households,} \\ \text{government,} \\ \text{and exports} \end{pmatrix} + \begin{pmatrix} \text{demand of industries} \\ \text{outside key sectors,} \\ \text{current and} \\ \text{capital account} \end{pmatrix}$$

The conditions of the problem are grouped into six general categories, A-F. Equations of type B, C, D, and F are essentially definitional and could have been eliminated through a preliminary data processing step:

A) *Flow of item i during target year*

Net current production, old plants		Net current production, new plants		(Imports) $\geq$	Final demand, outside key sectors		Demand for investment good i within key sectors
d_i	$+$	$\Sigma_j a_{ij} x_j$	$+$	$y_i \geq$	q_i	$+$	$0.15\, v_i$

B) *Demand for investment good i during the decade*

$$\sum_i b_{ij} x_j = v_i$$

C) *Definition of demand for input k*

Row k	Activity defined in row k	Definition of input k	Examples of k
CDA	ZZDA	1972, domestic, current account	operating labor
CMA	ZZMA	1972, imports, current account	royalties proportional to domestic production
CDB	ZZDB	1962–72, domestic, capital account	construction labor
CMB	ZZMB	1962–72, imports, capital account	machinery types with negligible prospects for domestic production, 1972

CXB   ZZXB   1962–72, total capital account

CTMQA   ZZTMA   1972, current account labor cost for machinery producing industries[6]

D) *Equations for predetermined values of d_i and q_i*

For bookkeeping and computational reasons, it was convenient to insert two restrictions, DW and DQ, and also two unknowns, WW and QQ. These restrictions and unknowns ensure respectively that the parameters d_i and q_i will be at their predetermined values.

E) *Resource availability restrictions*

Three resources were regarded as available in limited quantities: waste paper, sulfite, and northern iron ore. Upper bounds on the use of these three items are written in the form of restrictions *EPADES*, *EPACSI*, and *EHAMN*.

F) *Definitions of minimand*

The two final equations define the two alternative minimands, foreign exchange and total input costs, respectively. In cases 1 to 6, the six basic computations, these were defined on the basis of 12.5 MN per DL and 15 per cent per year gross return on capital invested during the decade:

$$\left(\begin{array}{c}FFDIV\\10^9DL\\\text{per}\\\text{year}\end{array}\right) = 1.0 \left(\begin{array}{c}ZZMA\\10^9DL\\\text{per}\\\text{year}\end{array}\right) + .15 \left(\begin{array}{c}ZZMB\\10^9DL\\\text{per}\\\text{decade}\end{array}\right)$$

and

$$\left(\begin{array}{c}FFCSTS\\10^9MN\\\text{per}\\\text{year}\end{array}\right) = 1.0 \left(\begin{array}{c}ZZDA\\10^9MN\\\text{per}\\\text{year}\end{array}\right) + .15 \left(\begin{array}{c}ZZDB\\10^9MN\\\text{per}\\\text{decade}\end{array}\right)$$
$$+ 12.5 \left(\begin{array}{c}ZZMA + ZZTMA\\10^9DL\\\text{per}\\\text{year}\end{array}\right) + (.15)(12.5) \left(\begin{array}{c}ZZMB\\10^9DL\\\text{per}\\\text{decade}\end{array}\right)$$

[6] This category of inputs was defined separately from CDA in order to facilitate calculations of the effect of labor costs in the machinery producing sector.

For case 7 (20 per cent protection), the accounting value of foreign exchange was raised from 12.5 to 15.0 in the definition of FFCSTS. The setup for case 8 (20 per cent return on capital) is facilitated by the fact that the unknown ZZXB measures the peso value of the total capital stock added over the decade. The only change necessary for case 8 is therefore to introduce an extra term of .05 (ZZXB) into the definition of FFCSTS.

V. GENERAL STRUCTURE OF THE PROGRAMMING MATRIX

Because of its size, it appeared impractical to reproduce the entire matrix in this report. Instead, a summary of the structure is given in Table 4. This table was not prepared directly from the original data, but rather from a computer-generated report on each of the rows and columns.[7] Through visual scanning of this computer report, it was possible to detect errors in signs and numerical magnitudes among the four thousand original coefficients. Fortunately, only a few errors were brought to light with this check.

Each of the blocks of Table 4 refers to a particular *group* of activities (columns) and *group* of items (rows). The fact that there is a negative sign in, say, the column group MQ (machinery) and the row group EL (electricity) means that it takes electricity as a current account input to produce machinery. The presence of both positive and negative signs in the column MQ and row MQ means that the machinery sector is both a producer of machinery and a current account consumer.

Unlike a Leontief input-output matrix, there are positive signs in certain off-diagonal blocks. For example, in the column group y_i (imports), positive signs are shown in each of the row groups except for cement, foundries, electricity, and railroads. In all other sectors, commodity imports are considered as direct alternatives to domestic production. The number 66 at the head of this column group indicates that there are altogether 66 importing activities included within the model.

In certain sectors, the positive signs in off-diagonal blocks refer to cases of joint production. For example, the positive sign in column group HA and row group PQ is a result of the fact that certain petrochemical products (ammonium sulfate, benzene, toluene, and xylenes) may also be produced as by-products of the steel industry's coke ovens.

Through a comparison of the number of activities and of items within each industry group, it is possible to obtain a rough idea of the degree of

[7] The routine is known as a "bedsheet program" and was provided through the courtesy of the Electronic Computing Center, Standard Oil Company of California.

substitutability built into the domestic production processes. There is no substitutability considered in the machinery sector (26 activities and also 26 items for the MQ group). On the other hand, there are significant substitution possibilities shown within paper (13 activities and 4 items), petroleum (26 activities and 17 items), and others.

The pattern of empty and of nonempty blocks in Table 4 reveals the omissions—either deliberate or inadvertent—in the description of intersectoral flows. For example, both electricity and petroleum products appear as current inputs into virtually all other sectors. On the other hand, paper products are neglected as explicit inputs anywhere within the key sectors. Railroad services are counted as inputs only within the steel sector. There is a flow from petrochemicals only into petroleum.

Empty blocks also appear with a distinctive pattern in the demand for capital goods, activity group v_i. Out of the 103 items produced within the key sectors, only 32 are regarded as capital goods. These originate in the cement, steel, copper, aluminum, and machinery sectors.

As a result of the capital goods, the structure of demand loses a considerable amount of triangularity. For example, in current account flows, the model shows that there are inputs from electricity into machinery but not vice versa. Once the feature of endogenous capital formation is included within the model (row group B and column group v_i), there exists a two-way linkage between this pair of sectors.

VI. SPECIFIC RESULTS—THE MACHINERY SECTOR

In order to illustrate the detail that underlies the aggregate results, some more specific results will now be reported for one of the individual sectors —machinery. This is a case in which Mexico has had only a limited amount of domestic production experience, and so both the current inputs and the capital coefficients have been extrapolated from U.S. sources: the *U.S. Census of Manufactures* [17], the 1947 input-output table, and R. N. Grosse [6]. In order to make use of Grosse's data, the classification scheme for the machinery sector has followed that of the U.S. input-output table for 1947. Production is measured in terms of 1958 dollars.

In the category of labor costs for the machinery sector, it is particularly dubious whether U.S. data can be extrapolated directly to Mexico. There are two conflicting factors to be considered here: Mexico's lower wage level and her lower average level of output per man-hour. In all calculation shown in Table 2 above, it had been assumed that for 1972 these factors would exactly offset each other. That is, in all of these cases, U.S. labor costs per unit of output have been translated into domestic inputs at the

Table 4. General Structure of the Programming Matrix

Items (rows) / Number of rows in group		x_i, level of operation, new plants, target year												y_i imports, target year	v_i investment demand, decade	z_k definition of inputs	FFDIV, FFCSTS, minimand
Activities (columns) / Number of columns in group		PA	QP	PQ	PT	CE	HA	CO	AL	FN	MQ	EL	FC				
		13	3	16	26	2	17	5	5	5	26	7	2	66	32[a]	6	2
A PA paper	4	+												+			
QP heavy chemicals	4	−	+	−	−				−					+			
PQ petrochemicals	16			+−	+−		+							+			
PT petroleum	17	−	−	+−	+−	−	−	−				−	−	+			
CE cement	2	−	−			+−	−										
HA steel	13				−		+−	−		−	−			+			
CO copper	5							+−		−	−			+	−		
AL aluminum	5								+−	−	−			+	−		
FN foundries	5									+	−			+	−		
MQ machinery	26				−						+−			+	−		
EL electricity	4	−	+−[b]	−	−	−	−	−	−	−	−	+			−		
A FC railroads	2						−						+				

Items (rows) — Number of rows in group ↘ Activities (columns) — Number of columns in group		x_j, level of operation, new plants, target year												y_i imports, target year	v_i investment demand, decade	z_k definition of inputs	FFDIV, FFCSTS, minimand
		PA	QP	PQ	PT	CE	HA	CO	AL	FN	MQ	EL	FC				
Number of columns in group		13	3	16	26	2	17	5	5	5	26	7	2	66	32[a]	6	2
B[b] investment demand, decade	32	+	+	+	+	+	+	+	+	+	+	+	+		−		
C input definitions	6	−	−	−	−	−	−	−	−	−	−	−	−	−	−[d]	+ −[d]	
D bookkeeping restrictions	2																
E[c] resource availability	3	+					+										
F minimand	2															−	+

[a] Thirty of the activities in this group are identified in the appendix with the prefix VV. The remaining two activities classified here are those identified as PQB and PTBREF.

[b] The positive sign in this block is the result of an electricity by-product from activity QPCSO.

[c] The convention on signs of coefficients is as follows: in row groups A, C, and F, an input is denoted with a negative sign and an output with a positive sign. The reverse holds for row groups B and E.

[d] The negative signs in this block occur in row 140, CXB, total capital requirements, 1962–72.

standard rate of 12.5 pesos per dollar. At this wage cost, domestic production of machinery turned out to be uniformly optimal—regardless of the level of protection, the rate of growth of GNP, or the rate of return on capital. For this reason, a new case was calculated—one in which it was supposed that Mexico's lack of experience in machinery production would lead to an extremely low level of output per man-hour. In this case, all conditions were identical with that of case 2 (6 per cent growth rate, zero protection level, and 15 per cent gross annual rate of return on capital), except for wage costs in the machinery sector. The only change was to suppose that for each dollar's worth of U.S. wage costs, Mexico would incur 16 pesos of domestic costs. The results of the new case were identical with those of case 2. Domestic production of machinery remained optimal —even after this 28 per cent increase in labor cost per unit of output.

Probably a more serious drawback to domestic production of machinery is that of the small size of the internal market. We now turn to some specific results for twelve machinery industries in which Mexico relied primarily upon imports during 1962. Within the machinery sector, there is little direct evidence upon the way in which aggregate costs depend upon aggregate levels of output. From the 1958 *U.S. Census of Manufactures* [17], however, we do obtain some clues as to representative plant sizes within the U.S. For present purposes, a "representative" plant size is defined as the largest one such that 50 per cent or more of the industry's 1958 total shipments came from plants equal or larger in size. For example, in the case of internal combustion engines (excluding automotive), the *Census* provided the information shown in Table 5. In order to account for 50 per cent or more of the industry's total shipments, the class of 1,000 to 2,499 employees is selected as the representative size. The dollar value of annual shipments per plant is therefore taken as $\frac{357}{12} = 30$ millions. A similar calculation of plant size was made for each of the other eleven machinery industries considered as candidates for domestic production by 1972.

As an exceedingly crude substitute for direct measurement of economies-of-scale, the following procedure was adopted: one series of linear programming optimizations was performed without placing any restrictions upon the scale of the domestic production activities. If, in this initial series of calculations, the level of domestic production fell below the critical size for a "representative" plant, that line of domestic production was suppressed altogether, and a second optimization was run. This procedure led to two unexpected outcomes. (1) There was not a single instance in which a domestic production activity exceeded the critical size on the first round

Table 5. United States Size Distribution of Establishments in Industry 111
(SIC 3519), Internal Combustion Engines (Excluding Automotive)

| | All establishments, total | Establishments with the following annual number of employees | | | | | | | | | |
		1–4	5–9	10–19	20–49	50–99	100–249	250–499	500–999	1,000–2,499	2,500 and over
Number of establishments	112	18	12	7	21	4	14	8	11	12	5
Value of annual shipments, millions of dollars	1,056[a]	1	1	1	10	8	52	40	171	357	414

SOURCE: *U.S. Census of Manufactures*, 1958, Vol. I, p. 2–49.
[a] Due to rounding, total does not add.

of calculations and then fell below that size on the second round. (2) The identical group of three industries fell below the critical size—regardless of variations in the growth rate, level of protection, or rate of return in capital shown above in Table 1.

Table 6 gives the machinery sector results for case 2 (6 per cent growth rate, zero level of protection, and 15 per cent rate of return on capital). The three sectors in which the 1972 domestic market appears insufficient to support even a single representative-sized plant are turbines and gen-

Table 6. The Market Potential for 12 Machinery Industries

1947 U.S. input-output identification number	Industry	Imports, c.i.f values	Market size Case 2, 1972 activity levels	
			New plants, domestic production f.o.b. factory	Size of representative U.S. establishment[a]
			(10⁶DLS/year)	
110	Turbines and generators[b]	18		122
149	Ships	30		87
150	Locomotives	26		94
	Imports, total	74		
111	Internal combustion engines[b]		34	30
112	Industrial and agricultural tractors		77	20
114	Machinery for mining and construction		191	27
116	Metal-cutting and metal forming machine tools		91	8
117	Cutting tools, jigs, and fixtures		37	4
118	Machinery for special industries: food, textiles, paper, cement, and others		210	7
120	Elevators, cranes, and conveyors		65	27
122	Power transmission equipment[b]		56	5
134	Welding apparatus		22	4
	Domestic production, total		783	

[a] Wherever more than one 4-digit U.S. *1958 Census* industry is included within a given category, the representative-sized establishment is shown as the largest plant size among the individual industries.

[b] Excluding automotive.

erators, ships, and locomotives. According to the model, therefore, these three industries should either be delayed by Mexico, or else initiated co-operatively with the other members of the Latin American Free Trade Area.

From the viewpoint of a market analysis of the machinery sector, both the U.S. input-output table for 1947 and the present model are based upon an exceedingly coarse level of aggregation. For example, in order to produce the full range of machine tools classified in Ind. 116, it is certain that a single plant with an annual output of 8 million dollars (the "representa-tive" size) would be uneconomical. On the other hand, the model indicates that Mexico's 1972 market for machine tools could accommodate an annual value of production of 91 million dollars, the equivalent of eleven representative-sized plants. If these results are to be believed, there are similar possibilities for multi-plant production—hence a wide spectrum of products—in most of the nine sectors that exceed the critical size for a single plant.

One final observation: this rough-and-ready analysis of the machinery sector is no substitute for more detailed studies of production functions and cost curves. The sector is a challenging one to study and has attracted far less attention from econometricians than such continuous process in-dustries as chemicals, petroleum, steel, and electricity.

VII. Computer Generation of Reports

In interpreting the numerical results of this model, a human being tends to be swamped both by the mass of detail and by the wide variety of units: pesos, dollars, kilowatts, tons, barrels, both on current and on capital ac-count. In order to aid the human, two special computer programs were written: one for a column-by-column and the other for a row-by-row analysis.

The row analyses represent *aggregate* supply-demand balances for each equation. Table 7 illustrates this in the case of one of the 148 items, AKW, guaranteed electric power before transmission and distribution. All activi-ties are grouped into a relatively small number of headings. The supply-demand balance is expressed in the unit common to this row: 10^6 kilowatts. All seven possible power-producing activities appear within the category EL, and the 1972 output from new plants in this sector is shown as 1.397 10^6 kilowatts. Among the power-consuming activities are the groups PA (13 paper activities), QP (3 heavy chemicals activities), and ND (103 dis-

Table 7. Supply-Demand Balance
for the Row AKW, Case 2 (6 per cent GNP
growth, zero protection, 15 per cent return on capital)

Group of activities (new plants only)	Power production (+) or consumption (−) (10^6 kilowatts).
PA, paper	− .078
QP, heavy chemicals	− .065
PQ, petrochemicals	− .077
PT, petroleum	− .060
CE, cement	− .083
HA, steel	− .531
CO, copper	− .003
AL, aluminum	− .084
FN, foundries	− .011
MQ, machinery	− .212
EL, electricity	+1.397
ND, disposal of surplus	− .194
Net total (rounded off)	0

posal activities).[8] Some such form of report generation seems essential if the computer is to manipulate a large volume of underlying detail, and yet the human being is to keep track of the major implications of the model.

A typical column analysis is illustrated in Table 8 for the activity ELH, hydroelectric generation before transmission and distribution. The original data specify that this activity produces joint products of 1.0 10^6 kilowatts and 6.0 10^9 kilowatt-hours per year. The only current account input here is one of .050 10^9 MN per year for item CDA, miscellaneous operating expenses. The remaining inputs are all on capital account: .807 10^6 tons of cement (BCEM), .270 10^6 tons of nonflat steel (BHANP), and .00445 10^9 dollars of miscellaneous imported capital goods (CMB).

In order to convert these diverse coefficients into common units (pesos' worth of costs), the program applies the implicit prices from a typical solution and then furnishes a percentage breakdown of the relative worth of all inputs and outputs. For example, 8.5 per cent of the annual costs are attributed to the initial capital investment in the item BMQ110, turbines and generators. Zero money benefits are assigned to the production of item AKW, guaranteed electric power, which happens to be in surplus supply. The activity ELH is one of those included in the optimal solution for case 2, and so the total money value of the benefits is equal to that of the costs.

---

[8] In case 2, the optimal solution calls for the disposal of .194 10^6 kilowatts of guaranteed power. This item happens to be a joint product with AKWHR, electrical energy.

Table 8. Analysis of the Column ELH

Row identification	Coefficient in row[a]	Exponent of 10	Unit of measurement	Implicit price for row (10^6MN/year)	Percentage distribution of benefits and costs
				Linear programming results (case 2)	
AKW	1.0	6	kilowatts	0	0
AKWHR	6.0	9	kilowatt-hours/year	72.44	+100.0%
CDA	−.050	9	MN/year	1,000.00	−11.5
BCEM	.807	6	tons	−17.58	−3.3
BHANP	.270	6	tons	−135.40	−8.4
BMQ099	6.75	6	DLS	−1.33	−2.1
BMQ110	17.95	6	DLS	−2.06	−8.5
BMQ114	69.25	6	DLS	−1.41	−22.4
BMQ132	8.10	6	DLS	−1.57	−2.9
BMQ133	7.56	6	DLS	−1.40	−2.4
CDB	−1.05975	9	MN	150.00	−36.6
CMB	−.00445	9	DLS	1,875.00	−1.9
				Net total benefits minus costs } = 0.0	

[a] The convention on signs of coefficients is as follows: in rows identified by the first character A or C, an input is denoted with a negative sign and an output with a positive sign. The reverse holds for rows identified with the letter B.

VIII. Sources of Data

For each of the sectors included in this model, there exists an individual methodology memorandum. These memoranda outline the sources of data, the principal assumptions, and the major limitations of the work done on the sector.

From one sector to another there was considerable variation in the degree of reliance upon domestic versus foreign sources of data. In the machinery industry (a new branch of activity for Mexico), all of the coefficients were derived from United States sources. On the other hand, in the electric power sector, through the cooperation of the Comisión Federal de Electricidad, it was possible to rely entirely upon Mexican sources.

Generally, it was possible to find domestic sources of economic-engineering information on the current flow coefficients a_{ij} for new plants. There were major obstacles, however, in estimating the capital stock coefficients b_{ij} from domestic data. Typically, these b_{ij} were derived through pooling two sources: (1) a Mexican estimate of the total capital cost per unit of capacity, and (2) a United States source, R. N. Grosse (1953), for the percentage breakdown of the total cost among the individual sectors that produce capital goods. In addition to Grosse, a number of other published items proved to be useful. These are listed in the references below.

For most of the heavy industries analyzed here, it is believed that there are considerable economies-of-scale with respect to the individual producing unit. Numerical data were available on size-cost relationships within several sectors: electricity, cement, chemicals, and others. In order to introduce a size-cost effect into the model, the usual procedure was to postulate a "typical" plant size. For example, after reviewing a twenty-year plan of development for the electricity sector (SOFRELEC [13]), it was concluded that the typical size of thermal power plants to be installed during the period 1965–72 would be of the order of 75 megawatts. Accordingly, all coefficients for the thermal electric power activities were based upon this plant scale.

In petrochemicals, there was a particularly acute problem of economies-of-scale. In all likelihood, there will be no more than a few plants of each major type constructed in the entire country during the course of a decade. Accordingly, three sets of coefficients were constructed—based, respectively, upon small, medium, and large plant sizes. The initial series of linear programming calculations was run with the coefficients for medium-sized plants. Once the model's results were available for the total ten-year expansion of capacity in each branch of petrochemicals, it was possible to modify the initial assumptions with respect to plant size and to adopt a more appropriate set of coefficients.

In estimating the various numbers, the usual practice was to postulate not only a "typical" size of plant, but also a typical location. For example, there are five activities that consume various types of iron ore. Those identified as HA30 and HA33 are based upon northern ore, HA31 and HA32 upon southern ore, and HA34 upon imported ore. For each of the three ore types, an individual location is postulated for an integrated iron and steel complex—either north, south, or center. In turn, depending upon the location and the type of iron-making process, a transport coefficient was estimated. Per ton of iron produced, these coefficients summarize the total rail freight ton-kilometers required for the movement of the coal, limestone, iron ore, scrap, and finished products.

The iron-and-steel sector was one in which there had been a recent intensive study of plant location in Mexico, and it was therefore comparatively easy to estimate the interdependence between processes, plant location, and transport requirements. The existing data were less satisfactory in other sectors, and the general practice was to postulate a "typical" distance for the movement of raw materials and/or products. For example, it was assumed that both crude petroleum and natural gas would be shipped in pipelines for a typical distance of eight hundred kilometers to arrive at the ultimate consumer. In those sectors, such as machinery, where transport is known to form a small fraction of total production costs, the transport requirements within the key sectors were neglected entirely.

IX. FINAL DEMAND ESTIMATES

The final demand estimates q_i were constructed according to the following arbitrary mechanical rules:

1. The total demand for an item was averaged for the years 1950–52 and for the years 1960–62. The past rate of growth was defined through dividing the latter by the former average.

2. A series of *ad hoc* estimates were drawn up, splitting the 1962 base year demand for an item into two components: the total inside and outside the key sectors. The latter constitutes the 1962 final demand.

3. If the GNP were to grow from 1962 to 1972 at a 5.0 per cent annual rate, the economy's aggregate performance would be similar to that experienced in the immediate past. With a 5.0 per cent assumption for GNP, the 1962 final demands for most items were extrapolated to 1972 using the compound growth rate actually experienced for that item during the period 1950–62. This procedure was modified in the case of those items (mostly chemicals) where the past rates of demand had been abnormally high. For extrapolation purposes, the growth rate for all items was limited to a maximum of 12 per cent per annum.

4. In order to predict the effects of an acceleration in the GNP from a growth rate of 5.0 to one of 6.0 or 6.5 per cent, a series of elasticity estimates was needed. Of those available, the most directly useful seemed to be those of Chenery (1960). His estimates had been derived by pooling the census data for individual manufacturing sectors from a cross-section of up to fifty-one countries. (Mexico lies well within the extremes of this sample—both in terms of population and in her per capita GNP.) The elasticity estimates adopted are those shown in Table 6, col. 11, of Chenery's paper.

No doubt, there is considerable room for refining the precision of the final demand estimates and for introducing factors other than secular trends and GNP elasticities. Perhaps even more important than sharpening the econometric techniques would be to improve the quality of the basic data on Mexican demand. In particular, a more careful job could have been done to arrive at the 1962 split between the key sectors and the rest of the economy on an item-by-item basis.

REFERENCES

1. Banco de México, S.A. *Informe Anual*. México, D.F., 1963.
2. Chenery, H. B. "Patterns of Industrial Growth," *American Economic Review*, L (September, 1960).
3. Chenery, H. B., and Kretschmer, K. "Resource Allocation for Economic Development," *Econometrica*, XXIV (October, 1956).
4. Ferrocarriles Nacionales de México. *Informes Mensuales* E–1.
5. Frisch, R. "Oslo Decision Models." University Institute of Economics, Oslo, June, 1957. (Mimeographed.)
6. Grosse, R. N. "Capital Requirements for the Expansion of Industrial Capacity." Washington, D.C.: U.S. Bureau of Budget, 1953. (Mimeographed.)
7. Manne, A. S. "Key Sectors of the Mexican Economy, 1960–70," Ch. 16 in A. S. Manne and H. M. Markowitz (eds.), *Studies in Process Analysis*. New York: Wiley, 1963.
8. Nacional Financiera, S.A. *Informe Anual*. México, D.F., 1962.
9. Naciones Unidas. "La Indústria Química en América Latina." E/CN.12/628 + 3 addenda, August and November, 1962. (Mimeographed, preliminary.)
10. Navarrete, R. A. "El Modelo de México de Desarrollo Industrial 1960–1970 Elaborado en Nacional Financiera," *Mercado de Valores*, Nacional Financiera, México, D.F., July, 1963.
11. Nelson, W. L. *Petroleum Refinery Engineering*. New York: McGraw-Hill, 1958.
12. Sandee, J. *A Long-Term Planning Model for India*. New York: Asia Publishing House, and Calcutta: Statistical Publishing Company, 1960.
13. SOFRELEC. *Plan Nacional de Electrificación de México*, Paris, 1963.
14. United Nations. "Programming Data and Criteria for the Pulp and Paper Industry," ST/ECLA/CONF.11/L.19, December, 1962. (Mimeographed, preliminary.)
15. United Nations. "Pre-Investment Data on the Aluminum Industry," ST/ECLA/CONF.11/L.24, January, 1963. (Mimeographed, preliminary.)
16. United Nations. *Studies in Economics of Industry: Cement/Nitrogenous Fertilizers Based on Natural Gas*. Sales No. 63 II B.3, ST/ECA/75. 1963.
17. *U.S. Census of Manufactures*. Washington, D.C.: Department of Commerce, 1958.

COMMENT

ERIK THORBECKE, IOWA STATE UNIVERSITY (AMES)

Professor Manne's contribution is a "process analysis" type model of the Mexican economy with emphasis on twelve key sectors (paper, heavy chemical, petro-chemicals, petroleum, cement, steel, copper, aluminum, foundries, machinery production, electricity, and railroad services). The reason for concentrating on the above sectors follows from the fact that the model was developed for, and in cooperation with, Nacional Financiera S.A., Mexico's official industrial development bank: The selected sectors are those of most immediate concern to Financiera. The bank's main function consists of channeling long-term capital from domestic and foreign sources into enterprises in both the public and the private sectors according to economic efficiency and social welfare criteria. The implementation of this function necessitates the construction of a bridge between the micro- and macro-effects of investment decisions—hence the need for and the desirability of formulating a model of the present type which can analyze quantitatively the independence between investment decisions in different sectors.

The model is highly disaggregated, consisting of 148 items (rows) and 446 activities (columns). Out of the 148 items, 103 are produced by the key sectors. A ten-year time horizon is selected in this model, 1962 being the base year and 1972 the target year.

The general structure of the programming matrix takes the following form. The rows are subdivided into six main groups: (*a*) the key sectors, (*b*) the investment demand during the decade, (*c*) definitions of demand for specific inputs, (*d*) equations predetermining the value of specific items, (*e*) resource availability restrictions for three resources, and (*f*) definitions for the two alternative minimands (foreign exchange and total input costs, respectively). The activities columns are subdivided into five main categories: (*a*) the level of operation of the new plants of the key sectors in the target year, (*b*) the level of imports in 1972, (*c*) the investment demand over the decade, (*d*) definition of inputs, and (*e*) the minimand.

The demand of the key sectors for their own products on both current and capital accounts are treated endogenously while the current and capital account demands of industries outside of the key sectors and elements of final demand (household, government, and export demand) are treated exogenously. The model is formulated in such a way that it can be solved so as to minimize foreign exchange requirements, total input costs at conventional prices, and total input costs at various shadow prices for foreign exchange and capital. This is an improvement over an earlier version of this model which was based upon the single criterion of satisfying exogenous demand within a minimum input of foreign exchange to the key sectors.

The foreign exchange demand and the total input costs in 1972 (as well as the total capital requirements necessary between 1962 and 1972) are computed for eight different cases. These eight cases are based upon different assumptions with respect to (*a*) the annual growth rate of GNP which is to prevail in Mexico between 1962 and 1972, (*b*) the level of protection, and (*c*) the gross rate of return on capital. The alternatives selected were, respectively: 5, 6, and 6.5 per cent for the growth rate of GNP, zero, 20 per cent, and infinity[1] for the level of protection and 15 and 20 per cent for the rate of return on capital.

---

[1] This last alternative implies that foreign exchange demand is the sole criterion to be minimized.

The aggregative results of the computations provide an insight into the range of substitution existing between imports and domestic production. Interestingly enough the foreign exchange demands in 1972 do not appear to be very sensitive to a relatively low level of protection. Thus, comparing the case of 20 per cent protection as opposed to zero protection, foreign exchange demands dropped from $536 million to $499 million, assuming a 6 per cent rate of growth of GNP between 1962 and 1972 and a 15 per cent rate of return on capital. The fact that imports did not decline much on the aggregate, assuming a 20 per cent level of protection (as opposed to zero), does not mean that certain commodity imports are not highly sensitive to small changes in the level of protection. Quite the contrary, as is shown by the tremendous decline in iron-ore imports from $52 million in the case of no protection to zero in the case of a 20 per cent protection level.

Besides the aggregative results discussed above specifying the foreign exchange demands and total domestic input costs as functions of alternative rates of growth of GNP, levels of protection, and rates of return on capital, certain specific results for the machinery sector are presented in some detail. According to the model, nine out of twelve machinery industries in which Mexico was primarily dependent on imports in 1962 will by 1972 have a sufficiently large internal market to justify producing domestically with the "representative" plant size in the U.S. in 1958 as a standard. In other words, the size of the projected internal market in 1972 will be larger (for nine of these industries) than the plant size of a "representative" (efficient) U.S. firm. (In most of these industries the size of the 1972 market was considerably larger than the "representative" U.S. plant size.) The only industries for which the projected 1972 output demand did not exceed the critical size for a single plant were turbines and generators, ships, and locomotives.

Professor Manne's model addresses itself to two of the most crucial questions in economic development, namely, that of the interdependence between investment decisions in different sectors and that of the desirability of embarking on policies of import substitution. Very few multisectoral models have been constructed at the level of disaggregation for developing countries which the present one possesses. It appears that the "process analysis" approach may become an important addition to the tool-kit of the development economist since it permits a more detailed diagnosis and understanding of the structure of an economy than alternative techniques. The model, nevertheless, contains a number of limitations and relatively arbitrary assumptions about the magnitudes of key structural parameters, which the author probably recognizes better than anyone else.

In the first place the amount of technical information (i.e., the input-output coefficients and incremental capital-output ratios) and of behavioral information (i.e., income elasticities of demand) required at the level of disaggregation of the model is very large. In a number of cases data were extrapolated directly from U.S. sources (as, for instance, in the machinery sector) or derived on the basis of very rough linear time trend extrapolation (i.e., income elasticities of demand over the period 1962–72 were assumed to correspond to those observed over the decade 1952–62). The reliability of the quantitative results forthcoming from the model is limited by the quality of the data used. In this connection it would have been desirable to test the sensitivity of the results to some of the more questionable parameters selected in the model. How sensitive, for instance, are the results to the assumption of a 15 per cent stock-flow conversion factor in the target year (1972) or to different values of the capital-coefficients and income elasticities?

The applicability of this model to countries at a lower level of development than Mexico may be hampered by the scarcity of national data and greater limitations inherent in using information based on international cross-sectional studies.

Another shortcoming of the model is the complete neglect of labor as an input. The incorporation of labor as a factor would have permitted measurement, on the demand side, of the potential employment creation in the key sectors and, on the supply side, of the availability of labor by types (particularly skilled labor) to the key sectors. It is clear that if a model of the present type is to be used as a guide to policy formulation in a developing country the employment effects should be explicitly introduced. If the welfare function of the policymaker is known in terms of the relative weights attached to the various macroeconomic objectives (i.e., growth of GNP, balance of payments, income distribution, level of employment, price stability, static economic efficiency) then the inclusion of labor as an input would make it possible to use Professor Manne's model as a first step in deriving alternative policies (with respect to the level of protection) which would maximize the welfare function.

The combination of talents and skills needed to formulate a "process-analysis" type model of a developing economy is very scarce, but one which Professor Manne possesses to a high degree.

11. EXPERIMENTS WITH LINEAR AND PIECE-WISE LINEAR DYNAMIC PROGRAMMING MODELS*

I R M A   A D E L M A N , NORTHWESTERN UNIVERSITY
F R E D E R I C K   T.   S P A R R O W , THE JOHNS HOPKINS UNIVERSITY

I. INTRODUCTION

Of all the formal techniques for development planning, the programming approach is by far the most powerful, the most detailed, the most complex, and the most elegant. For any specified objective function, it can be used to determine the optimal sectoral levels of domestic production, imports, fixed capital formation, inventory accumulation, labor use, and over-all foreign capital inflow as functions of time. Thus, the end result of the computations performed with programming models is a pattern of resource allocation through time which best meets the over-all planning objectives, given the constraints under which the economy must operate.

Generally, in a programming model an objective function is specified and is optimized subject to a set of linear constraints representing the economic and technological limitations upon policy. The constraints are of several types. One set specifies that, in the optimal program, the economy cannot use more than its supply of productive capacity, labor, foreign exchange, and savings. A second set limits the exports from each industry, and a third specifies, for each industry, minimum levels of investment and

* The authors are indebted to Michael Bruno, Hollis Chenery, and Karl Fox for their helpful comments. The research was supported by the Agency for International Development and by the Ford Foundation. The National Planning Association assisted in the construction of the investment-output matrix used in this study, and William F. Long and Dwight Wolkow helped with the computations. Final responsibility for conclusions rests, of course, with the authors.

291

of production for domestic consumption. In addition, linear production functions and linear objective functions are assumed, although nonlinear functions may be approximated by a series of linear functions valid over different ranges of the variables. A wide variety of objective functions is, of course, possible. Examples of objective functions optimized in such models are GNP, consumption, and net foreign capital inflows.

To arrive at a set of policy recommendations one must explore both the sensitivity of the optimal strategy to changes in constraints and the variation of the optimal strategy with changes in objective function. In this process, one looks for effects which are relatively insensitive to these changes and can then recommend policies with a certain amount of assurance. When, on the other hand, strategies are found which are quite sensitive to changes in objective functions or constraints, more careful scrutiny of goals and constraints is required before one can reasonably make policy recommendations from these calculations.

The present paper is devoted to an exploration of the sensitivity of optimal strategies to the linearity of the objective function and to the choice of economic characteristics to be optimized. For this purpose, two dynamic programming models are formulated, one with a linear objective function and one with a step-function approximation to a nonlinear objective function. Both models are applied to Colombian data for the 1950's, in order to investigate the effects of specification biases in the shape of objective function. In addition, the linear model is used to determine the sensitivity of the optimization calculations to changes in the nature of the goals the economy is assumed to pursue. It is found that, with identical constraints, the effects of specification biases introduced by the linearity of the objective function are less than one might have anticipated a priori. By contrast, the optimal economic profiles appear to be fairly sensitive to differences in economic goals.

The next section is devoted to the mathematical formulation of a generalized programming model, which includes both the strictly linear objective function and the step-function nonlinear approximation as special cases. The linear model is used, in the third section, to calculate the optima corresponding to four different objectives: the maximization of GNP and of consumption and the minimization of unemployment and of net foreign capital inflows. In the fourth section of the paper, for the case in which the goal is to maximize the economy's GNP, the results of the "nonlinear" and the linear calculations are contrasted, and attempts are made to see how sensitive the "nonlinear" results are to the elasticities assumed in the "nonlinear" approximations.

II. The Mathematical
Formulation of the Model

Piece-wise Linear Approximations of Nonlinear Functions

Before proceeding with the mathematical formulation of the model it may prove useful to explain the procedure used in piece-wise linear approximations. Let the nonlinear function to be approximated be represented by $f(x)$ in Figure 1. To carry out the approximation, the range of variable x is first divided into N segments, and a new variable x_k is defined on the kth segment. Next the end points of the intervals are projected onto (x), and the projections are connected by straight lines. The slopes resulting from these connections then become the coefficients associated with each of the x_k in the piece-wise linear approximation of $f(x)$. Suppose, for

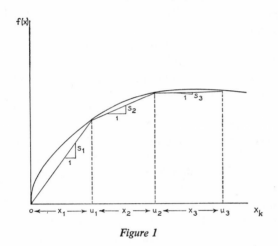

Figure 1

example, that a suitable approximation for $f(x)$ in Figure 1 can be achieved by three segments,[1] whose end points are U_1, U_2 and U_3. The slopes of the appropriate lines then are s_1, s_2, and s_3. The function $f(x)$ can now be replaced by a new (linear) function $f(x) = s_1 x_1 + s_2 x_2 + s_3 x_3$ where $x_1 \leq U_1$, $x_2 \leq (U_2 - U_1)$, and $x_3 \leq (U_3 - U_2)$.[2] One additional constraint would seem necessary: that, for all k, $x_k = 0$ unless $x_{k-j} = U_{k-j} - U_{k-j-1}$, where $j = 1, \ldots, k - 1$. In other words, no segment can be filled up until all the previous segments have been completely utilized. Fortunately, if the

---

[1] The larger the number of segments, of course, the better the approximation.

[2] All variables are also constrained to be nonnegative.

function $f(x)$ is convex, and if it is used in conjunction with an optimization problem, this constraint will automatically be satisfied. For the optimizing process itself would never call for the introduction of a variable whose coefficient in the objective function is smaller than that of another, otherwise identical, variable.

The Model

To avoid excessively complex notation, time subscripts are omitted from all variables except where necessary for clarity. Unless stated otherwise, the definitions of variables hold for each period included in the planning horizon and are measured in pesos. No descriptions are given for the quantities introduced in order to convert inequalities into equalities, except when they are economically significant.

The Endogenous Variables. The economy is disaggregated into fourteen sectors: (1) Primary (ISIC 0, 1); (2) Food, Beverages, and Tobacco (ISIC 20, 21, 22); (3) Textiles (ISIC 23); (4) Footwear and Clothing (ISIC 24); (5) Wood, Cork, and Furniture (ISIC 25, 26); (6) Printing and Publishing (ISIC 28); (7) Rubber and Rubber Products (ISIC 30); (8) Chemicals and Petroleum (ISIC 31, 32); (9) Nonmetallic Mineral Products (ISIC 33); (10) Mechanical and Metallurgical (ISIC 34, 35, 36, 37, 38); (11) Other (ISIC 27, 29, 39); (12) Residential and Nonresidential Nonplant Construction (ISIC 40); (13) Plant Construction; (14) Electrical Energy (ISIC 51). As in many analyses of this type, the service, transport, and trade sectors are not considered. This omission is not serious, however, since the extent of interdependence between these sectors and the included sectors is generally minimal.

The endogenous variables of the model represent the production, investment, import, and, for selected industries, export activities in each of the fourteen sectors of the economy. The symbols used to denote each of these activities are:

X_j = the total domestic production in the jth sector.
M_j = the total imports of the jth commodity. Any commodity other than construction, housing, and electrical energy can be imported. No capacity can be imported directly, although domestic capacity can be supplemented indirectly by imports.
S_B = the foreign exchange surplus carried over into the next period.

The three sectors of the economy where nonlinear effects are important enough to warrant inclusion are the export, investment, and consumption sectors. The symbols used to denote these activities are:

E_{mj} = the mth segment of the variable representing exports of the jth commodity. Only petroleum, coffee, and bananas can be exported. $m = 1, \ldots, 5$.

I_{lj} = the lth segment of the variable representing investment in the productive capacity of the jth sector, measured in pesos worth of output. Since construction was assumed to require no fixed capacity, investment in sectors 12 and 13 cannot take place. $l = 1, 2$.

S_{nj} = the nth segment of the variable representing the amount of output of the jth industry earmarked for final demand over and above the lower limit required by the plan. $n = 1, \ldots,$ 5 for the large sectors 1 and 2 and $n = 1, 2$ for $j = 3, \ldots,$ 14.

The Exogenous Variables. A number of economic and technological constraints must be met by the optimal program. These constraints are of two distinct types: (1) they specify the limit upon the availability of primary resources (labor, capital, and foreign exchange) at the start of each planning period, and (2) they set minimal sectoral goals for production and investment and upper limits on exports. These limits and goals are specified exogenously by:

K_j = the productive capacity of the jth type available for utilization during the period, measured in pesos worth of output. (This quantity is exogenous for a given period, but endogenous for the whole planning horizon, since for simplicity, it was assumed that any capacity-incrementing activity must be undertaken in the period previous to its first utilization.) Construction sectors 12 and 13 were assumed to have no capacity limits.

D_j = the amount of depreciation of the capital stock of the jth sector, expressed in terms of loss of output in pesos. For simplicity, straight-line depreciation was assumed, even though this method tends to overstate the amount of economic depreciation in a growing economy.

L_k = the supply of the kth labor skill available during the period, measured in man-years. The skill classes distinguished were proprietors, administrators and technicians, workers, and salesmen. A uniform, exogenously set, growth rate in the supply of each type of labor is assumed for the planning horizon.

F = the net foreign capital commitments upon which the economy can draw during the period. This quantity, together with the accumulated foreign exchange reserves, determines the maximum permissible discrepancy between imports and exports of goods for the period. It includes all foreign aid available to the economy.

Y_j = the amount of final demand for the output of the jth sector which the plan must produce.

I_j^L = the lower limit on investment in the jth industry.

I_{lj}^U = the upper limit of the lth segment of investment in the jth sector's capacity. Note that, if, for the last segment, I_{lj}^U is finite, an upper limit upon total investment in the jth sector is imposed. These upper limits have been selected so that their sum, $\displaystyle\sum_l I_{lj}^U$, constrains investment in each of the j sectors to not more than 150 per cent of actual investment in that sector during the base period.[3]

E_{mj}^U = the upper limit of the mth segment of the jth export. The piecewise linear approximations were based upon price elasticities of .25 for coffee and bananas and 1 for petroleum. $\displaystyle\sum_m E_{mj}^U$ is 112 per cent of actual exports for coffee and bananas and 110 per cent of actual exports for petroleum.[3]

S_{nj}^U = the upper limits imposed in the nth segment of the jth industry upon the production for final demand in excess of that required to meet the plan. When nonlinear relations were assumed to hold, the S_{nj} were based on elasticities of unity in sectors 1 and 2, 1.5 in sectors 3, 4, 5, 6, 11, and 14, and 2 in the remaining sectors.[4] $\displaystyle\sum_n S_{nj}^U$ was set equal to 25 per cent of Y_j; for $j = 1$, 2; for $j = 3, 4, 5, 6, 11$, and 14, $\displaystyle\sum_n S_{nj}^U = .4Y_j$; for the remaining sectors $\displaystyle\sum_n S_{nj}^U = .5Y_j$.

The Constraints. All the constraints incorporated into the model are linear. They express the accounting, technological, and resource balance

[3] These limits and elasticities are arbitrary and are used merely to study the properties of the model.

[4] These limits and elasticities are arbitrary and are used merely to study the properties of the model.

restrictions which the optimization process must obey. The constraints summarized below are written for the tth period; analogous constraints apply to each of the other time periods included in the planning horizon.

The total use-total availability equalities specify that, for each sector, the total amount of product available from production, imports, and opening inventories must equal its total use in intermediate production, capacity-incrementing uses, exports, final consumption, and stockpiling activities. The constraints can be expressed as:

$$X_j + M_j = \sum_i a_{ij}X_i + \sum b_{ij} \sum_{l=1}^{2} I_{lj} + \sum_{m=1}^{5} E_{mj}$$

$$+ Y_j + \sum_{n=1}^{5} S_{nj} \qquad \text{for all } j.$$

In the above equation,

$a_{ij} =$ the coefficients of the input-output matrix, assumed to be constant over time; they represent the peso value of input from the ith sector required to produce a peso's worth of output of the jth industry.

$b_{ij} =$ the coefficients of the investment-output matrix, also assumed constant over time; they represent the peso value of inputs from the ith industry required to increment the capacity of the jth sector by one peso.

The capacity inequalities state that domestic production in the jth sector in the tth time period is limited by the capacity available in that sector during that period. The available capacity is set equal to the initial capacity at the start of the plan plus the net investment from all previous periods. Formally, one can state this constraint as

$$X_j \leq K_{jt} = K_{jo} + \sum_{\tau=0}^{t-1} \sum_l I_{lj\tau} - \sum_{\tau=0}^{t-1} D_{j\tau} \qquad \text{for all } j$$

where

$K_{jt} =$ capacity available for production in the jth sector during the tth period.

$\sum_l I_{lj\tau} =$ gross investment in the jth sector during period τ.

$D_{jt} =$ depreciation of the capacity of the jth sector during period τ.

The above method of calculating available capacity incorporates implicitly the unrealistic assumption that current investment can be used only to increment capacity in the next planning period. A better, but less simple, approximation would have been to assume that a certain fraction of current investment does mature during the same planning period. Alternately, of course, one can use a shorter planning period.

The labor supply inequalities. Since the sum of labor of a given skill demanded for production or capacity-incrementing activities cannot exceed the availability of labor of that grade during the period, we require that

$$\sum_j l_{jk} X_j + \sum_j l'_{jk} \sum_l I_{lj} \leq L_k \qquad \text{for all } k$$

where

l_{jk} = the fraction of man-years of the kth labor skill required to produce a peso's worth of the jth commodity. These coefficients, like the a_{ij} and the b_{ij}, are assumed to be constant through time.

l'_{kj} = the fraction of man-years of the kth labor skill required to increment the capacity of the jth industry by one peso's worth of output. These coefficients are also taken to be constant over time.

The balance of payments constraint. For each time period, the total peso value of imports must be equal to the total peso value of exports, the net foreign capital commitments available, and the accumulated balance of payments surplus. That is,

$$S_{B_t} + \sum_j m_j X_j + \sum_j m'_j \sum_l I_{lj} + \sum_j M_j$$

$$= \sum_j \sum_m e'_{mj} E_{mj} + F_t + S_{B_{t-1}}.$$

In the above equation

m_j = the peso value of imports required to produce one peso's worth of output in the jth sector.

m'_j = the peso value of imports required to increment capacity by one peso in the jth sector.

e_{mj} = the value, in pesos, of a unit of the mth segment of the jth export. In the nonlinear case, the e_{mj} are based upon the elasticities assumed for exports. In the linear case, the e_{mj} are all unity.

S_{B_t} = the foreign exchange surplus carried over into the next period. For the terminal period of the planning horizon, a nonzero value of S_{B_t} is interpreted to represent repayment of foreign capital.

The savings-investment constraint differs from the other constraints in the model, as it represents a behavioral rather than a technological limitation upon the system. It expresses the requirement that the number of pesos used for investment shall not exceed the finance available for this purpose from domestic savings and from foreign sources. This requirement is always satisfied *ex post*, since savings are calculated as residual. It becomes a behavioral constraint, however, when savings are calculated from a savings function, as done here, rather than as the accounting difference between GNP and consumption. It should be noted that, *ex post*, the actual savings ratio need not be equal to the average propensity to save assumed in this constraint.

Mathematically, this constraint can be written as

$$\sum_j \alpha_j \sum_l I_{lj} \leq s(GNP^*) + F_t - S_{Bt} + S_{Bt-1}$$

where

α_j = capital per output ratio of the jth industry.
s = the average propensity to save out of that portion of GNP which originates in the fourteen sectors included.

$$GNP^* = \sum_j Y_j + \sum_. \alpha_j \sum_l c_{lj} I_{lj} + \sum_j \sum_n d_{nj} S_{nj}$$

$$+ \sum_j \sum_m e_{mj} E_{mj} - \sum_j m_j - F.$$

c_{lj} = the value, in pesos, of a unit of the lth segment of additions to capacity in the jth industry. In the linear case, the c_{lj} are all unity. In the nonlinear case, $c_{1j} = 1$ and $c_{2j} = .05$.
d_{nj} = the value, in pesos, of a unit of the nth segment of extra final demand produced in the jth industry. In the nonlinear case, the values of d_{nj} are based upon the elasticity assumptions made for the corresponding S_{nj}. In the linear case, the d_{nj} are all unity. Note that the term GNP*, as calculated here, differs from the normal GNP by excluding commerce, transport, and services.

Lower limits on investment. Investment in every industry is constrained not to fall below prescribed limits.[5] The relation used in this model is

$$\sum_{l} I_{lj} \geq I_j^L \quad \text{for all } j.$$

The investment constraints. The lth segment of investment in the productive capacity of the jth sector cannot exceed its upper limit,

$$I_{lj} \leq I_{lj}^U \quad \text{for all } l, j.$$

This implies, of course, that total investment in each sector cannot exceed an upper limit.

The export constraints. The mth segment of exports of the jth commodity is not allowed to exceed its upper limit. That is,

$$E_{mj} \leq E_{mj}^U \quad \text{for all } m, j.$$

Total exports are also constrained as a result.

The final demand constraints. The nth segment of final demand of the jth commodity (over and above Y_j) cannot exceed its upper limit:

$$S_{nj} \leq S_{nj}^U \quad \text{for all } n, j.$$

In each sector total production for final demand is therefore constrained by an upper limit.

The Objective Functions. Four different objective functions, typical of the goals which are usually explicit or implicit in development planning, were used in our calculations. Specifically, the planners are presumed to wish to do one of the following:

1. Minimize the discounted[6] sum of net foreign capital inflows:

$$\text{Max} \sum_{t=1}^{T} (1 + r)^{5(t-1)}(S_{Bt} - S_{Bt-1}).$$

S_{B0} was assumed to be zero.

2. Maximize the discounted (see footnote 6) sum of GNP:

$$\text{Max} \sum_{t=1}^{T} (1 + r)^{5(t-1)} GNP_t^*.$$

[5] These limits were set equal to the levels of investment which were actually realized in each sector of the economy during the relevant period.

[6] The rate of discount used in all the calculations in Table 1 was 5 per cent per year (in real terms). The qualitative results are not sensitive to the specific choice of discount rate over a reasonable range of values.

3. Maximize the discounted (see footnote 6) sum of consumption:

$$\text{Max} \sum_{t=1}^{T} (1 + r)^{5(t-1)} C_t = \sum_{t=1}^{T} (1 + r)^{5(t-1)} \left[GNP_t^* \right.$$

$$\left. - \sum_j \alpha_j \sum_l C_{lj} I_{lj} + F_t - S_{Bt} + S_{Bt-1} \right].$$

4. Minimize the average level of unemployment of labor:

$$\text{Min} \sum_{t=1}^{T} \sum_k S_{1kt}$$

where S_{1kt} is the unemployment of labor in the kth class during the tth period.

The Basic Model and Its Variations may now be summarized. One of our four objective functions is maximized, subject to the following constraints for each of the T periods:

(1) $\quad X_j + M_j = \sum_i a_{ij} X_i + \sum_i b_{ij} \sum_l I_{lj} + \sum_m E_{mj}$

$$+ \sum_n S_{nj} + Y_j \quad (j = 1, \ldots, 14).$$

(2) $\quad X_j \leq K_{jo} + \sum_{\tau=0}^{t-1} \sum_l I_{lj\tau} - \sum_{\tau=0}^{t-1} D_{j\tau} \quad (j = 1, \ldots, 11, 14).$

(3) $\quad \sum_j l_k X_j + \sum_j 1_{jk} \sum_l I_{lj} \leq L_k \quad (k = 1, \ldots, 4).$

(4) $\quad \sum_j m_j X_j + \sum_j m_j' \sum_l I_{lj} + \sum_j M_j + S_{Bt}$

$$= \sum_j \sum_m e_{mj} E_{mj} + F_t + S_{Bt-1}$$

(5) $\quad \sum_j \alpha_j \sum_l I_{lj} \leq s (GNP^*) + F_t - S_{Bt} + S_{Bt-1}$

(6) $\quad \sum_\cdot I_{lj} \geq I_j^L \quad (j = 1, \ldots, 14).$

(7) $\quad I_{lj} \leq I_{lj}^U \quad$ (for $l = 1, 2$ and $j = 1, \ldots, 14$).

(8) $\quad E_{mj} \leq E_{mj}^U \quad$ (for $m = 1, \ldots, 5$ and $j = 1, \ldots, 14$).

(9) $S_{nj} \leq S_{nj}^U$ (for $n = 1, \ldots, 5$ and $j = 1, \ldots, 14$).

To keep the size of the model manageable, two five-year periods were used for the planning horizon.

The basic model is linear. In this model, the coefficients c_{lj}, d_{nj}, and e_{mj}, which appear in the definition of GNP^*, in the balance of payments constraint, and in objective functions 2 and 3 above, are set equal to unity for all l, n, m, and j.

In addition, two variants of the basic model were studied:

Variant 1—The Nonlinear Model: This model is identical to the basic model, except that the c_{lj}, d_{nj}, and e_{mj} vary according to the elasticity assumptions stated above.

Variant 2—The Nonlinear Model without Upper Limits: This model is identical to Variant 1, except that the upper limits to investment and final demand in each sector are omitted by making the last segments of I_{lj} and S_{nj} infinite for all j.

III. Sensitivity of Optimal Strategies to Differences in Objectives

The linear form of the model formulated in Section II is used in this section to investigate the variations of optimal development strategies which result from changes in objective functions.

The basic data inputs required for the practical implementation of the model consist of the input-output coefficients (a_{ij}), the investment-output coefficients (b_{ij}), the primary resource inputs per unit of output for both current production and investment (l_{ij}, l'_{ij}, m_{ii}, m'_{ij}), and the values of the exogenous variables (Y_j, I_j^L, I_e^U, E_{mj}^U, S_{nj}^U, E_j^U, K_j, L_K, D_j and F_t). A brief description of the bases upon which the input data were derived is presented in the Appendix.

In Table 1 the sensitivity of the optimal development strategy to the choice of objective function is displayed. Each entry in the table, unless labeled otherwise, represents the level (in hundreds of millions of 1953 pesos) at which the corresponding activity is to be operated in the appropriate period for the optimal plan corresponding to the objective function given at the top of the column. The various activities are grouped in such a way as to permit the reader readily to assess how much should be produced, imported, and invested in each sector for the pertinent objective function. At the bottom of the table some of the relevant implications of the plans for the over-all economy are given. In particular, the scarce primary resources (labor by skill and capacity by sector, plus foreign exchange and savings) are specified, together with their shadow prices. These shadow prices permit, for each objective function, an evaluation of the benefits to be gained from the relaxation of the corresponding bottleneck.

While there appears to be a significant variation in the optimal development strategy according to the goals which the economy is trying to pursue, certain broad structural themes run through all of these optimal development programs. In general, the optimal pattern of production appears to be considerably less industrialized than is the existing structure, as all objective functions specify a significant expansion in the relative share of the primary sector.[7] Furthermore, within the manufacturing sector, relatively more emphasis is placed upon the production of light consumer goods and relatively less on basic industry.[8]

Looking at the specific optimum plans, we find substantial variation in development strategies with development goals, despite the fact that the scope for variation has been severely constrained in the present model by the imposition of upper limits on production, investment, and exports, by sector.

Not surprisingly, the minimization of aid produces a minimal economy. The levels of GNP and consumption attained with this strategy are the smallest of the four optima, and the level of unemployment is the largest. To attain its goals, the economy embarks upon a vigorous program of import substitution coupled with a somewhat less active export expansion plan. It exports as much crude petroleum as it can, given the upper limits upon demands for exports, but the shadow price of primary capacity in the second period is so high relative to that of foreign exchange that exports of coffee and bananas fall well below their upper limit during the second period optimum. The import substitution program entails the highest degree of industrialization of all our optima and the greatest relative emphasis upon basic industry. In accordance with the economy's objective, investment over and above that specified by the lower limits occurs only in export industries (primary) and import substitute industries (textiles, nonmetallic minerals, and "other" manufacturing). Interestingly enough, all types of labor resources are in excess supply under this program. They remain unused in the optimal plan, since the export-expansion-import-substitution program is constrained most severely by inadequate capacity, By the criterion specified, the economy performs quite well; it exports a significant amount of foreign capital—2.5 per cent of its GNP.

[7] The share of primary production in Colombia in 1953 was less than 50 per cent.

[8] The one exception to this statement is given by the "maximize consumption" case, for which the percentage of basic industry in total manufacturing is approximately equal to that which existed in 1953.

Table 1. Alternative Development Strategies—Variation with Objective Function

	Max GNP		Max Consumption		Min Aid		Min Unemployment	
	Period 1	Period 2	Period 1	Period 2	Period 1	Period 2	Period 1	Period 2
Activities								
Domestic Production[a]								
Primary	2275[b]	2402[b]	2275	2402	2275[b]	2402[b]	2275[b]	2402[b]
Food, beverages, tobacco	851	1206[b]	851	1121	659	865	851	1206[b]
Textiles	229[b]	370	229[b]	252	215	289	229[b]	426
Footwear, clothing					158	213	220	232
Wood, cork, furniture	46[b]	69[b]	46[b]	54	26	41	19	40
Printing, engraving			63	44	34	45	23	56
Rubber	26[b]	34[b]	26[b]	34[b]	17	23	26[b]	
Chemicals, petroleum	115		231	196	169	252	104	
Nonmetallic minerals	26[b]	39[b]	23	31	18	28	26[b]	39[b]
Mechanical, metallurgical	169[b]	83	144	180	97	162	165	233
Other manufacturing		154	127	90	87	116	127	
Electrical energy[c]	915	1338	922	1280	555	787	766	860
Nonplant construction	51[b]	114[b]	51[b]	114[b]	51[b]	114[b]	52[b]	114[b]
Plant construction	43	42	16	30	14	28	39	30
Investment[a]								
Primary	127[b]	127[b]	127[b]	85[d]	127[b]	85[d]	127[b]	85[d]
Food, beverages, tobacco	53[b]	53[b]	44	36[d]	6[d]	36[d]	53[b]	36[d]
Textiles	245[b]	245[b]	29	163[d]	107	163[d]	245[b]	163[d]
Footwear, clothing	28[b]	28[b]	27	26[d]	5[d]	26[d]	28[b]	26[d]
Wood, cork, furniture	19[b]	19[b]	2[d]	13[d]	2[d]	13[d]	19[b]	13[d]
Printing, engraving	48[b]	48[b]	6[d]	33[d]	6[d]	33[d]	33[d]	33[d]
Rubber	3[d]	16[d]	3[d]	16[d]	3[d]	16[d]	21	16[d]
Chemicals, petroleum	97[b]	97[b]	11[d]	65[d]	69	65[d]	80	65[d]
Nonmetallic minerals	99[b]	99[b]	11[d]	65[d]	11[d]	65[d]	97[b]	65[d]
Mechanical, metallurgical	126[b]	126[b]	102	89[d]	16[d]	89[d]	126[b]	89[d]

Other manufacturing	63[b]	63[b]	52	42[d]	16	42[d]	63[b]	42[d]
Electrical energy[c]	600[b]	300[b]	600[b]	300[b]			600[b]	300[b]
Imports[a]								
Primary	199		642		478		386	58
Food, beverages, tobacco								
Textiles				10			114	
Footwear, clothing	158	213	158	212				
Wood, cork, furniture	34	45					6	
Printing, engraving			7				14	
Rubber	61	260		56			70	23
Chemicals, petroleum								257
Nonmetallic minerals								
Mechanical, metallurgical								
Other manufacturing			14					106
Exports[a]								
Petroleum	258[b]	301[b]	258[b]	301[b]	258[b]	301[b]	258[b]	301[b]
Coffee, bananas	610	150	610		610	125	610	62

Shadow prices of scarce resources

Labor								
Proprietors	4.2	4.8	3.23	3.78			0	1.03
Managers	13.7						0	5.89
Professionals							0	
Workers							0	
Salesmen							0	0
Capacity								
Primary	.98	.74	.75	.76	.95	.71	0	
Food, beverages, tobacco								
Textiles	.14		.22	.15		.04	0	.02
Footwear, clothing								
Wood, cork, furniture				.01				

Table 1. continued

	Max GNP		Max Consumption		Min Aid		Min Unemployment	
	Period 1	Period 2	Period 1	Period 2	Period 1	Period 2	Period 1	Period 2
Printing, engraving			.08					
Rubber								
Chemicals, petroleum			.08	.03		.09		
Nonmetallic minerals								
Mechanical, metallurgical								
Other						.02	0	
Foreign exchange	1.03	.78	.8	.8	1.0	.75	0	0

[a] 10^7 1953 pesos.
[b] At upper limit.
[c] 10^7 KWH.
[d] At lower limit.

As with the minimization of foreign capital inflows, the optimal strategy for GNP maximization is foreign trade-oriented. But, by contrast with the earlier strategy, the current goal is best implemented by greater emphasis upon export expansion[9] rather than upon import substitution. Not surprisingly, the optimal strategy for the maximization of GNP is one of specialization according to the economy's existing comparative advantage. The optimal pattern of production corresponding to this objective is therefore quite specialized. In this plan, all the economy's final demands for footwear and clothing and for printing and engraving and substantial fractions of the requirements for chemicals and mechanical and metallurgical products are satisfied by imports. In addition, the best strategy corresponding to the "maximize GNP" objective is one in which heaviest reliance is placed upon primary production. As a result, the present optimal pattern is also the least industrialized of all four programs.

Naturally, the level of GNP attained in this manner is the highest and the amount of investment the heaviest. The economy's rate of growth over the planning horizon is disappointingly low, however (less than 1 per cent per year), since the objective function discounts future GNP relative to present GNP.

The strategy for the maximization of consumption differs from that for GNP maximization in that, as expected, investment in the second period is reduced to the minimum level. More emphasis is placed on import substitution; printing and engraving is now a domestic industry and the lion's share of the economy's demand for chemicals and petroleum is now satisfied by domestic production. Since, with the current strategy, the economy's ability to produce is more limited by its industrial capacity than with the other development programs, the shadow prices of the other two scarce resources (managers and foreign exchange) are correspondingly reduced.

The strategy for unemployment minimization is implemented by an industrialization program, even though in terms of direct labor requirements the primary sector is the third most labor-intensive sector. The key industries under this program are textiles, footwear and clothing, and mechanical and metallurgical, all of which are greatly expanded. Investment is not used as a public works program, even though plant construction is quite labor-intensive, because construction also makes heavy demands upon the economy's bottleneck resource—its technical manpower.

In the first period of the plan, the economy achieves full employment. Since, in this period, an optimum optimorum has thus been reached, the

[9] Even with this program, however, coffee and banana exports are not at their upper limits. They are the largest of all four optima though.

shadow prices of all resources are zero, even when they are not in excess supply. The shadow prices of the second period indicate that a major constraint upon the economy's ability to achieve full employment is the availability of entrepreneurial talent and the supply of high-level manpower. Indeed, each additional manager creates approximately six new jobs and each additional proprietor provides employment for one more worker. The supply of foreign exchange imposes no effective constraint upon the economy's ability to achieve full employment.

In summary, it is apparent that important differences in development strategies emerge when the economy's development goals are changed. These differences are both quantitative and qualitative in nature. In particular, the optimal degree of industrialization, the division between light and heavy industry, the degree of reliance upon export expansion as compared with import substitution, and the extent of diversification of the industrial pattern of production, all show significant variation between the four optimal programs. Despite these differences, however, the shadow prices of the two most important resource constraints, foreign exchange and primary capacity, show remarkably little variation with changes in objective function.

IV. SENSITIVITY OF OPTIMAL STRATEGIES
TO THE SHAPE OF THE OBJECTIVE FUNCTION

As is well known, the most obvious deficiency of dynamic linear programming for development planning is in the linear character of the functions specified in the model. In particular, the production functions assumed are of a strictly complementary, constant coefficient, Leontief type. This implies, first of all, that, in a given industry, no substitution between alternative inputs can take place. For the economy as a whole, substitution between labor-intensive, capital-intensive, and import-intensive technology does occur, but only as a result of shifts in the industrial composition of the total output. In addition, both economies of scale and external economies are ruled out by the linearity of the postulated production functions. This deficiency seriously limits the usefulness of linear programming in development planning, because much of successful development strategy consists of expanding production in industries which give rise to pecuniary and technological external economies.

Another consequence of the linear character of the model is perhaps even more important. The model values the output of each sector and each resource at the same constant price over the entire range of its production or use. As a consequence of this unrealistic specification, the relative marginal and average social utility of various products is held constant, independent of the amount manufactured. There is therefore a tendency for the optimal programs to overstate the extent of desirable changes from any initial position. In many cases, the overstatement is so gross that the entire structure of the economy is distorted.

To explore the extent to which distortions are introduced by the linearity of the linear programming model, the piece-wise linear approximation to the nonlinear model described under Variant 1 of Section II was used to calculate optimal development strategies for GNP maximization. It will be recalled that this model differs from the linear case by the introduction of diminishing returns to production for final demand, to investment, and to exports.

The most important features of these calculations are described in Table 2. Columns 4 and 5 of this table summarize the optimal results when GNP is maximized with the piece-wise linear approximation to the nonlinear model. The optimum obtained, under identical constraints, with the linear model is reproduced in columns 2 and 3 of the table in order to facilitate comparison.

It is apparent that the major effect of the selective introduction of diminishing returns is to force the pattern of production to become somewhat more diversified. The lion's share of final demand for footwear and clothing is now satisfied by domestic production rather than by imports. Domestic manufacture of food, beverages, and tobacco and of textiles is cut back somewhat, and mechanical and metallurgical production is significantly expanded. Thus, important differences arise in the optimal pattern of production. The structure of investment is affected very little by the nonlinearity. The diminishing returns to exports, on the other hand, lead to the complete elimination of the marginal export activity (coffee and bananas in the second period of the optimal plan). Thus, the optimal strategy now relies more heavily on import substitution for the maintenance of the economy's balance-of-payments position.

It is evident, then, that the linearity assumption tends to affect even the qualitative nature of the optimal results. Before one can urge the more general use of "nonlinear" models, however, one must explore the sensitivity of these models to the precise elasticities used in the derivation of the piece-wise linear approximations. Columns 7 and 8 of Table 2 describe the optima obtained for the "nonlinear" model with a different set of elasticities. The results of this calculation indicate that the optima are quite sensitive to the particular choice of elasticities. Indeed, the difference between the two sets of "nonlinear" results is at least as pronounced as the difference between the linear and the "nonlinear" models. The derivation of

Table 2. Sensitivity of Development Strategies to the Shape of the Objective Function and to Constraints when GNP is Maximized

	Linear O. F. Basic Case		"Nonlinear" O. F. Case 1		"Nonlinear" O. F. Case 2		"Nonlinear" O. F. No Upper Limits	
	Period 1	Period 2	Period 1	Period 2	Period 1	Period 2		
Activities								
Domestic Production[a]								
Primary	2275	2402	2275	2402	2275	2402	2275	3014
Food, beverages, tobacco	851	1206	819	1162	915	1291		
Textiles	229	370	229	285	229	305		
Footwear, clothing	46	69	148	131	101	129		
Wood, cork, furniture			46	70	35	54		
Printing, engraving					17			
Rubber	26	34	26	35	25	34		
Chemicals, petroleum	115		191		202			
Nonmetallic minerals	26	39	23	30	26	32		
Mechanical, metallurgical	169	83	130	188	137	200		
Other manufacturing		154	93	109	106	116		
Electrical energy[b]	915	1338	905	1298	713	1066	1300	1600
Nonplant construction	51	114	51	114	51	114	51	114
Plant construction	43	42	39	40	39	40	85	95
Investment[a]								
Primary	127	127	127	127	127	127	1474	11597
Food, beverages, tobacco	53	53	53	53	53	53	6	36
Textiles	245	245	219	245	219	204	29	163
Footwear, clothing	28	28	28	28	28	30	27	27
Wood, cork, furniture	19	19	19	19	19	24	2	13
Printing, engraving	48	48	48	48	48	40	6	33
Rubber	3	16	3	16	3	16	3	16
Chemicals, petroleum	97	97	80	80	80	80	11	65
Nonmetallic minerals	99	99	82	82	82	82	12	65
Mechanical, metallurgical	126	126	126	126	126	126	16	89

Other manufacturing	63	63	63	63	63	63	7	42
Electrical energy[b]	600	300	600	300	600	300	300	300
Imports[a]								
Primary	199		369		410	12		
Food, beverages, tobacco							151	225
Textiles	158	213	9	82	56	84	158	213
Footwear, clothing							16	26
Wood, cork, furniture	34	45	38	49	18	53	32	46
Printing, engraving								24
Rubber	61	260		273		251		
Chemicals, petroleum							166	227
Nonmetallic minerals							18	28
Mechanical, metallurgical							160	223
Other manufacturing							51	67
Exports[a]								
Petroleum	258	301	258	301	258	301	258	301
Coffee, bananas	610	150	610		610		646	789
Shadow prices of scarce resources								
Labor								
Managers	4.2	4.8	4.4	4.0	4.0	4.0		
Professionals	13.7		5.8		5.9			
Workers							58.0	43.2
Capacity								
Primary	.98	.74	.94	.71	.94	.71	.75	
Textiles	.14		.12		.19			
Wood, cork, furniture				.004				
Electrical energy							.04	.03
Foreign exchange	1.03	.78	1.0	.75	1.0	.75	1.0	.75

[a] 10^7 1953 pesos.
[b] 10^7 KWH.

qualitatively valid results with "nonlinear" models therefore clearly presupposes accurate sectoral estimates of price and income elasticities. It is not at all obvious that there is a net gain in using a nonlinear model based on poor elasticity estimates.

Another interesting question is the extent to which the use of "nonlinear" models can serve as a substitute for the expedient generally adopted by linear programming practitioners in search of sensible solutions of imposing upper and/or lower limits upon the optimal values of the decision variables of the program. To explore this question the "nonlinear" model was run without upper limits on investment and on final demand (see columns 8 and 9 of Table 2). These results show that the diminishing returns assumed are not sufficient to overcome the tendency for seeking out extreme solutions inherent in any linear program.

V. Summary and Conclusions

This paper reports experiments performed with several linear programming models of a standard variety in order to explore the sensitivity of optimal strategies to some of the usual arbitrary assumptions concerning objective functions. We find that both the nature of the goals the economy is assumed to pursue and the shape of the objective function postulated exert significant influences upon the optimal results. Perhaps not surprisingly, however, the effects upon the optima of changes in the economy's aims appear to be more important than the consequences of variations in the shape of the objective function used to represent a given aim.

These results suggest that before even qualitatively valid recommendations can be made, a careful exploration of the economy's planning goals is in order. The need for good elasticity estimates upon which to base "nonlinear" models is also underscored by the results of our study.

Appendix

The Data Used in the Calculations

The input-output matrix for Colombia was aggregated from a somewhat more detailed (17 x 17) matrix constructed for 1953 by the Economic Commission of Latin America. Since no data could be found for the vectors of input requirements for plant construction, nonplant construction, and electrical energy for Colombia, the published data had to be supplemented by estimates based on existing practices in other economies. For a combination of reasons, it was decided to base the first two vectors on U.S. technology and the third on Japanese data.

No investment-output matrix was available for Colombia. Indeed, such data exist for only three noncommunist economies—Japan, India, and the United States. Since the accuracy of both the Japanese and Indian data is admittedly poor, it was decided to base the investment-output coefficients upon U.S. data. The 183 x 183 National Planning Agency investment-output matrices was aggregated for the United States into a "Colombian" investment-output matrix by using Colombian domestic use weights. The detailed data on both domestic production and imports required for this purpose were derived from Colombian monthly statistical bulletins.

This gross approximation may not be too bad for new investment, in which generally modern technology tends to be used; but, since the efficiency of the capacity-incrementing process will generally be overstated by the use of U.S. data, a certain amount of bias will still be introduced in the process.

Labor inputs by four skill categories were computed on the basis of local census data. The category of "relatives," which appears in the published statistics, was distributed proportionately among other skill classes. (Otherwise, the optimal program might have ground to a halt for want of a sufficient number of relatives!) The distribution of labor requirements by skill for the construction sector was another input which had to be estimated on the basis of U.S. data. Since Colombian construction represents a relatively large proportion of over-all economic activity, this approximation may also tend to bias our results.

Imports were broken down into two categories: noncompetitive and competitive. Noncompetitive import requirements for current production were derived from the import vectors of the interindustry tables. It was assumed, in addition, that, for each industry, half of the required mechanical and metallurgical inputs into investment had to be imported, in accordance with Colombian practice in the base period.

The final demand constraints on production for the first period were set equal to approximately five times the production of consumer goods in the base year in each economy. A 5 per cent yearly increase in consumption was assumed to derive the final demand constraints for the second period.

The lower limits on investment for the first period were fixed at five times the base year investment. For the second period in Colombia the actual increase in over-all investment observed for 1955–59 was assumed; it was prorated by sector in accordance with the 1953 distribution of investment to arrive at the second period lower limits.

The upper limits on exports for both periods were set at their actual levels (in constant pesos).

Descriptions of the rate of underutilization of capacity in the base period were available for most sectors of the Colombian economy. These were utilized to set upper limits on the first period capacity. The initial capacity of the primary sector was set at 130 per cent of the base period production.

For labor, the working assumption for the basic calculations was to provide each economy with 120 per cent of the amount of each labor skill which would have been required to produce the actual output in the base period with the as-

Table 3. Interindustry Matrix (I-A)[a]

	Primary	Food, Beverages, tobacco	Textiles	Footwear, Clothing	Wood, Cork, Furniture	Printing, Engraving	Chemicals, Petroleum	Rubber	Non-metallic minerals	Mechanical, Metallurgical	Other Manufacturing	Residential[b] Nonplant Constr.	Electrical[c] Energy	Plant[d] Constr.
Primary	+.959380	-.548000	-.126510	-.320390	-.106216		-.289227	-.020317	-.098102	-.002357	-.140021	-.005000		-.000700
Food, beverages, tobacco	-.004122	+.934700	-.000073		-.000052		-.007801			-.000213	-.000273	-.000010		
Textiles	-.002998	-.005617	+.965160	-.320260	-.004607	-.001602	-.000688	-.051280		-.000859	-.008472	-.007590	-.000020	
Footwear, clothing				+1.0										
Wood, cork, furniture	-.000300	-.000056	-.000749	-.003240	+.688147	-.001827	-.006790		-.002139	-.014942	-.001359	-.000680	-.001390	-.000540
Printing, engraving				-.000102		+1.0	-.004460							
Chemicals, petroleum	-.000957	-.002592	-.083939	-.002337	-.005754	-.000703	+.965940	-.000330	-.023245	-.000179	-.000030	-.013400	-.014720	-.015410
Rubber				-.004247	-.000085	-.000323	-.002622	+.996800		-.007433	-.015894	-.001870	-.000168	-.002400
Nonmetallic minerals	-.003644				-.002865		-.006059		+.967069	-.001642	-.000302	-.004500	-.000150	-.162130
Mechanical, metal-lurgical	-.003345									+.954327	-.000165	-.010727	-.003280	-.298160
Other manufacturing	-.000025				-.007988	-.001405	-.004900		-.002139	-.003486	+.880700	-.000770		
Residential, nonplant construction	-.005165		-.002234	-.145132	-.000918	-.012505	-.011700	-.011206	-.038520	-.010727		+1.0	-.001690	
Electrical energy[e]	-.143000						-.092400		-.695000	-.124000	-.179000	-.018000	+.881000	-.032500
Plant construction			-.321600											+1.0

[a] Aggregated from "Analyses and Projections of Economic Development of Colombia" (U.N., ECOSOC) Vol. VIII, Table 8-45.
[b] This vector based on U.S. technology. Aggregated from NPA, PARM input-output coefficients for multiple unit housing (PARM 301200).
[c] This vector based on Japanese technology.
[d] This vector based on U.S. technology. Aggregated from NPA, PARM input-output coefficients for eight steel frame buildings (PARM 302400).
[e] "Analyses," Statistical Appendix, p. 156.

Table 4. Capital Coefficients and Primary Resource Requirements per Unit of Investment[a]

	Primary	Food, Beverages, Tobacco	Textiles	Footwear, Clothing	Wood, Cork, Furniture	Printing, Engraving	Chemicals, Petroleum	Rubber	Non-metallic Minerals	Mechanical, Metallurgical	Other Manufacturing	Plant Constr.
Primary							.000337		.000476	.000141		.000013
Food, beverages, tobacco	.00004						.000007					
Textiles												
Footwear, clothing	.00074	.000173	.000096	.000081	.000095	.000250	.000719	.001294	.000058	.000276	.000098	.000050
Wood, cork, furniture		.000054										
Printing, engraving												
Chemicals, petroleum					.000025		.000150			.000001		
Rubber	.00001						.000010	.105000		.000001		
Nonmetallic minerals		.019000					.015072		.000360	.001336	.000014	.000028
Mechanical, metallurgical	.003300	.000055	.029000	.012000	.016000	.026000	.063000	.000074	.035000	.025000	.013000	.005474
Other manufacturing	.000001				.000008	.000371	.000018		.000030	.000023		.000001
Residential, nonplant construction												
Electrical energy												
Plant construction	.005640	.029700	.047900	.008300	.043430	.031050	.085090	.165170	.060010	.037800	.024550	.009084
Primary resources												
Labor: workers[b]	.0090	.0178	.0140	.0050	.0086	.0120	.0643	.0520	.0500	.0320	.0136	.0500
Imports[c]	.0033	.0190	.0290	.0120	.0170	.0260	.0620	.1040	.0350	.0250	.0130	

[a] Aggregated from 183 x 183 capital coefficient matrix of National Planning Agency PARM MF 024019. Converted into a five-year matrix by dividing annual coefficients by five.
[b] Includes only labor requirements for equipment installation.
[c] Set equal to half of total mechanical and metallurgical requirements.

Table 5. Primary Resource Inputs

Primary Resources	Primary[a]	Food, Beverages, Tobacco	Textiles	Footwear, Clothing	Wood, Cork, Furniture	Printing, Engraving	Chemicals, Petroleum	Rubber	Non-metallic Minerals	Mechanical, Metallurgical	Other Manufacturing	Residential Non-plant Constr.[b]	Electrical Energy	Plant Constr.[b]
Labor[c]														
Proprietors		.0252	.048	.606	.6513	.094	.03464	.047	.147	.258	.195	.415	.0005	.415
Administrators and technicians	1.3	.0305	.101	.050	.0741	.151	.1009	.055	.091	.106	.0875	.837	.029	.837
Workers		.2321	.661	.807	1.0717	.926	.0318	.326	1.015	.927	.5895	2.784	.016	2.784
Salesmen	1.0	.001124	.023	.125	.01141	.005	.0144	.0001	.002	.004	.00946	.028		.028
Capacity	1.0	1.0	1.0	1.0	1.0	1.0	1.0	1.0	1.0	1.0	1.0		1.0	
Imports	.0042	.0129	.0153	.0033	.0240	.2710	.1140	.2190	.0420	.2410	.0780			
SOURCES:														

a Estimated on the basis of employment data for agriculture given in "Analyses," p. 230.

b Total labor/output requirements estimated on the basis of Colombian employment and output data given in *Boletín Mensual de Statística*. Skill breakdown prorated on the basis of U.S. data (NPA-PARM activities 302400 [light steel frame building] and 301200 [multiple unit building]).

c Employment figures by skill were derived from the 1953 Industrial Census (*Boletín Mensual de Statística*, July 1955, pp. 28–31) and divided into the production figures for each industry given in "Analyses." The class "familiares" was allocated proportionately among the other skill categories. 10⁴ man-years per 10⁷ pesos.

sumed technology. A 2 per cent per year growth in the labor force was hypothe-
sized to set upper limits on labor availability for the second period.

The rate of depreciation assumed for each sector was arbitrarily set equal to
half the rate of depreciation allowed by the U.S. Internal Revenue Code for
plant and equipment in the corresponding sector.

Net foreign capital commitments were treated as a parameter.

COMMENT

KARL A. FOX, IOWA STATE UNIVERSITY (AMES)

I. THE SENSITIVITY OF OPTIMAL DEVELOPMENT STRATEGIES TO CHOICES AMONG GOALS AND ALTERNATIVE SPECIFICATIONS OF STRUCTURAL CHARACTERISTICS OF THE ECONOMY

The authors' basic model describes the Colombian economy in terms of fourteen production activities, twelve investment activities, and a number of constraints, involving some fifty-one equations or inequations in each of two five-
year periods. Evidently the results of any development strategy can be expressed
as a set of values of 102 time-specific variables, and the locus of all such sets of
values for which at least one constraint is binding may be regarded as a *production
possibilities surface* for the economy represented by the model.

On what basis shall the policymaker select one particular point on this surface
as better than all others? We may ascribe to him an *objective function*, the arguments of which are sets of values of the 102 variables. If this objective function
is tangent to the production possibilities surface at a single point, this point may
be seen as an optimum, and the set of measures necessary to arrive at it constitutes
an optimal economic policy.

In principle the marginal rates of substitution between x_i and x_j ($i, j = 1, 2,
3, \ldots 102, j \neq i$) at various points on the policymaker's objective function need
have no relation to the internal pricing system of the economy. For example,
Van Eijk and Sandee [10] postulate an objective function which, over specified
ranges of values of the variables, states that the policymaker would accept any
one of the following undesirable effects in order to reduce the balance-of-payments deficit by 100 million guilders: (1) a 1.33 per cent increase in consumer
prices; (2) a 2 per cent decrease in real wages; (3) an 0.5 per cent decrease in
employment; (4) an increase of 200 million guilders in the government deficit; (5)
a reduction of 400 million guilders in government expenditure; or (6) a reduction

of 500 million guilders in domestic investment. These *barter terms of trade* between different variables clearly could not be derived from the internal pricing system of the Dutch economy but were inferred by Van Eijk and Sandee on the basis of current discussions of economic policy in the Social Economic Council and in the government in the second half of 1956.

In principle, a positive model of an economy could be disaggregated into a great many sectors. It could incorporate downward-sloping demand curves for many categories of consumer goods; it could use input-output relationships to translate wage increases into increases in producers' prices and these into changes in prices charged to consumers. The food and agricultural sectors of such a model could incorporate lagged responses of production to prices received by farmers, as well as the stochastic effects of weather on crop yields.

The sensitivity analyses by Adelman and Sparrow fall into two logically distinct categories. In the first category, four different objective functions are tried. Each is a linear combination of some of the 102 variables included in the basic model. GNP, consumption, and foreign aid are all measured in dollars at constant prices; employment is measured in numbers of workers. Given the upper and lower limits on production and domestic consumption specified for most of the fourteen industries, each objective function includes a single aggregative *target variable* in the Tinbergen sense [9]; all other variables are incidental or irrelevant. Each objective function leads to the selection as optimal of a different point on the same production possibilities surface.

In the second category, different assumptions are made concerning the presence and extent of "diminishing returns to production for final demand, to investment, and to exports." These are different assumptions concerning the structure of the Colombian economy and those aspects of the world economy which influence the demand for Colombian coffee, bananas, and petroleum. Full implementation of these assumptions would require the incorporation into the basic model of mechanisms for determining changes in prices, wage rates, consumer income, and perhaps other variables. If we assume a free market economy, consumer prices and quantities consumed will be determined by continuously downward-sloping demand functions and by the corresponding production functions and wage-price adjustment equations. These relationships (empirically validated, we presume) should largely replace the arbitrary upper and lower limits on consumption and production for each industry which serve to keep the authors' basic linear model literally within bounds.

Once prices are permitted to vary with physical output, physical consumption, or physical exports, differences in GNP or consumption as *dollar magnitudes* resulting from alternative policies are no longer unequivocal indicators of welfare change. At the least we must compare two GNP or consumption figures in terms of constant prices, raising some familiar index number problems.

To say that consumer expenditure is a quadratic function of the market-clearing quantities of different commodities sold to consumers would be an observation about the positive structure of the economy, subject (in principle) to empirical test. But this statement, true or not, has no necessary implications for the objective function of the policymaker who is selecting what he regards as an optimal development strategy. This is quite clear if the policymaker chooses to minimize unemployment or foreign aid. There is more danger of confusion if the policymaker chooses to maximize GNP or consumption. In this event he might well choose to maximize these measured at constant prices, which would have no necessary relationship to the actual market prices resulting from his policy measures. Or the policymaker might choose to maximize real GNP subject to restrictions on the rate of price inflation—or to maximize some weighted combination of change in real GNP and change in the price level.

I am not implying that the authors are basically unaware of this distinction, but I believe they lose sight of it momentarily when they say that "both the nature of the goals . . . and the shape of the objective function exert a significant influence on the optimal results." For what they here regard as changes in the shape of the objective function are in fact changes in their assumptions concerning the structure of the economy.

As noted earlier, the authors chose four alternative target variables (GNP, consumption, foreign aid, and unemployment) to be maximized or minimized one at a time. These are useful for displaying the properties of the model. In formulating real policy alternatives we could, of course, take account of two or more target variables simultaneously as did Van Eijk and Sandee. For example, we could maximize GNP subject to the constraint that unemployment not exceed 3 per cent of the labor force. This would approximate an objective function containing two target variables, one fixed (if the 3 per cent constraint on unemployment is binding) and the other (GNP) flexible.

Alternatively, we might choose to extremize some linear combination of two or more of the target variables—for example, $W_1 = 0.67$ investment $+ 0.33$ consumption, or $W_2 = 0.80$ investment in basic industry $+ 0.20$ consumption $- \lambda$ unemployment. W_1 implies "barter terms of trade" (in the policymaker's judgment) such that a \$1.00 increase in investment is as important as a \$2.00 increase in consumption. W_2 implies that a \$1.00 increase in investment in basic industry is as important as an increase of \$4.00 in consumption and as important as a reduction of λ man-years in unemployment. It seems to me that this would give the equivalent of a multiple target objective function in the sense of Van Eijk and Sandee.

II. Suggested Improvements in
Development Planning Models: Demands
for Domestic Consumption and Exports

The present version of the paper includes some experiments with step-function approximations to downward-sloping demand curves. The authors rightly observe that "the derivation of qualitatively valid results with 'nonlinear' models . . . clearly presupposes accurate sectoral estimates of price and income elasticities."

There is an extensive literature on price elasticities of demand and another, quite distinct, literature on income elasticities of demand. So far, neither of these seems to have been tapped in connection with development planning models, with the notable exception of Johansen's model for Norway [8].

Many of the constraints imposed by Adelman and Sparrow (lower limits on consumption and investment for each industry, upper limits on exports) are defenses against the strict linearity of their model. Some of these constraints could be dispensed with if the model itself included demand curves which were not only downward sloping but continuous.

The permissible exports from Colombia are coffee, bananas, and petroleum. A realistic submodel including domestic demand curves in Colombia, in the United States and Canada, in Europe and in the rest of the world, the corresponding supply curves, and provision for administrative interventions of certain types could be devised for each of these commodities. It is important to note that the primary realities in an international trade model are the demand and supply curves in each country. "Elasticities of export or import demand" are by-products without any direct structural significance [3].

Apart from coffee, bananas, and petroleum, all production in the model is for domestic use. Household demand could be represented by downward-sloping linear demand curves (consumption$_i$ = a_i + b_i price$_i$) and upward-sloping consumption-income curves (consumption$_i$ = c_i + d_i income) which approximately satisfy the homogeneity condition at the base period level of consumption. At the simplest, we could linearize and otherwise adapt the following elasticities:[1]

	Weight (w_i)	Own-price Elasticity (η_i)	Sum of Cross-price Elasticities	Income Elasticity (γ_i)
Food	w_1	−0.6	0	0.6
Clothing	w_2	−1.2	0	1.2
Housing	w_3	−0.8	0	0.8
All other	w_4	−1.6	0	1.6

Consumption theory provides us with certain constraints for a single consumer

Thus if $\sum_i w_i = 1.00$, $\sum_i w_i \eta_i = -1.00$. Also $\sum_i w_i \gamma_i = 1.00$.

Thus, if income is identical with consumption expenditures or if consumption expenditures are a constant percentage of disposable income, that part of total capacity in each sector which was needed to supply household demand, directly or indirectly, would be generated as a result of effective household demand.

I do not understand the reluctance of economists to include a few downward-sloping and continuous linear demand curves in a development planning model. The Fox-Taeuber spatial equilibrium model of the United States livestock and

---

[1] The income elasticities are based on Houthakker [7]; use of the homogeneity condition to derive a complete set of income and price elasticities of demand was suggested by Frisch [6] and implemented in a particular case by Brandow [1].

feed economy [5] included ten consumer demand functions for livestock products, ten producer demand functions for feed, and ten supply functions for livestock products. Each of these thirty equations included either three or four
variables, and the system was interdependent. By organizing the computations
in a common-sense iterative sequence we were able to obtain solutions quite easily
using ordinary desk calculators. Once an initial solution was obtained representing approximate 1949–50 conditions, it was found possible to obtain equilibrium solutions for other sets of initial conditions (sets of values of the exogenous variables) in a short time.

If the Colombia model were revised as suggested, the determination of prices,
and possibly of wages, would require some further attention. GNP produced
in each sector would be distributed to households (and depreciation), so the
revised model would be more nearly closed than that of Adelman and Sparrow.
The household sector would become essentially endogenous. Demand curves for
exports would slope downward, perhaps only slightly for petroleum but significantly for coffee and bananas. The demand and supply curves in countries other
than Colombia would shift for reasons exogenous to the Colombian economy.

III. Sensitivity Analysis and the Specification of Production Processes: The Anatomy of a Technology Matrix

In Table 1 I have tried to suppress a good deal of distracting detail from the
authors' interindustry matrix (I-A), presented in their Table 3. My presumption
in approaching any matrix which strives (properly) for comprehensiveness is that
"there is less to it than meets the eye."

If we suppress all coefficients in the Adelman and Sparrow Table 3 which are
either smaller than 0.01 or round to 0.01, the number of "important" off-
diagonal coefficients is reduced to twenty-five. Further, the 14 by 14 matrix can
be arranged in strictly lower triangular form. Finally, the matrix can be par-
titioned into four 7 by 7 blocks, of which one is diagonal and another null.

This form permits exceedingly simple manipulations of this part of the model,
using a desk calculator or simply pencil and paper. The small effects of suppressing some coefficients are suggested by the following tabulation:

Kind and Size of Coefficients	Number of Coefficients	Algebraic Sum of Coefficients
On major diagonal:	14	13.20
Off major diagonal:	182	−4.61
Rounding to −0.02 or more[a]	25	−4.34
Rounding to −0.01	17	−0.17 (est.)
Between −0.005 and −0.001	31	−0.08 (est.)
Less than −0.001[a]	32	−0.02 (est.)
Zero	77	0

[a] In absolute value.

Table 1. Interindustry Matrix of Adelman and Sparrow, Modified by Suppressing All Coefficients in Their Table 3 Which Are Smaller in Absolute Value than, or Round to, −0.01

Which Are Smaller in Absolute Value than, or Round to, −0.01

Industry	6	12	14	8	4	2	5	10	9	3	11	7	1	13
6 Printing	1.00													
12 Res. constr.		1.00												
14 Plant constr.			1.00											
8 Rubber				1.00										
4 Clothing					1.00									
2 Food						+.93								
5 Furniture							+.69							
10 Mech., metal			−.30					+.95						
9 Nonmetal, min.			−.16						+.97					
3 Textiles										+.97				
11 Other mfg.				−.05	−.32				−.04		+.88			
7 Chem., petrol.					−.15				−.02	−.13	−.02	+.97		
1 Primary						−.55	−.11	−.24	−.70	−.32	−.14	−.29	+.96	
13 Electricity				−.02					−.10		−.18	−.09		+.88
Imports	−.27	−.02	−.03	−.22	−.32	−.14	−.02	−.12	−.04	−.02	−.08	−.11		
Value added[a]	0.73	0.98	0.49	0.71	0.21	0.24	0.56	0.59	0.07	0.50	0.46	0.48	0.96	0.88

B. Proportion of Total Resource or Capacity Needed to Support 10^7 Pesos Gross Output

	6	12	14	8	4	2	5	10	9	3	11	7	1	13
Proprietors	.00027	.00119	.00119	.00013	.00174	.00007	.00187	.00074	.00042	.00014	.00056	.00010	0	b
Admin. tech.	.00055	.00302	.00302	.00020	.00018	.00011	.00027	.00038	.00033	.00036	.00032	.00036	0	.00010
Workers	.00019	.00057	.00057	.00007	.00016	.00005	.00022	.00019	.00021	.00014	.00012	.00001	.00027	b
Salesmen	.00011	.00061	.00061	b	.00002	.00002	.00025	.00009	.00004	.00050	.00021	.00031	0	0
Capacity	.02083	—	—	.03125	.00429	.00058	.01961	.00585	.01695	.00552	.01000	.00543	.00044	.00088
Imports	.00028	0	0	.00022	b	.00001	.00002	.00025	.00004	.00002	.00008	.00012	0	0

C. Selected Capital Coefficients

	6	12	14	8	4	2	5	10	9	3	11	7	1	13
Mach., metal	.0260	.1050	.0120	.1050	.0120	.0190	.0160	.0190	.0350	.0290	.0130	.0630	.0033	.0055
Plant const.	.0311	.1652	.0083	.1652	.0083	.0297	.0434	.0378	.0600	.0479	.0246	.0851	.0056	.0091
Labor	.0120	.0520	.0050	.0520	.0050	.0178	.0086	.0320	.0500	.0140	.0136	.0643	.0090	.0500
Imports	.0260	.1040	.0120	.1040	.0120	.0190	.0170	.0250	.0350	.0290	.0130	.0620	.0033	.0000

[a] Approximate contribution to GNP per 10^7 pesos gross output

In final calculations, all well-substantiated coefficients should probably be used. But the twenty-five off-diagonal coefficients in part A of my Table 1 account for at least 94 per cent of the sum of the 105 off-diagonal coefficients in the Adelman-Sparrow table so solutions obtained by manipulating the matrix in Table 1 should not seriously mislead us. Adding the diagonal and off-diagonal coefficients without regard to sign, we may estimate that Table 1 preserves

$$\frac{17.54}{17.81} = 98.5 \text{ per cent of the total information in the orginal matrix.}$$

We next proceed to Table 5 of the Adelman-Sparrow paper, the matrix of inputs of basic resources including four kinds of labor, "capacity," and imports. Here the situation can be illuminated by adapting to our purposes a normalization procedure or short cut, first demonstrated (I believe) by Frederick V. Waugh [11]. In this case, we divide each coefficient in the table by the appropriate total capacity figure. For each industry or resource these figures tell us what proportion of the total capacity or of the total amount of the resource is required to support a gross output of 10^7 pesos from each industry. The largest figure in each column in part B of Table 1 is the most limiting single resource with respect to that industry.

Industries 1, 2, 4, 12, and 13 figure prominently in the Period 2 solutions when the objective is to maximize GNP. Why do these particular industries enter the optimal program?

Some favorable though not necessarily decisive factors may be noted. Industries 1 and 13 (primary products and electricity) make—in my simplified Table 1 —no demands on other domestic industries, so (except for the small or negligible imports in Table 5) their total net outputs go directly into GNP. Along with Industry 12 (residential construction) they make the highest contributions to GNP per unit of gross output. The most limiting factor for Industry 1 is *less* limiting than the most limiting factor for Industry 13. Industry 12 makes unusually heavy demands on workers per unit of gross output.

If part C of Table 1 is correct, capacity in Industry 13, electricity, can be expanded with very moderate demands on domestic capital-goods industries and none on imports. Thus, when certain extremands are used, output of Industry 13 expands sharply. Industry 1 also expands output, as the costs of expanding capacity by one unit in Industry 1 are (according to the Adelman-Sparrow Table 4) among the smallest of any industry.

Industries 4 (footwear and clothing) and 2 (food, beverages, and tobacco) make very light demands on imports per unit of output and of value added. The requirement for workers per unit of value added is moderate in Industry 2 and average or above in Industry 4.

It is possible to see fairly readily how the authors' model produces its results, if some of the smallest interindustry coefficients are suppressed and if F. V. Waugh's short cut is used. The resulting model is simple enough so that it can be curbed or "second-guessed" by good judgment at any step.

IV. LIMITATIONS OF DEVELOPMENT PLANNING MODELS AS DESCRIPTIONS OF THE CURRENT AND EVOLVING STRUCTURE OF AN ECONOMY

As always, the assumption of unchanging interindustry and factor inputs per unit of output (constant coefficient structure) is undesirable.

If we have lots of information about current production practices and available alternatives, the recursive programming approach of Richard H. Day [2] appears very promising. The new methods do not appear in Day's optimal programs until and unless they are sufficiently profitable to justify a place in the optimal program. Even though we lack specific studies for a given country, we should be able to adapt coefficients from studies made in other countries. Disaggregation to the process analysis level may be the only fully satisfactory way to illuminate the problem of changing coefficients.

V. SPATIAL ASPECTS OF THE DEVELOPMENT PROCESS AND IMPLICATIONS FOR DEVELOPMENT PLANNING MODELS

Adelman and Sparrow omit the transportation, trade, and service sectors of the Colombian economy in order to focus more sharply on the primary and manufacturing industries, foreign trade, and foreign aid. In the United States about half of the total labor force is employed in the trade, service, and transportation sectors. Regional and urban economists dealing with an area of a few hundred or a few thousand square miles in the United States would call these sectors *residentiary*, while the primary and manufacturing sectors would form the area's *export base*, "exports" in this context meaning for the most part shipments to other areas within the same country.

The process of urbanization in a primarily agricultural region, coupled with improved transportation of workers, shoppers, peddlers, and the like has the following effects:

1. Village monopolies are broken down and competition among retailers in neighboring villages is increased. The villages in a progressively larger geographic area become linked into a "low-density city" or urban-oriented labor market area and community. Dualism is gradually transformed into monism.

2. In these larger market areas, larger and more complex establishments become possible in retailing, wholesaling, and local government. These can help develop administrative talent and labor skills; factories are not unique in this respect.

3. As constraints on the size of labor market and retail trade areas are relaxed, some towns grow much more rapidly than others. A limited number

become major "growth points," with labor forces sufficiently large and diverse to accommodate the entry of fairly large manufacturing firms. Some villages and hamlets lose population or turn into retirement centers for elderly and immobile people. A predevelopment pattern of small villages of roughly similar sizes and functions is transformed into a hierarchy of central places of different sizes, each size or level providing characteristic services in addition to those available in towns of the next smaller size.

The import of these hypotheses is that progress toward usefulness of the Adelman and Sparrow model for development programming would require further disaggregation and that this disaggregation should take account of spatial and trade-hierarchic aspects of the structure of the Colombian economy which will change systematically during the process of economic development and urbanization.

The Adelman and Sparrow paper makes a very useful contribution toward quantifying the implications of alternative policy goals. Given an accurate model of the economy, the policymaker could be presented with these implications—after which he might modify his goals. However, errors in specifying the true structure of the economy would lead us to present the policymaker with a set of alleged outcomes which would not have materialized in fact.

There is evidently a need for systematic and symmetrical analyses of the consequences of differences in goals and of errors in specifying various components of the models of real economies. A "management game" developed along these lines might be highly useful to the profession, its students, and its advisees.

REFERENCES

1. Brandow, G. E. *Interrelations among Demands for Farm Products and Implications for Control of Market Supply.* Pennsylvania State University Agricultural Experiment Station Bulletin 680, August, 1961, pp. 11–22.
2. Day, Richard H. *Recursive Programming and Production Response.* Amsterdam: North-Holland Publishing Co., 1963. Table 5 in the Appendix to Chapter 7 (precedes page 221).
3. Fox, Karl A. "Some Uses of Econometric Models in Appraising Foreign Trade Policies," Chapter 8, pp. 154–69, in *Econometric Analysis for Public Policy.* Ames: Iowa State University Press, 1958.
4. Fox, Karl A. "Spatial Price Equilibrium and Process Analysis in the Food and Agricultural Sector," Chapter 8, pp. 215–33, in *Studies in Process Analysis: Economy-Wide Production Capabilities.* (Cowles Foundation Monograph 18.) New York: Wiley, 1963.
5. Fox, Karl A., and Taeuber, Richard C. "Spatial Equilibrium Models of the Livestock Feed Economy," *American Economic Review*, LXV (September, 1955), 584–608.
6. Frisch, R. "A Complete Scheme for Computing all Direct and Cross Demand Elasticities in a Model with Many Sectors," *Econometrica*, XXVII (April, 1959), 177–96.
7. Houthakker, H. S. "An International Comparison of Household Expenditure Pat-

terns Commemorating the Centenary of Engel's Law," *Econometrica*, XXV (October, 1957), 532–51.

8. Johansen, Leif. *A Multi-Sectoral Study of Economic Growth*. Amsterdam: North-Holland Publishing Co., 1960.

9. Tinbergen, J. *On the Theory of Economic Policy*. Amsterdam: North-Holland Publishing Co. 1952 (rev. ed. 1955).

10. Van Eijk, C. J., and Sandee, J. "Quantitative Determination of an Optimum Economic Policy," *Econometrica*, XXVII (January, 1959), 1–13.

11. Waugh, Frederick V. "The Minimum-Cost Dairy Feed," *Journal of Farm Economics*, XXXIII (August, 1951), 299–310.

12. A PROGRAMMING MODEL FOR ISRAEL

MICHAEL BRUNO, HEBREW UNIVERSITY AND BANK OF ISRAEL*

I. INTRODUCTION

This paper analyzes a multisector programming model in which foreign trade plays a major role. Although the model and the analysis are based on data for the Israeli economy, most of the structural features are applicable to open, developing economies in general.

The model has considerable affinity with similar work done in this field in recent years. Sandee [11], Manne [10], Chenery and Uzawa [6], and others have been important sources of inspiration. This is a thirty-sector model (roughly comparable to a two-digit industry classification). The main variables for which optimal values for the planning period are sought are the levels of output, consumption, investment, exports, and imports by sector and by type of commodity group and the prices of commodities and primary factors. The main constraints of the model are:

1. Input-output relations of the Leontief type.
2. Demand schedules for private consumer goods based on expenditure elasticities and an over-all savings constraint.

* The paper is based on research mainly carried out at the Bank of Israel and the Hebrew University in Jerusalem. An earlier version of the model and some preliminary results have been described in [3] and [4].

The present paper was written during my stay as Visiting Professor at M.I.T. and Research Associate at the Center for International Affairs, Harvard University. I am indebted to the latter's Project for Quantitative Research in Economic Development for supporting supplementary computations.

Mordecai Fraenkel of the Bank of Israel has contributed much more to this paper than ordinary research assistance, and his help is gratefully acknowledged. I am also indebted to Christopher Dougherty, now at Harvard University, and Amnon Bar-Shua of the Computation Centre, the Israel Ministry of Defence, for their faithful assistance. Last but not least, thanks go to Clopper Almon, Hollis Chenery, Richard Eckaus, Jan Sandee, Alan Strout, and Jean Waelbroeck for helpful comments on an earlier version of this report.

3. A capital-output matrix for determination of investment demand. Housing is a function of consumer demand.

4. A set of import coefficients for each sector and type of final good, with allowance for import substitution.

5. An export demand curve for each commodity. For most industries this takes the simple form of minimum and maximum bounds for each commodity with the minimum based on 1964 figures and the maximum rate of growth based on past performance and expert advice.

6. A limitation on the supply of foreign exchange.

7. A limitation on the supply of labor by skill category. Labor co-efficients are projected into the future on the basis of past productivity performance and expert advice. Alternative formulations have also been tried.

Optimal programs are obtained by maximizing total consumption at the end of the planning period, subject to the given constraints. The model is set up and solved for two end-years, 1970 and 1975. Technical coefficients and exogenous variables are changed between the two years. However, the model is "static" in the sense that for any single optimal solution all variables relate to the same year, or end of a planning period.

Rather than providing one optimal solution and a set of shadow prices, the model is used to explore *schedules* of optimal solutions and prices under alternative assumptions about the availability of scarce factors or about the demand and supply functions. Using parametric programming we can trace production possibility frontiers for the economy even though the exact form of the social welfare function may not be known.

Our discussion will be mainly concerned with the structure and general implications of this type of model and less with the policy content of the specific numerical results. Another paper of mine [5] discusses in greater detail the analytical implications of the model for optimal trade and development patterns.

II. Summary Description of the Model

The Variables

We start by enumerating the groups of endogenous variables, or activities, appearing in the model (see Table 1). Since we have a thirty-sector breakdown, the subscript i runs from 1 to 30, though for most groups of variables some empty cells are ignored. Column 3 of the table indicates the number of variables in each group.[1]

Table 1. The Endogenous Variables

Notation	Definition	Number of variables in group
(1)	(2)	(3)
X_i	Output of commodity i	(30)
C_i	Private consumption of domestically produced commodity i	(27)
M^c	Direct imports for private consumption	(1)
V^c	Direct value added in private consumption	(1)
C	Total private consumption	(1)
E_i	Exports of commodity i	(26 + 1)
E	Total exports	(1)
I_i	Gross investment (from sector i)	(27)
M^I	Direct imports for investment	(1)
V^I	Direct value added in investments	(1)
I	Total gross investments	(1)
$I_{1,i}$	Net investments in fixed assets (excluding roads and housing) from sector i	(19)
$I_{3,22}$	Investment in housing	(1)
$I_{5,i}$	Change in inventories	(19)
R_i	Import substitute i (measured from its lower bound $\underline{S_i}$	(4)
M	Total imports	(1)
V	Total GNP	(1)
Z_i	Disposal or artificial activities	(189)

The main exogenous or controlled variables are defined as:

G_i = Public consumption domestically produced (commodity i).

M^G = Direct imports for public consumption.

G = Total public consumption.

N = Total population.

L_0 = Total supply of labor force.

L_1 = Supply of skilled labor.

F = Foreign capital inflow (including all transfers and loans).

P = Private restitution transfers from abroad (included in F).

$I_{4,i}$ = Investment in road construction and replacements of fixed assets.

[1] Table 5 in the Appendix gives a classification of industries and variables in the model.

All money variables (with the exception of F) are measured in millions of Israeli pounds at 1962 prices and relate to the year 1970 or 1975. F is supposed to be measured in millions of dollars at current 1970 or 1975 prices.

The Constraints

Next we give the summary list of constraints, by groups, written in standard form, with the constants (including the exogenous variables) appearing on the right-hand side and the disposal activities immediately to the left of the equality sign. On the far right we indicate the actual number of constraints (rows) appearing in each group.

Group Number	Disposal	Constants or controlled variables	Number of Constraints
(a) *Output determination*			
(a.1) $(a_{ii} - 1)X_i + \sum_{j \neq i} a_{ij}X_j$ $+ C_i + I_i + E_i + R_i$	$+ Z_i$ (a.1)	$= -G_i - \underline{S}_i$	30
(b) *Consumer demand and savings*			
(b.1) $-C_i + \left(\epsilon_i \dfrac{C_i^0}{C^0} \right) C$		$= N\left[\dfrac{C_i^0}{N^0}(\epsilon_i - 1) \right]$	27
(b.2) $-M^c + \left(\sum_i \epsilon_i' \dfrac{M_i^c{}_0}{C^0} \right) C$		$= N\left[\sum_i \dfrac{M_i^c{}_0}{N^0}(\epsilon_i' - 1) \right]$	1
(b.3) $-C + \Sigma C_i + M^c$	$+ V^c = 0$		
(b.4) $-C + (1 - s)V$	$+ Z$ (b.4)	$= G - C_0 - G_0$ $+ (1 - s)V_0$	1
(c) *The demand for investment goods*			
(c.1) $I_i - I_{1,i} - I_{3,22} - I_{5,i}$		$= I_{4,i}$	27
(c.2) $I - \sum_i I_i - M^I - V^I$		$= 0$	1
(c.3) $-10I_{1,i} + \sum_j k_{ij}X_j$	$[+ Z_i$ (c.3)$] = 0$		19
(c.4) $-10I_{3,22} + \left(\dfrac{\epsilon_k K_3^0}{C^0} \right) C$	$[+Z$ (c.4)$] = N\left[\dfrac{K_3^0}{N^0}(\epsilon_k + \epsilon_p - 1) \right]$ $-P\left(\dfrac{\epsilon_p K_3^0}{P^0} \right)$		1
(c.5) $10M^I - \sum_j k_{32,j}X_j - 10\delta_5 M$		$= 10I_{4,32}$	1

(c.6) $10V^I - \sum_j k_{33,j} X_j$ $= 10 I_{4,33}$ 1

(c.7) $I_{5,i} - \eta_i X_i$ $= 0$ 19

(d) *The demand for imports*

(d.1) $M - \sum_j m_j X_j - M^c - M^I$ $= M^G - \sum_i d_i \underline{S}_i$ 1

         $+ \sum_i d_i R_i$

(d.2) R_i $+ Z_i \,(\text{d.2}) = \bar{S}_i - \underline{S}_i$ 4

(e) *Export constraints*

(e.1) $E - \sum_i E_i$ $= V^E$ 1

(e.2) $- E_i$ $+ Z_i \,(\text{e.2}) = -\underline{E}_i$ 26

(e.3) E_i $+ Z_i \,(\text{e.3}) = \bar{E}_i$ 26

(f) *Foreign exchange constraint*

(f.1) $u_M M - \Sigma u_i E_i$ $+ Z \,(\text{f.1}) = F + u_E V^E$ 1

(g) *Labor constraints*

(g.1) $\sum_j 1_{sj} X_j$ $+ Z_s \,(\text{g.1}) = L_s$ $(s = 0, 1)$ 2

(h) *The determination of total GNP*

(h.1) $M - C - I - E + V$ $= G$ 1

Output Determination (a) comprises the thirty commodity balances for domestic production. Public consumption (G_i) is taken as exogenously given by government social and defense policies.[2] The variable R_i is a transformation of an import substitution variable (S_i) to make it take on only nonnegative values. Thus, if $\underline{S}_i \le S_i \le \bar{S}_i$, where $\underline{S}_i$ may be negative, we transform $R_i = S_i - \underline{S}_i \ge 0$ [see also constraint (d.2)]. The input-output coefficients of domestic intermediate goods are a_{ij}. These are mainly derived from a 1962 base-year table but take into account predictable technical changes in the input of power (24) and water (25) between 1962 and the target years 1970 and 1975. Both of these rows of input coefficients have shown systematic variation in the past, and a detailed separate analysis of each was carried out.

Consumer Demand and Savings (b). The equation (b.1) is the tangential approximation to the logarithmic relationship $C_i/N = (\text{constant})(C/N)^{\epsilon_i}$ at a forecast reference point (C^0/N^0, C_i^0/N^0) on this curve (ϵ_i = expenditure elasticity for commodity i, estimated from cross-section and time series

[2] Alternative solutions for alternative values of G_i (and M^G) can be worked out.

analyses of consumer behavior). The reference point was derived from previous solutions to the model. Although the further any actual solution of the model gets from this point the less accurate the tangential approximation, the error involved is in most cases quite small (different reference points are used for 1970 and 1975). Equation (b.2) does the same for the weighted total of imported consumer goods and (b.3) is a definitional equation. We have explicitly introduced the population level (N) on the right-hand side of these constraints to allow for parametric variations in the level of immigration, a problem of particular importance in Israel.

The last constraint in this group (b.4) expresses the over-all savings limitation, $S - S_0 \leq s(V - V_0)$, where s is the marginal propensity to save. In the recent past, s has been around 0.19 and the model is run for the following alternative future values: $s = 0.20, 0.25, 0.30$ where the increase over 0.19 is implicitly assumed to consist of additional net government taxes. In other words, s is considered a policy parameter subject to political limitations. A level of 0.25 for 1970 and 0.30 for 1975 might reasonably estimate these bounds. One way of improving the model is to introduce explicitly the determination of the various savings components (private, corporate, and public).

A more restrictive feature of the above specification of consumer demand is its failure to consider the price elasticity of demand for each commodity group, though import substitution is allowed, at least in principle. At our level of aggregation this assumption may not be as unrealistic as may first appear, but it seems advisable to experiment with alternative, more flexible, formulations. Yet, bringing in prices explicitly is obviously impossible at present because the future behavior of relative *market* prices is unknown and *shadow* prices have to be determined from the solution itself. Short of proceeding by a trial and error method, we shall allow for some variation around the Engel curves.[3] This is done (for a 10 per cent variation) in constraints (b.1)$'$ and (b.1)$''$:[4]

(b.1)$'$ $\qquad\qquad\qquad -C_i + 0.90\beta C \leq 0.90\alpha$

(b.1)$''$ $\qquad\qquad\qquad C_i - 1.10\beta C \leq -1.10\alpha$

where $\qquad\qquad \alpha = N\left[\dfrac{C_i^0}{N^0}(\epsilon_i - 1)\right]$ and $\beta = \epsilon_i \dfrac{C_i^0}{C^0}.$

[3] See also Sandee [11].
[4] The figure of 10 per cent is, of course, quite arbitrary. A more satisfactory procedure would be to assume different variations for different commodity groups to take account of different price elasticities.

These constraints replace (b.1). There is no need to replace (b.2) since import substitutability is in principle already allowed. In this case, however, an explicit equation must be added to determine V^c.[5]

The economic implication of this alternative specification is that, within a ± 10 per cent range of variation around the Engel curve, the consumption pattern automatically adjusts itself to relative factor scarcities. As we shall see below, this alternative specification removes an unrealistic knife-edge property of the present model.

The Demand for Investment Goods (c) is divided into four broad groups:

1. Investments in roads and replacements $(I_{4,i})$, exogenously determined.
2. Investments in fixed assets (I_1), determined through a capital-output matrix (k_{ij}) (equations c.3, c.5, c.6).
3. Investments in housing $(I_{3,22})$, which is a function of (C) and Restitution transfers from abroad (P), (equations c. 4).[6]
4. Investment in inventories $(I_{5,i})$, assumed a fixed proportion of output (equation c.7).

The equations (c.1) and (c.2) are definitional. The stock of capital is assumed to grow at a rate of 10 per cent during the terminal year, t. The factor 10, wherever it appears, is a conversion factor from the required stock of capital at the beginning of the year to the investment flow during the year. Some such solution of the terminal-period problem is common to all finite horizon programming models.[7] We also implicitly assume that the degree of capacity utilization will remain the same as it was in the base year 1962.

This formulation of the demand for investment leaves much to be desired, particularly from the point of view of capital theory, since it amounts to regarding capital as an intermediate good. One way to improve the model is to solve it simultaneously for a number of years while keeping the

[5] This consists of an "exogenous" term, the services of nonprofit institutions, and the consumption of housing services. In the previous formulation the elasticity of this residual term is implicitly made to come out "right."

[6] This equation, which is similar in structure to (b.1), is based on an unpublished study by J. Paroush of the Bank of Israel, estimating the elasticity of demand for housing with respect to total consumption (ϵ_k) and restitution payments (ϵ_p). We have, approximately, $\epsilon_k = \frac{1}{2}, \epsilon_p = \frac{1}{16}$. Since P is expected to go down over time whereas C rises, this distinction is of some importance. The propensity to consume out of P has been found by M. Landsberger to be very small.

[7] See, for example [10] and [11]. Usually investments in the terminal year are made to depend on investments in the preceding planning period. Our present formulation seems more satisfactory from the pricing point of view.

stocks of capital of each year fixed for the duration of the year and determined by past years' investment (see Eckaus [9]).[8]

The Demand for Imports (*d*). Equation (d.1) sums up the demand for imports of the various types of final goods after deducting import substitutes (R_i). The coefficient d_i measures the ratio of the price of the imported commodity (at the official exchange rate) to the domestic production cost price. Although R_i takes only nonnegative values, import substitution (defined as $R_i - \underline{S}_i$) can take up negative values, depending on the optimal choice within the model. Because of the linearity of the model this will usually be an "all or nothing" choice. This is the rationale for the lower and upper bounds on S_i, and therefore an upper bound on R_i in (d.2). Another justification for this formulation is the fact that our commodity groups are not homogenous and the choice between domestic production or imports is usually confined to a very narrow range of commodities within the broader groupings. One disadvantage of our formulation, however, is the need to make some prior guesses as to the values of $\underline{S}_i$ and $\overline{S}_i$.[9] In the Israeli case, in any event, the remaining possibilities for choice in this field are considered to be very small.[10] We have incorporated this variant in our model for a few illustrative cases mainly to see how the model works.

Export Constraints (*e*) are summed up in equation (e.1). V^E is an exogenous estimate of direct value added in exports (mainly interest and dividends), a small amount. Equations (e.2) and (e.3) are again linear substitutes for what are essentially nonlinear constraints on either supply or demand. For most commodities, we just have lower and upper bounds on total exports of the commodity in question. The lower bound is taken to be the 1964 level or some low rate of increase,[11] and the upper bound is based on an assessment of past performance and on expert advice. In the case of

---

[8] Such formulation of our model is now being tried out, but is still in exploratory stage and will not be discussed here. In Section III, where some price implications of our present formulation are being discussed, it will be mentioned that this can also be rationalized in terms of imposing an exogenously given rate of interest on the model (see also [5]). Another formulation allowing for substitution between labor and capital has been discussed in [3].

[9] An alternative procedure is to incorporate a detailed import matrix within the model and let the model decide on the implied total commodity requirements. See [3]. The weakest link in the system, however, will remain, namely the empirical estimation of d_i.

[10] Empirical analysis has shown that, whereas industrial and agricultural development in earlier years has been characterized by considerable import substitution, this is no longer the case. The major share of imports now consists of raw materials and, to a lesser extent, equipment, almost all of which is of the type which a small country could not afford to produce under any relevant price ratios.

[11] This is because of the reasonable premise that it will hardly ever pay to actually *decrease* exports in absolute value because of resulting excess capacities (exports are usually specialized goods). Another argument may be the existence of vested interests.

citrus fruits (E_3), in which Israel commands a considerable share of the market, a sloping demand curve must be assumed. This curve is approximated here by a step function with only two steps. The result is shown in the marginal revenue curve:[12]

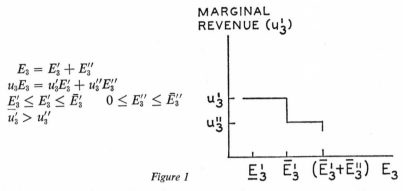

$$E_3 = E_3' + E_3''$$
$$u_3 E_3 = u_3' E_3' + u_3'' E_3''$$
$$\underline{E_3'} \le E_3' \le \bar{E}_3' \quad 0 \le E_3'' \le \bar{E}_3''$$
$$u_3' > u_3''$$

Figure 1

Finally, we should add that for two industries, land transportation (26) and trade (30), the export entry is an overhead cost and the constraint takes the simplified form: $E_i - \alpha_i E = 0$ (where $i = 26, 30$ and we have, approximately, $\alpha_{26} = \alpha_{30}, = 0.01$).

Foreign Exchange Constraint (f) is expressed in current $(t$ year) dollar terms in equation (f.1). For this reason export and import figures have to be multiplied by the dollar price coefficients u_i.[13] The variable F (foreign capital inflow) includes unrequited receipts, transfers, and loans. A future modification of the model is envisaged in which a supply schedule for F will be incorporated explicitly, bringing in the cost of borrowing. In the present analysis we confine ourselves to parametric changes over a wide range of F values, thus regarded as gifts or transfers.

Labor Constraints (g). At present we only have a breakdown of labor into two categories, "skilled"[14] and "unskilled." The total labor equilibrium condition is given by $s = 0$, and the specific "skill" constraint is given by $s = 1$ in (g.1). The total labor coefficient is estimated from time series regressions and the expected future breakdown between the two types of labor is mainly based on expert studies for the various sectors.

[12] In principle one could add any number of steps to approximate a smooth sloping marginal revenue curve.

[13] Import prices are assumed to remain constant, thus u_M reflects the official exchange rate. For some exports (primarily citrus) an exogenous price reduction has been assumed.

[14] Roughly speaking, the "skilled" group includes the types of labor for which an extra training period of at least two years (in addition to ordinary schooling) is required. An attempt is now being made to provide a finer breakdown of the labor force. Data, however, are very scant.

As long as the training period for a particular type of labor is shorter than the total planning period, any supply shortage could in principle be remedied by allowing for an additional training activity in the model. This is a subject for further refinement. For the moment, our estimate of the supply of skilled labor is based on what the "normal" output of skilled labor up to the year t is likely to be, on the basis of government forecasts. Alternative solutions of the model are worked out for parametric changes in L_1. An alternative production function specification is discussed in Section VI.

Determination of Total GNP (h) is defined by equation (h.1). This does not place any additional restriction on the model.

The Solution of the Model

The solution of the model consists of finding a maximum value of total private consumption subject to the above constraints. The model has been run with different sets of parameters for 1970 and 1975. The main method has been to look at patterns of solutions with variations in some of the most important exogenous variables (F, L_1, N, and L_0, E_i) and also some key parameters (such as labor inputs, consumption expenditure elasticities, and export prices). Only some of these experiments are discussed here and those will only be considered from certain selected aspects.

III. The Implications of Variations in Capital Inflow

In the experiments which follow we fix the expected value of all exogenous variables (including factor supplies, and the like) and also the value of F, the total expected foreign capital inflow. We obtain a maximum value of C, total private consumption, for the end year (1970 or 1975, each time using a different set of parameters). We now alter the value of F, keeping all other exogenous variables fixed. As we increase F, resources (labor, capital, and foreign exchange) can be freed from export industries[15] and diverted to increasing the over-all level of consumption in the economy. For simplicity we start off by assuming that the savings constraint (b.4) is not effective (i.e. let s be completely endogenous). A further increase in F will lead to a further increase in C, but with diminishing returns, since resources now have to be freed from relatively more productive export

---

[15] Formally import substitution is just like exports. In the present experiment no import substitution was introduced, however.

activities. We thus get a transformation frontier between F and optimal C levels.[16]

Figure 2 introduces four such series of experiments, two for each planning year, one (B-curve) with the supply of skilled labor held fixed at its forecast level, and one (A-curve) without the skilled labor constraint and with only the total labor force kept fixed.[17] All the curves in the F-C plane are upward sloping and concave to the origin. The experiment here has been conducted by shifting F upward at $50 million intervals. In actual fact these curves consist of piece-wise linear segments, unequal in length, each corner representing a change of basis as we expand or contract an export industry.[18] As we shall see below, industries enter or exit in order of their comparative advantage which can be given a very simple formula.

The slope of the curves at each point indicates the shadow price or marginal productivity of foreign exchange $\frac{\partial C}{\partial F} = p_\$$. We note that this is relatively high before the point of full employment (maximum total export ceiling) is reached, since any additional unit of foreign exchange contributes directly to an increase in consumption by permitting the imports of additional raw materials which could not be achieved through additional exports. Selected values of C, F, the shadow price of foreign exchange ($p_\$$), and the shadow prices of labor (w_0) and skill (w_1) for the four sets of solutions are given in Table 2.[19]

So far we have not said anything about the savings constraint. The curves in Figure 2 are the optimal transformation curves only if savings can be made to adjust. The required level for the policy instrument s (the marginal savings ratio) can be worked out for each point on these curves by applying the relation (b.4) as an equation defining s. We have marked the points corresponding to the three representative values of s (.20, .25, .30) on the curves B_{70} and B_{75} of Figure 2 (these are the same, for any given F, also for the A-curves).

Let us now recognize that the government may be limited in its capacity

---

[16] A corresponding curve in the E-F or E-$p_\$$ (exchange rate) planes could also be drawn. For data see Table 6.

[17] The implied labor skill adjustment is here assumed to take place at zero cost. This would be consistent only if it represents a variation in the skill composition of future immigration.

[18] In [5] these segments are worked out explicitly. Owing to faults in the parametric programming computer program that was used here, pseudo-parametrization of the above kind had to be employed.

[19] A more complete set of aggregate solutions is given in Table 6. Individual sector output and commodity price figures, though of considerable interest, have not been reproduced here.

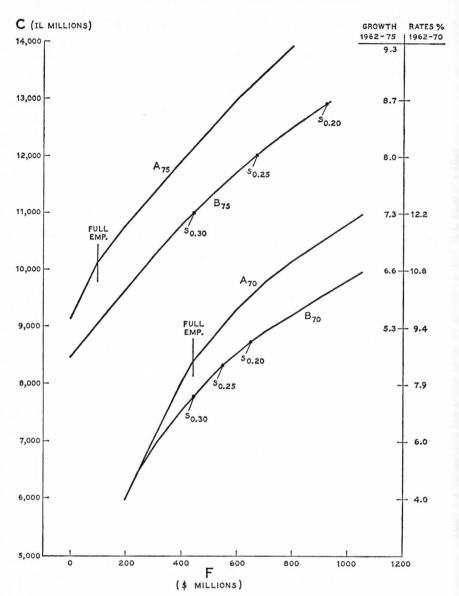

Figure 2. Optimal Values of C *as a Function of* F, *under Different Labor Constraints,
1970 and 1975*

Table 2. Consumption and Factor Prices for Selected Values of F, 1970 and 1975

F	0	100	200	300	400	450	500
1970							
$C(A)$			4.0	6.0	7.9	8.6	9.1
$C(B)$			4.0	5.8	7.0	7.5	8.0
$w_0(A)$			0	0	0	6.66	8.34
$w_1(B)$			10.27	14.68	19.40	19.40	22.22
$p_\$(A)$			10.27	10.27	10.27	6.67	5.77
$p_\$(B)$			5.87	6.90	5.82	5.82	5.17
1975							
$C(A)$	5.8	6.7	7.2	7.6	8.0	8.2	8.4
$C(B)$	5.2	5.8	6.3	6.7	7.2	7.4	7.6
$w_0(A)$	0	7.21	9.49	10.93	10.93	10.93	10.93
$w_1(B)$	20.87	23.53	23.53	23.53	27.33	28.12	29.20
$p_\$(A)$	9.93	7.07	6.17	5.60	5.60	5.60	5.60
$p_\$(B)$	6.33	5.87	5.87	5.87	5.22	5.08	4.90

F	550	600	700	800	900	1000
1970						
$C(A)$	9.5	9.9	10.6	11.1	11.5	12.0
$C(B)$	8.4	8.7	9.3	9.8	10.2	10.6
$w_0(A)$	8.87	9.51	10.77	12.87	12.87	12.87
$w_1(B)$	24.50	27.80	29.99	31.47	31.47	31.47
$p_\$(A)$	5.48	5.13	4.46	3.32	3.32	3.32
$p_\$(B)$	4.65	3.89	3.39	3.05	3.05	3.05
1975						
$C(A)$	8.6	8.7	9.0	9.3		
$C(B)$	7.7	7.9	8.2	8.4		
$w_0(A)$	12.26	12.28	13.28	13.67		
$w_1(B)$	31.24	31.24	35.48	38.29		
$p_\$(A)$	5.07	5.06	4.66	4.51		
$p_\$(B)$	4.54	4.54	3.81	3.33		

Definitions and units:

F = Foreign capital inflow ($ million).
C = Private consumption (annual rate of growth since 1962).
w_0 = Price of unskilled labor (Israeli thousand pound per man-year).
w_1 = Price of skill (Israeli thousand pound per man-year).
$p_\$$ = Price of foreign exchange (Israeli pound per $).

to promote private savings or to levy additional taxes, also public consumption (G) is taken as exogenous and fixed. The actual optimal solutions for C will then lie below the transformation curves whenever the savings constraint becomes effective. This is indicated by a sharp bend below the curve to the left of the respective s_i points in Figure 1. If, for example, $s \leq 0.20$, the shadow price of foreign exchange when $F \leq F(s = 0.20)$ will be considerably higher than the cost of production of additional exports or import substitutes at that point, as given by the slope of the respective A or B curve.[20] A reasonable upper limit on s is, of course, a matter of judgment. An increase in s from 0.20 to 0.25 over a five-year period (1965–70) and to 0.30 over the subsequent period 1970–75 seems perfectly feasible. It turns out that this is approximately what may be required in the Israeli case.

In 1964–65 Israel was running a deficit on current account of about 500 to 550 million dollars (out of a total level of imports of some 1,200 million dollars), with the capital inflow slightly higher than that. The latter had been rising in the past at an average annual rate of some 8 per cent, but is now expected to remain more or less constant until about 1970 and then gradually decline in the 1970's while imports increase approximately like GNP. A reasonable assumption about the average expected path of F is that it will go through a level of some 500–550 by 1970 and 400–450 by 1975.[21] The corresponding optimal growth for C in our model (see Figure 2, curves B_{70} and B_{75}; rates of growth of C appear on the right-hand side) is 8.0–8.4 per cent for 1962–70 and 7.2–7.4 per cent for 1962–75, implying a growth rate of 3.5–4 per cent in consumption per capita for the decade 1965–75 compared to some 6 per cent in recent years,[22] while GNP goes on increasing at a 5–6 per cent per capita rate.[23] The policy implication is the need for a considerable increase in domestic savings (mainly public)[24] and in exports (15–16 per cent growth rate), particularly of manufactures (20 per cent rate of growth).

---

[20] A fuller treatment of the modified transformation curve for such cases is given in [5].

[21] These are somewhat higher than the official estimates, which have been downward biased in the past; even then the above estimates may be too low.

[22] A difference of around 1 per cent growth rate for the two solutions 1962–70 and 1962–75 is quite consistent with a same per capita growth rate for the two implied future planning periods 1965–70 and 1970–75. This is due to two factors: a lower expected population growth rate of 2.9 per cent for 1970–75 as against 3.6 per cent until 1970, and the fact that during 1962–65 C had been growing at 10–11 per cent, which biases the 1970 growth rates by more than the 1975 ones.

[23] See Table 6 in Appendix.

[24] The required levels for s in that case are, in fact, around 0.25 for 1970 and 0.30 for 1975. These conform to our prior judgment as to feasible savings rates which was made independently of the forecast of "reasonable" F levels.

From a comparison of these B-curve solutions with the corresponding A-curve ones, we note that a skilled labor shortage implies a gross loss of around 1 per cent of annual growth rate in consumption (except for very low F values). An analysis of the shadow prices for labor in the two types of solutions also brings out quite clearly how important the skill limitation is. The difference in price indicates the costs it would pay to incur in order to train more labor. The range of values of F and C between the A and B curves (for each year) corresponds to solutions in which L_1 (the supply of skilled labor) is given intermediate values between the forecast level and the level at which skill becomes relatively redundant (with $w_1 = 0$).[25]

Returning to the specific range of solutions discussed earlier ($F = 500$–550 for 1970, 400–450 for 1975), we find that the shadow price of foreign exchange for both years would be around 5.60 ($IL/\$$) if skill is a free good and about 10 per cent lower if skilled labor is constrained.[26] This should be viewed against the official rate of 3.00 ($IL/\$$), or a somewhat higher effective rate today (say 3.50). In our model this effective rate would be about the right shadow price for 1970, for example, if an F value of some 700–750 would be expected. In that case consumption could be expected to rise at a rate of 9–9.5 per cent or 5–6 per cent per capita (with $s <$ 0.20). In many ways such a situation would correspond to what the economy might look like if the foreign capital inflow (F) could be increased at the annual rate at which it grew in the past. One empirical test that a planning model should be subjected to is its ability to reproduce the existing dynamic structure of the economy under the assumption of no policy change. It is reassuring to find that our model passes this test.

The price solutions to our model also indicate that the market price of unskilled labor in Israel is higher and that of skilled labor lower than the implied marginal productivities, after discounting to the present at a 4 per cent growth rate. This is probably another reflection of a relatively abundant present foreign exchange supply which obviates the need to go into more costly export industries.

This may be a convenient stage to stress that we believe the usefulness of a planning model such as ours does not lie in giving one or two sets of optimal solutions for all variables but rather in tracing out *the area of choice* of feasible and efficient policies and the respective *range* of prices. We could even go so far as to say that our choice of objective function,

---

[25] The corresponding experiment with F held fixed and parametric change in L_1 has also been conducted (see below).

[26] The marginal productivity of foreign exchange is higher when more of complementary factors is available. These rates refer to constant 1962 domestic (IL) prices, current t year world ($\$$) prices.

the maximization of C, is only a device for drawing out an efficient transformation curve over the whole range of F (and other factor supplies). We cannot single out any one point on this curve and suggest it as the optimal solution for a government to follow. Theoretically, what is lacking is a specification of the "true" social welfare function, in which a function of C, F, and perhaps some other variables is being maximized.[27] The absence of information on such a function does not detract from the usefulness of our present exercise. All that has to be kept in mind is that we need some additional judgment to supplement our range of numerical solutions before making a specific policy recommendation.

Most insight into the working of a model of this kind can be gained by looking at the price structure, that is, the dual problem. This forms the basis for the analysis of the optimal trade pattern in another paper [5] and will be mentioned only briefly here. Just like in any other Leontief technology, the shadow prices of commodities in the model equal the costs of production in terms of direct and indirect use of the four primary factors of production: foreign exchange, unskilled labor, skill, and capital. The specific form in which capital enters our model can be shown to be equivalent to pricing the capital input in terms of its costs of production (by means of the other three primary factors) and a *fixed 10 per cent rate of interest.*[28]

Applying this framework to an export good (or import substitute), we can distinguish between domestic costs of production (direct and indirect use of labor, skill, and the domestic flow part of the capital input) and the net foreign exchange earned, per unit (gross sales minus the total import component). In case of an import substitute we have to talk in terms of net foreign exchange *saved*. The order of exit (or entry) of foreign trade activities along the transformation curve is determined precisely by the ratio of the domestic resource cost to the net foreign exchange earned (or saved). This obviously is what one would expect on the basis of comparative advantage theory. A comparison of export rankings along the four transformation curves of Figure 2 also reveals the important issues of relative factor scarcity and comparative advantage (in particular, the importance of the skill composition) and the question of dynamic comparative advantage (see [5] and [4]).

---

[27] If this is a function of only C and F, in terms of Figure 2 we could envisage this welfare function taking the form of a set of indifference curves which are upward-sloping and convex to the origin. The marginal rate of substitution between C and F on such indifference curves would be a function of financial and of other possible social trade-offs. The true optimal solution would then be given at a tangency point of the highest indifference curve on the relevant transformation curve of Figure 2.

[28] This equality of the rate of interest and the terminal growth rate of the capital stock, a "Golden Rule" property, is commented on in [5].

Finally, although we would regard the experiment underlying Figure 2 useful for the purpose of establishing the likely range of values of $p_\$$ (and other factor prices) and C with changes in F, not too much reliance for planning purposes should be placed on any one specific export industry result. Even with twenty-five export activities, our model is highly aggregated and the linearity-cum-boundary assumption is a very crude approximation to nonlinear realities. In the real world the curve consists of an infinite number of tiny linear segments, each derived from a tiny linear segment of the demand (or supply) curve of a homogeneous commodity, of which there are thousands. Yet we believe that we have got the approximate curvature and height of our curves right even with the present model.[29]

IV. INFLEXIBILITIES AND SUBSTITUTION IN THE MODEL

We now trace optimal solutions of the model by varying L_1, the supply of skill, keeping all other exogenous variables (including F) fixed. In theory we would expect to find another rather smooth curve (in the L_1– C plane) tracing out a gradual change in the marginal productivity of skill (w_1). In practice, however, the prices of both unskilled labor (w_0) and skill (w_1) change quite abruptly, or do not change at all, and what is worse, hardly ever are both of these prices positive. Table 3 gives the results of such an experiment for three alternative values of F in 1970.[30]

The table shows that in only one case ($F = 800$, $L_1 = 375,600$) do both w_0 and w_1 turn out positive (that is, there is a range of at most 10,000); otherwise the change from $w_0 = 0$ to $w_1 = 0$ is very abrupt.[31]

The structure of the model indicates reasons for its almost knife-edge property. Because of the inflexible consumption pattern, there is one and only one input combination of the two types of labor corresponding to each level of C. The only way substitution of these two factors comes in is in the indirect "production" of the third factor—foreign exchange—be-

[29] We believe that the general changes in the composition of sector output that emerge from our model (not reproduced here) are on the whole reliable. Nonetheless we feel that the more one aggregates back the results of the model the more credence can be placed on them for policy purposes. At the present state of our knowledge the use of multisectoral models should be confined to improvement of our knowledge of aggregate relationships (such as transformation curves) and assessment of shadow prices for the key primary factors, as indicators for decentralized investment decisions. Even this statement, however, should be qualified, as will be seen from our next section.

[30] The starting point in the analysis, in all of these cases, lies on curve B_{70} of Figure 2 and the end point on curve A_{70}, and the path in that figure is along a vertical line. L_1 has been changed by 5,000 (man-years) with each solution.

[31] At the same time we note that the price of foreign exchange ($p_\$$) is quite insensitive to changes in L_1 (except for $F = 300$ which is an unemployment situation right through).

Table 3. Sensitivity
of Factor Prices to Changes in
the Supply of Skill (1970 Model)

| L_1 | | $F = 300$ | | | | $F = 550$ | | | | $F = 800$ | | |
	C	w_0	w_1	$p_{\$}$	C	w_0	w_1	$p_{\$}$	C	w_0	w_1	$p_{\$}$
345,600	6,901	0	14.7	6.90	8,350	0	24.5	4.65	9,237	0	31.5	3.05
350,600	6,975	0	14.7	6.90	8,470	0	22.9	5.02	9,394	0	31.5	3.05
355,600	7,014	0	0	10.27	8,583	0	22.2	5.17	9,551	0	31.5	3.05
360.600	7,014	0	0	10.27	8,694	0	22.2	5.18	9,709	0	31.5	3.05
365,600	7,014	0	0	10.27	8,800	0	19.4	5.82	9,866	0	31.3	3.10
370,600	7,014	0	0	10.27	8,897	0	19.4	5.82	10,018	0	30.0	3.39
375,600	7,014	0	0	10.27	8,993	0	19.4	5.82	10,159	5.5	16.7	3.45
380,600	7,014	0	0	10.27	9,050	8.9	0	5.48	10,166	12.9	0	3.32
385,600	7,014	0	0	10.27	9,050	8.9	0	5.48	10,166	12.9	0	3.32

Definitions and units: L_1 = Skill (man-years). C = Private consumption (*IL* million). w_0 = Price of unskilled labor (*IL* thousand per man-year). w_1 = Price of skill (*IL* thousand per man-year). $p_{\$}$ = Price of foreign exchange (*IL* per \$). F = Foreign capital inflow (\$ million).

cause of the choice of alternative export industries.[32] Although factor proportions vary considerably over different export industries, substitution is limited by the boundaries imposed on the range of use of these activities.

Figure 3 illustrates what is involved.[33] The two axes measure the input of L_0 and L_1 respectively. The point D_1 corresponds to some given endowment of L_0 and L_1 ($= L_1'$). The curves C_0, C_1, and so forth, are isoconsumption curves, and their distinct property is the limited range of factor variability (the ranges are A_0B_0, A_1B_1, etc.). The latter is determined by the extent of effective substitution allowed in the foreign trade sector. Clearly, the larger any given F, the more scope there is for choice in foreign trade and thus the wider will be the factor variability portion of the curves.[34] This explains why, when $F = 800$, we get one intermediate case (see Table 3) in which both w_0 and w_1 are positive. This would correspond to the point D_2 (with $L_1 = L_1'' = 375,600$) in Figure 3, whereas at D_1 ($L_1' = L_1'' - 5,000$) $w_0 = 0$ and at D_3 ($L_1''' = L_1'' + 5,000$) we already have $w_1 = 0$ $w_0 > 0$.

There are a number of ways to go about this problem and introduce more flexibility into the model. One way is to introduce factor substitution on an industry level. In principle there is no difficulty in introducing piece-

[32] As mentioned before, import substitutes come under the same category as exports.

[33] This is a slight variation of a diagram suggested by M. Fraenkel. The situation is reminiscent of the Eckaus factor proportions problem [8].

[34] We can also say that for a given F the lower the consumption level the wider is the range of choice. This, however, is of no help since we want to maximize consumption.

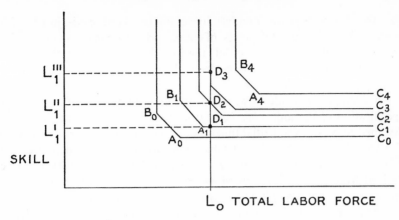

wise linear approximations to a neoclassical production function into our model.[35] There is only the problem of obtaining good empirical estimates of these functions.[36] Another way, which we have adopted at the present stage, is to allow for substitution in consumption, along the lines suggested in Section III, by introducing some flexibility into our Engel curves. We have experimented with a ±5 per cent and a ±10 per cent variation of parameters. The modified attempt at the analysis underlying Table 3 does give a considerably wider scope of variation in the 10 per cent case.[37] Even then, however, the degree of substitutability remains rather limited. Perhaps this is the way the real world actually works. After all, there would not otherwise be such emphasis on the need for training and education of the labor force.

V. OTHER EXPERIMENTS AND CONCLUDING REMARKS

As mentioned earlier, the model treats *import substitution* just like exports. In the Israeli case the scope for import substitution is rather limited, and we have confined ourselves in our experiments to only four such activities: meat (6), chemicals (13), basic metals (17), and machinery (19). Of these, machinery, to a limited extent, is considered a likely candidate for import substitution. Meat is a possible case for negative import substitution (an increase in imports and reduction in domestic production), and

---

[35] A Cobb-Douglas example has been discussed in [3].

[36] In the case of Israel's manufacturing industries these do not exist so far; however, there is some work in progress.

[37] Another by-product is some rise in the optimum consumption levels.

the other two sectors are boundary-line cases. In all four cases, just as with exports, the actual result depends, of course, primarily on the shadow price of foreign exchange. In any event, the introduction of these alternatives does not significantly alter the results, and the analytical implications have already been dealt with.

An attempt was made to work out the implication of using a different specification of the unit *labor input function*. In the present model this is assumed to be an exponential function of time, in each sector. An alternative view is to assume the unit labor input to be itself a function of the scale of operation, for example, $L = AX^\beta$, with $0 \leq \beta \leq 1$, which can be derived from time series regressions. Since this function is concave (decreasing marginal costs) it was incorporated in our model by approximating the implied curve by the tangent at a forecast "reference" point. There are sufficient additional restrictions in the model to prevent it from turning out extreme results. On the other hand, such a formulation does affect the relative prices of factors as the general tendency is to raise the marginal productivity of labor and lower the price of foreign exchange.[38] Which of the two alternatives is a better representation of reality is an open question, and the answer may be different for different industries.

The *population level* enters the consumer demand schedules (equations (b.1), (b.2), and (c.4)) and the supply of labor (constraint (g.1)). In the Israeli case such a variation would come about through a change in immigration. Even when we assume automatic skill adjustment it seems that under the present formulation additional immigration causes a net excess demand for scarce factors since the level of consumption per capita decreases somewhat with the increase in population. This would not be the case, however, if we assume a skill limitation and a relatively skilled immigrant group. A different result is also obtained when the increasing returns to labor assumption is taken. In the latter case an increase in population also raises consumption per capita. An interesting experiment, which we have not conducted, would be to let the population level be determined by the model and to look for a solution which maximizes consumption per capita.

The optimal level of C is not very sensitive to a relaxation of the *export minima*, mainly because the implied rates of growth of exports are so high that the base year level is only a fraction of the final year result. On the other hand, solutions can be quite sensitive to assumptions about *changes in world prices*. A fall in price, for example, will not only decrease the level of C and raise p_s but may also affect the ranking of export industries since what is at stake is the net and not the gross foreign exchange revenue per

---

[38] See also [3].

unit. Moreover, information on the future behavior of world prices may be even more difficult to come by than correct estimates of future productivity growth rates.

We shall briefly mention again areas where the present formulation of the model looks least satisfactory and where additional work is envisaged.

The model could, in principle, be *dynamized* in quite a straightforward manner by bringing in the whole planning period explicitly. Our model structure would be repeated for each year, and an output capacity limitation would be brought in with capacity determined by cumulative investments made up to the year in question. Final year capacity would then have to be fixed in advance (or brought into the objective function) and the objective function would involve maximization of discounted consumption (or other combination of variables) over time (see [9] and [7]). The main problem with this kind of extension is that the size of the problem becomes somewhat unmanageable.[39] One way out is to aggregate the basic model, but we then lose some of the realism which only a minimum of disaggregation can give.[40]

An attempt is being made to break down the *foreign capital inflow* into its various components (gifts and transfers, loans by interest, length of repayment period, and the like). The idea is to bring in the cost of foreign borrowing[41] explicitly and let the model decide on optimal patterns of foreign aid.

For *domestic savings*, too, some improvement in formulation is being thought of. The least one can do is to incorporate a fixed marginal personal savings rate, corporate savings as a function of value added in manufacturing, say, and a government tax function. The latter are tentative ideas on which no work has yet been done.

Some estimates exist on the *cost of training* for various types of labor in Israel. Much work still remains to be done in the breakdown of demand for different types of labor, by sector. The important problem here is not so much to obtain a very fine breakdown by type of skill, but rather to isolate those parts of the labor force for which a relatively longer period of training is required or for which training costs are specific.[42]

[39] If we use our present model as a basis we reckon that for each year we would have about 250 constraints, thus running up to several thousands for any reasonable time span.

[40] One line of attack, now being tried by M. Fraenkel, is using the kind of structural analysis presented in Section IV to express the model in terms of final commodities and primary factors only (leaving out the interindustry part). This, however, has the disadvantage of leaving out specific sector capacity limitations.

[41] In principle F should come into the objective function (with a negative entry), especially since it does not only involve interest payment but may have a social cost element such as "loss of political independence" (how is that measured?).

[42] For two recent studies on this subject, see S. Bowles [2] and I. Adelman [1].

The order in which these four topics were mentioned probably also corresponds to the order of comparative ease of implementation in the present case. Even without these improvements, however, we believe that experiments on a model of the kind discussed here can be of help in understanding some of the development policy problems of an open economy and not only the shortcomings of this and other models at the present state of knowledge. After all, programming models, if not used mechanically, can do at least all the things that development forecasters and planners do anyway and some other things besides. Moreover, once set they do it rather quickly.[43]

APPENDIX

Base Period Figures

Table 4. Base-Year
(1962) Aggregates and Average
Annual Growth Rates (1958–63)

	Percentage rate of growth 1958–63	1962 figures[a] (IL million current prices)
Private consumption	9.8	4,364
Public consumption	10.8	1,558
Gross investment	8.8	2,098
Exports	22.0	1,609
Total uses	11.3	9,629
GNP	10.7	6,698
Imports	12.9	2,931
Population ('000)	3.55	2,288
Employment ('000)	4.6	777
B.O.P. Deficit on current account ($ million)	8.0[b]	455
Official exchange rate (IL/$)		3.00
Marginal propensity to save (1958–64)		0.19

ᵃ Figures have been slightly adjusted to conform with the definitions in the model. Imports are uniformly evaluated at the new official rate of *IL* 3.00 per dollar although devaluation took place in February, 1962. In addition, exports have been evaluated at the prices various commodities fetch on the domestic market (the total is some 17 per cent higher than the normal f.o.b. value), so as to achieve a uniform evaluation of the various commodities in the input-output tables. The G.N.P. figure is adjusted accordingly.

ᵇ This figure relates to the period 1958–62. A similar rate of growth applies to the period 1958–64. 1963 was an exceptionally low year.

[43] In our recent experiments (using a Philco 212 computer) computing time was cut down to $1\frac{1}{2}$ minutes per solution.

Assumptions About Exogenous Variables

In the choice of values for the main exogenous variables we rely on information compiled from various sources, mainly from estimates prepared by the government ministries involved. The following are the estimates for the most important variables:

Population and the Labor Force (N, L_0, L_1). The natural increase accounts for about 1.6 per cent rate of growth in population, the rest coming from immigration, which is expected to go down in the period 1970–75. Labor force participation rates are expected to continue increasing during the period with a slightly lower rate toward the latter part. Another factor accounting for a higher rate of growth in potential employment in the earlier part of the period is a continued decrease in the level of frictional unemployment. (Unemployment stands at a level of about 3 per cent today.) The following figures account for our estimates of N, L_0, and L_1 in the model (absolute figures are in thousands; rates of growth in percentages):

	1962	1970	1975	Rate of Growth 1962–70	1970–75	Notation
Population	2,288	3,034	3,505	3.6	2.9	N
Labor force	808	1,125	1,323	4.2	3.3	
Per cent frictional unemployment	3.8	2.5	2.5			
Potential employment	777	1,097	1,290	4.4	3.3	
Labor supply, all industries[a]	626	884	1,039	4.4	3.3	L_0
Of which: skilled		346	406			L_1

[a] Excluding nonprofit institutions and government employees which are exogenous in the model.

Foreign Capital Inflow (F). Strictly speaking, F stands for the "permissible" deficit on current account after allowing for a reasonable minimum level of foreign exchange reserves. Current forecasts of the Ministry of Finance point to a value of about $450 million for F in 1970 and $400 million in 1975. Past forecasts of actual foreign capital inflow have usually turned out to be on the low side.

Export Constraints $(\underline{E_i}, \overline{E_i})$. These are based on an inspection of past time series for the various commodities and on expert opinion, mainly

Table 5. Classification of Industries and Variables in the First Model

Code (1)	Industry Definition (2)	Output (3) X_i	Private Consumption (4) C_i	Exports (5) E_i	Total Investment (6) I_i	Fixed Investment (7) $I_{1,i}$	Housing (8) I_3	Change in Inventories (9) $I_{5,i}$	Import Substitutes, Total Imports, and G.N.P. (10)
(1)	Field crops	1	31	61	88	118		—	
(2)	Livestock	2	32	62	89	119		—	
(3)	Citrus	3	33	63,158	90	120		138	
(4)	Other agriculture	4	34	64	91	121		139	
(5)	Mining	5	35	65	92	122		140	
(6)	Meat and dairy products	6	36	66	93	—		141	159
(7)	Other food products	7	37	67	94	—		142	
(8)	Textiles	8	38	68	95	—		143	
(9)	Wood products	9	39	69	96	123		144	
(10)	Paper and Printing	10	40	70	97	124		145	
(11)	Leather products	11	41	71	98	—		146	
(12)	Rubber and plastics	12	42	72	99	125		147	
(13)	Chemicals	13	43	73	100	—		148	160
(14)	Fuel	14	44	74	101	—		149	
(15)	Cement and ceramics	15	45	75	102	126		150	

		(M^c) / (V^c) / (C)	(V_E) / (E)	(M^i) / (V^i) / (I)				(M) / (V)
Diamonds	(16)	16	—	76	103	—		151	
Basic metals	(17)	17	—	77	104	127		152	170
Metal products	(18)	18	46	78	105	128		153	171
Machinery	(19)	19	47	79	106	129		154	
Household equipment	(20)	20	48	80	107	130		155	
Vehicles	(21)	21	49	81	108	131		156	
Housing	(22)	22	50	—	109	—	137	—	
Construction	(23)	23	—	—	110	132		—	
Power	(24)	24	51	—	—	—		—	
Water	(25)	25	52	82	—	—		—	
Land transport	(26)	26	53	83	111	133		—	
Shipping and aviation	(27)	27	54	—	—	—			
Other transport.	(28)	28	55	84	112	134		—	
Services	(29)	29	56	85	113	135		—	
Trade	(30)	30	57	86	114	136			
Imports			58(M^c)	—	115(M^i)				59(M)
Value added			(V^c)	Constant(V_E)	116(V^i)				(V)
Total use			60(C)	87(E)	117(I)				

Table 6. Selected Aggregate Solutions (1970)

F	200	250	300	350	400	450	500	550	600	650	700	750	800	850	900	950	1000	1050
A_{70}																		
C — Per	4.0	5.0	6.0	7.0	7.9	8.6	9.1	9.5	9.9	10.2	10.6	10.8	11.1	11.3	11.5	11.8	12.0	12.2
I — cent	7.3	7.7	8.0	8.4	8.7	8.9	8.8	8.9	8.9	9.0	9.1	9.1	9.1	9.1	9.2	9.2	9.2	9.3
E — rate	18.3	18.3	18.3	18.3	18.3	17.9	16.9	16.5	15.9	15.2	14.5	14.0	13.5	13.0	12.5	12.0	11.5	11.0
M — of	9.9	10.3	10.6	10.9	11.2	11.3	10.9	11.0	11.0	10.8	10.7	10.7	10.7	10.7	10.7	10.8	10.8	10.8
V — growth	8.2	8.7	9.2	9.6	10.1	10.4	10.4	10.5	10.6	10.7	10.7	10.8	10.8	10.8	10.8	10.9	10.9	10.9
P$ (IL/$)	10.27	10.27	10.27	10.27	10.27	6.67	5.77	5.48	5.13	4.53	4.46	3.59	3.32	3.32	3.32	3.32	3.32	3.32
w_0 or (y_0)[a]	(122.85)	95.82	68.80	41.77	14.74	6.66	8.34	8.87	9.51	10.63	10.77	12.37	12.87	12.87	12.87	12.87	12.87	12.87
$(-y_1)$[b]	−14.90	−3.42	8.06	19.53	31.01	36.60	35.24	34.53	34.34	33.07	30.70	30.85	30.56	30.98	31.41	31.83	32.25	32.68
B_{70}																		
C — Per	4.0	5.0	5.8	6.5	7.0	7.5	8.0	8.4	8.7	9.0	9.3	9.5	9.8	10.0	10.2	10.4	10.6	10.8
I — cent	7.3	7.7	7.8	7.8	8.0	8.1	8.1	8.2	8.2	8.2	8.2	8.2	8.2	8.2	8.2	8.3	8.3	8.3
E — rate	18.3	18.3	17.7	16.8	16.2	16.2	15.2	14.8	14.1	13.6	13.0	12.4	11.8	11.3	10.7	10.2	9.6	9.0
M — of	8.2	8.7	9.0	9.1	9.3	9.4	9.5	9.6	9.6	9.7	9.7	9.7	9.7	9.7	9.7	9.7	9.7	9.7
V — growth	9.9	10.3	10.1	9.8	9.7	9.7	9.8	9.8	9.8	9.7	9.8	9.6	9.7	9.7	9.7	9.7	9.8	9.8
P$ (IL/$)	10.27	10.27	6.90	6.32	5.82	5.82	5.17	4.65	3.89	3.67	3.39	3.05	3.05	3.05	3.05	3.05	3.05	—
w_1 or (y_1)[c]	(14.90)	3.42	14.69	17.24	19.40	19.40	22.22	24.50	27.80	28.79	29.97	31.47	31.47	31.47	31.47	31.47	31.47	44.77
(y_0)	122.85	95.82	83.77	79.23	73.62	71.70	70.77	69.61	70.28	69.95	69.39	70.38	71.42	72.46	73.49	74.52	75.57	76.49

[a] (y_0) = Unemployment of unskilled (thousands). Figures not in parentheses relate to w_0 (IL thousand per man-year).

[b] $(-y_1)$ = Additional skill requirements.

[c] (y_1) = Unemployment of skilled (thousands). Figures not in parentheses relate to w_1 (IL thousand per man-year).

Table 7. Selected Aggregate Solutions (1975)

F	0	50	100	150	200	250	300	350	400	450	500	550	600	650	700	750	800
A_{75}																	
C Per cent	5.8	6.3	6.7	6.9	7.2	7.4	7.6	7.8	8.0	8.2	8.4	8.6	8.7	8.9	9.0	9.2	9.3
I cent	8.4	8.5	8.7	8.7	8.6	8.6	8.6	8.7	8.7	8.7	8.8	8.8	8.8	8.8	8.9	8.9	8.9
E rate	16.4	16.4	16.4	16.2	15.8	15.4	15.3	15.1	14.9	14.8	14.6	14.5	14.3	14.1	13.8	13.5	13.3
M of	10.2	10.3	10.5	10.4	10.3	10.0	10.1	10.1	10.1	10.1	10.2	10.2	10.2	10.2	10.0	10.0	10.0
V growth	9.1	9.3	9.4	9.5	9.5	9.6	9.6	9.6	9.7	9.7	9.7	9.8	9.8	9.8	9.9	9.9	9.9
$p_\$$ (IL/\$)	9.93	9.93	7.07	6.46	6.17	5.89	5.60	5.60	5.60	5.60	5.60	5.07	5.06	5.06	4.66	4.59	4.51
w_0 or (v_0)[a]	(37.65)	17.82)	7.21	8.74	9.49	10.19	10.93	10.93	10.93	10.93	10.93	12.26	12.28	12.28	13.28	13.47	13.67
$(-y_1)$[b]	38.87	47.49	54.89	53.32	52.40	50.36	50.13	49.54	48.95	48.36	47.77	47.53	46.70	47.51	45.13	43.32	42.30
B_{75}																	
C Per cent	5.2	5.5	5.8	6.0	6.3	6.5	6.7	7.0	7.2	7.4	7.6	7.7	7.9	8.0	8.2	8.3	8.4
I cent	7.8	7.9	8.0	8.0	8.1	8.1	8.1	8.2	8.2	8.3	8.3	8.3	8.3	8.3	8.3	8.4	8.4
E rate	15.2	15.0	14.9	14.7	14.6	14.4	14.3	14.1	14.0	13.8	13.7	13.5	13.2	13.0	12.8	12.6	12.4
M of	9.2	9.1	9.1	9.2	9.2	9.2	9.3	9.3	9.3	9.3	9.4	9.4	9.3	9.3	9.3	9.3	9.3
V growth	8.6	8.7	8.7	8.8	8.8	8.9	8.9	9.0	9.0	9.1	9.1	9.2	9.2	9.2	9.2	9.2	9.2
$p_\$$ (IL/\$)	6.33	6.01	5.87	5.87	5.87	5.87	5.87	5.87	5.22	5.08	4.90	4.54	4.54	3.81	3.81	3.81	3.33
w_1	20.87	22.74	23.53	23.53	23.53	23.53	23.53	23.53	27.33	28.12	29.20	31.24	31.24	35.48	35.48	35.48	38.29
(v_0)	111.55	105.84	103.17	101.88	100.63	99.36	98.09	96.82	94.60	92.49	90.67	92.89	94.97	95.51	94.73	93.94	95.60

[a] (y_0) = Unemployment of unskilled (thousands). Figures not in parentheses relate to w_0 (IL thousand per man-year).
[b] $(-y_1)$ = Additional skill requirements.

from estimates prepared by the Ministry of Industry and Trade and the Economic Planning Authority. Although exports have in the past achieved higher maximal rates of growth, something like an over-all rate of 18 per cent is considered an absolute maximum.[44] Maxima assumed for different commodities do, of course, vary quite considerably round this over-all figure, and a lower maximum rate is applied to the whole period 1964–75 (about 16 per cent).[45]

REFERENCES

. A delman, I. "A Linear Programming Model of Educational Planning: A Case Study of Argentina," this volume, pp. 385–412.
2. Bowles, S. "The Efficient Allocation of Resources in Education: A Planning Model with Application to Northern Nigeria." Unpublished Ph.D. thesis, Harvard University, 1965.
3. Bruno, M. "A Model of Resource Allocation for Israel." Mimeographed paper, Jerusalem, 1964.
4. Bruno, M. "The Optimal Selection of Export Promoting and Import Substituting Projects," United Nations document ISDP.1/A/R.3 (to be published in Report on UN Inter-regional Seminar on Planning of the External Sector, Ankara, September, 1965).
5. Bruno, M. "Optimal Patterns of Trade and Development," *Review of Economics and Statistics* (forthcoming).
6. Chenery, H. B., and Uzawa, H. "Non-linear Programming in Economic Development," in K. J. Arrow, L. Hurwicz, and H. Uzawa, *Studies in Linear and Non-Linear Programming.* Stanford: Stanford University Press, 1958.
7. Chenery, H. B., and MacEwan, A. "Optimal Programs of Growth and Aid: The Case of Pakistan," this volume, pp. 149–78.
8. Eckaus, Richard S. "The Factor Proportions Problem in Underdeveloped Areas," *American Economic Review*, XLV (September, 1955), 539–65.
9. Eckaus, Richard S. "Planning in India." Mimeographed paper, Massachusetts Institute of Technology, 1965.
10. Manne, A. S. "Key Sectors of the Mexican Economy, 1960–1970," in A. S. Manne and H. Markowitz, *Studies in Process Analysis.* New York: McGraw-Hill, 1963.
1. Sandee, J. *A Demonstration Planning Model for India.* New York: Asia Publishing House, 1960.

[44] The figure of 22 per cent for the period 1958–63 is misleading. It is an average of high rates at the beginning of the period, in growing from very low initial levels, and rates of 15–18 per cent later on. The main problem here is the falling share of citrus and the need for very rapid expansion of manufacturing exports.

[45] For more detailed data see [5].

COMMENT

ALAN M. STROUT, AGENCY FOR INTERNATIONAL DEVELOPMENT

My principal complaint with this paper is that the author has usurped most of a discussant's task by drawing out, clearly and concisely, the major lessons from the analysis as well as exposing most of the weakness still remaining in the model. My enthusiasm for the paper is nevertheless unbounded. I think it is certainly one of the most interesting studies we have had before us. Part of this I attribute to the author's experimental use of his model for exploring two phenomena of great interest, the transformation of foreign capital into domestic consumption and the effect of factor scarcity on the international comparative advantage of individual industries. Part of the interest results also from the fact that this is one of the most "mature" models presented at this session. The author has successfully overcome many of the data and specification hurdles which are often the despair of model builders.

In discussing Michael Bruno's study I find it useful to contrast it with another exceedingly interesting model presented to this conference, that of Hollis Chenery and Arthur MacEwan. In one sense the two models are diametric opposites. Bruno's is extensively disaggregated by industry, on both the supply and demand sides, and gives little attention to optimization over time. The Chenery model optimizes over a twenty-year time span but contains almost no sectoral detail. The advantages of each are obvious. Chenery and MacEwan can make many interesting statements about the time-phasing strategies of foreign aid, but their treatment of absorptive capacity and developments in "trade amelioration" lacks the conviction of a more disaggregated model. Bruno, on the other hand, can deal in depth with import-substituting and export-promoting possibilities, but his model is bothered by problems of specifying terminal conditions and lacks a sense of the best strategy for exploiting over time the various trade possibilities.

As one example, Bruno finds that increased foreign capital can increase Israel's investment and hence its growth rate. Investment increases in the model at a slower rate than does GNP, and the terminal investment ÷ GNP ratio falls as growth increases between the initial and terminal years. Lower investment ÷ GNP ratios imply lower terminal GNP growth rates, and so we have the peculiar combination of lower terminal GNP growth accompanying higher intervening GNP growth rates. This may have been intentional and in any case it is not particularly serious. But I suspect that it is unintentional and results from the usual difficulties in specifying appropriate terminal constraints for a static model of this type.

In other respects the two models are quite similar. They can both be used to describe a transformation function between net foreign capital and domestic consumption. Bruno's curve B_{70}, when plotted after expressing C in dollars (at 3£/$) has a slope of 3.4 until the "full employment" point. The slope falls off to less than two units of C for one unit of F at actual anticipated 1970 capital inflow ($500–$550 millions), and it then decreases further to a final ratio of almost 1:1. When the labor skill constraint is relaxed, a different industry mix permits greater investment, GNP growth, and hence consumption. The B_{70} curve shifts upward to A_{70} in Figure 2.

Some of the Chenery-MacEwan results may be interpreted in a similar manner. Runs 1, 4, and 7 may be regarded as variations in which cumulative discounted foreign capital is limited, respectively, to 39, 26, and 20 billion rupees. All other constraints and objective functions for these three runs are identical. Cumulative discounted consumption found for these three points turns out to be 598, 571, and 556 billion rupees, for a marginal consumption per foreign capital ratio of 2.0. Similarly, when the constraint on investment is lifted, as in Run 6, the average consumption per foreign capital ratio increases, and one suspects that alternative runs would show an upward shift of the transformation curve in a manner analogous to Bruno's shift from B_{70} to A_{70} or B_{75} to A_{75}.

The reason, of course, is the same in both models: A relaxation of absorptive capacity permits higher investment and greater growth. The difference is mostly that Bruno's skill limits offer a more convincing explanation of this absorptive capacity phenomenon than does Chenery's rather arbitrary limit on the maximum investment growth rate. It is also worth noting the interesting similarity in the slopes of the Bruno and Chenery transformation curves, particularly in the range of Bruno's "expected" 1970 and 1975 foreign capital levels (2.0 for Chenery *vs.* 1.5–1.9 for Bruno). One may suspect, however, that the slope from the Chenery-MacEwan model may be connected with their use of a 2.0 weight relating consumption to foreign capital in the objective function.

In conclusion I find that the Bruno and Chenery-MacEwan papers complement one another in a particularly satisfactory manner, and I wonder whether this does not suggest a profitable direction for further model developments. Instead of building one immensely complicated and difficult-to-comprehend model combining many sectors and many years, it may be preferable to have separate models for disaggregations over time and among industries. Terminal conditions and other time-phasing restrictions can then be determined by the time path models while realistic possibilities for implied structural change can be explored through the multisector model.[1]

---

[1] It is rather a pity that this conference has not been exposed to a modern simulation model, in which simultaneity is relaxed and time phasing and nonlinearities are introduced by sequential decision rules. This class of models may avoid some of the successive imposition of restrictions often needed before a linear programming model "behaves sensibly." Because its solution does not depend on the inversion of a large matrix it may permit a manageable combination of many sectors and many time periods. Formal optimizing is precluded in such a model, but successive runs employing variations in the structural relations, constraints, and decision rules may suggest suboptimizing possibilities of considerable practical usefulness to policymakers.

13. PROGRAMMING MODELS FOR THE PLANNING OF THE AGRICULTURAL SECTOR

E A R L O. H E A D Y , IOWA STATE UNIVERSITY (AMES)
N A R I N D A R S. R A N D H A W A , U.N. FOOD AND
AGRICULTURAL ORGANIZATION
M E L V I N D. S K O L D , KANSAS STATE UNIVERSITY

Mathematical programming models provide a promising potential for planning the economic development of agriculture. Even relatively simple linear models can help to improve planning with current data being applied in plans through other methods. Since agriculture is made up of many commodity and regional or spatial sectors, even a degree of refined planning to consider the interdependence of these many sectors is possible only through programming models. These models have great advantage over conventional input-output and time-series regression models because the planning goal ordinarily is to change greatly the mix of products produced, the regional proportions of commodities, the proportion of resources used, and other structural relationships. The basic assumptions of input-output models are inadequate for agriculture where the direct aim is to change the ratio of capital and labor to land and where productivity of capital such as fertilizer and irrigation is diminishing. Regression models, usually impossible because of inadequate time-series data, have the effect of tying the plan too much to the past.

Lack of data is also a large problem for programming models, and the demand of the analyst for data will always be nearly insatiable. In countries where formal planning is taking place and will continue, available data can be used with modifications and extensions, and development and specification models could be a great aid in organizing future data collection. We include a small model applied to India which illustrates the uses for data already being employed for planning purposes.

Varying degrees of refinement in programming models can be developed in the future, depending on the specific need. For example, to aid the planning of U.S. agricultural policy, we are now synthesizing the data and developing computer routines which incorporate demand functions and will generate, with a normative framework on the supply side, equilibrium prices and quantities for the nation and optimal production patterns by regions and farms within regions. However, this degree of refinement is scarcely needed in developing countries; an objective function with constant weights and demands represented by a "fixed bill of goods" from agriculture ordinarily will be sufficient. "Parameterization" of the restraints representing the discrete demand quantities also can be used to test different plan assumptions. Under decomposition computer routines, linear models now can incorporate several thousand equations, and the constraint in application of programming is becoming much more one of data than of computing capacity.

We illustrate the potential of programming in planning with two relatively modest models for India and the United States. Both refer only to crop production and the restraints mainly represent land and discrete demand quantities. We are completing solutions of models for the United States with livestock products and capital and labor restraints added, which extend up to 4,000 equations. However, results of these are not yet available for interpretation, and the examples presented suggest both the potentials and the limitations of programming models for agricultural policy planning. Emphasis in the two empirical models presented is on interregional production patterns and optimum land use to meet specified demand quantities for the various products.

I. INDIVIDUAL FARM MODEL

Conceptually, each farm in a nation could be incorporated into a single programming model. The model could be used to specify optimum commodity and resource mixes under different demand conditions or assumptions, or to estimate normative commodity supply and resource demand functions. Data and computational limitations prevent application of such detailed models so we have used two substitute but quite unlike approaches. One approach is based on a sample of farms for a region in which programming models can be used to estimate normative commodity supply functions or resource demand relationships for individual farms; these are then weighted into regional aggregates. At the other extreme, we have used models which initially consider the region as the producing unit or the basis of restraints, with aggregative relationships estimated directly for it.

We have used the individual farm and sample approach for three U.S. studies, which we will review briefly.[1] First, random samples of farms are

[1] While initial consideration has been given to correction terms which may be added to the estimates of supply quantities for the *average* farm, to provide more realistic esti-

drawn in arbitrarily defined producing areas or regions. Next, farms of the samples are allocated to r strata or sample domains deemed to be "homogeneous" in respect to certain production characteristics (largely resource restraints such as land and capital and type of farm or tenure). A single "representative" farm is selected for each of the r strata. Stepped supply functions, with prices varied in parametric fashion, are then estimated for these representative farms, via a firm linear programming model which considers competing products or investment alternatives and optimizes on the basis of profit maximization. Each farm used has its own restraints, usually averaging about forty. The results for the individual farms then are aggregated into area totals by means of strata weights based on the number of farms in the sample (or by means of weights based on census enumerations). Hence the regional supply function, $F(S)$ effectively is

$$(1) \qquad F(S) = \sum_{i=1}^{r} q_i f_i(s_i)$$

where q_i is the estimated number of farms in the ith strata and $f_i(s_i)$ is the supply function estimated for the representative farm of the ith strata.

Typically in the individual farm models, each producing unit will have restraints to represent land of various classes, buildings for different classes of livestock, and so forth. The farm operator starts out with a given amount of family labor and capital. He can hire or purchase additional resources, including land and labor. Capital can be borrowed, but always in some fixed ratio to the type of asset and the initial capital supply. Hence, family labor in different periods of the year, since farm production is seasonal, and capital provide several restraints for each farm. The individual farmer can hire labor, purchase capital items, and borrow funds from supplies which are apart from other farms. However, if he purchases land and increases the magnitude of this restraint, the quantity of land must be reduced on another farm in our model. In summary form, then, we have the follow-

---

mates of the average supply quantities of all farms in the domain, the method supposes parametric programming against the resource "restraints" which vary among farms but which generally do not define the *average* farm. If several such "restraints" are important, the method becomes burdensome or prohibitive in the amount of computation involved. For example, see J. C. Anderson and Earl O. Heady, *Normative Supply Functions for Milk and Agricultural Adjustment Possibilities in Northeastern Iowa* (Iowa Agricultural Experiment Station, Bulletin, forthcoming); Earl O. Heady, Ronald D. Krenz, and Ross V. Baumann, "Normative Supply Functions by Linear Programming," *Agricultural Economics Research*, XIV (1964) 13–18; Ronald D. Krenz, Earl O. Heady, and Ross V. Baumann, *Profit-Maximizing Plans and Static Supply Schedules for Fluid Milk in the Des Moines Milkshed* (Iowa Agr. Exp. Sta. Bul. No. 486); J. C. Anderson and Earl O. Heady, *Normative Supply Functions and Optimum Farm Plans for Northeastern Iowa* (Iowa Agr. Exp. Sta. Bul. No. 537).

ing structure of the model. The ith farm strata has m restraints, s_{ik}, relating to its individual limiting resources as:

(2a)
$$\sum_{j=1}^{n} a_{i1j}x_{ij} \leq s_{i1}$$

$$\vdots \qquad \vdots$$

(2b)
$$\sum_{j=1}^{n} a_{ikj}x_{ij} \leq s_{ik}$$

$$\vdots \qquad \vdots$$

(2c)
$$\sum_{j=l}^{n} a_{imj}x_{ij} \leq s_{im}$$

where a_{ikj} is the technical coefficient for the jth activity and kth restraint and x_{ij} is the level of the jth activity on the ith farm. Hence, with r strata of farms and m scarce resources, the system includes mr relations of the above type defining the production possibilities of each representative farm in the model. There are also n equations of the form

(3)
$$S_j = \sum_{i=1}^{r} q_i x_{ij} \qquad (j = 1, 2, \ldots n)$$

to allow direct summation of the aggregative output of the jth product in the r regions. With p types of land which can be exchanged among farmsl there also is an exchange equation of the following form for the gth soi> type:

(4)
$$E_k = \sum_{i=1}^{r} \sum_{j=n+1}^{n+2} a_{ijk}q_i x_{ij} \qquad (g = 1, 2, \ldots p)$$

where a_{ijk} is -1 for $j = n + 1$ to denote land purchase and is $+1$ for $j = n + 2$ to denote land sale by the ith representative farm. For the index k in (2), particular soil types are indicated since these serve as restraints on individual farms, but k does not range from 1 to n.

While various objective functions might be used, the one employed in a parametric approach to determining supply quantities for a region is

(5)
$$\text{Max} f(x) = \sum_{i=1}^{r} \sum_{j=1}^{n} c_j q_i x_{ij}$$

subject to the over-all matrix relation

(6) $$AX \leq S$$

where A is the matrix of input-output coefficients for the r farms and is of order $mr + n + p$ by $rn + 2p$, X is a vector of activity levels and S is a vector of restraints of conforming order. The variables and parameters involved are defined as follows:

c_j = net price unit of jth product.

q_i = number of farms in the ith strata.

s_{ik} = restraint for the kth resource on the ith representative farm (i.e., the "typical" farm representing the ith strata).

x_{ij} = amount of the jth product produced by the individual representative farm of the ith strata.

a_{ikj} = the amount of the kth required to produce the jth activity on the ith representative farm.

S_j = the aggregate regional output of the jth product.

E_k = the amount of the kth land type (restraint) exchanged.

This model has distinct disadvantages, but can be applied only where the regions are small (farms at great distances are not easily merged) and/or soil types are homogeneous. It can be used to program normative supply responses, factor demand, farming structure, income, and costs or other items under alternative projections of demand, technical coefficients, and others. In general, this approach to programmed estimates of normative regional relationships involves a large amount of data for generation of technical coefficients and restraints for individual farms. Hence, it is not likely to be used widely over many regions of a nation. Obvious problems in sampling and weighting also exist.

II. MODELS WITH REGIONAL PRODUCING SECTORS

An alternative approach is consideration of entire regions as the relevant producing units. Although these models only "cover up" certain of the data and empirical problems mentioned above, they are more easily manageable from the standpoint of computations and can serve effectively for certain broad policy, planning, and developmental problems of agriculture. The extent to which they are realistic and useful for particular policy purposes depends on the amount of disaggregation allowed in them. Specification of the farming regions composing the different sectors of the interregional model is, of course, simply a special problem in aggregation over inputs. A major problem here is the extent to which soils of different types and qualities, and the resources more or less attached to land, can be aggregated into particular geographic producing regions. The number of distinct soil areas specified over the nation by agronomists is far too great to be handled with existing research resources and computing facilities, should we attempt to use them to define regional boundaries. Furthermore, data are not available for separating all of these regions, or for defining relevant coefficients within them. Classification by soils criteria, while one important base, is not always sufficient as it actually combines and separates groups of soils which are similar or dissimilar in respect to (1) physical production functions, and (2) price functions for factors and commodities.

The interregional programming model uses the region as the producing unit and ordinarily optimizes the objective function at the national level. The restraining resources of individual farms are summed to regional totals under the implied possibilities of constant scale returns, as suggested later.

These models, which we are beginning to use for some large studies in the U.S., are not selected as "the optimal technique," but as one which is manageable and useful in providing greater insight into regional interdependencies and policy possibilities.

III. INTERREGIONAL MODELS FOR AGRICULTURE

As a first review of interregional programming models applied to agriculture, we will summarize a relatively simple model for India.[2] Increases of as much as 12.5 per cent in food supply are suggested simply from the application of a formal model which considers interrelationships among regions and relative production possibilities within regions. The model is restricted to the same data involved in less formal methods actually used and does not suppose a different technology or greater capital investment. In brief, we might attribute the implied potential gains in production to the greater precision of the formal model in specifying optimum regional allocations of production. Implied gains, perhaps, could be even greater than those indicated if restrictions were relaxed. Boundary conditions were incorporated into the model to (1) hold change to a pace which could be absorbed by various producing regions, and (2) provide a *welfare eco-*

[2] See M. S. Randhawa and Earl O. Heady, "Interregional Programming Models for Land Use Planning under Agricultural Development," *Journal of Farm Economics*, XLVI (1964), 137–49.

nomics or *Pareto-better condition* wherein total gain could be realized but with no individual region of cultivators sacrificing in income.

Agriculture, because it represents a large share of national income and employment, has received increasing emphasis in recent five-year plans in India, especially its regional aspects. However, the methods of analysis employed are largely informal and subjective. Our purpose in this study was testing the application of formal programming models as a means of improved regional planning in Indian agriculture. We attempted to answer the question: How much can agricultural efficiency be improved by use of more systematic planning models to consider the specific comparative advantage of particular regions? In this investigation, then, we do not imply alternative technologies and investments. We simply test whether food output might be increased from a given current collection of resources, should relatively simple formal programming methods be applied in allocating production among regions. While the data are imperfect, they are generally those used for less formal planning methods.

We do not specify an optimized solution in terms alone of maximum food output from given resources in order that the *Pareto-better conditions* might be allowed. Finally, we place upper bounds on the extent of interregional reallocations of production so as to avoid extreme adjustments.

IV. THE MODEL FOR INDIA

The model used to meet the specified conditions can be summarized as follows:

$$(7) \qquad \text{Max:} \sum_{L=1}^{U} \sum_{j=1}^{P} C_j^L X_j^L$$

where $U = 17$ regions, $P = 16$ crops, X_j^L is the level of the jth activity in Lth region (an activity unit is taken as one acre of a crop) and C_j^L is the income per acre from the jth crop in the Lth region subject to:

$$(8) \qquad X_j^L \geq A_j^L \text{ (min)}$$

$$(9) \qquad X_j^L \leq A_j^L \text{ (max)}$$

$$(10) \qquad \sum_{j=1}^{P} X_j^L = A^L$$

$$(11) \qquad \sum_{j=1}^{P} C_j^L X_j^L \geq I^L$$

$$(12) \qquad \sum_{L=1}^{U} \sum_{j=1}^{8} Y_{j_{(f)}}^{L} X_{j_{(f)}}^{L} \geq F$$

$$(13) \qquad \sum_{L=1}^{U} Y_{j_{(s)}}^{L} X_{j_{(s)}}^{L} \geq S$$

$$(14) \qquad \sum_{L=1}^{U} Y_{j_{(c)}}^{L} X_{j_{(c)}}^{L} \geq C$$

$$(15) \qquad \sum_{L=1}^{U} Y_{j_{(g)}}^{L} X_{j_{(g)}}^{L} \geq G$$

$$(16) \qquad \sum_{L=1}^{U} \sum_{j=12}^{16} Y_{j_{(o)}}^{L} X_{j_{(o)}}^{L} \geq O$$

$$(17) \qquad X_{j}^{L} \geq O$$

A^L, the cropped area for region L, is available to all crops in that region. $A_{j(\text{min})}^{L}$ and $A_{j(\text{max})}^{L}$ respectively are the minimum and maximum level of acreages for the jth crop in the Lth region. Y_{j}^{L} represents the yield per acre of the jth crop in the Lth region. F, S, C, G, and O are the minimum quantities of food grains, sugar cane, cotton, jute, and oil seeds specified at the national level. I^L indicates the minimum income level for the Lth region, below which income of that region is not allowed to decline. Manual and bullock labor, chief sources of power on farms, are not included in the system of restrictions because of their large-scale underemployment and unemployment, reported by a number of studies. The dual solution is:

$$(18) \quad \text{Min:} \sum_{L=1}^{U} V^{L} A^{L} - \sum_{L=1}^{U} \sum_{j=1}^{P} V_{j(\text{min})}^{L} A_{j(\text{min})}^{L} + \sum_{L=1}^{U} \sum_{j=1}^{U} V_{j(\text{max})}^{L} A_{j(\text{max})}^{L}$$

$$- \sum_{L=1}^{U} \delta^{L} I^{L} - P_{f}F - P_{f}S - P_{c}C - P_{g}G - P_{o}O$$

subject to

$$(19) \quad \gamma^{L} - \gamma_{j(\text{min})}^{L} + \gamma_{j(\text{max})}^{L} - \delta^{L} C_{j}^{L} - P_{f} Y_{j_{(f)}}^{L} - P_{s} Y_{j_{(s)}}^{L} - P_{c} Y_{j_{(c)}}^{L}$$
$$- P_{g} Y_{j_{(g)}}^{L} - P_{o} Y_{j_{(o)}}^{L} \geq C_{j}^{L}$$

$$(20) \qquad \gamma^{L}, \gamma_{j(\text{min})}^{L}, \gamma_{j(\text{max})}^{L}, \delta^{L}, P_{f}, P_{s}, P_{c}, P_{g} \text{ and } P_{o} \geq O \, .$$

In the dual, γ^L is the general gross rent per acre of land in the Lth region. $Y^L_{j(\min)}$ is the specific rent for the jth crop in the Lth region if the minimum acreage limit for that crop is binding. Similarly $\gamma^L_{j(\max)}$ is the specific rent for crop j if the upper acreage limit for a crop is effective. δ^L is the proportion by which income per acre for a crop in the Lth region should be raised to meet the region's minimum income requirement. This minimum income might be attained through programs of subsidies: P_f, P_s, P_c, P_g and P_o are the subsidy prices for food grains, sugar cane, cotton, jute, and oil seeds respectively, which must be added to the respective regional prices to induce regions to produce the commodities at their minimum levels. The magnitudes of P_f, P_s, P_c, P_g and P_o will be greater than zero only if constraints six, seven, eight, nine, and ten, respectively, are binding. In case these values exceed zero, existing price relations among commodities are not consistent with the composition of the agricultural production sought. These subsidy prices would provide the adjustment factors to bring the prices in line with the objectives of the policy.

C^L_j, income per acre of the jth crop in the Lth region has been estimated by multiplying the yield per acre of a crop by the corresponding regional price per unit of the main produce of a crop. Net income might have been employed for C^L_j. However, capital costs represent a minor proportion of the inputs for crops and farm production in the country. Hence, regardless of whether the C^L_j are based on either value of the main produce or on net income, the resulting programmed cropping plans will be highly similar, if not identical. This would be less true had we considered large new capital outlays for improvements in technologies. In addition the farm work force is very large, has high underemployment, and lacks alternative opportunities.

The primal solution has 214 activities and 467 restraints of types (8 to 16) above. The solutions for several levels of change allowed (e.g., ± 10 per cent, ± 20 per cent, ± 40 per cent) were obtained by parametric programming methods.

Base Period and Coverage

The base period for acreage restraints and average commodity prices for each region is 1956–57 to 1960–61, the period covered by the second five-year plan. Production coefficients Y^L_j are based on data for 1960–61. This particular year was selected to take into account technological improvements brought about during the second five-year plan. Furthermore, 1960–61 is the base year for the third five-year plan currently in operation and is considered to be, broadly, a normal year.

Programming Results

The programming solutions provide many interesting details of potential crop reallocation among and within regions. Space prevents us from presenting detailed data by regions, and we emphasize a summary of results at the national level. Tables 1 and 2 summarize, at the national level, but built up from the regional patterns, the acreage and percentage distribution of major crops (1) during the base year, and (2) under change in allocation allowed in the programming model.

Table 1. Distribution of Acreages among Different
Groups of Crops for All Regions, in Million Acres (actual and programmed)

Commodity Group	Under Original Distribution		Under Programming Solutions					
			± 10% Changes		± 20% Changes		± 40% Changes	
	Area	Dis.[a]	Area	Dis.[a]	Area	Dis.[a]	Area	Dis.[a]
Food grains	229.8	79.8	227.4	79.0	225.5	78.3	221.1	76.8
Sugar cane	5.2	1.8	5.7[b]	2.0[b]	5.7[b]	2.0[b]	6.2[c]	2.2[c]
Cotton	19.5	6.8	20.6	7.2	21.7	7.6	24.0	8.3
Jute	1.7	0.6	1.9	0.7	2.1	0.7	2.4	0.8
Oil seeds	31.7	11.0	32.3	11.2	33.0	11.5	34.2	11.9

[a] Percentage distribution.   [b] ± 10 per cent change.   [c] ± 20 per cent change.

Only food grains decrease in acreage. Jute increases to the maximum acreage allowed and sugar cane nearly does so. Cotton has moderate increases under each level of allowed change.

Increases in production and income suggested under the various solutions of the model are presented in Tables 3 and 4. These results suggest the

Table 2. Indices of Acreages for Different Commodity Groups

Commodity Group	Under Original Acreage	Under Programmed Solutions		
		± 10% Changes	± 20% Changes	± 40% Changes
Food grains	100.00	99.0	98.1	96.2
Sugar cane	100.00	110.0	110.0[a]	120.0[b]
Cotton	100.00	105.7	111.5	123.0
Jute	100.00	110.0	120.0	140.0
Oil seeds	100.00	102.0	103.9	107.9

[a] ± 10 per cent change.   [b] ± 20 per cent change.

Table 3. Production of Different Commodity Groups
for All Regions, in Million Maunds

Commodity Group	Under Original Allocation	Under Programmed Solutions					
		±10% Changes		±20% Changes		±40% Changes	
		Quantity	Inc.[a]	Quantity	Inc.[a]	Quantity	Inc.[a]
Food grains	1,876.7	1,903.5	1.4	1,934.1	3.1	1,991.4	6.1
Sugar cane	210.1	231.1	10.0	231.1[b]	10.0[b]	252.1[c]	20.0[c]
Cotton	79.2	84.1	6.2	89.1	12.5	98.9	25.0
Jute	21.9	24.1	10.0	26.3	20.0	30.6	40.0
Oil seeds	164.9	173.1	4.9	181.4	10.0	197.8	19.9

[a] Percentage increase over original production of existing pattern.
[b] ± 10 per cent change.
[c] ± 20 per cent change.

increase in value of product under planning procedures which, given the specified objective function and the boundary conditions discussed earlier, more formally recognize the comparative advantage and interdependencies among regions. Even greater potential gains in production and income might be realized if acreage changes for any one crop and region were not limited to 40 per cent. On an over-all basis, the model solutions suggest some important increases in production and income—to as much as 12 per cent without adding resources—if land were allocated by regions and crops as specified by our results.

The magnitude of improvement varies with the amount of change allowed by crop and region. When change is restricted to 10 per cent of the

Table 4. Income from Different Commodity
Groups for All Regions, in Million Rupees

Commodity Groups	Under Original Allocation	Under Programmed Solutions					
		±10% Changes		±20% Changes		±40% Changes	
		Income	Inc.[a]	Income	Inc.[a]	Income	Inc.[a]
Food grains	28,877.4	29,517.0	2.2	30,207.1	4.6	31,535.4	9.2
Sugar cane	3,402.7	3,742.9	10.0	3,742.9[b]	10.0[b]	4,083.1[c]	20.0
Cotton	2,652.6	2,821.7	6.4	2,991.7	12.8	3,330.8	25.6
Jute	531.7	584.9	10.0	638.1	20.0	744.4	40.0
Oil seeds	3,202.1	3,351.5	4.7	3,503.8	9.4	3,805.1	18.8
Total	38,666.6	40,018.0	3.5	41,083.6	6.3	43.498.8	12.5

[a] Percentage increase over original income of existing pattern.
[b] ± 10 per cent change
[c] ± 20 per cent change

original or base period acreage, the total increase in value of crop production for the nation is 3.5 per cent. However, when change of 40 per cent is allowed, the increase in value of production rises to 12.5 per cent. In general, the gain is expected to come from the collection of resources already in agriculture and does not imply large capital outlays. It results almost entirely from a reallocation of crop production to conform with regional production possibilities and comparative advantage.

The programming solutions for food grains specify a decrease in total acreage. However, because their production is allocated more efficiently, both production and income from grains rise. Substitution in value among the eight food grains more than offsets decreases in acreages, in terms of total value of output produced. The crops which gain in acreage are generally "superior" food grains (rice and wheat) and losers are mostly "inferior" ones (jowar and bajra). Hence, apart from increases in physical production the composition of the food grain mix is improved.

Regional Results

Regional production and income are given in Tables 5 and 6. Though not uniform, an increased income is specified for all regions. Food grain pro-

Table 5. Food Grain Production in Different Regions, in Million Maunds

Region	Under Original Allocation	Under Programming Solutions		
		±10% Changes	±20% Changes	±40% Changes
Andhra Pradesh	152.4	157.8	163.4	174.4
Assam	43.8	43.7	43.7	43.7
Bihar	157.8	159.0	160.5	163.2
Guzrat	43.3	42.1	40.9	38.5
Jannu and Kashmir	12.8	13.0	13.3	13.7
Kerala	28.5	28.6	28.8	29.0
Madhya Pradesh	217.7	222.6	227.6	237.6
Madras	124.8	130.8	136.8	148.7
Maharashtra	166.5	164.5	162.6	158.7
Mysore	81.3	82.8	84.2	87.2
Orissa	104.0	104.6	105.2	106.4
Punjab	158.3	160.2	162.6	166.9
Rajashtan	114.0	121.1	128.3	142.6
Uttar Pradesh	319.0	320.2	323.8	328.5
West Bengal	143.4	143.3	143.3	143.2
Delhi	1.7	1.8	1.8	1.9
Himachal Pradesh	7.3	7.3	7.2	7.1
Total	1,876.7	1,903.5	1,934.1	1,991.4

Table 6. Income in Different Regions, in Million Rupees

Region	Under Original Pattern	Under Programming Solutions		
		±10% Changes	±20% Changes	±40% Changes
Andhra Pradesh	3,335.9	3,526.8	3,693.8	4,051.4
Assam	755.9	769.8	778.6	800.9
Bihar	3,227.9	3,301.5	3,356.5	3,485.1
Guzrat	1,861.0	1,958.1	2,052.2	2,243.4
Jannu and Kashmir	195.3	200.6	205.7	216.0
Kerala	421.5	423.4	424.1	426.8
Madhya Pradesh	3,665.4	3,748.2	3,826.8	3,988.2
Madras	2,898.9	3,009.8	3,108.6	3,317.9
Maharashtra	3,740.6	3,848.8	3,923.5	4,106.4
Mysore	1,968.4	2,070.8	2,157.4	2,346.4
Orissa	2,112.1	2,126.2	2,138.3	2,164.3
Punjab	2,921.5	3,047.2	3,148.7	3,375.9
Rajasthan	1,808.7	1,924.3	2,036.9	2,265.2
Uttar Pradesh	6,417.8	6,691.1	6,830.5	7,243.2
West Bengal	3,187.8	3,221.0	3,249.1	3,310.1
Delhi	27.8	28.9	29.9	32.1
Himachal Pradesh	120.2	121.5	122.8	125.4
Total	28,666.6	40,018.0	41,083.6	43,498.8

duction is increased in all regions except Assam, Guzrat, Maharashtra, and West Bengal, but their decline in food grain production is not large relative to increases in other regions and would create no substantial transport problems. Food grains still are grown on 77 to 88 per cent of the total cropped area.

Regional income restrictions and national availability constraints were not binding in the solutions. Thus δ^L, P_f, P_s, P_c, P_g, and P_o are all zero and indicate that the programming results would improve each region's income.

Planning Application

The availability of the data allowed consideration of only current techniques and of some fairly aggregative producing regions. Nevertheless, planning models which consider interrelationships among regions and among crops within regions promise a greater product from given resources without additional large capital investments. Even then, the gain indicated underestimates the full potential from application of models such as the one illustrated. Further gain would result if the 17 regions were further subdivided in terms of climate, location, soil productivity, and other variables which relate to relative production possibilities. The regional groupings were simply those used previously in India for construct-ing five-year plans and for which data were currently or readily available. Since interrelationships among the same regions have not been formally considered in the planning procedures actually used, the results from our model suggest the high payoff possible from formal programming models for this purpose.

Informally and somewhat subjectively, plans of the conventional type are based on data of the kind needed for linear programming models. They could be more systematically organized to conform with modern computa-tional capabilities and mathematical models and could then give sufficient attention to differentials in regional resource productivities and investment alternatives. But even without this degree of detail, the data used in con-ventional or less formal approaches in agricultural planning can serve equally well for programming models. Or, stated conversely, the results could not be worsened, and would certainly be improved, if data now being used for informal planning methods were incorporated into formal models allowing more systematic analyses.

V. MODELS FOR THE UNITED STATES

We have completed some large-scale interregional programming models for the United States and have numerous others under way. Models initiated recently (including demand functions and nonlinear production functions) are perhaps of most interest, but since solutions for them are not yet complete, the following pages are restricted to a few for which computa-tions are finished. To date, we have completed solutions for over two dozen interregional models for U.S. agriculture represented by major field crops. The new models include livestock as well as field crops for 157 regions. While several years are required to build up the basic data required, we believe that the data and models now being used have promise of con-siderable power and usefulness in interregional analysis of American agri-culture and in designing policies for it. The data are greatly more ex-tensive and detailed than those for the Indian model and provide more precise indications of prospective interregional shifts in production and land use.

A basic purpose of the studies is to provide an empirical base for ana-lyzing and devising agricultural policies and for estimating the extent of adjustment needed in the U.S. farming industry. The findings reported here represent only one phase in the broader study. While programming models and large-capacity computers simplify the task, a major require-ment is that of assembling data and defining coefficients for the different regions and commodities. Even with the coefficient matrix used for this study, the task of assembling data was very large and required several man-years of time. The process of assembling and refining data will continue, and models and results will be extended and improved.

The Nature of the Study

The following pages summarize results from an interregional linear programming model where the specific purposes are to determine (1) which field crops should be produced in the 144 agricultural regions; (2) the total acreage required to produce the nation's food and fiber requirements; (3) the amount of land which should be shifted from crop production if the nation were to cease accumulation of surplus stocks; and (4) the location of this land. Production of major field crops (corn, wheat, oats, barley, grain sorghum, tobacco, and cotton) has been under acreage or output control most of the time for thirty years. The resulting pattern of production is not consistent with current technical and economic development in agriculture since production quotas tend to remain in a historic mold.

The empirical models have the common objective of determining the optimal pattern of agricultural production and product shipments that satisfies all of the regional demands at the least possible cost.[3] For each model the production and shipment patterns differ, depending on demand and other assumptions. We have computed models for numerous points in time, including 1955, 1965, and 1975. Our projections to 1975 indicate land areas and production patterns needed at that time, in order that current agricultural policies may properly direct adjustment of resources. We review the model and empirical results for one set of 1975 projections in this report. Results among regions are highly similar to those for models referring to 1955 and 1965. Crops included in the analysis are wheat, cotton, soybeans, and feed grains (corn, oats, sorghum, and barley). How-

[3] For details on other models, see: Alvin C. Egbert and Earl O. Heady, *Regional Adjustments in Grain Production, A Linear Programming Analysis* (USDA Tech. Bul. No. 1241); Earl O. Heady and Alvin C. Egbert, "Activity Analysis in Allocation of Crops in Agriculture," in A. S. Manne and H. M. Markowitz, eds., *Studies in Process Analysis* (Cowles Foundation Monograph 18) (New York: Wiley, 1963), pp. 161–214, Alvin C. Egbert, Earl O. Heady, and Ray F. Brokken, *Regional Changes in Grain Production, An Application of Spatial Programming* (Center for Agricultural and Economic Adjustment, Report 14T); Alvin C. Egbert and Earl O. Heady, *Regional Analysis of Production Adjustments in Major Field Crops, Historical and Prospective* (bulletin, forthcoming); Earl O. Heady and Alvin C. Egbert, "Programming Regional Adjustments in Grain Production to Eliminate Surpluses," *Journal of Farm Economics*, XLI (1959), pp. 718–33. No. 4; Earl O. Heady and Alvin C. Egbert, "Mathematical Programming of Regional Production Patterns," (forthcoming) (Mimeo, 1962).

ever, for one model not presented here, we allowed all regions to attain the same level of technology. The Southeast then increases production greatly at the expense of the Great Plains and West.

Regions. Producing and Transfer Activities

Historically, the 144 production or programming regions used in this study (Figure 1) account for about 95, 97, 93, 84, 99, 99, and 99 per cent of

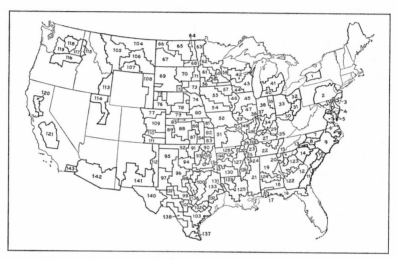

Figure 1. Location and Boundaries of the 144 Programming Regions

the United States production of wheat, corn, oats, barley, grain sorghum, soybeans, and cotton, respectively. The model also includes 31 spatially separated consuming or demand regions (Figure 2) for the three final demand categories: wheat, feed grains, and oil meals. Consuming regions follow state boundaries and are either comprised of one state or of several states within the same geographic proximity. It was necessary to choose a sufficient number of demand regions to accurately reflect the interregional flows of these products, but to choose few enough that the computational burden was not too great. In most cases, demand regions are unique to an individual state. In cases where they are not, the states are adjoining and are closely related economically.

Production homogeneity within regions originally was approximated by grouping state economic areas and individual counties, in some cases, in terms of: (1) those having relatively the same number of tractors, combines, and corn pickers per thousand acres; (2) those with similar proportions of

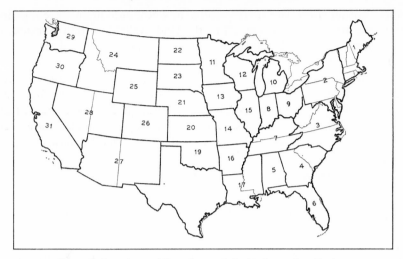

Figure 2. Location and Boundaries of the 31 Consuming Regions

total cropland planted to particular field crops; (3) those with similar yields of the seven field crops considered; and (4) to an extent, regions with similar soils. In the production regions in Figure 1, the large areas without numbers were excluded from the programming model because either they are mountains or arid grazing lands, they do not produce a significant quantity of the products studied, or they produce these commodities in "limitational" quantities tied to particular conditions. (These areas have been included in the models which incorporate livestock activities.)

Five possible production activities exist for each producing region: wheat, feed grain rotation, feed grain-soybean rotation, soybeans, and cotton. The existence of a certain activity within a region is dependent upon the region's historical record in the production of that particular crop. The models contain 31 wheat-to-feed-grain transfer activities, one for each consuming region. Wheat may be used as livestock feed if it is the cheapest source of livestock nutrients. Transportation activities for each of the three demand categories allow for the movement of grains between consuming regions. Theoretically there exist 930 transportation activities for each commodity, for a potential total of 2,790 transportation activities. Some of these activities are eliminated, however, by the physical potentials of the regions concerned. A demand restraint is specified in all 31 consuming regions for each of the demand entities, wheat, feed grains, and oil meals. In addition, a United States demand requirement for cotton lint is specified. A land restraint is defined for each of the 144 programming or producing regions to reflect the total amount of land available for use of these five activities. The model permits the wheat, feed grain, or feed grain-soybean activities to occupy all of the land available within a region, if necessary for the optimum solution. The soybean activity is limited to 50 per cent of the total land available in any region.

A very large amount of detail went into building up the technical co-efficients for the crop activities of the various regions. These were based on yields and inputs such as labor, fertilizer, seeds, machinery, tractors, fuel, and all other operating costs. About five man-years of time have been required to build up the coefficients for the several models now in use.

Summary of the Model

The objective function of the interregional model can be stated as:

$$(21) \quad \text{Min } f(c) = \sum_{i=1}^{144} \sum_{k=1}^{5} c_{ki}x'_{ki} + \sum_{m=1}^{31} d_m y_m + \sum_{l=1}^{3} \sum_{\substack{m'=1 \\ m' \neq m}}^{31} \sum_{m=1}^{31} b_{lmm'} z_{lmm'}$$

where,

c_{ki} = cost per acre of producing the kth activity in the ith programming region,

x'_{ki} = level of production of the kth activity in the ith programming
region,

d_m = cost per unit of transferring wheat into feed grains in the mth
consuming region,

y_m = quantity of wheat transferred into feed grains in the mth consuming region,

$b_{lmm'}$ = cost of transporting a unit of the lth product from (to) the
mth consuming to (from) the m'th consuming region,

$z_{lmm'}$ = quantity of the lth product transported from (to) the mth
consuming region to (from) the m'th consuming region.

Equation (21) is minimized subject to the linear restraints:

$$(22) \quad D_{1m} = \sum_{i=1}^{r} a_{1i}x'_{1i} - h_m y_m \pm \sum_{m'=1}^{s} t_{1mm'} z_{1mm'} ;$$

$$(23) \quad D_{2m} \leq \sum_{i=1}^{r} a_{2i}x'_{2i} + \sum_{i=1}^{r} a_{3i}x'_{3i} + h_m y_m \pm \sum_{m'=1}^{s} t_{2mm'} z_{2mm'} ;$$

$$(24) \quad D_{3m} \leq \sum_{i=1}^{r} a_{2i}x'_{3i} + \sum_{i=1}^{r} a_{4i}x'_{4i} + \sum_{i=1}^{r} a_{5i}x'_{5i} \pm \sum_{m'=1}^{s} t_{3mm'}z_{3mm'} \; ;$$

and

$$(25) \quad D_c \leq \sum_{i=1}^{144} a_{5i}x'_{5i} \; .$$

D_{lm} = demand for the lth product in the mth consuming region in which: $l = 1$ refers to wheat demand; $l = 2$ refers to feed grain demand; and $l = 3$ refers to oil meal demand.

a_{ki} = yield per acre of the kth producing activity in the ith programming region for which:

$\quad\quad k = 1$, wheat,
$\quad\quad k = 2$, feed grains,
$\quad\quad k = 3$, feed grain-soybeans,
$\quad\quad k = 4$, soybeans, and
$\quad\quad k = 5$, cotton.

x'_{ki} = level of production acres of the kth activity in the ith programming region,

r = number of programming regions in the mth consuming region,

h_m = amount of wheat transferred into feed grains per unit of the wheat to feed grain transfer activity in the mth consuming region,

y_m = level of the wheat to feed grain transfer activity in the mth consuming region,

$t_{lmm'}$ = amount of the lth product transported from (to) the mth consuming region to (from) the m'th consuming region per unit of the lmm'th transportation activity,

$z_{lmm'}$ = level of the lmm'th transportation activity, i.e., the activity which transports the lth product from (to) the mth consuming region to (from) the m'th consuming region, and

D_c = national demand for cotton lint.

In addition, equation (21) must be minimized given the land restraints:

$$(26) \quad L_{Ti} \geq \sum_{k=1}^{5} x^t_{ki} \; ,$$

$$(27) \quad L_{Ci} \geq x'_{5i} \; ,$$

(28) $L_{Si} \geq x'_{4i}$,

where

> L_{Ti} = total amount of land available for the $k = 5$ producing activi-
> ties in the ith programming region,
> L_{Ci} = amount of land available for cotton production in the ith pro-
> gramming region,
> L_{Si} = amount of land available for the soybean activity in the ith
> programming region, and

all other symbols are as defined above. Finally, we have the conditions that:

(29) $x'_{ki} \geq 0; y_m \geq 0; z_{lmm'} \geq 0.$

The model as outlined has a coefficient matrix of $402 \times 1,923$ order with-out slack vectors. To assure against an infeasible solution in some of the high-demand empirical models, 93 artificial activities were introduced (one for each of the three final demand categories in the 31 consuming regions) which enabled the demand in any consuming region to be met at a very high cost artificially, if the producing regions were not able to satisfy the demand. It was necessary to set the cost on these artificial activities at a level considerably higher than the highest producing activity plus trans-portation cost that may be a potential supplier to that particular consum-ing region. Although these artificial activities were not utilized in the solu-tions to any of the empirical models, they are potentially very valuable in problems of this size.

In establishing the demand requirements at the national level for the model it was assumed that the United States population in 1975 would be 221,968,000. Real per capita income is assumed to be 150 per cent of 1955. Per capita consumption of farm products is projected to increase in accord-ance with this change in per capita income. Trends in converting feed into livestock products are expected to follow the pattern set in the 1940–60 period. Exports of wheat, feed grains, and oil meals are expected to be the same as the 1956–61 average export levels (other models have been applied which allow various assumptions on exports). On the cost and output side, per acre yields are assumed to follow the 1940–62 per acre yield trends. The trend in real cost per unit of output is expected to follow the 1949–61 trend.

Results of the Model

Solutions for the programming model provide a vast array of regional and national data, which, including the shadow prices from the dual, have important implications for education and policy. However, because of limited space we will not include numerical results and will provide only a few graphic summaries of results.

Table 7 indicates the amount of land (in thousands of acres) which can be shifted from cotton, soybeans, wheat, and feed grains to grazing, forestry, or recreation under the projections and assumptions of the model. Most of the South Atlantic states, the Delta states, and parts of Kentucky, Tennessee, southern Indiana and Illinois, eastern Ohio, eastern Kansas and Oklahoma, southeastern Missouri, South Dakota, and southeastern Montana can shift large regions from the crops specified to grass, trees, or recreation.

The projections for 1975 indicate that the nation may have as many as

Table 7. Thousands of Acres of Land Available to Shift from Crops to
Grazing, Forestry, or Recreation by Regions

Region	Land	Region	Land	Region	Land
7	335	51	1,803	108	509
10	471	54	2,226	110	408
11	337	56	1,229	113	1,730
12	4,673	62	1,308	115	447
14	289	64	2,012	122	209
15	141	65	5,846	123	1,041
16	448	66	120	124	403
17	190	67	4,021	125	1,366
18	544	68	100	126	1,521
19	1,746	69	1,751	127	1,274
20	141	70	3,918	128	16
21	2,381	71	1,382	130	149
22	1,223	72	918	131	28
23	193	73	465	133	496
24	312	78	914	134	87
26	213	81	1,232	135	115
27	1,069	82	1,006	136	177
28	281	83	883	141	223
30	593	84	1,095	144	49
31	415	86	746	—	—
32	1,162	87	34	—	—
34	830	90	448	—	—
40	333	91	2,618	—	—
41	2,057	93	497	—	—
42	994	105	1,777	—	—
48	1,718	106	419	—	—
49	1,471	107	415	—	—

74 million acres now in the crops analyzed (or in governmental control programs) which are surplus for these purposes by then. The acreage would be distributed among regions in the manner indicated in Table 7. (Absence of a region in Table 7 indicates that surplus acreage does not exist within it.) Models computed for the present time show about 50 million acres surplus for the field crops under analysis. The two sets of figures can be used in national policy; for example, in using present large subsidies for agriculture to help finance the mammoth land use adjustments implied. To make large shifts to less intensive crops over broad areas requires financial aid in helping farmers to invest in grazing herds, forestry, and other investments. It also requires aid in mobility, since the latter crops require a much smaller labor force and population in the numerous regions.

Areas normally in feed grains and indicated to be withdrawn from these crops include the specified areas of eastern Ohio, Kansas, Oklahoma, and southwestern Missouri. They often are considered to be marginal areas with respect to feed grain production. The physical limitations of the land in these regions, rolling hills and rough topography, make farming costly relative to other land and regions.

Land typically in wheat but specified to be retired from this crop is in the Dakotas and Montana. Yield variability due to weather extremes, which leads to lower average yields, is projected to cause these Northern Plains states to lose out in competition with the Southern Plains states in supplying the nation's wheat.

In general, the projected crop production pattern follows an expected pattern. Feed grain production is concentrated in the Corn Belt, soybean production is found in the South and in the fringes of the Corn Belt, and cotton production is allocated to the Delta states, Texas, Arizona, and California. Wheat is produced in the Southern and Central Plains, northern Montana, the Pacific Northwest, and in California and Arizona. On the other hand, the model departs from tradition in the sense that wheat is specified in California and Arizona and not in the North Plains; feed grain is specified in southern Texas, and not in southern Illinois, Indiana, and eastern Ohio. These changes in production patterns are undoubtedly due to the spatial aspect of the study. When transportation costs and population growth are considered, more of the products are projected to be raised nearer their point of consumption, if suitable land is available.

In general, some large-scale adjustments in interregional production patterns and land use are specified. Cotton production would be shifted importantly from the Southeast to the West. Field crops would be contracted generally in the Appalachian region and the Delta states. The central Corn Belt area would become relatively more important in the nation's agriculture than at the present when production is dispersed over the country through the existing policy structure. The large acreage which could be shifted from cotton, feed grains, and wheat would allow more grazing and beef production, to mesh with changes in demand under growth in per capita incomes.

Interregional flows can be specified for each commodity. Maps showing flows for feed grains and oil meals (from cotton and soybeans) are shown in Figures 3 and 4. (Figures on the flow lines indicate quantities in thousands of tons.) In computing interregional flows, producing regions have been aggregated into consuming regions, with the flows indicated only

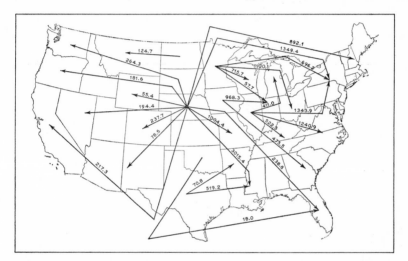

Figure 3. Interregional Flows of Feed Grains (Thousands of Tons of Feed Units)

between consuming regions. Because the number of regions adapted to soybeans is much more restrained than for feed grains, the pattern of interregional movements specified for the former is much more complex than for the latter.

While the step is not taken here, data of the type generated in the study can be used to indicate the optimum location of storage and processing facilities for the various commodities. These specifications can be made as an interdependent part of a model such as that used here, or they can be made after forthcoming solutions from the current model are known. Many other data were derived from the model but are not presented here because of space limitations. One set of useful data are the shadow prices

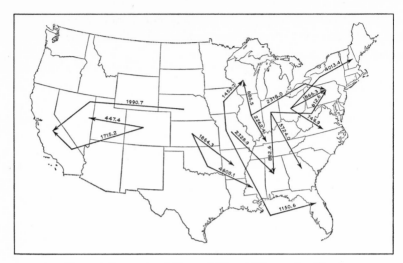

Figure 4. Interregional Flows of Oilmeal (Thousands of Tons)

from the dual, indicating the subsidies which might be required to compensate farmers for shifting land among various uses. Models computed for a 1965 date are being used especially for these purposes.

Limitations and Other Models

Our aggregation of producing and consuming regions is "uneven." Use of only 31 consuming regions offset some of the detail obtained by use of more regional producing sectors. The interregional production pattern specified by greater detail in consuming regions would not have differed greatly from that specified. However, in more recent models we are using more consuming regions. Our interest was especially in detail for producing regions, in order that we might specify the locations and amounts of surplus land acreage. These quantities can be useful both in the formulation of policies to encourage the long-run adaptation of crop patterns to prospective needs and to eliminate government surpluses. They also can be used in educational programs designed for local areas to foster structural adjustments of agriculture.

We believe that our results are generally useful in these directions. However, the studies reviewed above, designed especially for comparison of outcomes under different models and assumptions, have other limitations of which we are aware. These include problems in regional and crop aggregation, acreage restraint specifications, exclusion of certain competitive crops and livestock, and others. The work we have initiated on other models, however, helps overcome numerous of these difficulties. These models include several thousand of both equations and real variables. They involve livestock activities, differential soil types within producing region, individual farms, and larger transportation matrices. Also, as mentioned earlier, some new models include demand functions rather than discrete requirements for each region. While the data required are great, we believe the solutions which can be forthcoming shortly will pave the way for a steady stream of improved and useful results.

COMMENT

WALTER P. FALCON, HARVARD UNIVERSITY

There is nothing like the array of formal planning models presented at this conference to give one particularly interested in the agricultural sector even more neuroses than he might already have. These anxieties are of a diverse nature, but they center on two main issues: (1) within an aggregate model, what specification of the agricultural sector is required to assure correct conclusions? (2) How much sophistication is required in a sectoral model of agriculture to insure that its results provide appropriate policy guidelines to planners of rural development?

Although Professor Heady's paper is more concerned with the second of these dilemmas, the first question seems of sufficient importance to be raised, if not completely answered, at this conference.

The sheer size of the agricultural sector—30 to 50 per cent of GNP in most underdeveloped countries—means that the problem cannot be passed off lightly. Furthermore, several structural characteristics of agriculture make it rather special and should cause immediate concern to builders of either consistency or optimizing models. First, agricultural production is typified by the wide range of input substitutions which are technically possible—*not* by fixed coefficients. Secondly, one of the primary objectives of an agricultural development program is to change the input-output coefficients (a_{ij}'s) associated with agricultural production; therefore, to extrapolate inputs or outputs on the basis of historically derived average coefficients for agriculture, as has several times been done, is to violate the basic premise of the entire rural-development program. Couple these two factors with the innovational difficulties involved in getting millions of peasant cultivators to adopt technically known production processes and there is still further reason to worry about the handling of the agricultural sector in aggregate models. All of these factors are particularly bothersome when the projected growth rates are large and cover long periods of time.

My point is not to argue that economy-wide models cannot, or should not, be built. Rather my plea is for additional sensitivity work on all parts of the tableau to test how the assumptions made about the agricultural sector affect the major conclusions of these models—conclusions on import substitution, on the shadow price of foreign exchange, on saving rates, and others.

Since several other conference papers deal more directly with aggregate models, it is perhaps appropriate if the remainder of this comment focuses on programming models for the agricultural sector. In this regard, Professor Heady's regional model of Indian agriculture is an excellent example with which to illustrate some of the facets of the second question raised.

The Indian model in its present unqualified form, if not wrong, is at least terribly misleading to planners. (I should add that my comments, though critical, are very sympathetic. I helped produce a similar agricultural model for the Khaipur region of West Pakistan which is subject to many of the same limitations; moreover, I have had to live with that unsatisfactory model at the Pakistan Planning Commission for the last sixteen months!) The major methodological point at issue is Professor Heady's contention that "even in simple linear form, these models can allow great improvement of planning activities with current data." The most important conclusion which emerges, however, is that programming models, *unless adequately founded on specific micro studies of particular agricultural regions*, are more likely to lead planners away from truth than toward it.

Consider, for example, the Indian model which gives the outward appearance of being a very detailed formulation. It deals with seventeen separate regions involving data on the yields, acreages, and prices of sixteen different commodities. Varying constraints are placed on cropping pattern changes in each region, aggregate planning targets are imposed for five key commodity groups, and in addition, regional income constraints are applied. Professor Heady concludes that if individual crops within regional cropping patterns can change by as much as 40 per cent, national agricultural income could be increased by over 12 per cent.

In considering this model in anything but a demonstration context, there are two points which should be raised: (1) whether the regional changes which the model postulates are technically feasible and (2) whether this formulation provides agricultural planners in India with a useful course of policy action.

With regard to technical feasibility, it is quite clear that the model is sufficiently misspecified to cast very serious doubts upon the results it generates. In the model, land is the only physical limitation within each region. Even disregarding the problem of great intraregional variations of soils and climates, land is not even the major constraint in vast areas of the Indian subcontinent. In many of the more productive regions, there are large amounts of fallow land in all of the crop seasons (which are not distinguished in the model), and irrigation water is the binding resource. This single fact explains both the direction and magnitude of Professor Heady's conclusions. For example, the model indicates that within the food crop category, the "inferior" commodities (bajra, jowar, gram) are reduced to the minimum levels in most regions. One need not be perfectly Schultz-ian[1] to be surprised at the present misallocation of resources implied by such a statement or to question this result. Even neglecting the important practical question of how these crops fit into the livestock economy, a more adequate account must be taken of the differential water requirements. Bajra, for example, can grow in the *kharif* (spring-planted) season in many areas with fourteen acre-inches of water, whereas rice in the same season and region may need forty acre-inches or more. Not surprisingly, rice produces a higher value *per acre*, and, since only land is considered in the program, one acre of rice replaces one acre of bajra in meeting the model's aggregate food target. However, the relevant comparison is between one acre of rice and about three acres of bajra. If each crop in the model had appropriate water coefficients and if each region had seasonal water constraints, it is quite clear that the optimal solution would be very different from the one given by the present version of the model. While it would be foolish to argue that no gains are possible from regional shifts in cropping patterns, a properly specified model would probably show much less than the 12 per cent gain in aggregate income.

Additionally, the regional formulation for India does not contain any transportation costs. This omission, which is recognized, is another reason why the model overstates the net income gains. Moreover, in the foreseeable future there are likely to be important physical limitations on transportation in India. Although virtually nothing complimentary has ever been written about subsistence agriculture, it does have one redeeming feature: it helps to minimize transport needs. The large changes contemplated in one version of the model (and 40 per cent variations in cropping patterns are *very* large) would put a terrific strain on the Indian transportation network. The importance of this point can be found in recent discussions of famine and in the conclusion that internal transportation difficulties are a primary factor limiting India's ability to absorb Public Law 480 commodities.

Finally, there are questions to be raised about the policy implications of the model. This concern stems from a personal conviction that a "good" planning model is by definition one that provides a useful course of action to planners and policymakers. In this regard, three features of the Indian conclusions appear worrisome. First, it seems very dangerous to tell policymakers in South Asia that it is somehow possible to increase agricultural output significantly *without any additional inputs or investments*. To reinforce the agriculture-doesn't-need-investment-funds argument, already prevalent in many circles, is to ask for additional agricultural troubles for the future. This, of course, is a personal judgment, but perhaps a sound one given the relative neglect of Indian agriculture during the Third Plan period. Secondly, the discussion hints that Indian agricultural planners should be especially concerned with the gains from regional specialization. Although they cannot disregard such an issue, it does seem of minor importance relative to other aspects of agricultural development. The gain from re-

---

[1] See Theodore Schultz, *Transforming Traditional Agriculture* (New Haven, 1964).

gional shift is of the once-and-for-all variety. The increase—perhaps on the order of 5 per cent when transportation costs and water requirements are taken into account—is really quite small when compared to the agricultural growth target for even one five-year plan. Lastly, there is some suggestion in the paper that a system of taxes and subsidies should be used as the policy instrument for achieving this regional orientation. Given the difficulties with the existing system of agricultural controls in India and the other limitations of the bureaucracy, the thought of further government involvement in agricultural production is frightening. Thus, even if one believed the results of the model, they provide only the most questionable lines of policy action for Indian planners.

With the immense and excellent model for United States agriculture described in the last portion of Professor Heady's paper, it is perhaps unwarranted to have labored over the Indian model so long. It might have been better, for example, to have considered the latter a demonstration model, even though it was not really presented in that form, and to have concentrated instead on the U.S. model which meets many of the previous objections. Nevertheless, the contrast with the U.S. model perhaps illustrates the most important point of this discussion. Unless there is an adequate base of micro studies which specify the real constraints on production and which indicate how peasant farmers will react when the constraints are lifted, programming models for the agricultural sectors of backward countries should be constructed and used only with extreme caution.

14. A LINEAR PROGRAMMING MODEL OF EDUCATIONAL PLANNING: A CASE STUDY OF ARGENTINA

I R M A A D E L M A N , NORTHWESTERN UNIVERSITY*

I. INTRODUCTION

The importance of the human element in economic development has been stressed by many scholars. It was brought home forcefully to this author in an earlier programming study of the Argentine economy,[1] in which a sensitivity analysis of the impact of high-level manpower endowments revealed a dramatic *qualitative* change in the optimal pattern of production as the supply of high-level manpower was altered. In that study a 20 per cent increase in the availability of technical and managerial manpower transformed the optimal production structure from one rather less industrialized and with less emphasis upon basic industry than the pattern of the actual base period to one much more industrialized and with a larger proportion of manufacturing production concentrated in heavy industry.

In the present work a dynamic linear programming model is developed for educational planning and applied to Argentine data to explore, with the aid of a realistic pilot study, the potential usefulness of this approach in determining the optimal extent and composition of resource allocation to education. This is a four-period, twenty-year dynamic programming model, with investment in education optimized simultaneously with investment in real capital. The optimal time patterns of production, imports, and exports for each of the several sectors of the economy are also determined concurrently. Thus, by contrast with the real world, the model not only gener-

* The author is indebted to the Ford Foundation and to the Agency for International Development for financial support. She is also grateful to her husband, Frank L. Adelman, for his comments and to Dwight Wolkow for computational assistance. The paper also benefited from comments made on an earlier version by Samuel S. Bowles.

[1] I. Adelman and Frederick T. Sparrow, "Dynamic Linear Development Planning: Two Case Studies" (mimeographed, 1965). This study was sponsored by the Agency for International Development.

ates optimal numbers of graduates of each type, but also allocates them most efficiently throughout the entire economy. To that extent, it tends to overstate the benefits from education.

Philosophically, the model formulated is a cross between the "manpower-requirements" approach[2] to educational planning and the "benefit-cost" approach.[3] As in the manpower-requirements approach, the model described generates its demands upon the educational system from the production side of the economy and uses fixed labor-output coefficients for each class of manpower and for each sector of the economy. In the manpower-requirements approach, however, the pattern of causality runs unilaterally from a projection of the productive profile of the economy to a manpower-training strategy; the present model more realistically provides for an interaction between the two in which both are optimized at the same time.

There are also some similarities with the benefit-cost approach. Just as in that approach, the extent of resources to be devoted to education is determined in the present model by comparing the marginal social benefit of each type of education with its marginal social cost. However, while most other benefit-cost analyses rely, of necessity, upon historical benefit-cost data, the current approach allows both the marginal social benefit and the marginal social cost to vary dynamically with the structure of production and with the extent of resource allocation to education. This advantage is of special importance in the planning of education in a developing economy, where the structure of production may undergo rapid change. It should be noted, however, that only the strictly economic contribution of education—its effect upon future output—is included in the model, and that only formal educational programs are treated. The effects of on-the-job training, in-service educational programs, and extension schools, which increase the over-all stock of skills, are not considered. Also, it is assumed that all manpower formation is domestic;[4] there exists no explicit mechanism for importing higher level manpower through such measures as technical assistance and immigration, although the model could easily be extended to include these possibilities. The net effect of the first limitation

---

[2] A good description of this technique is given in William G. Bowen, "Assessing the Economic Contribution of Education: An Appraisal of Alternative Approaches," *Economic Aspects of Education* (Princeton, 1964).

[3] Carl S. Shoup, *et al.*, *The Fiscal System of Venezuela* (Baltimore, 1959). For a general discussion of the benefit-cost approach see Theodore Schultz, *The Economic Value of Education* (New York, 1963), and references cited therein.

[4] This is not a serious deficiency for a country at Argentina's level of human resource development.

is that the model tends to understate the social value of investment in education as compared with the real world. The cumulative effect of the last two deficiencies leads the model to overstate, to some extent, the optimal level of educational investment.

II. The Model

General

The present model treats investment in education in a manner entirely analogous to investment in real capital. The pattern through time of resource use in education is optimized simultaneously with the structure of production, investment, imports, and exports for the entire economy. The optimization is carried out under a set of linear constraints which represent the economic, technological, and socio-cultural limitations upon policy. The end result of the computations is a description of the dynamic pattern of investment in human resources which best meets the over-all planning objectives, given the constraints under which the economy must operate.

The general structure of the model is as follows. An objective, such as the maximization of the economy's rate of growth, the maximization of GNP, or the minimization of unemployment, is specified. The appropriate objective function is optimized subject to a set of linear constraints of several types. For the educational system, the major exogenous constraints are the initial supply of teachers for each type of school, the supply of school buildings, and the school-age population. Production functions for the educational system, which specify the "technological" conditions for the transformation of matriculants of a given school level into graduates, must also be satisfied. In addition, because the initial experiments were characterized by radical shifts in the utilization of the several types of secondary schools between periods, it was necessary to subject the optimization to a set of socio-economic constraints which stipulate that enrollments in each type of school be nondecreasing through time. These latter constraints serve also to provide an appropriate set of terminal conditions for the calculations.

For the productive sectors of the economy, the constraints specify the technological conditions of production and investment. They also limit the economy's use of primary resources to available stocks for productive capacity (by sector), manpower (by skill), and foreign exchange and savings. The optimal program is required to obey certain behavioral constraints: it must provide certain minimal amounts of each industry's product for domestic consumption; it must not exceed specified absorptive capacity constraints upon investment in each sector; and it cannot export more than a certain amount of each industry's output. Finally, certain (modest) terminal conditions must be met by the optimal program: sectoral investment in the last period of the program must cover at least that period's depreciation.

The maximization process results in a specification of the optimal levels at which all the endogenous variables in the system must be operated in each period of the program. The decision variables for the educational system allocate graduates and dropouts[5] in each time period to a particular type of employment: labor of a given skill or retention within the school system (either as a student or as a teacher). In setting the levels of these decision variables, the driving force for the educational part of the model is basically the over-all labor scarcities by skill generated in the rest of the model. The demand for labor of each class is translated into educational requirements through the assignment of different productivities to different levels of schooling within labor of a given skill. Not surprisingly, anticipated student, teacher, and school-building requirements and availabilities also have a strong impact upon the optimal levels of production and the use of graduates and dropouts.

As is usual in a model of this type, the decision variables relating to the noneducational portion specify the optimal sectoral levels of domestic production, imports, fixed capital formation, inventory accumulation, labor use, and over-all foreign capital inflow as a function of time.

The labor-availability-labor-use constraints provide the major link between the educational and the noneducational portions of the model. Some feedback is also provided through the demands upon construction and savings which arise in the educational sector.

Even though only six educational processes are considered in an economy disaggregated into a mere nine productive sectors, the resultant model specification still involves about 70 equations per period. The complete four-period, twenty-year model contains 284 equations and requires approximately forty minutes of 7094 time to generate an optimal solution. The machine-time cost therefore imposed a severe limitation upon the number of parametric studies which could be carried out with the present model.

---

[5] This decision is subject to a socio-cultural constraint which specifies a rate of leakage of educated and semieducated into activities not normally considered economically productive, such as housewifery.

Description of the Argentine School System

The Actual System. The primary education course in Argentina is seven years in length, free, and compulsory for children between the ages of seven and fourteen.

The general secondary schools are academic in orientation. They are free, except for fees for registration, supplies, and equipment, and they can be entered only by primary school graduates. The secondary program is generally five years in length.

Commercial schools prepare students for clerical jobs (commercial secretary, bookkeeper, and white collar jobs) and for entrance into the University Faculty of Economic Sciences. Courses can be three, four, five, or six years in length. The industrial schools prepare students for technical supervisory positions in industry, as well as for entry into the engineering and scientific faculties of the university. These courses are five years in length.

Teachers for elementary schools receive their training in normal schools, also in a five-year program; graduates are eligible to enter a university.

Vocational and trade schools may be entered after completion of primary school. These schools train men for jobs as skilled workmen, technicians, and foremen and women for domestic service. There is a three-year and a six-year course for men and a five-year course for women. Students in these schools generally work part-time.

To qualify for a university or for the superior[6] schools, students must complete a five-year secondary course and must pass an entrance examination. The duration of university courses varies with the specialty chosen and ranges from two years for actuaries and social workers to six years for engineering, architecture, and medicine. University and superior schools train secondary teachers and professionals; only the universities can supply university teachers.

The Stylization. Since all decision periods in the program must be of the same length, and since the average school course is five years, a five-year period has been chosen for the calculations.

In the model, the Argentine educational system is disaggregated into the following types of schools: (1) primary; (2) general secondary; (3) commercial and industrial (technical); (4) normal (primary teacher training); (5) vocational and trade; (6) university and superior.

A flow-diagram of the Argentine educational system, as portrayed in our calculations, is displayed in Figure 1.

---

[6] These schools train secondary school teachers.

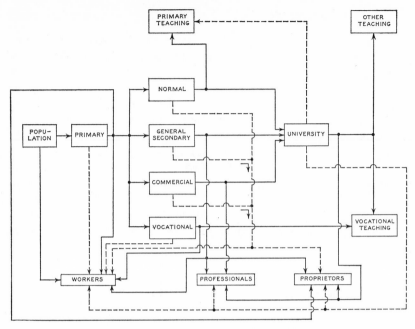

*Figure 1. Education Flow Diagram (Solid Lines Are for
Graduates; Dashed Lines Are for Dropouts)*

Mathematical Formulation

To avoid excessively complex notation, time subscripts are omitted from all variables except where necessary for clarity. Unless otherwise stated, the definitions of variables hold for each period included in the planning horizon. No descriptions are given for the quantities introduced in order to convert inequalities into equalities, except when those quantities have economic significance.

The Endogenous Variables in the educational system represent, for each school, the numbers of new students, new teachers, and new graduate and dropout workers by skill category. The symbols used to represent each of these variables are:

N_p = new students in schools of type p.

N_{pq} = new students in schools of type q originating from schools of type p.

W_{pk} = new workers of skill class k originating from schools of type p.

T_{pr} = new teachers originating from schools of type p and available in schools of type r.

Z_{pk} = new dropouts from schools of type p who enter labor skill class k.

R = new uneducated, unskilled workers.

The endogenous variables in the rest of the model represent peso values of production, investment, imports, and, for selected industries, exports in each of the nine sectors[7] of the economy. The symbols used to denote each of these activities are:

X_j = the total domestic production in the jth sector.

M_j = the total imports of the jth commodity. Any commodity other than construction, housing, and electrical energy can be imported. No capacity or labor can be imported directly, although domestic capacity can be supplemented indirectly by imports.

E_j = the total exports of the jth commodity. Only certain products can be exported: primary products, textiles, chemicals, processed foods, and "other."

S_j = the amount of the output of the jth industry stockpiled for future use. Electrical energy, construction, and housing cannot be stockpiled.

S_B = the foreign exchange surplus carried over into the next period.

L_k = the supply of the kth labor skill available during the period, measured in man-years of standard efficiency. The skill classes distinguished were: (1) workers; (2) managers, white collar workers, and professionals; and (3) proprietors.

I_j = investment in the expansion of productive capacity in the jth sector, measured in terms of pesos worth of output. The index $j = 1, \ldots , 9$ is for the productive sectors given in footnote 7; $j = 10$ represents investment in buildings for primary and secondary schools; and $j = 11$ indicates investment in university buildings.

The Exogenous Variables. A number of economic and technological constraints must be met by the optimal program. These constraints are of two distinct types: (1) they specify the limits upon the availability of primary

---

[7] The economy was divided into the following nine sectors: (1) primary; (2) food, beverages, and tobacco; (3) textiles, footwear, and clothing; (4) wood, cork, furniture, printing and publishing, and other manufacturing; (5) rubber, rubber products, and non-metallic minerals; (6) mechanical and metallurgical; (7) chemicals, petroleum, and electrical energy; (8) construction; (9) transportation and services. The principle used to aggregate the 23 two-digit ISIC sectors of the input-output matrix into the above nine groups was the extent of similarity in their labor requirements by skill category.

resources (school-age population, teachers, school buildings, labor, capital, and foreign exchange) at the start of the program and at the beginning of each planning period; and (2) they set minimal sectoral goals for production and investment in the terminal period and upper limits upon investment and exports. These limits and goals are specified exogenously by:

T_{ro} = the stock of school teachers for schools of type r available at the start of the plan, in man-years.

L_{ko} = the supply of the kth labor skill available at the start of the plan, measured in man-years of standard efficiency.

P = the school-age population in the age group 5 to 14.

K_j = the productive capacity of the jth type available for utilization during the period, measured in pesos worth of output. (This quantity is exogenous for a given period, but endogenous for the whole planning horizon, since, for simplicity, it was assumed that any capacity-incrementing activity must be undertaken in the period previous to its first utilization.) As with investment, the index j ranges from $j = 1, \ldots, 11$ for this variable.

D_j = the amount of depreciation of the capital stock of the jth sector, expressed in terms of loss of output (in pesos). For simplicity, straight line depreciation was assumed, even though this method tends to overstate the amount of economic depreciation in a growing economy. For this variable, too, $j = 1, \ldots, 11$.

I_j^U = the upper limit set on investment in the jth industry, $j = 1, \ldots, 11$.

Y_j = the amount of final demand for the output of the jth sector which the plan must produce.

E_j^U = the upper limit on exports of the jth commodity.

F = the net foreign capital commitments upon which the economy can draw during the period. This quantity, together with the accumulated foreign exchange reserves, determines the maximum permissible discrepancy between imports and exports of goods for the period. It includes all foreign aid available to the economy.

The Constraints. All the constraints incorporated into the model are linear. They express the accounting, technological, socio-cultural, and resource balance restrictions which the optimization process must obey. The constraints summarized below are written for the tth period; analogous constraints apply to each of the four time periods included in the planning horizon. For the educational sector, we have the following constraints.

Conservation equalities for graduates. These equations specify that, for each type of school, the total number of new graduates available[8] to the system from the previous period must be precisely equal to the sum of those allocated to the work force, to teaching, and to continuation in school in the current period. These constraints may be written as

$$(1 - d_p)(1 - h_p)N_{pt-1} - \sum_{q=p+1}^{6} c_{pq}N_{pqt} - \sum_{k=1}^{6} e_{pk}W_{pkt} - \sum_{r=1}^{6} f_{rp}T_{prt} = 0$$

for all p .

In all equations of this model the subscript p has the following meaning:

$p = 1$ represents primary schools.
$p = 2$ represents general secondary schools.
$p = 3$ represents commercial and industrial schools.
$p = 4$ represents normal schools.
$p = 5$ represents vocational and trade schools.
$p = 6$ represents university and superior schools.
d_p = the dropout rate for schools of type p, a fraction.
h_p = the leakage rate into housewifery, etc., for students of type p, a fraction.
$c_{pq}, e_{pk}, f_{pr} = 1$ or 0 (see Table 1).

Conservation equalities for dropouts. These constraints state that the total number of dropouts available to the system from each type of school must be precisely equal to the sum of those allocated to various categories of the work force, or, for university dropouts, the work force and primary teaching. It is assumed that, on the average, dropouts leave school during the middle of each period. These constraints may be written as

$$d_p(1 - h_p)N_{pt-1} - \sum_{k=1}^{3} g_{pk}Z_{pkt} - s_p T_{61t} = 0 \qquad \text{for all } p .$$

$g_{pk}, s_p = 1$ or 0 (see Table 2) .

[8] That is, the graduates who do not disappear from the system into housewifery, etc.

Table 1. Possible Assignments of Graduates Remaining in School or Entering the Labor Force
(values for c_{pq}, f_{rp}, e_{pk})

t / $t-1$	c_{pq}					f_{rp}						e_{pk}		
	S $q=2$	C $q=3$	N $q=4$	V $q=5$	U $q=6$	T_1 $r=1$	T_2 $r=2$	T_3 $r=3$	T_4 $r=4$	T_5 $r=5$	T_6 $r=6$	Workers $k=1$	Managers Profes-sionals $k=2$	Employers $k=3$
Primary $p=1$	1	1	1	1	0	0	0	0	0	0	0	1	0	1
General secondary $p=2$	0	0	0	0	1	0	0	0	0	0	0	1	1	1
Commercial $p=3$	0	0	0	0	1	0	0	0	0	0	0	0	1	0
Normal $p=4$	0	0	0	0	1	1	0	0	0	0	0	0	0	0
Vocational $p=5$	0	0	0	0	0	0	0	0	0	1	0	1	0	0
University $p=6$	0	0	0	0	0	1	1	1	1	1	1	0	1	1

Table 2. Possible Assignments of Dropouts
g_{pk}, s_p

$t-1$ \\ t	Workers $k=1$	Managers Professionals $k=2$	Employers $k=3$	T_1 (s_p)
Primary $p=1$	1	0	0	0
Secondary $p=2$	1	0	1	0
Commercial $p=3$	1	0	1	0
Normal $p=4$	1	0	1	0
Vocational $p=5$	1	0	0	0
University $p=6$	1	1	1	1

Accounting equation for sources of university entrants states that

$$\sum_{p=2}^{4} N_{p6} = N_6 .$$

Teacher constraints require that the number of students who can enroll in a school of type r is limited by the number of teachers available for that kind of school. This limitation may be expressed as

$$u_r v_r N_r \leq T_{r0}(1 - \lambda_r)^{t-\tau} + \sum_{\tau=1}^{t}\sum_{p} f_{rp}T_{pr\tau}(1 - \lambda_r)^{t-\tau}$$

$$\text{for } r = 1, \ldots, 6, \text{ and } \tau = 1, \ldots, t$$

u_r = factor used to convert the number of entrants into school of type
    r at the beginning of the five-year period into an average annual
    enrollment in that school category.

v_r = teacher-student ratio in school of type r.

λ_r = death and retirement rate for teachers of school type r.

The school-building constraints limit the number of students enrolled in primary and secondary schools to the number which can be accommodated by the stock of primary and secondary school buildings.

$$\sum_{p=1}^{5} u_p n_p N_p \leq K_{10,0} + \sum_{\tau=0}^{t-1} I_{10,\tau} - \sum_{\tau=0}^{t-1} D_{10,\tau}$$

Similarly, the number of university students must obey the analogous constraint:

$$u_6 n_6 N_6 \leq K_{11,0} + \sum_{\tau=0}^{t-1} I_{11,\tau} - \sum_{\tau=0}^{t-1} D_{11,\tau} .$$

In the above equations

$n_p =$ the building-student ratio, in pesos per student.

The population constraint states that the number of entrants into primary schools plus those entering the work force with no education cannot exceed the population in the 5 to 14 age group.

$$N_1 + R \leq P$$

Socio-cultural constraints state that enrollments in each type of school must be nondecreasing through time. They express the socio-cultural requirement for a certain amount of continuity in school enrollments and provide terminal constraints for the educational system.

For each p, we require that

$$N_{pt} \geq N_{pt-1} .$$

In addition, for the sake of realism, the number of entrants into university from commercial schools is limited to no more than 20 per cent of commercial school graduates.

$$N_{36t} \leq .2(1 - d_p)(1 - h_p)N_{3t-1}$$

The labor force change equations provide the main link between the educational system and the productive sectors of the economy. They define the contribution of graduates and dropouts from schools of a given type to the supply of labor of a particular skill. Differential productivities were assumed for various grades of graduates and dropouts. These will be varied parametrically in further calculations under the program. The constraints may be written recursively as

$$L_{kt} = (1 - \alpha)L_{kt-1} + \beta_k R_t + \sum_{p=1}^{6} e_{pk}W_{pkt}\pi_{pk}$$

$$+ \tfrac{1}{2} \sum_{p=1}^{6} g_{pk}\phi_{pk}(Z_{pkt} + Z_{pkt-1}) + \sum_{\tau=t-1}^{t} (q_{k\tau}W_{51\tau} + r_{k\tau}Z_{51\tau-1})$$

for each skill class k .

In the above equation

π_{pk} = productivity of laborers of educational level p in labor skill of type k. These productivity coefficients are used to convert labor in man-years into labor in efficiency units. They are normalized in such a way that the base period supply of the kth labor grade measured in efficiency units is numerically equal to the base period supply of the kth grade of labor in man-years. For later periods, these last two quantities, of course, tend to diverge as the educational composition of each labor skill is altered in the course of the optimization process.

ϕ_{pk} = productivity of dropouts from school of type p in labor skill k. Dropouts were assumed to enter the labor force in the middle of the period during which they drop out of school.

α = the mortality rate of the labor force.

β_k = a constant which is zero for $k = 2, 3$ and which equals the productivity of the uneducated for $k = 1$.

$q_{k\tau}, r_{k\tau}$ = constants used to adjust the equation for the fact that vocational school enrollees work half-time while in school. These constants are zero for $k = 2, 3$.

The first right hand side term of the previous equation indicates the decrease in the supply of labor of the kth grade due to death and retirement. The second term, which appears only for $k = 1$, represents the increase in skilled and unskilled labor due to newly entering uneducated workers. The third term measures the contribution to the kth skill category of graduates of different educational levels. The fourth term represents the contribution of dropouts; the coefficient of $\frac{1}{2}$ preceding this term arises because of our assumption that they drop out in the middle of each period; the term in Z_{pkt-1} is required to adjust the current work force for the fact that, in the previous period, dropouts were assumed to work for only half the period. The final sum in this equation appears because students in vocational schools work half-time while in school.

The noneducational portion of the model consists, as usual, of the following sets of constraints.

The total use–total availability equalities. These restrictions specify that, for each sector, the total amount of product available from production, imports, and opening inventories must equal its total use in intermediate production, investment, exports, final consumption, and stockpiling activities. The constraints can be expressed as:

$$X_j + M_j + S_{jt-1} + \sum_{i=1}^{9} a_{ij}X_i + \sum_{i=1}^{11} b_{ij}I_i + E_j + Y_j + S_{jt}$$

$$(j = 1, \ldots, 9).$$

In the above equation

a_{ij} = the coefficients of the input-output matrix.

b_{ij} = the coefficients of the investment-output matrix; they represent the peso value of inputs from the ith industry required to increment the capacity of the jth sector by one peso. Sectors 10 and 11 are the building sectors for education.

S_{jt} = the inventories of the jth type at the end of the tth period.

The capacity inequalities state that domestic production in the jth sector in the tth time period is limited by the capacity available in that sector during that period. The available capacity is set equal to the initial capacity at the start of the plan plus the net investment that has taken place during all previous periods. Formally, one can state this constraint as

$$X_j \le K_{jo} + \sum_{\tau=0}^{t-1} I_{j\tau} - \sum_{\tau=0}^{t-1} D_{j\tau} \qquad \text{for all } j = 1, \ldots, 9 \,,$$

where

K_{jt} = capacity available for production in the jth sector during the tth period.

$I_{j\tau}$ = gross investment in the jth sector during period τ.

$D_{j\tau}$ = depreciation of the capacity of the jth sector during period τ.

The above method of calculating available capacity incorporates implicitly the assumption that current investment can be used only to increment capacity in the next planning period.

The labor supply inequalities. Since the sum of labor of a given skill demanded for production or capacity-incrementing activities cannot exceed the availability of labor of that grade during the period, we require that

$$\sum_{j} l_{jk}X_j + \sum l'_{jk}I_k \le L_k \qquad \text{for all } k \,,$$

where

l_{jk} = the fraction of man-years of the kth labor skill required to produce a peso's worth of the jth commodity.

l'_{jk} = the fraction of man-years of the kth labor skill required to increment the capacity of the jth industry by one peso's worth of output.

The balance of payments constraint. For each time period, the total peso value of imports must be equal to the sum of the peso value of exports, the net foreign capital commitments available for the period, and the accumulated balance of payments surplus.

That is,

$$S_{B_t} + \sum_j m_j X_j + \sum_j m'_j I_j + \sum_j M_j = \sum_j E_j + F_t + S_{B_{t-1}}.$$

In the above equation

m_j = the peso value of imports required to produce one peso's worth of output in the jth sector.

m'_j = the peso value of imports required to increment capacity by one peso in the jth sector.

S_{B_t} = the foreign exchange surplus carried over into the next period. For the terminal period of the planning horizon a nonzero value of S_{B_t} is interpreted as repayment of foreign capital.

The savings-investment constraint differs from the other constraints in the model, as it represents a behavioral rather than a technological limitation upon the system. It expresses the requirement that the number of pesos used for investment shall not exceed the finance available for this purpose from domestic savings and from foreign sources. This requirement is always satisfied *ex post*, since savings are calculated as residual. It becomes a behavioral constraint, however, when savings are calculated from a savings function, as done here, rather than as the accounting difference between GNP and consumption. It should be noted that, *ex post*, the actual savings ratio need not be equal to the average propensity to save assumed in this constraint.

Mathematically, this constraint can be written as

$$\sum_{j=1}^{11} k_j I_j \leq s(GNP) + F_t - S_{Bt} + S_{Bt-1}$$

where

k_j = capital per output ratio of the jth industry.

s = the average propensity to save.

$$GNP = \sum Y_j + \sum k_j I_j + \sum_j (S_{j_t} - S_{j_{t-1}}) + \sum E_j - \sum M_j - F$$

The export constraints. Exports of the jth commodity are not allowed to exceed a preassigned upper limit.

Formally, we write that

$$E_j \leq E_j^U \qquad \text{for all } j .$$

Upper limits on investment. Investment in every industry is constrained not to exceed prescribed limits. These are behavioral constraints and reflect the role of absorptive capacity limitations in restraining the economy's ability to increment its capital stock. The relations used in the model are

$$I_j \leq I_j^U \qquad \text{for all } j .$$

Lower limits on investment in the terminal period. These constraints require that the final period's investment cover at least the final period's depreciation in each sector.

$$I_{jt} \geq D_{j0} + \sum_{\tau=1}^{3} (1 + d_j)^{4-\tau} I_{j\tau} \qquad \text{for all } j ,$$

where d_j is the rate of depreciation in the jth sector per period.

The objective functions. Three different objective functions, typical of the goals which are usually explicit or implicit in development planning, were used in our calculations. Specifically, the planners are presumed to wish to do one of the following:

1. Maximize the discounted[9] sum of *GNP*:

$$\text{Max} \sum_{t=1}^{T} (1 - r)^{5(t-1)} GNP_t^* .$$

In the above expression, GNP^* differs from the normal GNP since GNP^* includes the capitalized value of social gains from investment in education after the end of the program. This amendment was introduced in order that investment in human capital be viewed in a manner more nearly analogous to investment in real capital. Otherwise, it would appear that all social benefits from investment in education must accrue during the lifetime of the program. This would have biased the calcu-

---

[9] The rate of discount used in all the calculations was 5 per cent (in real terms). The qualitative results are not sensitive to the specific choice of discount rate over a reasonable range of values.

lated results against investment in education, especially in the later periods of the plan.

In principle, the imputed gains from education should be valued at the shadow price of the corresponding activities and the calculation repeated till the initial and final shadow prices of education converge. This was not done for the numerical results discussed below, since it is not clear that convergence can be obtained. Instead, the gains from education for each type of schooling were taken to be the capitalized differences in productivity over the next highest educational level in labor class 1. This labor class includes entrants from all educational levels, and the assumed productivity differentials in this skill category were the largest. Mathematically,

$$GNP^* = GNP + \{(1 + r)^{5(10-t)} N_1[(1 - h_1)(1 - d_1)(\pi_{11} - \beta_1)$$
$$+ (1 - h_1)d_1(\phi_{11} - \beta_1)]$$
$$+ (1 + r)^{5(9-t)} \sum_{p=2}^{5} N_p[(1 - h_p)(1 - d_p)(\pi_{pt} - \pi_{11})$$
$$+ (1 - h_p)d_p(\phi_{pt} - \pi_{11})]$$
$$+ (1 + r)^{5(8-t)} N_6[(1 - h_6)(1 - d_6)(\pi_{61} - \pi_{21}) + (1 - h_6)d_6(\phi_{61} - \pi_{21})]\}P_1,$$

where P_1 is the shadow price of unskilled labor. An iterative process was employed till the initial and final values of P_1 converged.[10] The above calculation assumes a life expectancy of 50 years in the labor force for primary school graduates, 45 for secondary school graduates, and 40 for university graduates.

2. Maximize the change of GNP:

$$\text{Max } GNP_T^* - GNP_0^*$$

where GNP_0^* is the value of GNP^* in the base period.

3. Minimize the discounted sum of net foreign capital inflows:

$$\text{Max } \sum_{t=1}^{T} (1 + r)^{5(t-1)}(S_{Bt} - S_{Bt-1})$$

S_{Bo} was assumed to be zero.

The Basic Model. The basic model used to investigate optimal educational strategies can now be summarized as follows. We optimize the objective function subject to the following constraints for each of the T periods:

---

[10] The numerical results in our calculations, are based upon a zero value for P_1, since workers were in excess supply. The actual values of GNP^* and GNP therefore coincided.

$$(1) \quad (1 - d_p)(1 - h_p)N_{pt-1} - \sum_{q=p+1}^{6} c_{pq}N_{pqt} - \sum_{k=1}^{6} e_{pk}W_{pkt}$$

$$- \sum_{r=1}^{6} f_{rp}T_{prt} = 0 \qquad (p = 1, \ldots, 6).$$

$$(2) \quad d_p(1 - h_p)N_{pt-1} - \sum_{k=1}^{3} g_{pk}Z_{pkt} - s_pT_{61t} = 0 \qquad (p = 1, \ldots, 6).$$

$$(3) \qquad\qquad \sum_{p=2}^{4} N_{p6} = N_6$$

$$(4) \quad u_r v_r N_r \le T_{r0}(1 - \lambda_r)^{t-\tau} + \sum_{\tau=1}^{t} \sum_{p=1}^{6} f_{rp}T_{1 r\tau}(1 - \lambda_r)^{t-\tau}$$

$$(r = 1, \ldots, 6).$$

$$(5) \qquad \sum_{p=1}^{5} u_p n_p N_p \le K_{10,0} + \sum_{t=0}^{t-1} I_{10,\tau} - \sum_{\tau=0}^{t-1} D_{10,\tau}$$

$$(6) \qquad\qquad u_6 n_6 N_6 \le K_{11,0} + \sum_{\tau=0}^{t-1} I_{11,\tau} - \sum_{\tau=0}^{t-1} D_{11,\tau}$$

$$(7) \qquad\qquad\qquad N_1 + R \le P$$

$$(8) \qquad\qquad N_{pt} \ge N_{pt-1} \qquad (p = 1, \ldots, 6).$$

$$(9) \qquad\qquad N_{36t} \le .2(1 - d_p)(1 - h_p)N_{3t-1}$$

$$(10) \quad X_j + M_j + S_{jt-1} = \sum_{i=1}^{9} a_{ij}X_i + \sum_{i=1}^{11} b_{ij}I_i + E_j + Y_j + S_{j_t}$$

$$(j = 1, \ldots, 9).$$

$$(11) \qquad X_j \le K_{j0} + \sum_{\tau=0}^{t-1} I_{j\tau} - \sum_{\tau=0}^{t-1} D_{j\tau} \qquad (j = 1, \ldots, 9).$$

$$(12) \quad \sum_j 1_{k_j} X_j + \sum_j 1'_{j_j} I_j \le (1 - \alpha) L_{kt-1} + \beta_k R_t + \sum_{p=1}^{6} e_{pk} W_{p_{pk}} \pi_{pk}$$

$$+ \tfrac{1}{2} \sum_{p=1}^{6} g_{pk} \phi_{pk} (Z_{pkt} + Z_{pkt-1}) + \sum_{\tau=t-1}^{t} (q_{k\tau} W_{51\tau} + r_{k\tau} Z_{51\tau})$$

$$(k = 1, \ldots, 3).$$

$$(13) \quad \sum_j m_j X_j + \sum_j m_j I_j + \sum_j M_j + S_{Bt} = \sum_j E_j + F_t + S_{Bt-1}$$

$$(14) \quad \sum_{j=1}^{11} k_j I_j \le s\, GNP + F_t - S_{Bt} + S_{Bt-1}$$

$$(15) \quad E_j \le E_j^U \quad (j = 1, \ldots, 4, 7).$$

$$(16) \quad I_j \le I_j^U \quad (j = 1, \ldots, 11).$$

In addition, for the final period of the program we have the constraint that

$$(17) \quad I_{jT} \ge D_{j0} + \sum_{\tau=1}^{3} (1 + d_j)^{4-\tau} I_{j\tau} \quad (j = 1, \ldots, 11).$$

Even though the model was disaggregated into only six educational activities and only nine productive sectors, it still includes 68 equations for each time period. To keep the size of the model manageable, therefore, it was decided to use four five-year periods for the planning horizon. A longer time span with smaller time steps would, of course, have been preferable.

III. Results

Caveat

Before we examine the results, it should be emphasized that the output of the optimization calculations must not be taken too literally. The discussion which follows is intended merely to illustrate the nature and range of conclusions which can be drawn from the application of a model of this nature to a practical economy. It should not be taken as a policy document for Argentine education, even though the results may indicate conclusions which, if valid, would have obvious policy implications.

There are many reasons for this caution. The well-known theoretical limitations arising from the linearity of all the functions of the model and the exclusion of technical change are, of course, important, but they are perhaps less restrictive with respect to the educational subsystem than they are with respect to the noneducational sectors of the model.[11] The most important limitations for the present calculations are on the data side. Relatively old input-output and investment-output relationships were used in the optimizing program. In some cases, "guesstimates" of crucial parameters (e.g., the productivity differentials) had to be made on the basis of similar information for other economies at a corresponding level of development. In other cases, since no information was available, crude approximations (e.g., the assumption of uniform "leakage rates" by sex, independent of educational level[12]) had to be used. For all these reasons, the results of the optimization calculations discussed below can provide only qualitative insights into the functioning of the educational sector of an economy, the broad characteristics of which are typified by the choice of data in this study. It does not necessarily apply to the real Argentina.

To the extent that the data used do approximate the structure of the Argentine economy, and providing that the results are not too sensitive to small errors in the statistical inputs, the calculated optima may offer some guidance for desirable directions of change in Argentine education. However, the purpose of the discussion is not to provide a statement of optimal educational strategy for Argentina; it is rather to indicate the potential usefulness of a model of this nature in educational planning.

Optimal Educational Strategy

The shadow prices of various labor skills indicate that the primary labor bottleneck in the Argentine calculations is the supply of high-level manpower. Indeed, except for the case in which the economy's goal is the maximization of its growth rate, the availability of managerial and professional talent constitutes the *only* binding labor constraint. And, even in the "maximize growth rate" calculations, the ratio of the shadow price of managerial and professional labor to employer labor (the next most important constraint) lies between 6 to 1 and 4 to 1!

Because of the overwhelming importance of the high-level manpower shortage in our calculations, the optimal educational strategy was found

---

[11] For the educational production functions, the constant-coefficient character of the model and the exclusion of "technical change" is, I believe, not unrealistic for an economy at Argentina's level of human resource development. In addition, one form of technical change in the noneducational sectors, that induced by improvements in education embodied in a given grade of labor, is an important decision variable in the model.

[12] The average leakage rate h_p varies by educational level, but only as a result of changes in the sex composition of enrollments.

to be invariant with respect to both changes in goals and (qualitatively) to changes in constraints. The entire educational system is geared to the most efficient alleviation of the high-level manpower bottleneck. Since, in our basic calculations, the productivity of managers and technicians with university degrees was assumed to be about three and a half times that of those with secondary school certificates,[13] the most effective solution turned out to be to produce as many university-trained managers and professionals as possible. The production of university graduates was then limited only by the school-age population as neither the building nor the teacher constraints were binding. The scale of the entire educational system was therefore set by the school-age population.

The calculated optima all indicate the economic desirability of universal primary education. All primary graduates who do not leave the system by leakage are sent on to obtain a secondary education. As large a fraction of secondary school graduates as possible, given the graduation and leakage rates, enter a university.

The secondary school system is rationalized to only two rather than four types of schools. The commercial and the vocational schools, which offer specialized forms of education, are never used. Instead, preference is given to the academically oriented general secondary education. Once the teacher constraint on general secondary enrollments becomes binding, the excess students enter normal school. The normal schools are used, however, as adjuncts to the general secondary schools, rather than as teacher training institutes. Upon graduation from normal school, students are sent into university rather than into primary teaching. The primary teaching force is replenished through university dropouts, who are generated as a by-product of university training.

Marginal Social Benefit from Investment in Education

Formally, the shadow price of each resource constraint in a linear program indicates the change in the objective function which would result from an additional unit of the resource indicated by the constraint. The shadow prices of the conservation equalities for graduates (dropouts) from the several educational processes therefore indicate the marginal social products of graduates (dropouts) from the respective schools. When the objective function maximized is the discounted value of GNP, the social benefit is measured in terms of the discounted peso value of additional product which could be generated by an additional graduate (or dropout)

---

[13] Another parametric variation which assumed that the relative productivity of university *vs.* high school graduates was 2:1 was tried, but yielded an unfeasible solution.

over the twenty years of the program. When the objective pursued is the minimization of foreign capital inflows, the social benefit from education is expressed in terms of the number of units of foreign exchange (in pesos) which could be saved by an additional graduate or dropout from each school process. When the objective is the maximization of the economy's rate of growth, the social benefit from education is measured in pesos of the final period's output which could be produced by an extra graduate or dropout.

The relevant shadow prices, averaged over the first two periods of the calculation,[14] are given in Table 3 for each of the three objective functions. An examination of this table reveals several interesting facts:

Table 3. Shadow Prices of Graduates and Dropouts
(average over first two periods of program)

Graduates	Max. GNP[a]	Max. Growth Rate[a]	Min. Foreign Capital[b]
Primary school	1,360	520	360
Secondary school	4,370	1,340	1,030
Commercial school	4,370	1,190	660
Normal school	4,370	1,340	1,030
Vocational school	0	105	0
University	6,920	1,950	1,510
Dropouts			
Primary school	0	0	0
Secondary school	0	0	0
Commercial school	0	0	0
Normal school	0	0	0
Vocational school	0	0	0
University	6,380	1,550	1,680

[a] 1950 pesos per student per five years.
[b] 1950 pesos' worth of foreign exchange per student per five years.

1. In general, the shadow prices of commercial and vocational school graduates are considerably lower than those of secondary and normal school graduates. This explains why these schools are not utilized in the optimal school network.

2. The shadow price of university dropouts is quite large relative to that of university graduates. Indeed, in the "minimize aid" calculations, the shadow price of university dropouts actually exceeds that of graduates! Since the characteristics of dropouts in our calculations are that

[14] Only the first two periods' shadow prices have meaning, since the shadow prices for the subsequent periods are heavily influenced by the terminal constraints.

they are available for work for half the period during which they enter their respective course, and their productivity is halfway between that of secondary and university graduates, these calculations suggest the desirability of instituting extensive two- to three-year junior college programs. This conclusion hinges heavily upon the particular productivity assumption chosen and would have to be explored further by appropriate investigations.

3. The difference between the shadow price of graduates and dropouts from each type of school sets an upper limit to the subsidy which it would be economically desirable to pay in order to reduce the dropout rate. To the extent that students are compelled to leave schools for economic reasons, the difference between these two shadow prices indicates the maximal grants which could be offered to keep students in school. For secondary school students, for example, the grants could be as high as 875 pesos per year, as apparent from the "maximize GNP" calculations.

4. The difference between the shadow prices of graduates of various types and their respective average earnings may offer an indication of the extent to which the market incentives reflect the true marginal social benefit of each type of education. It should be pointed out, however, that an excessive divergence between market prices and shadow prices most probably implies that some constraint has been incorrectly stated, and thus serves as a diagnostic device for the validity of the model rather than for the optimality of the real economy.

Marginal Social Cost

The data in our calculations can also be used to evaluate the marginal social cost of a student of each type. The major elements are the opportunity cost of student and teacher time and the opportunity cost of school buildings. To carry out illustrative calculations for the maximize GNP objective function in the first period of the program, the opportunity cost of student time was valued at the shadow price of the most productive employment open to a representative student of each category had he not been enrolled in school. Since the uneducated can only become unskilled workers, and the shadow price of unskilled labor is zero in the program, the social opportunity cost of primary student time is zero. Similarly, since primary graduates can, at best, become employers and the shadow price of employers is also zero, the social opportunity cost of secondary student time is also negligible in our calculations. The opportunity cost of university students, on the other hand, is quite high. Since high school graduates can become managers and professionals with a productivity of .8, and a shadow price of 142 (1950) pesos per year, the opportunity cost of each year of university student time is 114 pesos' worth of output.

The social cost of a teacher was measured at the next most socially productive employment open to a person with equivalent education.[15] For primary teachers, who need only be educationally equivalent to normal school graduates, the social opportunity cost per year is equal to that of a university student. Secondary and university school teachers, on the other hand, are university graduates. The opportunity cost of their time, therefore, is their productivity in the managerial and professional class: $3 \times 142 = 426$.

School buildings were assumed not to be transferable to any other use; their marginal social cost is therefore their shadow price, which, in the first two periods of the program was zero.

The results of this calculation are displayed in Table 4. In terms of cost per productive graduate, normal school and general secondary are the cheapest of all secondary courses, which, of course, accounts for their being chosen in the optimal program. University education is less than twice more expensive than secondary education. Since the productivity of university graduates is assumed to be more than twice that of high school graduates, this explains why the entire educational system in our calculations is geared to produce university graduates.

A comparison with the social rate of return from education in Table 3 indicates that all forms of education pay off, even at the margin.

Investment in Education

It may be interesting to compare the extent of investment in human capital with investment in physical assets over the twenty years of our program.[16] In estimating the amount of investment in education, student and teacher costs are measured at their social opportunity cost, as before, and investment in buildings is taken at its actual value in the optimal program. When enrollments in primary school are limited to the school-age

---

[15] This assumes, contrary to the adage, that those who teach can do!

[16] No comparison with the actual educational program in Argentina is made in the text in order not to change the flavor of the discussion, which is intended merely to illustrate what can be learned from the application of a model of this nature to real world data. However, for whatever it is worth, in 1950–1955 (the first period of our calculations) approximately 2.4 million children were enrolled in primary schools, 460,000 in secondary schools (excluding adult education), and 140,000 in universities in Argentina. The comparable figures in our calculations are 3 million for primary, 580,000 for secondary, and 210,000 for university (see Table 5).

Table 4. Marginal Social Cost per Student
(1950 pesos, max. GNP objective function)

	Opportunity Cost of Student Time	Opportunity Cost of Teacher Time	Opportunity Cost of School Buildings	Total
Primary School				
Cost per student year	0	5.6	0	5.6
Cost per graduate[a]	0	84	0	84
Cost per productive[a] graduate	0	242	0	242
General Secondary				
Cost per student year	0	56	0	56
Cost per graduate[a]	0	673	0	673
Cost per productive[a] graduate	0	1,048	0	1,048
Commercial School				
Cost per student year	0	61	0	61
Cost per graduate[a]	0	800	0	800
Cost per productive[a] graduate	0	1,266	0	1,266
Normal School				
Cost per student year	0	42	0	42
Cost per graduate[a]	0	309	0	309
Cost per productive[a] graduate	0	1,075	0	1,075
Vocational School				
Cost per student year	0	42	0	42
Cost per graduate[a]	0	512	0	512
Cost per productive[a] graduate	0	1,500	0	1,500
University				
Cost per student year	114	13	0	127
Cost per graduate[a]	1,136	126	0	1,262
Cost per productive[a] graduate	1,671	185	0	1,856

[a] With an expected value of one graduate. If the criterion used were a given probability (e.g., .95) of obtaining at least one graduate, the cost per graduate would be quite different.

population, optimal investment in education is 21 per cent of investment in physical capital (see Table 5). If the imputed cost of student time, which is not included in conventionally computed school budgets, is subtracted from the figure for educational investment, the ratio of investment in education to investment in productive capacity is reduced to 12 per cent, a reasonable value.

Table 5. Investment in Education
(1950 10^6 pesos, for the maximize GNP calculations)

	Primary	Secondary and Normal	University	Total
Basic Case (1950 School-Age Population Limit)				
Number of students per period	3,040,000	577,000	210,000	
Opportunity cost of student time	0	0	118	
Opportunity cost of faculty time	47	93	7	
Investment in school buildings	.320		0	
Total	47	93	125	265
Investment in physical capital				1,265
Optimum Unlimited by School-Age Population				
Number of students per period	4,400,000	854,000	311,000	
Opportunity cost of student time	0	0	175	
Opportunity cost of faculty time	68	138	10	
Investment in school buildings	.918			
Total	68.5	138.5	185	392
Investment in physical capital				1,364

In order to investigate the optimal extent of investment in education if a certain amount of adult primary education were also permitted, another set of calculations was made in which the school-age population constraint upon enrollments was removed. The results of this experiment are summarized at the bottom of Table 5. The "optimum optimorum" educational effort rises by 50 per cent, and educational investment mounts to 28.7 per cent of investment in real assets (when all educational social costs are taken into account).

Educational Level of the Labor Force

The allocation of graduates and dropouts from different schools to labor of various skill classes is determined endogenously in our model. It is therefore interesting to inquire into the educational level of labor force additions during the lifetime of the program. A typical assignment pattern results in additions to the entrepreneurial group having, on the average, nine years of formal education,[17] with 28 per cent university dropouts and 62 per cent high school dropouts. The managerial and professional category is staffed entirely with university graduates (55 per cent) and university dropouts, leading to an average of 14.5 years of formal education. Additions to skilled and unskilled labor, on the other hand, are almost wholly uneducated; their average number of years of schooling is less than one, with 12 per cent secondary school dropouts and the rest with no formal education whatsoever.

While no data on the actual composition of the labor force in Argentina could be found, the general impression is that the pattern chosen by the program would lead to an upgrading in the quality of the economy's high-level manpower, a deterioration in the quality of its skilled and unskilled labor, and a virtually unchanged employer class. This upgrading in the quality of the economy's scarcest labor resource at the expense of the quality of its slack labor resources, is, of course, eminently rational. While a strategy of this nature would therefore be followed in any model of this type, not much should be made of the particular pattern chosen in our basic calculations since it depends upon the specific (rather arbitrary) productivity differentials assumed.

Coupling of the Educational and Industrial Portions of the Model

As we saw under "Optimal Educational Strategy," above, the present calculations display a significant lack of sensitivity of the educational optima to the details of the industrial structure of the economy. For the economy described in our calculations, one can therefore formulate a reasonable educational plan without reference to developments in the noneducational portion of the model. This does not mean, of course, that such a procedure is indicated in the more general case in which one feature of the economy (in this instance, the scarcity of high-level manpower) does not completely dominate all other considerations. What our results suggest, then, is a multistage approach of the following nature. The first step is to ascertain, by any means whatever, whether or not some particular aspect of the economy exerts an overwhelming influence upon the optimal development plan. If it does, the conclusions are obvious. If not, it appears desirable to explore the situation with a fairly coarse model of the educational subsector coupled with a rather aggregative description of the rest

---

[17] The numbers cited in the text are based upon the assumption that primary education is five years in length, since, in our calculations, the primary course has been stylized to a five-year duration.

of the economy, as in the present work. The final stage of the analysis would utilize the shadow prices obtained in the fairly aggregative calculations to set up an objective function which maximizes the net benefit from education (as done by Bowles[18]) subject to a considerably more detailed model of the educational subsector.

The complementary question to the one discussed above is the extent to which the development plan for the productive sectors of the economy can be programmed without including the educational sectors. To investigate this point for the economy of our calculations, the model was run without the educational sector, with the supply of each labor skill growing exogenously at the rate of 2 per cent per year. A comparison of the optimum obtained for this case with that obtained with the same initial conditions when the educational subsector is included, indicates that the omission of the educational sector from the model tends seriously to distort the allocation of resources in the productive sectors at both late and early periods of the plan. In our calculations, the economy constrained by the need to educate its labor force devoted a significantly smaller percentage of its resources to investment, achieved a considerably lower rate of growth, was more agricultural, and concentrated a larger share of its industrial product in light consumer-goods industries.

COMMENT

SAMUEL BOWLES, HARVARD UNIVERSITY

Professor Adelman's model for educational and economic planning breaks new ground in a number of important respects. Although the emphasis on allocation decisions in the education field is no longer particularly novel, Professor Adelman's treatment of the problem of educational and economic planning differs significantly from most previous contributions to the literature on this subject. First, her model allows for some substitution in production between labor of different educational levels. Thus it differs from most of the existing planning approaches, which rely on fixed input coefficients in the economy for labor of various educational or occupational levels.

Second, Professor Adelman's model allows for the simultaneous computation

[18] S. Bowles, "The Efficient Allocation of Resources in Education: A Planning Model with Application to Northern Nigeria" (Unpublished Ph.D. dissertation, Harvard University, 1965).

of an optimal pattern of growth in the economy and an optimal pattern of enrollments and resource use in the educational system. The demands for educated labor are generated endogenously by the optimum pattern of economic and educational growth. In this respect her paper makes an important and fruitful contribution.

In the following critical comments, I will confine myself to Professor Adelman's treatment of the educational sector and its relationships with the economy. I will suggest:

1) that there may be some substantial problems involved in giving any concrete empirical content to the parameters representing the relative productivity of various types of labor;

2) that the specification of direct substitution possibilities in production raises serious problems, as does the assumed constancy of the marginal rates of substitution between labor of various types;

3) that the treatment of the terminal conditions is unsatisfactory; and

4) that the model in its present form is not particularly helpful in coping with many of the actual policy problems facing the educational planner.

The demand for educated labor is generated in the model on the basis of relative productivity coefficients for laborers with various levels of education. If these productivity figures are intended to represent relative social marginal productivities, Professor Adelman's approach is based on the marginal rate of substitution in production between types of labor classified by educational level and occupational group. Use of the fixed marginal rates of substitution allows her to treat the persons in each occupational group as only one factor of production, even though the occupational group is composed of a number of distinctly different types of labor when classified by educational attainments. The productivity coefficients also form the standard of valuation of the terminal stock of human capital (the summation of education's contribution to lifetime productivity following the end of the planning period). In view of the absolutely central role which the productivity coefficients play, Professor Adelman owes it to us to present the figures which she used and to describe the methods of estimation underlying them. If the estimated productivity figures are no more than guesses (as she implies), then Professor Adelman might suggest how in principle these data could be collected. Had she gone to these lengths, I think that a number of problems involved in her method might have become more clear to the reader. In particular, I suspect that the only feasible method for estimating these relative productivity coefficients is based on the relative earnings of laborers with various levels of education. Estimation of the productivity differentials on these grounds would raise the familiar but serious questions concerning the relationship between market wages and social marginal productivities. Additional problems are raised by the possibility that the difference in observed earnings or in estimated productivity among laborers classified by educational level may be explained to a significant degree by noneducational factors. These are major problems, and while they are not peculiar to Professor Adelman's approach, it seems unwise to launch a model of this type without explicitly mentioning the difficulties involved.

A second set of problems arises from the treatment of the possibility for substitution between labor inputs of various educational levels. Although it is often unrealistic to suppose (as many educational and economic planners do) that there is no substitutability whatever between inputs of labor of various educational or occupational levels, Professor Adelman's approach, which accommodates both perfect substitutability and zero substitutability, raises problems too. She has assumed that the marginal rate of substitution between any two educational categories of labor within an occupational group is constant over any feasible range of input proportions. At the same time she has assumed no substitutability whatever between occupational groups. Thus, for example, within the "managers and professional" occupational group, secondary school graduates are substitutable for university graduates at the rate of approximately 3.5 to 1 *ad infinitum* while there is no direct substitutability whatever allowed between "managers and professionals" and any other occupational group. There are two somewhat implausible implications of this procedure: first, that "managers" with a university education cannot change their occupational group and become, say, "employers," regardless of relative earnings, and second, that there can be no direct substitution in production of "employers" for "managers" regardless of the relative wages of each group.[1] The choice of complete substitutability in one case and none in the other requires some explanation.

The dichotomous treatment of substitutability is particularly noticeable within the educational system, where despite the identical educational backgrounds required of teachers in the four types of secondary-level schools, it is assumed that there is no substitutability between the teaching inputs in these schools.

The constant marginal rates of substitution between labor with different levels of education within a given occupational group imply that the relative marginal productivities of each type of labor within an occupational group do not depend on the rate of capital accumulation or the relative scarcity of each type of labor, or structural change in the economy or any other variable in the model. Strictly speaking, a necessary condition for this assumption is that the marginal productivity functions for labor classified by educational level are infinitely elastic. Even this stringent assumption, however, is not sufficient. Intellectual and other relevant abilities may be distributed so that any major change in educational enrollments is likely to affect the quality of the student intake and to alter the expected marginal productivity of the educational outputs. Thus, even if movement out along a marginal productivity of labor curve does not lead directly to any appreciable fall in the marginal productivity, it may induce a downward shift in the entire function, through a lowering of the average quality of the educational outputs.

In her evaluation of the terminal human capital stock, Professor Adelman must assume implicitly that despite the major changes in the educational com-

---

[1] Indirectly, of course, substitution is possible through changes in the structure of production.

position of the labor force suggested by the solutions to the model, the relative marginal productivities of each type of labor will remain unchanged, not only over the twenty-year planning period, but over a period extending forty or fifty years beyond that. The assumption of constant marginal productivities may be defensible for short-term problems and for the consideration of minor changes in the outputs of the educational system, but it surely requires more defense when used in a long-term model of the type proposed by Professor Adelman.

A number of somewhat peculiar results of the model can be attributed directly to the assumption that the relative marginal productivities of each type of labor within occupational groups do not depend on the amounts of educated labor produced. For example, the assumption that a university graduate working as a "manager" or a "professional" is 3.5 times as productive as a secondary school graduate in the same position and the estimate that the costs of producing a university graduate are less than 3.5 times the unit costs of secondary education explain why the model yields the unlikely result that the entire body of "professionals and managers" are either college graduates or college dropouts. (In the U.S. in a similar occupational category only 55 per cent were similarly educated.) Over the twenty-year period covered by the model, the relatively high levels of production of higher education and the saturation of one of the three occupational categories with its products can be expected to place a downward pressure on the productivity of university graduates and dropouts relative to other types of labor in the economy, and thus to alter the (assumed constant) marginal rates of substitution between labor of each type. A further peculiarity which can be attributed to the constant marginal rates of substitution is that, with the notable exception of the university activity, the educational system contributes no graduates to the labor force outside of the educational system itself. All of those who successfully complete an educational course are used as teachers or are channeled into higher education. Only the dropouts enter the non-teaching labor force.

Third, Professor Adelman has valued the increment in the stock of human capital at the end of the period by the discounted productivity differentials attributable to the education produced over the period. Whereas no economist in the planning field can claim to have discovered a satisfactory operational solution to the problem of terminal conditions, the approach used by Professor Adelman is arbitrary and inconsistent. The terminal human capital stock is valued at the present value of future benefits, while the increment in the terminal physical stock is not valued at all. The terminal conditions with respect to physical capital merely prevent disinvestment in the last period. The asymmetry between the treatment of physical and human capital amounts to counting benefits associated with educational expenditures and failing to count the analogous benefits from investment in plant and equipment. It is therefore surprising that Professor Adelman explains that her treatment of the terminal condition with respect to human capital is intended to render it "more nearly analogous to investment in real capital."

Aside from the inconsistent treatments of physical and human capital, the valuation of the post-terminal year stream of benefits appears to be somewhat arbitrary. There are three occupational or skill levels used in the model and hence three different sets of coefficients measuring the relative productivity of workers of various educational backgrounds within each occupational level. In valuing the terminal human capital stock, Professor Adelman chose to use the relative productivity figures from Group 1 ("workers"), but there is clearly no reason to use a figure for this occupational group as opposed to any other group. Professor Adelman has used a shadow price of "workers"[2] to convert the relative productivity coefficients to value terms. The shortcomings of the whole procedure are all too evident in this particular application as the shadow price for "workers" is zero in all years and for all runs thus far computed. The result is that the terminal human capital stock is valued at zero prices!

Abstracting for a moment from the above flaws in construction and problems of data, one may ask what relevance this model has to the actual concrete problems of educational planning? In the first place, the model is too highly aggregated to cope successfully with many of the real policy issues which arise on a year-to-year basis, and at the same time it appears to be more detailed than is necessary to generate the type of aggregate information which planners need for the long-run period (i.e., 20 years). The fact that the optimal solutions appear to be rather insensitive to changes in the pattern of growth in the economy suggests that a disaggregated model with a more detailed specification of the educational system would yield useful results. One hopes that Professor Adelman will follow up her suggestion to this effect.

Secondly, many of the components of the model which appear as parameters should, in any concrete planning situation, be regarded as policy variables. I am thinking particularly of dropout and failure rates, teacher-student ratios and other elements of the educational production functions. Professor Adelman might have devoted more attention to parametric variation and other experiments to determine the trade-offs between the main variables, and to test the sensitivity of the results to changes in the underlying data. The real value of a model of this type may not be so much in the optimal plan which it generates but in its usefulness in exploring relevant regions of the production possibility set of the economy and the educational system.

There is one last respect in which I feel that the present form of the paper is lacking. This is the somewhat cavalier treatment of the data. We are treated to a fascinating discussion of the results of the computations and yet we get not a single page devoted to a presentation of the basic data. The absence of data on the crucial parameters renders both comprehension and criticism more difficult.

Despite Professor Adelman's warnings, one suspects that a good part of the economics and planning professions will find it difficult to resist the temptation to take the results of the model seriously. It is therefore unfortunate that Pro-

---

[2] Although she refers to the shadow price, there are four shadow prices for this occupational group, one for each period. She gives us no indication of which price she intends to use; nor do I perceive any clear-cut theoretical grounds for using any particular year's price. This choice must also remain arbitrary.

fessor Adelman was not able to develop a more satisfactory empirical foundation for the work. On the basis of other studies on the Argentine labor market, it would appear that at least one crucial parameter, the ratio of the marginal productivity of university graduates to that of high school leavers in managerial and professional occupations, is considerably in error.[3]

Perhaps a word of clarification concerning the shadow prices should be added here. In her discussion of the marginal social benefit from investment in education, Professor Adelman suggests that when the objective function is the discounted value of GNP, the shadow prices measure the increment in discounted GNP over the twenty years of the planning period associated with the availability of an additional graduate or dropout. However, in Table 3 the shadow prices are defined in terms of pesos per student *per five years*. In fact, it would seem that neither of these interpretations is entirely correct. The shadow prices in Professor Adelman's model refer not to the annual or five-yearly or even twenty-yearly rental of a graduate or dropout, but rather to the purchase price of a graduate or dropout as a capital good; namely, the capitalized value of the entire stream of earnings over the life of the capital good extending not only over the twenty-year planning period but over the entire lifetime of the individual. The productivity of the individual in periods beyond the end of the planning period is taken account of in the valuation of the terminal human capital stock. For those individuals who graduate or drop out toward the end of the planning period the major component of the shadow price would presumably reflect the valuation of productivity in the post-terminal years. The confusion with respect to the shadow prices is illustrated, for example, by the statement: "The difference between the shadow prices of graduates of various types and their respective average earnings may offer an indication of the extent to which the market incentives reflect the true marginal social benefit of each type of education." It is clear that the relevant comparison is between the shadow price and discounted value of lifetime earnings.

A number of present weaknesses of the model (such as the four-year investment gestation lag, the five-year stylization of the educational system, and the unsatisfactory occupational categories) will be cheerfully accepted as the price one pays for a model of the scope and interest which Professor Adelman has presented. Many of the more serious shortcomings of the model fall into either of two categories: those which can be remedied in future editions of the model and those major problems which afflict any economist working in this field. Professor Adelman has handled a number of these major problems skillfully; and she has given us a model which holds out hope of fruitful empirical application.

[3] Jacob Mincer's unpublished work based on a survey of employment in large firms carried out by the Centro de Investigaciones Económicas in 1961 suggests that a ratio of 2:1 or lower is more correct than the 3.5:1 figure used in the model. It is disturbing to note that Professor Adelman experimented with a 2:1 figure and found that for that value no feasible solution exists.

INDEX

328, 334*n*, 337*n*, 340*n*, 342, 342*n*,
346*n*, 354*n*
Buck, J. L., 49, 49*n*, 50

C

Cairncross, A. K., 105
Capital: accumulation, 119, 127; effect of
foreign, on welfare function, 155–57;
foreign aid as, 149–78; to income ratio, 125; variations in supply of external, Pakistan, 171–75
—growth rate: and increase in labor force,
81–87; and industrialization, 79–80;
maximum, 75–76, 89
—intensity of use: 122, 125, 142: and industrialization, 78, 91; in Peru, 194,
203
—ratio to labor, 74–75, 80–81, 120–21:
and price ratio, 136; in private sector,
116; in public sector, 116
—ratio to output, 58–59, 60: foreign capital affecting, 158; in India, 252; in
Peru, 190*n;* in Zambia, 237
—resources: in agriculture, 24; in industry,
23
Capital stock: and population in United
Kingdom, 108
Cass, D., 114, 115, 128
Chakravarty, S., 241
Chambers, J. D., 55*n*
Chapman, Janet G., 94*n*
Chenery, Hollis B., 62, 62*n*, 149*n*, 150*n*,
151, 153, 153*n*, 165*n*, 169, 259*n*, 269,
285, 291*n*, 327, 327*n*, 347, 355
China: disguised unemployment in, 49;
maximum-speed development system
in, 67
Closed economy, 67
Cobb-Douglas production function, 10,
29, 31, 34, 61–62
Colombia: balance of payments in, 298;
consumption demands in, 319–21; dynamic programming model for, 292–
325; exports, 320; import substitution
in, 303; input-output system in, 297,
302, 312; investment in, 299–300; labor in, 298; variables in model, 294–
96. *See also* Dynamic programming
models
Comfort region: and wage rate, 73, 78, 81
Constraints: in dynamic programming
model, 296–300; in educational planning model, 387, 392; in Israel model,
330–36

Construction: in India, 248–49; in Zambia, 216
Consumption: African, 228; demands in
Colombia, 319–21; demands in Israel, 331–33, 356; and disposable income, 117–18; long-run equilibrium
standards, 83–86; maximization of,
307; by nonsterile workers, 20; per
capita, increase in, 12; per capita, and
real wage, 94; and population
changes, 12–15, 22; of private goods,
per man, 142; response to changes in
standards of, 71–73, 81; by sterile
workers, 20
Copper: royalties in Zambia, 213, 229
Credit system: in Zambia, 233–34

D

Davila, O., 99
Day, Richard H., 324
Deficiency region: and wage rate, 72, 81
Demand functions in economy, 119: Co-
lombian, 319–21
Determinism: and dualism, 36–37, 40
Difference equations: stochastic, 100
Differential-difference equations, 102–7
Disaggregation, 152–53: in Mexico, 286;
in Zambia, 211
Discount rates: in welfare function, 156
Discrimination: in employment, 97
Disguised unemployment, 4, 9, 10, 13: in
agrarianism, 4, 9, 13, 46; and capital-
output ratio, 58–59, 60; in China, 49;
defined, 49; and dualism, 46; in
Egypt, 49; in Greece, 50; indirect
measurement of, 49; in Italy, 49; nonsterile, 19; and rates of growth, 57-58,
59; and real income per capita, 56–57,
59, 64; and real wage rate, 54, 59;
sterile, 19; and wage and labor productivity, 73*n*
Domar, Evsey, 96*n*, 99
Dorfman, Robert, 149*n*
Dougherty, Christopher, 327*n*
Dovring, F., 55*n*
Dropouts: and educational planning, 393,
395, 405
Dualism, 3–43: allocation decisions in, 24;
backward and advanced sectors, 45–
66; causal order chart for, 35; central
feature of, 4; characteristics of, 23–
27; and determinism, 36–37, 40; development of, 27–37, 45–66; and disguised unemployment, 46; intersec-

Theory and Design of Economic Development

Edited by IRMA ADELMAN and ERIK THORBECKE

designer: Gerard Valerio
typesetter: Kingsport Press, Inc.
typeface: Times Roman
printer: Kingsport Press, Inc.
paper: P & S, GM, 95/R
binder: Kingsport Press, Inc.
cover material: Columbia Riverside Vellum RV-1370

DATE DUE

Withdrawn From
Ohio Northern
University Library

GAYLORD

PRINTED IN U.S.A.